P9-APM-566

GOVERNMENT AND MARKETS

International Studies in Economics and Econometrics

VOLUME 32

Government and Markets

Establishing a Democratic Constitutional Order and a Market Economy in Former Socialist Countries

edited by

Hendrikus J. Blommestein

University of Twente,
Netherlands Centre for Security
and Co-operation in Europe

and

Bernard Steunenberg

University of Twente,
Faculty of Public Administration
and Public Policy

KLUWER ACADEMIC PUBLISHERS
DORDRECHT / BOSTON / LONDON

Library of Congress Cataloging-in-Publication Data

Government and markets : establishing a democratic constitutional order and a market economy in former socialist countries / edited by Hendrikus J. Blommestein and Bernard Steunenberg.
p. cm. -- (International studies in economics and econometrics ; v. 32)
Includes indexes.
ISBN 0-7923-3059-5 (hard : alk. paper)
1. Europe, Eastern--Economic policy--1989- 2. Free enterprise--Europe, Eastern. 3. Post-communism--Europe, Eastern. 4. Europe, Eastern--Politics and government--1989- 5. Democracy--Europe, Eastern. I. Blommestein, H. J., 1950- . II. Steunenberg, Bernard. III. Series.
HC244.G64 1994
338.947--dc20 94-30156

ISBN 0-7923-3059-5

Published by Kluwer Academic Publishers,
P.O. Box 17, 3300 AA Dordrecht, The Netherlands.

Kluwer Academic Publishers incorporates
the publishing programmes of
D. Reidel, Martinus Nijhoff, Dr W. Junk and MTP Press.

Sold and distributed in the U.S.A. and Canada
by Kluwer Academic Publishers,
101 Philip Drive, Norwell, MA 02061, U.S.A.

In all other countries, sold and distributed
by Kluwer Academic Publishers Group,
P.O. Box 322, 3300 AH Dordrecht, The Netherlands.

Printed on acid-free paper

Printed in the Netherlands

Contents

Editors' Preface

In August 1992, the newly founded Netherlands Centre for Security and Cooperation in Europe (NCSCE) organized an international conference in Enschede, the Netherlands, on the development of markets and the role of democratic governments in formerly planned economies. At this conference, the authors of the essays in this volume presented their work to an audience of scholars and policymakers from the Baltic countries, Central and Eastern Europe, the U.S.A., Western Europe, as well as representatives of the Organisation for Economic Co-operation and Development (OECD), the International Monetary Fund (IMF) and the European Bank for Reconstruction and Development (EBRD). This volume is based on updated and sometimes significantly revised versions of these presentations.

The generous support of the principal sponsor of this conference and this volume, the Ministry of the Interior of the Netherlands as part of the Program for Cooperation with Eastern Europe, played a decisive role in the success of the conference and the publication of this volume. Support by *De Nederlandsche Bank N.V.*, the Board of Governors of the University of Twente, the Faculty of Public Administration and Public Policy of the same university, as well as the Province of Overijssel is also gratefully acknowledged. We are embedded to the Ministry of the Interior and the other sponsors for supporting this effort to understand the complexities and problems of the transformation process from plan to market. Finally, we thank Fenna Pols for her editorial assistance, and Gerri Stender and Jamila Younouss for finalizing the manuscript.

Hendrikus J. Blommestein and Bernard Steunenberg

Foreword

The Netherlands Centre for Cooperation and Security in Europe (NCSCE) was founded in 1991 as a response to the dramatic political and economic changes in Central and Eastern Europe. The principal objective of the NCSCE is to conduct and promote research on the transformation from a planned economy to a market-based democratic society. The transformation is studied from economic, political, legal, and sociological points of view. This multi-disciplinary orientation enables the NCSCE to serve as a focal point for studying in a systematic fashion the relations between the different dimensions of the transformation from plan to market.

The NCSCE also provides training and technical advice to policymakers in formerly planned economies and organizes on a regular basis conferences, seminars, and lectures on the transformation process. In the period 13-15 August, 1992, the NCSCE brought together scholars and policymakers from the Baltics, Central and Eastern Europe, the former USSR, Western Europe, and the U.S.A. as well as representatives of the OECD, IMF, World Bank, European Union and the European Bank for Reconstruction and Development for a conference on 'Democratic Governments and the Transition from Plan to Market.' The conference is part of the NCSCE's commitment to enhance the understanding of the transformation process as well as to contribute to the dialogue with scholars and policymakers from Central and Eastern Europe and the former USSR.

Hendrikus J. Blommestein
CVSE Professor of Economics
Director NCSCE

Contributing Authors

Rolf Alter is Senior Economist at the OECD Directorate for Financial, Fiscal and Enterprise Affairs. Prior to joining the OECD in 1991, he was a staff member of the IMF. He holds a doctorate degree from the University of Göttingen, Germany.

Timothy Ash studied economics at Manchester and worked as a Researcher in Agricultural Economics at Exeter University before joining the Centre for Economic Reform and Transformation at Heriot-Watt University (U.K.) in 1991.

Cees van Beers is Assistant Professor of Economics at the University of Leiden since 1991. He received his Ph.D. in Economics from the Free University of Amsterdam/Tinbergen Institute.

Hendrikus J. Blommestein is a Senior Economist at the OECD, Paris, France. He is also the CSCE Professor of Economics, Faculty of Public Administration and Public Policies, University of Twente, Enschede, The Netherlands. Before joining the OECD, he served as Deputy Head of the International Monetary Affairs Division of the Netherlands Ministry of Finance and prior to that, as an Associate Professor of Economics at the University of Twente, Visiting Professor at the University of Akron, and Visiting Scholar at the Smithsonian Institution.

Peter B. Boorsma is Professor in Public Finance at Twente University, in the Netherlands. He is a member of the OECD Advisory Group on Privatization and the Christian Democratic fraction of the Senate. As a Senator he is one of the speakers on Government Finance and Health.

James M. Buchanan earned his Ph.D. from the University of Chicago (1948). Is currently Advisory General Director, Center for Study of Public Choice, Harris University Professor, George Mason University, Fairfax, Virginia and holder of the Nobel Prize in Economic Sciences, 1986.

Anna Canning graduated in interpreting and translating at Heriot-Watt University, then worked in Hungary for three years for the Ecumenical Youth Council in Europe. In 1992 she joined the Centre for Economic Reform and Transformation at the Heriot-Watt University (U.K.).

Ron J.H.A. Crijns works at the Provincial Council of Overijssel and the Ministry of Waterways and Public Works. He served previously as an Assistant Professor at the University of Twente, in the Netherlands.

Huib M. de Jong is Professor of Law at the University of Twente, Faculty of Public Administration and Public Policy, in the Netherlands.

Paul G. Hare was educated at Cambridge and Oxford Universities and has spent most of his subsequent academic career in Scotland, first at Stirling University and since 1985 as Professor of Economics and, since 1990, as Director of the Centre for Economic Reform and Transformation at Heriot-Watt University (U.K.).

Max Kaase is Research Professor at the Wissenschaftszentrum Berlin für Sozialforschung, Germany. He obtained his Ph.D. in Political Science at the University in Cologne and his Habilitation (*venia legendi*) at the University of Mannheim. He was Director of ZUMA, a social science academic research institute, in Mannheim from 1974 to 1980 and then held a chair in Political Science and Comparative Social Research at the University of Mannheim until 1993.

George Kopits is the Senior Resident Representative of the International Monetary Fund in Hungary. Previously he was Chief of the Fund's Fiscal Operations Division. Earlier, he had served at the Office of the U.S. Secretary of Treasury and taught at the John Hopkins School of Advanced International Studies. He holds a Ph.D. in Economics from Georgetown University.

Timothy D. Lane is a Senior Economist with the European I Department of the International Monetary Fund. He received his Doctorate at the University of Western Ontario. Before joining the IMF, he served as an Assistant Professor at the University of Iowa and at Michigan State University.

James Langenfeld is Vice President of Lexecon, Inc. He received his Ph.D. in Economics from Washington University in St. Louis, U.S.A. He has served as the Director for Antitrust in the Bureau of Economics of the U.S. Federal Trade Commission and has worked at General Motors, the U.S. Interstate Commerce Commission, and Amtrak.

Laurence J. O'Toole Jr. is Professor of Political Science at the University of Georgia, U.S.A. He served previously on the faculties of the University of Virginia and Auburn University, in the United States.

Dick W.P. Ruiter is Professor of Constitutional and Administrative Law at the University of Twente, Faculty of Public Administration and Public Policy, in the Netherlands.

Tad M. Rybczynski is an Honorary Visiting Professor at the City University, London. He has been a Visiting Professor at the Surrey University 1968-1974 and at the City University 1974-1987. He was the Economic Adviser to Lazard Bros. & Co. Ltd. London 1973-1988, a director of Lazard Securities 1969-1986, and a member of the U.K. Monopolies and Mergers Commission 1978-1982.

Holger Schmieding studied Economics in Munich, London and Kiel, where he received his doctorate. Having worked at the Kiel Institute of World Economics and at the IMF in Washington D.C., he is presently Senior Economist at an international investment bank in Frankfurt am Main, Germany.

Bernard Steunenberg is Associate Professor of Public Finance at the University of Twente, the Netherlands, and holds a Ph.D. in Public Administration and Policy Analysis.

Jules Theeuwes is Professor of Economics at the University of Leiden, in the Netherlands. He worked as a Lecturer at the Free University Amsterdam and Erasmus University Rotterdam, and is a former Research Associate of the Centre for Operations Research and Econometrics at the University of Leuven, Belgium, Visiting Professor of Economics at the University of British Columbia (Canada) and the University of Wisconsin (U.S.A.), and Fellow at NIAS.

Dennis A. Yao is one of the five commissioners at the U.S. Federal Trade Commission. He is on leave from the Wharton School, University of Pennsylvania, where he is Associate Professor of Public Policy and Management and Associate Professor of Management.

1

Government and Markets: An Introduction

Bernard Steunenberg and Hendrikus J. Blommestein

> It will be one of our chief contentions that most of the rules of conduct which govern our actions, and most of the institutions which arise out of this regularity, are adaptations to the impossibility of anyone taking conscious account of all the particular facts which enter into the order of society (Hayek 1973: 13).

After the breakdown of the socialist regimes in Central and Eastern Europe and, somewhat later, the former Soviet Union these countries indicated that they were going to introduce as quickly as possible a market economy based on a democratic constitutional order. Initially, there was great enthusiasm and optimism in both East and West, and the general expectation was that the problems connected with such a transformation could be solved fairly smoothly and rapidly. However, the transformation from a planned socialist system into a civil market economy turned out to be a process fraught with many unexpected difficulties (Blommestein 1993a). The ultimate objective is clear: the introduction of a competitive market system with a much smaller and efficient public sector. The starting-point, however, appeared to be less clear in the sense that most reformers underestimated the problems associated with large inefficient bureaucracies and economies dominated by a noncompetitive industrial sector and an underdeveloped service sector.

Moreover, there are many social, political, economic, and budgetary obstacles to overcome. Policymakers face the task to find and suggest solutions that are supported by most groups in society. Given the heterogeneous and sometimes incompatible interests in these societies this is not a simple task. In addition, it is complicated by the following factors. First, the political system is being transformed from a 'one party' socialist model into a representative democratic system in which powers have to be shared. Not

H. J. Blommestein and B. Steunenberg (eds.), Government and Markets, 1–14.

only between legislative, executive and judicial branches of government, but also between different political parties which represent divergent views on the transformation process and its ultimate goals. Political powers are being dispersed, and this may reduce the speed of the transformation process. Second, many of the former socialist countries have inefficient and incompetent bureaucracies that are responsible for the implementation of reform. Moreover, as most of the bureaucratic agencies with administrative control over most sectors of the economy have to be abolished or privatized, their incentives to support and implement reforms may be weak or absent. These features do not promote a quick and successful change. Third, most of the economic and political entrepreneurs belonged to the social and political elites who supported and benefitted from the former regime. These entrepreneurs have to support and guide the process of transformation. Finally, the transformation process will provide economic agents with new opportunities to earn monopoly rents, which are the result of the regulation of market behavior, including the protection of newly privatized sectors. These rents serve as prices to be earned, and they will lead to investments in lobbying and other 'nonproductive' behavior in order to capture and secure these benefits (Buchanan et al. 1980; Tollison 1982; Mueller 1989: 229-246). Rent-seeking behavior will be an important driving force in the political decision-making process, and it does not necessarily promote a competitive political and economic order.

The government is an important actor in the transformation from plan to market. This leads to the following paradox (Blommestein 1993a). On the one hand, the ultimate aim is to reduce the role of government in the market process, which implies that most decisions about production, investments, savings and consumption have to be taken by private agents and not by public officials. On the other hand, the policymakers in these countries cannot rely completely on the spontaneous evolution of market-based institutions and practices, since the institutions and practices associated with a well-functioning market economy have been suppressed for decades. Policymakers face the task to create an environment in which markets can flourish.

This volume focuses on the role of government in the transformation process from plan to market, in particular its active, albeit very selective, institution building role. In this context, the following basic question will be addressed: how and to what extent are governments able to contribute to the emergence and development of the institutions of a market economy based on a democratic constitutional order?

In this introduction we will examine the analytical basis of the transformation and design of institutions. To that end, we shall first discuss the nature of social institutions and the extent to which they can be deliberately designed by man to serve its interests. Next, we study the role of government in a process of institutional changes and apply our insights to the development of a market economy based on a democratic political order. Finally, a number of important policy dilemmas in the transformation process from plan to market will be outlined.

Institutions and Institutional Change

To clarify the notion of social institutions a distinction has to be made between 'physical' and 'social' facts. Physical facts are observable and can therefore be considered as data for every individual. In contrast, social facts are not observable and will thus need to be explained to individuals who are not part of the corresponding social order. Although social facts are associated with specific symbols, signals or acts, which are observable, they cannot be understood without knowledge of the underlying behavioral rules. Thus, contrary to physical facts, social facts are only meaningful to those individuals who know the underlying behavioral rules and are willing to accept them. The existence of a chemical plant is clear to everyone, since it is tangible and visible. Even if someone denies that the object is a plant, it remains existent as an object. Ownership of this plant is a social fact, and its existence depends on the beliefs of the members of society, whereby they recognize and accept a set of rules called property rights. But if individuals just stop believing in the existence of property rights, these rights will not exist any longer and nothing will distinguish the former rightful owner from any other individual. This non-physical nature is typical for social institutions, and they are therefore logically related to individual behavior and beliefs (Rowe 1989: 20).

The non-physical nature of social institutions implies that they are man made. Furthermore, social institutions apply to social interaction, and can be described as the 'working rules' of society (Ostrom 1990: 51) or the 'humanly devised constraints that shape human interaction' (North 1990: 3).[1] Institutions as sets of rules governing social interaction have to be distinguished from behavior (see Ostrom 1986: 4-5; Ruiter 1994). This distinction is not always made, and institutions are sometimes typified by the behavioral

[1] Ostrom (1990: 51) distinguishes various types of these rules, such as '...rules that are used to determine who is eligible to make decisions in some arena, what actions are allowed or constrained, what aggregation rules will be used, what procedures must be followed, what information must or must not be provided, and what payoffs will be assigned to individuals dependent on their actions.'

regularities they induce.[2] These regularities or 'particular ways of acting' only indicate that individuals participate in some social institution. But these individuals, in some way, have to be familiar with the set of rules which constitutes a social institution in order to interpret behavior as 'regular' or 'predictable' in the sense of following or being constrained by a specific rule. Property rights, for example, do not just exist because someone's field was accidentally not trespassed for some time by individuals unfamiliar with these rights, but because individuals recognize and accept property rights, and will behave accordingly.

Social institutions and institutional changes are the result of human design and invention. This is not to say that the reasons for these changes are always known to the participants in some institution, or that institutions are designed for the purpose they appear to serve. The process of change is 'overwhelmingly' incremental, as North (1990: 83) indicates, and it continuously shapes the institutions of society. The question now arises whether, and to what extent, individuals are capable of creating or designing those institutions which they think will serve best their interests. Or, to put it differently, to what extent is it desirable and feasible to design an 'optimal' set of market institutions as the outcome of a well-defined optimization problem? If the design of optimal institutions is in principle possible, then policymakers are best advised to implement a detailed design of the market and other institutions on the basis of these 'optimal' blue-prints. However, this approach is fruitless and deceiving, since it is based on false assumption regarding knowledge and the human mind. As Hayek (1973) argues, all our knowledge is conjectural and that the human mind has a limited capacity to analyze information. No one knows *ex ante* what constitutes the 'best' solution to a social interaction problem. Consequently, only *ex post* will it be possible to determine whether a proposed solution will work as anticipated. Thus, a new institutional arrangement has to be regarded as a 'trial' in a process of testing, and only *ex post* will it be possible to determine its actual capacity to solve a well-defined set of problems.

[2] Rowe (1989: 21-22), for instance, describes social institutions as '...*identical to* ...some or other facet of human action and belief. A social institution is nothing more than a particular way of acting and believing for some agents who are thus said to be members of, or participants in, that social institution.' Also Schotter (1981: 11) stresses the importance of behavioral regularities, when he defines a social institution as '...a regularity in social behavior that ...specifies behavior in specific recurrent situations, and is either self-policing or policed by some external authority.'

The impossibility of constructing *ex ante* 'optimal' institutions, necessitates that one focuses on the process of change.[3] In this process different rules can be tested, and the problem-solving capacity of an *ex ante* rule can be compared with that of alternative solutions. Such a process of testing by trial and error allows institutions to be continuously adapted, refined or corrected in view of past experience. The extent to which such an evolutionary process is effective, determines the ability of a society to solve its problems associated with human interaction through time. As Alchian (1950) as well as Hayek (1960) indicate, a society which is able to generate the largest number of trials is most likely to solve these problems. In other words, an open process of trial and error, which is not *ex ante* restricted by any rules or values and, therefore, allows for various arrangements to be tried out, is most likely to be a more successful society than one that prohibits or restricts strongly alternative institutional arrangements on ideological or other grounds.[4]

An evolutionary process of institutional change governed by the principle of trial and error, may lead to unexpected outcomes. Consequently, the notion of deliberate institutional choice should be qualified with the observation that it is based on conjectural knowledge of individuals that operate in a 'reality' they cannot fully comprehend.[5] Moreover, as indicated above, institutional choice is restricted by 'values' (for instance, equity) which limit 'competition' between alternative institutional arrangements. The experience of centrally planned economies demonstrates the drawbacks of a system governed by values that severely restricts the competition between different institutional solutions. It also demonstrates, however, that values may dramatically change thereby facilitating institutional changes.

[3] See Blommestein (1992) for an application of this idea to the process of privatization.

[4] See Popper (1974) for a similar argument on scientific inquiry. However, as Vanberg (1993: 317) indicates, a key difference between scientific inquiry and an evolutionary process of social institutions is that our knowledge of the problem-solving capacity of alternative rules is '...not so much as explicit and articulated knowledge, but as experience that is implicit or embodied in time-tested rules and institutions.'

[5] In his work, Hayek (1973: 29-30) rejects 'constructivist rationalism' (or 'naive rationalism' in Popper's terminology) which implies that '...conscious reason ought to determine every particular action.' To Hayek this type of rationalism is based on the heroic and completely mistaken assumption of unlimited human abilities to understand itself as well as its environment, and it is distinguished from 'evolutionary rationalism' (or in Popper's terminology 'critical rationalism') which '...recognizes abstractions as the indispensable means of the mind which enable it to deal with a reality it cannot fully comprehend.'

The Role of Government in the Transformation Process

Policymakers in Central and Eastern Europe have to guide two different, albeit interdependent, processes of institutional change. First, these countries want to move toward a *democratic* order which is characterized by a stable set of rules for collective decisionmaking which promotes equity among individuals. Second, their aim is to establish a *market economy* as well, that is, a set of rules that makes possible and facilitates voluntary exchange among individuals and which is grounded on individual liberty. As Buchanan (1994) indicates, the independence of each individual from the coercion of the state can be achieved by setting constitutional limits to the authority of democratic government, which makes clear that both goals are interdependent and cannot be approached separately. The problem these countries face is to find a balance between individual liberty and equity, which affects the extent to which an evolutionary process is allowed to work. Based on these values, government has to find a way between intervention and spontaneous development or, as Hayek puts it, between *taxis* and *kosmos*.[6] This choice will affect the transformation from plan to market (Blommestein 1993a). Too much emphasis on *taxis* will hamper the development of a market economy and thus slow down the transformation process. On the other hand, a too passive government may reduce the transformation to competitive markets as well, since the starting-point for all these countries is a centrally planned economy.

Development of a Democratic Constitutional Order

The creation of autonomous and accountable government institutions are an often neglected, yet very crucial part of the development of a market economy. An important issue is the impact of government institutions and rules on the extent of rent-seeking in an economy. Incentives for rent-seeking are created by the overall manner in which the government runs its business and interacts with the economy. The degree of autonomy and accountability of a government, being part of the institutions constituting the political order, are the main determinants of the extent of rent-seeking. The rules constituting the political order offer opportunities of wealth distribution.

Weak states are characterized by weak institutions that are very vulnerable to political pressures (e.g. of well-organized special interest groups, including organized crime); weak or soft states will consistently underprovide economically desirable interventions. This in turn means that in the economies of

[6] In Hayek's terminology, *taxis* is the deliberate organization of individual actions, and *kosmos* represents the spontaneous evolution of institutions and rules (Hayek 1973: 36-38).

weak states significant resources are allocated to use political institutions and the political process in order to extract income and wealth from others in the society. These private efforts or activities distract valuable resources from socially productive use. For example, Bhagwati and Srinivas (1982) analyze the relation between government regulation, corruption and black markets. They argue that the main characteristic of so-called directly unproductive profit-seeking activities (e.g. corruption and other illicit transactions) is that they consist of ways of making profits which do not involve directly the production of any output. Baumol (1990) shows that the allocation between productive and nonproductive entrepreneurial activities is strongly influenced by the relative payoffs society offers to illicit transactions. The payoffs in turn are determined to a large extent by the enforcement of policies to combat illegal activities. In this context Blommestein (1993b) has argued that a necessary condition for the establishment of successful market based financial institutions in former planned economies is the implementation of adequate policies and safeguards against illicit transactions.

The redistribution of income and wealth is a driving force of the political process. Knight (1971) and others have noted that some basic measure of redistribution is a necessary condition for a stable order. On the other hand, experience shows that persistent redistributive activities undermine the liberal political order. Wide-spread black markets in market economies are *prima facie* evidence that governments have gone beyond a critical threshold of redistribution. Of greater concern is that some former communist countries may not have reached the point to establish the critical threshold of a civil economy in which political freedom and constitutional constraints on governmental authority provide a solid underpinning to the rules of the game and institutions of a market economy. In other words, rule by authority and arbitrary government has not yet been fully replaced by the Rule of Law. Instead, we are observing societies in which rent-seeking is widespread, many private and public agents are involved in semi-legal or illegal activities, government institutions are 'weak', political accountability is absent, and private ownership of productive resources is not (sufficiently) protected against political takings. Yet, the legal state (*Rechtsstaat*) is a vital component of a competitive order because it constitutes the basis for political rights and individual autonomy (De Jong and Ruiter 1994). In this context Buchanan (1994) has argued that the necessary conditions for the effective functioning of a market economy require that clearly defined limits are placed on the range and scope of the actions of the government, including constitutional constraints on the range and scope of political authority. These limits and constitutional constraints are part of the political, legal and economic order. This view also means that at an early as possible stage in the political transformation process, an active institution building role by the government and the politicians is required in order to limit the frequent intrusion of politics in the market. This means that the balance between *taxis* and *kosmos* in creating a democratic order should be in favor of the former.

Development of a Market Order

The creation of a democratic, market-based society means the building up of new institutions and rules, while transforming or eliminating existing ones. In a market economy most resources are controlled by private agents. A well-functioning market economy is characterized by a set of rules and institutions that constitutes an effective corporate governance structure for allocating these resources efficiently. Private property rights and market based institutions and practices (for instance, commercial banks, capital markets, bankruptcy proceedings and corporate laws) are important elements of effective corporate control mechanisms. In former centrally planned economies these mechanisms are (largely) missing. Consequently, the general objective of the transformation toward a market economy is to establish and develop the institutions and rules for an effective corporate governance structure in a political, legal and economic order dominated by private agents (Blommestein 1993a). The main task of privatization and the related development of market institutions is therefore to ensure that the transfer of property rights from the state to the private sector leads to effective control by private owners or their proxies. There are four main reasons for an active role of the government in the development of a competitive enterprise sector, including privatization.

First, the scale and scope of privatization is very wide in former planned systems. These economies possess significant concentrations of specialized productive capacity in state-owned hands. The speedy transfer of these assets to private agents requires therefore the introduction of privatization institutions and rules by the authorities. Examples include the introduction of a proper legal framework for the specification and enforcement of private property rights, the legal treatment of the liabilities of state-owned enterprises (for instance, debts, environmental damage), and the creation of privatization agencies. In addition, appropriate action by the government needs to be taken prior to the privatization of individual enterprises: a proper legal framework for the functioning of enterprises, including an effective bankruptcy law and reducing the power of workers' councils in the management of enterprises; eliminating highly subsidized services to workers; financial restructuring of the enterprises; splitting huge industrial conglomerates into autonomous components and so on (see Blommestein et al. 1993). However, it is important that the privatization framework is flexible enough to allow the adaption to new circumstances or a timely reaction to unintended consequences. This would argue in favor of spontaneous or bottom-up privatization mechanisms within the broader institutional framework. For example, the use of buy outs within a general legal framework for privatization. The challenge for the authorities is to strike as much as possible the right balance between *taxis* and *kosmos*. Unfortunately, the right balance is impossible to predict on the basis of existing knowledge. Inevitably, learning by doing will be an essential ingredient of privatization and the transformation process.

Second, the government has a key role to play in the establishment of the institution of private property, which is expected to improve the dynamic allocation of resources. Simply put, the entry of new private firms and the transfer of most public assets to the private sector is expected to lead to an increase in efficiency. This line of reasoning comes from an understanding of principal-agent relationships (Nuti 1991). The institution of private property subjects enterprise managers to three types of competitive pressure: contractual discipline imposed by shareholders, take-over discipline enforced by potential bidders, and bankruptcy discipline exerted by creditors. It is then easy to understand why the absence of such pressures has been put forward as a important reason for the inefficiency that characterized state-owned enterprises in former planned systems. In sum, theory and practice suggest that the proper incentives to allocate resources efficiently over time exist only under private ownership. Thus, a vital condition for creating efficient competitive markets is the rapid establishment of a private property base.

The extent to which private property produces efficient results depends on how, among other things, the other factors that influence effective corporate governance are implemented. This is the third area for an active institution building role by the government (see also Blommestein and Spencer 1993). For related reasons, for privatization to succeed at all in improving efficiency, the system of central control over enterprise management must be replaced by another control mechanism which not only provides managers with the resources to finance restructuring but also gives them the incentives to respond to market prices in the most efficient manner feasible. Market based financial institutions play a key role in achieving these objectives. Unfortunately, the financial system inherited from the system of central planning is in a very poor state (Blommestein 1992). The banking system in most former planned economies is plagued by large stocks of non-performing loans to state enterprises, low capital, bank staff that is largely unfamiliar with commercial practices, and loan portfolios that are concentrated geographically and sectorial. Banking supervision is inadequate. Equity and bond markets are either nonexistent or extremely small and illiquid. Payment systems are unsafe and inefficient (Blommestein and Summers 1994). Yet, the transformation process, in particular privatization, places tremendous demands on the financial system. The government has therefore an important role to play in the development of market based financial institutions. First, the authorities need to eliminate the structural obstacles that prevent or hamper the emergence of a reliable, stable, and efficient financial sector (Blommestein and Lange 1993). This would argue in particular in favor of providing a jump start to the development of a sound banking sector. Second, the government should encourage or allow financial institutions to play an important corporate governance role in order to overcome or mitigate principal-agent problems in privatized enterprises. These problems stem from the following situation, in many respects unique to the transformation process. The relatively broad distribution of shares in privatized firms and symmetries of information between the managers of firms, its shareholders, and its creditors create the potential for conflicts between these groups. These conflicts can fruitfully be discussed in terms of a principal-agent model in which, for example, the manager act as the agent for the principal, that is, shareholders or creditors (Blommestein and Spencer 1993). Agency conflicts and resulting costs can be alleviated by providing the principal with a mechanism for monitoring the behavior of the agent. Provided this monitoring ability is combined with an enforcement mechanism, second-best contracts can be designed which reduce agency costs. The challenge of privatization and, more generally, the development of competitive markets is to replace the direct control mechanisms of the state by market based mechanisms such as financial institutions. The potential for agency conflicts during and after the transition process provides the basic rationale for the corporate control function of financial institutions. The government needs therefore to move as rapidly as possible to eliminate the structural obstacles to an effective corporate control function by financial and other market institutions.

Fourth, public authorities have the task is to lay out clearly the principles and rules governing the operation of market institutions and to supervise compliance with (or, at least, provide the framework for supervision) and enforce these rules. For example, the legal underpinning of the modern property system improved the specification and enforcement of property rights by providing protection against arbitrary actions of governments. In addition, the current confusion in many former planned economies over 'who owns what' should be eliminated in order to reduce incentives for the current 'managers' of enterprises and farms from engaging in asset stripping and to distribute responsibility for existing liabilities. In general, failure to specify and enforce property rights acts as an impediment to privatization, foreign direct investment and the efficient utilization of the capital stock.

Dilemmas

The central objective of the political-economic transformation process is to reduce dramatically the influence of the state on individual activities. Nonetheless, the role of government in the development of a market economy is important. However, this role should be largely be limited to eliminating the obstacles to and putting in place the conditions for the emergence of a viable market economy. This does not mean that government should be passive in every respect. First, the introduction of a market economy requires an active, interventionist government in the initial stages of the transformation process. Second, the core of the structural reform program consists of conditions and institutions that promote the development of a democratic order. Both processes require a government that plays an active, albeit very selective, institution building role (Blommestein 1993a). This also means that government should implement clearly defined limits on the range and scope of public and political interventions.

The dilemma of government that should restrict the range and scope of political its own actions forms the basis of the chapters in this volume yet to come. Each of these chapters points to specific problems faced by the policymakers in these former centrally planned economies with respect to the development of a democratic constitutional order and a competitive market economy. The following policy dilemmas related to the transformation from plan to market can be identified.

The performance-expectations trap. Kaase (1994) concludes that citizens in the former socialist countries have attitudes which may form the basis of a stable democratic order. However, the political and economic problems in these countries are of such a magnitude that it is doubtful 'whether transitions will indeed lead to consolidated democratic polities.' Policymakers face the difficult task to convince their constituencies that reforms are on the right track while expectations about economic performance is falling and political discontent is rising.

Privatization and the development of market institutions. Policymakers in formerly centrally planned economies cannot fully rely on the spontaneous emergence of market institutions, since the institutions and practices of a well-functioning economy have been suppressed for decades. This implies that government has to play an active role in the privatization process. However, policymakers are faced with the dilemma that the more they interfere with the role of market institutions, the less likely that they will develop (Hare et al. 1994). In other words, policymakers need to strike a balance between *taxis* and *kosmos*.

Formal versus informal property rights. In the formerly socialist countries, state-owned enterprises and other assets were in many cases controlled at the local level. Important decisions about production, land use and so on, were made by managers, workers or local bureaucrats. As Schmieding (1994) points out, the combination of state-ownership and local control results in conflicts and tensions and will trigger intense local political resistance against changes initiated by the central authorities. Policymakers at the central level face therefore the task to balance formal and informal rights in developing privatization schemes.

Central government policies and local government interference. The government machinery is also being transformed. For example, in most countries in Central and Eastern Europe the local government is re-established after a period of one-party control from the center. Local government may provide the central policymakers with the opportunity for a decentralized approach for some of the transformation problems they face. However, local governments may also complicate central government policies, as shown by O'Toole (1994) in case of the privatization program in Hungary.

Competition agencies and market competition. Most countries in Central and Eastern Europe have passed competition laws and have established competition agencies. The main task of these agencies is to develop competitive markets. Since a market economy does not yet exist, these agencies are *de facto* playing an active, interventionist role (Langenfeld and Yao 1994). Policymakers in these agencies face therefore the dilemma that the more they regulate market behavior and the more they intervene in the market process, the lower the chances that competitive markets will develop.

Full employment syndrome. Government in the formerly socialist countries guaranteed all workers permanent jobs. The transformation to a market economy will, in the short run, lead to unemployment as a result of the process of restructuring. Also in the long run one should expect some unemployment (Van Beers and Theeuwes 1994). Policymakers are facing the problem to reduce government intervention in moving to a market economy while creating 'open' unemployment.

Privatization and macroeconomic management. As soon as the market-oriented transformation creates privately-owned and more autonomous enterprises in the former centrally planned economies, policymakers lose most of their capacity to suppress macroeconomic imbalances through traditional administrative measures. Furthermore, privatization will erode the traditional tax base, that is, the surpluses or profits of state-owned enterprises. This may lead to large budget deficits. In the absence of market-based monetary instruments (Rybczynski 1994; Lane 1994), these deficits together with price liberalization may generate hyper-inflation. Policymakers are facing the difficult task to accompany spontaneous market developments by the use of macroeconomic control instruments such as credit limits to banks, exchange rate controls, wage controls and fiscal limits (Kopits 1994).

References

Alchian, A.A. (1950) Uncertainty, Evolution and Economic Theory. *Journal of Political Economy* 58: 211-221.

Alter, R. (1994) *The Economic Role of Government.* In this volume.

Baumol, W.J. (1990) Entrepreneurship: Productive, Unproductive, and Destructive. *Journal of Political Economy* 98: 893-921.

Bhagwati, J.N. and T.N. Srinivas (1982) The Welfare Consequences of Directly-Unproductive Profit-Seeking (DUP) Lobbying Activities. *Journal of International Economics* 13: 33-44.

Blommestein, H.J. (1992) Sound Banks for a Strong Market. *OECD Observer* 177: 13-22.

Blommestein, H.J. (1993a) Government and Markets, Inaugural Lecture, Netherlands Center For Security Co-operation in Europe (NCSCE). Enschede: University of Twente.

Blommestein, H.J. (1993b) Illicit Transactions and Financial Markets, Statement read at a special session of the Antimafia Committee of the Italian Parliament. Roma.

Blommestein, H.J. (1994) *Markets and Governments in Advanced Market Economies: Experiences and Lessons.* In this volume.

Blommestein, H.J., R. Geiger and P. Hare (1993) *Privatising Large Enterprises: Overview of Issues and Case-Studies.* In: H.J. Blommestein, R. Geiger and P. Hare (eds.) *Privatising Large Enterprises.* Paris: OECD. 11-37.

Blommestein, H.J. and J.R. Lange (1993) *Balance Sheet Restructuring and Privatization of the Banks.* In: H.J. Blommestein and J.R. Lange (eds.) *Transformation of the Banking System: Portfolio Restructuring, Privatization and Payment System Reform.* Paris: OECD. 13-33.

Blommestein, H.J. and M.G. Spencer (1993) The Role of Financial Institutions in the Transformation to a Market Economy. Washington, D.C.: International Monetary Fund. IMF Working Paper WP/93/75.

Blommestein, H.J. and B.J. Summers (1994) *Banking and the Payment System.* In: B.J. Summers and H.J. Blommestein (eds.) *The Payment System: Design, Management, and Supervision.* forthcoming

Buchanan, J.M. (1994) *Democracy within Constitutional Limits.* In this volume.

Buchanan, J.M., R.D. Tollison and G. Tullock (eds.)(1980) *Toward a Theory of the Rent-Seeking Society.* College Station: Texas A&M Press.

De Jong, H.M. and D.W.P. Ruiter (1994) *Democracy, Legal State, and Constitutional Change.* In this volume.

Hare, P.G., A. Canning and T. Ash (1994) *The Role of Government Institutions in the Process of Privatization.* In this volume.

Hayek, F.A. (1960) *The Constitution of Liberty.* Chicago: University of Chicago Press.

Hayek, F.A. (1973) *Law, Legislation and Liberty: A New Statement of the Liberal Principles of Justice and Political Economy. Volume 1: Rules and Order.* Chicago: University of Chicago Press.

Kaase, M. (1994) *Political Culture and Political Consolidation.* In this volume.

Knight, F.H. (1971 [1921]) *Risk, Uncertainty and Profit.* Chicago: University of Chicago Press.

Kopits, G. (1994) *Monetary and Fiscal Management During the Transformation.* In this volume.

Lane, T.D. (1994) *Financial Sector Reforms: Banking, Securities, and Payments.* In this volume.

Langenfeld, J. and D.A. Yao (1994) *Competition Policy and Privatization: An Organizational Perspective.* In this volume.

Mueller, D.C. (1989) *Public Choice II: A Revised Edition of Public Choice.* Cambridge: Cambridge University Press.

North, D.C. (1990) *Institutions, Institutional Change and Economic Performance.* Cambridge: Cambridge University Press.

Nuti, D.M. (1991) *Privatisation of Socialist Economies: General Issues and the Polish Case.* In: H.J. Blommestein and M. Marrese (eds.) *Transformation of Planned Economies: Property Rights Reform and Macroeconomic Stability.* Paris: OECD.

Ostrom, E. (1986) An Agenda for the Study of Institutions. *Public Choice* 48: 3-25.

Ostrom, E. (1990) *Governing the Commons: The Evolution of Institutions for Collective Action.* Cambridge: Cambridge University Press.

O'Toole, L.J., Jr. (1994) *Privatization in Hungary: Implementation Issues and Local Government Complications.* In this volume.

Popper, K.R. (1974) *The Logic of Scientific Discovery.* London: Hutchinson.

Rowe, N. (1989) *Rules and Institutions.* Ann Arbor: University of Michigan Press.

Ruiter, D.W.P (1994) Economic and Legal Institutionalism: What Can They Learn from Each Other. In: *Constitutional Political Economy* 5: 99-115.

Rybczynski, T.M. (1994) *The Role of Banks and Financial Markets in the Process of Privatization.* In this volume.

Schmieding, H. (1994) *Property Rights, Institutions, and Market Reform.* In this volume.

Schotter, A. (1981) *The Economic Theory of Social Institutions.* Cambridge: Cambridge University Press.

Tollison, R.D. (1982) Rent Seeking: A Survey. *Kyklos* 35: 575-602.

Van Beers, C. and J. Theeuwes (1994) *Labor in Transition to a Market Economy.* In this volume.

Vanberg, V. (1993) *F.A. Hayek.* In: G.M. Hodgson, W.J. Samuels and M.R. Tool (eds.) *The Elgar Compagnion to Institutional and Evolutionary Economics: A-K.* London: Edward Edgar. 314-320.

2

Markets and Government in Advanced Market Economies: Experiences and Lessons

Hendrikus J. Blommestein*

> ...It seems demonstrable that both representative political institutions and free exchange and free enterprise are essential to the general framework of a truly moral social order... [A]ny great extension of state action in economics is incompatible with political liberty...
>
> Of course I do not believe in literal 'laisser-faire'; I know of no reputable economist who ever did. Certainly neither Smith and Ricardo nor Cobden and Bright would have restricted the state entirely to the negative functions of policing individual liberty and defence against outside attack (Knight 1948).

In this chapter I will identify and discuss several guidelines for policymakers responsible for designing market and government institutions in emerging market economies. The guidelines are based on the experience of a number of advanced market economies. The focus is on the role of governments in creating or fostering the development of market institutions and 'rules of the market game.' Yet, my contribution is not a recipe for the creation of markets or the transformation process in general. No blueprint will be outlined here. In any event, this would be a futile exercise because the transformation of planned economies is an extremely complex political, social, and economic process. It is characterized by many unexpected problems, unintended consequences, spontaneous processes including the emergence of new market institutions, errors, and learning-by-doing. It is, indeed, to a large extent

* The opinions expressed and arguments employed in this paper are the sole responsibility of the author and do not necessarily reflect those of the OECD or of the governments of its member countries.

H. J. Blommestein and B. Steunenberg (eds.), Government and Markets, 15–37.

sailing in uncharted waters. Although the objective or direction of change might in very general terms be clear, the exact road toward that goal is by definition less obvious.

The chapter is structured as follows. First, I will outline the main features of successful market economies. Next, I will explain why the building of market institutions is a very complex undertaking that goes far beyond the adoption of laws or decrees. I will do this by focusing on the OECD experience with market institutions, including the role of government in developing, protecting and fostering these institutions. In the final part of the chapter I will mention possible guidelines—perhaps even lessons for governments in Central and Eastern European countries based on the OECD experience with market institutions.

Features of Successful Market Economies

Successful market economies share the following important features[1]:

Rule of Law

The rule of law has replaced rule by authority. 'This means that government in all its actions is bound by rules fixed and announced beforehand—rules which make it possible to foresee with fair certainty how the authority will use its coercive powers in given circumstances...' (Hayek 1977: 72). The legal state (*Rechtsstaat*) constitutes the basis for political rights and economic freedoms. This means that individual rights are protected, the existence of independent courts, the protection of private property and the existence of laws that enforce private contracts. Moreover, 'entry' of enterprises is regulated by laws that permit enterprises to organize themselves as subsidiaries, joint ventures, joint stock and limited-liability companies, while 'exit' is regulated by bankruptcy laws.

Private Ownership

The means of production are predominantly privately owned. State-owned enterprises, in some cases accounting for as much as one-third or more of output, played a more important role during the early stages of reconstruction and development in OECD countries, when unemployment was still extensive and voluntary savings were still low, than more recently. State enterprises tend to be more efficient when they function in a competitive environment

[1] See Helliwell (1991) and Marer (1991) for excellent and more detailed overviews.

than when they are insulated from domestic and foreign competitive pressures. However, the operation of state-owned firms is difficult to insulate from political and bureaucratic pressures. In practice, many state-owned enterprises face soft budget constraints. Effective corporate governance of state-owned enterprises seems difficult to realize. Consequently, in recent years practically all the industrial countries and many developing economies in Latin America and Asia have implemented programs of privatization.

Competition

The most crucial feature of a market system is effective competition. Competition was found in all successful market economies to be a key ingredient for achieving productivity advances in the private sector. In some cases, foreign and domestic competitive pressures were used as substitutes. For smaller countries, the discipline of the international markets is crucial from the beginning. Although larger countries have a wider scope for achieving gains in efficiency through domestic competition, open regimes for international trade and foreign direct investment are also of great importance for larger economies.

Sound Currency

One of the essential functions of government is to provide a sound currency. This means a low rate of inflation and a credible program to move to partial and then to full convertibility. The rate of inflation can be kept manageable only with sound monetary and fiscal policies (Sargent 1986); the same is also a precondition for convertibility.

Reasonable price stability and the expectation that any existing or possible inflation will not get out of hand are necessary to motivate business firms as well as households in their capacity as savers and providers of labor services to take the long view and focus on real economic activities instead of devoting their energies to hoarding, speculation and other kinds of manipulation to protect the value of their assets.

Convertibility is essential to link the domestic economy with the world economy. Convertibility facilitates establishing correct relative prices and the efficient cross-border flow of goods, services, technology and people. No meaningful import competition or trade along the lines of comparative advantage is likely to occur without the currency being convertible. *Comparative advantage* is usually emphasized in relation to foreign trade, although it applies equally in principle to specialization and exchange within the domestic economy.

Savings, Financial Intermediation and Capital Accumulation

An adequate level of voluntary savings and an efficient financial intermediation of savings into productive investments are essential common features of sustained, positive economic performance. Efficient investment in physical and human capital is the engine of technical progress and productivity improvements. In the long run, all countries must rely on domestic savings to finance an adequate level of domestic investment. Foreign savings can assist a country only for a certain amount of time.

A market-based competitive financial system is essential for the efficient allocation of new savings on the basis of risk-return criteria but, also, as an important vehicle for effective corporate governance of the existing capital stock. This means a system that is largely private, with investors risking their own funds and seeking profits (Blommestein 1992). Moreover, savers and investors must be able to choose from an array of financial instruments (e.g. savings accounts, stocks and bonds and the like). Market-based financial institutions are also important components of the corporate governance structure in market economies (Blommestein and Spencer 1993).

Much emphasis is traditionally placed on the accumulation of physical capital, in the form of factories, housing, roads and telecommunication systems. Equally important, are the accumulation of human capital, chiefly represented by health, education and skills. Governments have traditionally played an important role by providing public goods in these areas.

Individual Liberty and the Role of Government

People can, in accordance with the freedoms of a constitutional democracy, determine their own destiny. This means that they possess the political and economic freedom to pursue goals as entrepreneurs, investors, professionals, and wage earners. Social mobility is key for people's goal-setting and sense of fulfillment. A rigid social order and lack of individual freedom hamper adjustments to changes in the economy, leading to inefficient allocations of resources. Free exchange and free enterprise also require that the role of government is 'restricted.' Buchanan (1994) argues that the necessary conditions for the effective functioning of a market economy require that the range and scope of democratic authority be limited. 'Big' and arbitrary governments pose a threat to individual liberties, including the freedom to run one's own business. Predictability of governmental policies and actions is also key for successful market economies because it reduces the type of uncertainty that is harmful for investors and entrepreneurs. Interventions by the government to correct market failures should be subject to cost-benefit analyses, in order to safeguard against the substitution of 'market failures' by 'government failures.'

Stable Political and Social Institutions

Individual liberties need to go together with stable political institutions. The experience of OECD countries underlines the importance of social cohesion and widespread support for the inevitable rigors of the reform process, and there are many different ways to achieve these supportive factors. Giersch (1990) emphasizes the importance of establishing a stable democratic system. The democratic process should help in setting realistic expectations for the reform process and articulating a common purpose. For example, Spain's reforms succeeded, despite a sequence of changing governments, because all of the parties backed a common objective, namely, to follow the models and forms of Western European political and economic systems (De la Dehesa 1990). In those models, the establishment of a stable democratic system is a necessary precondition for successful economic reforms.

Another aspect of stable social institutions is the establishment of a system of social safety nets. These systems have been prominent in Sweden and Finland (Lindbeck 1990; Vartia 1990); they appear to have played a much smaller role in Japan and Korea (Yoshitumi 1990; Park 1990). The basic challenge for governments in emerging market economies is to develop a social safety net that does not undermine: (1) the objective of budgetary consolidation; and (2) the introduction of a market-based incentive structure.

Political units need to be homogeneous enough to support a sense of shared purpose and to ensure that elected governments have a real chance of maintaining legitimacy. This raises the following complicated issue: in multiethnic and multinational states facing sustained and explosive tensions, is it worth accepting a proliferation of smaller independent national states or semi-independent regional governments in order to capture local loyalties as the glue for a binding consensus behind policies of transformation cum-modernization? Or might this instead lead to a major slowdown of the transformation process because fragmentation and politization lend to greater uncertainties, higher input and more opportunities for rent-seeking? An optimistic vision might be formulated as follows: allow maximal autonomy to ethnic or regional units by the creation of a democracy or legal state with strong constitutional constraints on the central (federal) and local governmental authorities. A quick transformation will result in a society in which free exchange and free enterprise dominate economic activities, so that ample opportunities are created for individuals from the different ethnic and regional units to increase their economic welfare.

OECD Experience with Competitive Markets

These features of successful market economies provide a first, general indication for the design of a successful market building strategy. The next step is to explain why this is a very complex undertaking. I will do this by drawing on the OECD experience with developing and fostering competitive markets as described in Blommestein and Marrese (1991b).

There is increasing recognition that it is extraordinarily difficult to create, in a short amount of time, conditions and institutions that promote the development of competitive markets. In 1989, this was not the case because people in the East and West were very confident that the introduction of the successful market model could be done easily and quickly. In 1990 this optimism already started to fade. By the end of 1990, popular domestic enthusiasm for the transformation of these economies had declined as people became more aware that economic transformation is a long and painful process. Competitive markets are not simply legislated into existence in one broad stroke and used 'as is' thereafter. Rather they are the ever-changing interplay of entrepreneurial actors conditioned by institutions, incentives and rules of the game that evolve over time and as a result of social bargaining among employers, employees and government representatives.

Thus, there is now widespread recognition that it is very hard to create, in a short amount of time, conditions and institutions that promote the development of competitive markets. However, initially this was not the case.

In 1989 there were high expectations. In 1989, the populations of Central and Eastern Europe had numerous reasons to be optimistic. The following three were mentioned frequently:

1. market reform movements would no longer be hampered by ideological constraints;
2. governments and enterprises would be run by more capable people who would understand how a market economy functions; and
3. the West would offer substantial assistance.

The events since 1990 clearly indicate that this optimism was premature. There are several reasons but in this presentation I will discuss only one important reason: misunderstandings about the operation of a market economy. Before 1989 those individuals who designed radical reforms shared certain misconceptions about how market economies operate that in some cases led to inflated expectations about the pace of introducing a market economy. For instance, the incentive structures in most of these radical reforms were based on profit-sharing without paying enough attention to the sources of profit. Often profit did not stem from responsiveness to market opportunities, innovative insights or the acquisition of new techniques, but rather from an ability to exploit bureaucratic connections. More generally, policymakers seemed to share, perhaps unwittingly, a naive belief in the model of perfect competition. While this model is useful in describing the informational role of prices, it assumes that all agents are profit- or utility-maximizing price-takers in an environment of given cost functions, demand functions, and technological expertise (Demsetz 1982). However, the actual success of a market economy is related to its ability to uncover and improve cost and technological parameters and to discover demand conditions.

This ability depends on the response of economic agents to prevailing conditions and incentives, which in turn are influenced by government policies and a country's institutions.

So while the people of Central and Eastern Europe correctly recognized the ineffective response of economic agents prior to 1989, they may not have realized that a system of competitive markets requires two dramatically different sets of economic actors than existed previously. First and above all, entrepreneurs are needed who ideally possess:

> An alertness to market opportunities; the motivation and ability to act on such alertness by organising inputs to produce goods and services, and having ideas that are appropriate responses to either an arbitrage opportunity or an innovative insight; a willingness to bear risk; and a deep-seated desire to be generously rewarded for entrepreneurial success (Marrese 1990: 101).

Second, policymakers are needed who ideally, among other things, define and enforce market-oriented rules that constrain entrepreneurs to interact in a way that benefits society as a whole. These new sets of actors cannot be created overnight, especially when many of the most privileged members of these societies were government functionaries or managers of state-owned enterprises in the pre-1989 system.

Moreover, there is no single theoretical model to describe these conditions and institutions. Michael Marrese and I decided therefore to address the issue of creating competitive markets by describing the OECD experience with five dimensions neglected by models of perfect competition:

1. the influence of property rights on incentives;
2. the effect of legal, political and regulatory institutions on savings and investment;
3. the impact of monopoly, oligopoly, and external effects on information and transaction costs;
4. the adverse consequences of asymmetric information; and

5. factors that promote dynamic efficiency (see Table 2.1 for an outline of these ideas).

With respect to the *first dimension*, the most fundamental consideration is to establish clearly defined and legally recognized property rights. In OECD countries, there is a long tradition of private ownership of homes, small businesses, and capital goods. However there are still ambiguities concerning the use of public property, the misuse of private property, and the protection of intellectual property rights. Public property includes state-owned firms, parks, waterways, and roads. For state-owned firms, the state is the residual claimant of income, but the reward structure of these firms defines the way in which state ownership affects the incentives of managers and employees. For instance, the economics literature compares the relative efficiency of state-owned firms to privately owned firms and also attempts to measure changes in technical and allocative efficiency due to privatization (Atkinson and Halvorsen 1986; De Alessi 1977; Fare et al,. 1985; OECD 1987a, 1989a, 1989b: 23-25, 1989c). The public ownership of educational institutions, parks, waterways and roads can lead to overcrowding and inefficient utilization of these resources unless usage rights, obligations and fees are specified to reflect the 'marginal social benefit versus marginal social costs' tradeoff. Work in this area is widespread and includes the utilization of: educational vouchers (Friedman 1962: 85-107); user charges (OECD 1990); improved procurement practices (Commission of the European Communities 1989); contracting out government services (OECD 1987c, 1987d); and the franchising and private financing of public infrastructure.

The misuse of private property touches on three issues found in Table 2.1. First, for how long should intellectual property rights be protected given that such protection can hinder the development of competition and the diffusion of new technologies? (Jorde and Teece 1990; OECD 1989e; Phillips 1990). Second, how can the environment be protected with market-oriented instruments such as tradeable emission permits? (OECD 1989g). Third, how can safety standards be influenced via requirements for the mandatory purchase of liability insurance by motorists, homeowners, and enterprise managers?

The *second dimension* promoting the development of competitive markets is the effect of legal, political and regulatory institutions on investment and savings. Seven important aspects can be mentioned.

First, an autonomous central bank, financially sound commercial banks, other financial intermediaries, and market-oriented supervisory agencies that oversee the activities of financial markets are important components of a monetary and financial system that protects the purchasing power of money and allocates savings effectively (OECD 1987a, 1989a, 1989f; Blommestein 1993, Villanueva and Mirakhor 1990).

Second, tax regulation affects decisions to supply and demand labor and to save and invest (OECD 1989a: 168-190, 347-364; Owens and Norregaard 1990).

Third, institutions and policies related to well-functioning labor markets are of great interest to investors. Such institutions and policies include: wage bargaining systems, unemployment insurance, lay-off and living restrictions, minimum wage provisions, and public-sector labor market policies (OECD 1987a, 1989a).

Fourth, no matter how wise legislation may be, unless it is enforced, it is worthless. Thus, institutions dedicated to the enforcement of property rights and laws are indispensable to investor confidence.

Fifth, competition law seeks to ensure that vertical integration, horizontal mergers, take-overs, inter-locking directorates, and joint ventures do not damage the public interest (OECD 1987b, 1988c, 1989b; Phillips 1990).

Sixth, corporate law encompasses bankruptcy provisions, enterprise restructuring rules and liquidation procedures, all of which contribute to the recycling of failed assets.

Seventh, a complex set of local, national and international institutions influence the extent to which international trade and capital flows contribute to investment and to the spread of new ideas and technologies (OECD 1984, 1987a; Park 1990).

The *third dimension* is the impact of market imperfections on information and transactions costs. For instance, subsidies contribute to inefficient market outcomes by driving wedges between prices for producers and those for consumers (Commission of the European Communities 1989; OECD 1989i). Tax distortions, a major concern of OECD countries, depend on the level and dispersion of tax rates, on agents' behavioral responses and on the elasticities of factor substitution in production (McKee et al. 1986; OECD 1987a: 356-364, 1987c, 1988d, 1988e, 1989a: 168-190). Trade distortions and restrictions on cross-border financial flows include: tariffs, non-tariff barriers, trade subsidies, restrictions on convertibility, and controls on foreign direct investment flows (Fukao and Hanazaki 1987; Laird and Yeats 1988; OECD 1989a, 1989b: 5-7). 'Efficiency-inhibiting' distortions in factor markets include: wage indexation, many of the benefits of the social safety net, interest rate controls, restrictions to entry and exit, reserve requirements, regulatory barriers between financial intermediaries, and quantitative credit controls (OECD 1987a, 1989a). In addition, externalities disturb the informational usefulness of 'prices formed in competitive markets' because such prices no longer reflect marginal social values. Pollution is a particularly visible externality. Policies designed to contain the failure of the market to take pollution fully into account include: deposit-refund systems, non-compliance fees, effluent charges, user charges, clean-air standards and resource-use

Table 2.1. Assessing the Impact of Policy and Institutional Changes on Competitive Markets in OECD Countries

a. *Influence of Property Rights on Incentives*
- ownership which is clearly defined and legally recognized
- state-owned enterprises versus private firms
- privatization
- reforming the public sector
- protecting intellectual property rights
- allocating environmental costs
- maintaining safety standards

b. *Effect of Legal, Political and Regulatory Institutions on Investment and Savings*
- regulating the monetary and financial system
- tax regulations
- regulating labor markets
- enforcing property rights and laws
- competition law
- corporate law, including provisions for liquidating bankrupt firms
- rules for international economic relations

c. *Impact of Market Imperfections on Information and Transactions Costs*
- subsidies
- tax-related distortions
- distortions in international economic relations
- distortions in factor markets
- externalities

d. *Adverse Consequences of Asymmetric Information*
- credit rationing
- price discrimination
- adverse selection
- restricted diffusion of innovations

e. *Factors Promoting Dynamic Efficiency*
- investment in human capital
- flexibility of factor markets
- innovations

Source: Blommestein and Marrese (1991b).

quotas (OECD 1989g). Externalities can also arise from government failure.

The *fourth dimension* deals with the adverse consequences of asymmetric information. For example, asymmetric information about the resources and integrity of potential investors may lead to credit rationing of even good customers, especially if they are geographically far from lending institutions. Villanueva and Mirakhor (1990) indicate that high inflation may hide the flaws of fundamentally weak bank portfolios from an understaffed regulatory apparatus, thus allowing 'insolvent' banks to try to recoup their solvency by providing unsound loans at high interest rates. Thus, the adverse consequences of these types of asymmetric information might be lessened by simultaneously lowering barriers for entry into the banking system and strengthening the quality of bank regulation. Another widespread problem is that 'under-informed' buyers, sellers, employers or employees might select or produce the 'wrong' product, job, house or service. Laws requiring more complete disclosure of product content, safety standards, and legal recourse against fraud are common measures taken by OECD countries in order to improve the functioning of competitive markets. A less obvious consequence of asymmetric information is that dominant firms may influence the diffusion of technologies by limiting the access of rivals to innovations.

The *fifth dimension* encompasses factors promoting dynamic efficiency. Among these factors, the quality of human capital has long been recognized by governments to be of fundamental importance to long-term growth and has begun to play a key role in growth models with endogenous technological change (Romer 1990). Another factor that promotes dynamic efficiency is the flexibility of capital and labor markets in response to new information such as price shocks and major technological innovation (Fama 1976; OECD 1987a, 1989a). Finally, innovations promote competition. Schumpeter (1942) argued that the kind of competition that really matters for enhancing welfare is the competition that is driven by new products and new processes.

Policymakers recognize the importance of innovation through their requests for information on per capita expenditures on R&D, the number of researchers per 1,000 members of the labor force, high-tech trade, output of high-tech industries, patent flows, and R&D capital expenditure per university researcher (OECD 1987a: 253-264).

There are three major lessons that may be extracted from our discussion thus far:

Lesson 1: The efficiency of market economies depends, among other things, on how the details of the above-mentioned five dimensions are 'worked out' endogenously by each society. This is an evolutionary process in which governments interact with entrepreneurs and households to produce a set of institutions and policies that strongly influence the competitiveness of markets.

Lesson 2: There is no unique set of policies and institutions that promote the development of competitive markets. More specifically, the role of government in creating or fostering the development of market institutions and 'rules of the market game' is far from uniform. However, OECD countries and developing countries offer a wealth of experience about how successful their sets of institutions and policies have been. In many countries, the size and scope of the public sector and government regulations had an adverse impact on the functioning of markets and durable economic growth. Moreover, each set of choices would imply different starting positions for various segments of the populations of Central and Eastern Europe. It is natural that there will be fierce debates about starting positions in society.

Lesson 3: Markets are not so much fixed, exogenous structures as combinations of rights and incentives which change over time. To the extent that governments play a role in affecting these changes, their policies should be predictable for market participants. This argues in favor of an institutional structure in which rules dominate discretionary actions by the government.

Strategy for the Creation of Competitive Markets

The endogenous interaction of economic agents is partly responsible for a country's particular set of policies and institutions. An important determinant of this interaction in Central and Eastern Europe is the degree of experience of entrepreneurs, employees and government officials in a market economy. This factor influences the speed and ultimate success of the transformation process. Nevertheless, Blommestein and Marrese (1991b) suggest that there are certain guidelines that Central and Eastern European countries should follow regardless of their previous experience with markets.

Private Property Rights

The first guideline is the establishment of the institution of private property. Simply put, the entry of new private firms and the transfer of most public assets to the private sector is expected to lead to an increase in efficiency. This line of reasoning comes from an understanding of principal-agent relationships. The institution of private property subjects enterprise managers to three types of competitive pressure: contractual discipline imposed by shareholders, take-over discipline enforced by potential bidders, and bankruptcy discipline exerted by creditors. It is then easy to understand why the absence of such pressures has been put forward as a key reason for the inefficiency that characterized state-owned enterprises in Central and Eastern Europe.

The likelihood of inefficient outcomes in a self-management system also seems high when one distinguishes between theory and practice. Yes, in theory there are many possibilities to enhance competition in an economy consisting of decentralized self-managed enterprises. However, the theory ignores two realities. First, in a self-management system there are no private owners of capital, yet it is precisely such private owners (or their surrogates) who have the incentives to allocate resources efficiently. Second, non-market interventions by the Communist party and bureaucracy did not diminish in Yugoslavia once self-managed decentralization was put in place. In practice, Yugoslav product and factor markets continued to be distorted under self-management.

In sum, theory and practice suggest that the proper incentives to allocate resources efficiently over time exist only under private ownership. Thus, the first vital condition for creating efficient competitive markets is the rapid establishment of a private property base. However the extent to which private property produces efficient results depends on how, among other things, the other guidelines in this section are implemented.

A Sound Currency and Payment System

Lenin was probably correct in his assessment that 'to destroy a bourgeois society, you have to destroy its monetary system.' Eucken said that 'all efforts to create a competitive system are in vain unless a certain stability of money is assured.' Thus, high priority should be given to the creation of an independent monetary authority with the mandate and means to preserve the purchasing power of the currency. More in general, a sound currency requires that the flow causes of excess demand are eliminated, in particular the reduction of budget deficits (Blommestein and Marrese 1991a). The creation of an efficient and safe payment system is also a key task for the monetary authorities (Blommestein 1993). This is not an easy task. However, the authorities in emerging market economies should not postpone central banking reforms, otherwise macroeconomic stability and structural reform objectives will be impossible or very difficult and very slowly attained.

Legal Aspects of Ownership

The third guideline is that a proper legal system will enhance economic efficiency by specifying and enforcing property rights (Yang and Wills 1990). From a historical perspective, the legal underpinning of the modern property system improved the specification and enforcement of property rights by providing protection against arbitrary actions of governments. In addition, the current confusion in Central and Eastern Europe over who owns what should be eliminated in order to reduce incentives for the current 'managers' of enterprises and farms from engaging in asset stripping and to distribute responsibility for existing liabilities. In general, failure to specify and enforce property rights acts as an impediment to privatization, foreign direct investment and the efficient utilization of the capital stock.

Regulatory Reform and Privatization

Part of the fourth guideline is that regulatory reforms may significantly contribute to the emergence of competitive markets and therefore to greater micro-economic flexibility and economic efficiency. One form of regulatory reform, deregulation, involves not only the elimination of price controls and output restrictions but also the abolition of barriers to entry and exit (Pera 1989).

The other part of the fourth guideline is that deregulation in Central and Eastern Europe should be accompanied by privatization (Blommestein et al. 1993). Three reasons stand out. First, deregulation is insufficient to attain allocative efficiency if a public enterprise enjoys an incontestable natural monopoly or one of the many first-mover advantages to deter entry (Sharkey 1982; Gilbert 1986). Second, a private enterprise is more likely to behave in a competitive fashion because of the discipline imposed by the private capital market and the market for corporate control. Third, privatization might restrain governments from distorting competition by reducing support for inefficient but politically important enterprises.

Price Liberalization

The fifth guideline is to implement price liberalization, meaning the market formation of scarcity prices. Price liberalization is necessary because without price flexibility, markets simply cannot function effectively (this is indeed the key insight in the model of perfect competition). However, to secure price liberalization's full benefits, it is important that the flow causes of excess demand (budget deficits, involuntary expansion of inter-enterprise credit, increase in the tax and social security arrears of enterprises) are eliminated and that more effective instruments for macroeconomic control are in place. These conditions for a stable macroeconomic regime assure that price deregulation will only lead to a one-time jump in prices and not to ongoing open inflation. In this way, a stable macroeconomic regime contributes to the smooth functioning of competitive markets and, conversely, micro-economic flexibility assists in attaining macroeconomic stability. In a successful transformation process the same virtuous circle is operative, although policymakers face extra challenges.

Liberalizing Foreign Economic Relations and Establishing Convertibility

The sixth guideline includes: convertibility and the selection of an appropriate exchange rate; the reduction of trade barriers; the creation of an open foreign direct investment regime; and removal of restrictions on cross-border capital flows. Such competition-enhancing policies would influence privatization in two ways. First, open regimes for international trade and foreign direct investment may be very effective mechanisms for quickly generating competition, even if the domestic production structure is still highly concentrated (a condition often cited as a reason not to privatize). For instance, Giersch (1990) notes that during 1948-1957, import pressure ensured workable competition in the Federal Republic of Germany. Imports created such pressure because importers had the legal right to purchase foreign exchange, without restriction, at an official exchange rate. In addition, a recent World Bank study shows that the best way to promote economic growth is to expose domestic producers to foreign competition (Papageorgiou et al. 1990). These examples argue for current-account convertibility at an early stage in the transformation process.

Second, lack of domestic capital may impede the process of privatization. If so, foreign direct investment could quicken the pace of restructuring domestic enterprises, thereby increasing their competitiveness.

Competitive Financial Markets

The seventh guideline stems from the observation that in the absence of central planning, the financial system becomes the centerpiece of resource allocation (Hinds 1990). The key issue is how to ensure that mobilized savings are efficiently allocated. The past record of Central and Eastern European economies—including those who pursued decentralized decision-making such as Hungary and Poland—shows that state-owned enterprises invested capital and used existing capital stock much less efficiently than private enterprises in market economies (Crane 1991). Thus, the creation of a competitive capital market is of crucial importance. Two steps are needed.

First, to improve the incentive framework for making investment decisions it is necessary that the number of state-owned enterprises be reduced through enterprise restructuring and privatization. Also, the free entry of new private business should be promoted. Second, to facilitate the intermediation between savers and investors, a competitive network of commercial banks should be a top priority (Brainard 1991, Blommestein 1992). This means that the program for the restructuring and privatization of state-owned banks should be implemented without delay (Blommestein and Lange 1993).

A competitive financial market provides information about the 'correct' price of capital to the owners of capital and potential investors. The experiences of both OECD countries and many developing countries clearly demonstrate the importance of well-functioning, competitive capital markets (Cameron et al. 1967). However, it seems likely that in the early stage of transformation, financial markets will remain distorted by problems related to asymmetric information. In particular, enterprises may face widely differing costs of external finance depending on whether they are urban versus rural or exporters versus importers. These cost differentials, which are related to access to domestic and international capital markets and arise due to the asymmetric distribution of information, can constrain investment behavior and depress the overall growth of productivity (Greenwald et al. 1990; McKinnon 1990; Calomiris 1990). The main policy strategy should be to reduce these imperfections and their adverse consequences. In particular, 'financial repression' should be avoided and the creation of well-supervised financial intermediaries for financing investment should be promoted (McKinnon 1973; Park 1990).

Two related policy issues emerge from the literature on asymmetric information and moral hazard and from experience in OECD countries and developing countries. First, high priority should be given to financial reforms that foster greater competition in the banking system and improve the efficiency of banking services. There is overwhelming evidence that the banking system accounted for the larger part of investment finance in all advanced market economies except the United States (Calomiris 1990). Although the developments of markets for equities and government bonds is also important (especially for financing government deficits and as a means of implementing privatization), it is highly probable that in the next decade the bulk of savings will be channelled through the banking system (Brainard 1991; Blommestein and Spencer 1993).

Second, in some circumstances financial markets should be liberalized gradually. For instance, in a situation of macroeconomic instability and inadequate supervision of the banking system it may be socially desirable that the monetary authorities 'impose a ceiling on standard loan (and deposit) rates of interest' (McKinnon 1988). The problem is that the interaction of macroeconomic instability and inadequate supervision of the banking system may increase moral hazard. In other words, the temptation for banks to provide risky loans at high interest rates would increase in the expectation that large losses would be covered by government authorities who provide some form of subsidized deposit insurance yet fail to monitor properly.

Economies in transition are particularly vulnerable to this second issue because of the overhang of bad assets in the portfolio of commercial banks; their legacy of lending to loss-making state-owned enterprises; their severe problems with asymmetric information between lenders and borrowers; the high costs of screening and monitoring borrowers during the early stage of the transformation process; weaknesses in the regulatory environment; undercapitalized banks; and macroeconomic instability (Blommestein 1993). Under these circumstances, the abolition of the pre-reform regulatory system and the complete liberalization of interest rates may well intensify moral hazard in the banking system and lead to the excessive provision of high-interest loans to lenders who have a high probability of defaulting. In addition, one of the prevailing conditions in economies in transition—the lack of working capital in newly established private enterprises—may result in highly-leveraged enterprises. Moreover, the indebtedness of the non-bank private sector may be further increased by privatization programs in which 'easy credit' is granted to enterprises and individuals for the purchase of 'highly risky' public assets. The resulting financial fragility would make it harder to reduce macroeconomic imbalances and therefore could undermine the entire transformation process.

Thus the seventh guideline indicates that the creation of a competitive financial sector should be front-loaded with effective bank supervisory and regulatory controls to minimize moral hazard. The evidence from market economies as well as analytical considerations indicate that simple regulatory structures, leaving relatively little scope for discretion, are likely to perform best (Stiglitz 1993). In addition, the complete liberalization of interest rates should be postponed until inflation is under control and banks are being properly supervised.

Labor Market Strategy

The eighth guideline is that a labor market strategy (retraining, access to job-related information, relocation financing, and so forth) should not be neglected in the first stage of the transformation process. A well-functioning labor market reacts to changes in relative prices. One of the most challenging tasks during the transformation will be the reallocation of labor across enterprises, occupations, sectors and regions. This indicates the desirability of a competitive labor market in which a highly mobile labor force can react to price signals.

The present mobility of labor in Central and Eastern Europe is low. The rigidity of labor markets is related both to labor laws and to many distortions in other markets including a rigid housing market and the absence of or obstacles to the creation of a competitive capital market. This underlines the importance of a comprehensive strategy for creating competitive labor markets. Failure to do so may result in persistent, long-term open unemployment. The OECD experience provides some useful lessons (OECD 1986, 1989; Lindbeck 1990).

Development of a Stable Tax Regime

The establishment of a new tax system that provides a stable source of revenue for the government is important for the transformation process. Tax reforms should support macroeconomic stabilization. Following the breakdown of the old tax system, a drastic improvement in the government's ability to collect tax revenue in a decentralized environment is a sine qua non for longer-term macroeconomic stability. On the other hand, tax reforms should also reflect the fundamental assumption of a market economy, namely that profits and high incomes for the larger part can be seen as 'positive contributions to the material well-being of society by individuals through better initiative, more risk taking, more effort and better economic decisions' (Tanzi 1991: 26).

The Creation of Autonomous and Accountable Government Institutions

The final guideline is somewhat elusive. Yet, it is a very important one. The key issue is the impact of government institutions and rules on the extent of rent-seeking in an economy. Incentives for rent-seeking are created by the overall manner in which the government runs its business and interacts with the economy. The degree of autonomy and accountability of a government, being part of the institutions constituting the political order, are the main determinants of the extent of rent-seeking. The rules constituting the political order offer opportunities of wealth distribution.

Weak states are characterized by weak institutions that are very vulnerable to political pressures (e.g. of well-organized special interest groups); weak or soft states will consistently underprovide economically desirable interventions. This in turn means that in the economies of weak states significant resources are allocated for the use of political institutions and the political process in order to extract income and wealth from others in the society; weak states are usually also characterized by a large share of illicit transactions, including widespread corruption. These private efforts or activities distract valuable resources from socially productive use.

Thus, the redistribution of income and wealth is a driving force of the political process. Knight and Buchanan have noted that some basic measure of redistribution is a necessary condition for a stable order. On the other hand, experience shows that persistent redistributive activities undermine the liberal political order. Widespread black markets in market economies are prima facie evidence that governments have gone beyond a critical threshold of redistribution. Of great concern is that some former communist countries may not have reached the point of establishing the critical threshold of a civil economy in which political freedom and constitutional constraints on governmental authority provide a solid underpinning to the rules of the game and institutions of a market economy. Instead, we are observing societies in which rent-seeking is wide-spread, many private and public agents are involved in illicit transactions, government institutions are 'weak,' political accountability is absent, and private ownership of productive resources is weakly protected against political takings.

Conclusions

Progress in creating competitive markets differs significantly across the emerging market economies, but certain common features are apparent.

First, property rights reform (including privatization) is proceeding much more slowly than expected. The reasons for the delay in privatization are illustrative of the more general difficulties involved in the transformation process. Decisions concerning the allocation of wealth must be made and technical institutional problems must be solved if the transformation is to progress much further. With respect to the technical institutional problems, OECD experience may be helpful, even though the countries of Central and Eastern Europe lack many market institutions that are taken for granted in OECD countries. *Second,* the inability to face up to the economic failures of the past via enterprise restructuring and bank restructuring has been a major impediment to pressuring state-owned enterprises to act as privately-owned firms. *Third,* governments in, for example, the former CSFR, Hungary and Poland have spent much more effort on macroeconomic stabilization than on competition-enhancing institution-building or policies to promote dynamic efficiency. *Fourth,* price liberalization and reduction of consumer and producer subsidies have had dramatic impacts on the reduction of budgetary expenditures and introduction of relative prices that reflect much less distorted scarcities. *Fifth,* foreign direct investment has not played the role anticipated. However, once the property right question is clarified and enterprises and banks are reformed, the flood of foreign direct investment into these countries should be substantial. *Sixth,* a stable political order and strong government institutions that minimize unproductive rent-seeking behavior are key elements for economic growth in the medium and longer term.

References

Atkinson, S.E. and R. Halvorsen (1986) The Relative Efficiency of Public and Private Firms in a Regulated Environment: The Case of US Electric Utilities. *Journal of Public Economics* 29: 281-294.

Blommestein, H.J. (1992) Sound Banks for a Strong Market. *OECD Observer* 177: 13-22.

Blommestein, H.J. (1993) *Financial Sector Reforms and Monetary Policy in Central and Eastern Europe*. In: D.E. Fair and J. Raymond (eds.) *The New Europe: Evolving Economic and Financial Systems in East and West*. Dordrecht: Kluwer.

Blommestein, H.J., R. Geiger and P. Hare (1993) *Privatising Large Enterprises: Overview of Issues and Case-Studies* In: H.J. Blommestein, R. Geiger and P. Hare (eds.) *Privatising Large Enterprises*. Paris: OECD. 11-37.

Blommestein, H.J. and J. Lange (1993) *Balance Sheet Restructuring and Privatisation of the Banks*. In: H.J. Blommestein and J. Lange (eds.) *Transformation of the Banking System*. Paris: OECD. 13-33.

Blommestein, H.J. and M. Marrese (eds.) (1991a) *Transformation of Planned Economies: Property Rights Reform and Macroeconomic Stability*. Paris: OECD.

Blommestein, H.J. and M. Marrese (1991b) *Developing Competitive Markets*. In: P. Marer and S. Zecchini (eds.) *The Transition to a Market Economy*. Paris: OECD. 44-62.

Blommestein, H.J. and M.G. Spencer (1993) The Role of Financial Institutions in the Transformation to a Market Economy. Paper presented at the IMF-World Bank Conference on Building Sound Finance in Emerging Market Economies, held in Washington D.C. on June 10-11.

Brainard, L.J. (1991) *Strategies for Economic Transformation in Central and Eastern Europe: The Role of Financial Market Reform*. In: H.J. Blommestein and M. Marrese (eds.) *Transformation of Planned Economies: Property Rights Reform and Macroeconomic Stability*. Paris: OECD. 95-108.

Buchanan, J.M. (1994) *Democracy within Constitutional Limits*. In this volume.

Calomiris, C.W. (1990) Government Policies to Improve Agricultural Capital Markets. Paper prepared for the World Bank Conference on Agricultural Reform in Eastern Europe, August 29-September 1, Budapest.

Cameron, R. et al. (1967) *Banking in the Early Stages of Industrialisation*. Oxford: Oxford University Press.

Commission of the European Communities (1988) *The European Economy, Report No. 35*. Brussels.

Commission of the European Communities (1989) *White Paper on Subsidies*. Brussels.

Corbo, V. and J. de Melo (1985) Overview and Summary. *World Development* 13: 836-866.

Crane, K. (1991) *Property Rights Reform: Hungarian Country Study* In: H.J. Blommestein and M. Marrese (eds.) *Transformation of Planned Economies: Property Rights Reform and Macroeconomic Stability*. Paris: OECD. 69-94.

De Alessi, L. (1977) Ownership and Peak-Load Pricing in the Electric Power Industry. *Quarterly Review of Economics and Business* 17: 7-26.

De la Dehesa, G. (1990) The Spanish Economic Transformation to a Full Market Economy, Paper prepared for the OECD Conference on The Transition to a Market Economy in Central and Eastern Europe, Paris, November 28-30.

Demsetz, H. (1982) *Economic, Legal, and Political Dimensions of Competition*. Amsterdam: North-Holland.

Fama, E.F. (1976) *Foundations of Finance*. New York: Basic Books.

Fare, R., S. Grosskopf and C. Mayer (1987) The Relative Performance of Publicly Owned and Privately Owned Electric Utilities. *Journal of Public Economics* 26: 89-106.

Friedman, M. (1962) *Capitalism and Freedom*. Chigago: The University of Chicago Press.

Fukao, M. and M. Hanazaki (1987) Internationalisation of Financial Markets and the Allocation of Capital. *OECD Economic Studies* 8: 35-92.

Giersch, H. (1990) Lessons from West Germany. Paper prepared for The OECD Conference on The Transition to a Market Economy in Central and Eastern Europe, Paris, November 28-30.

Gilbert, R.J. (1986) *Pre-emptive Competition* In: J.E. Stiglitz, J.E. and G.F. Mathewson (eds.) *New Developments in the Analysis of Market Structures*. London: McMillan.

Grossman, S.J. and Stiglitz, J.E. (1976) Information and Competitive Price Systems. *American Economic Review* 66: 246-253.

Hare, P. (1987) Economic Reform in Eastern Europe. *Journal of Economic Surveys* 1: 25-58.

Hayek, F.A. (1977) *The Road to Serfdom*. Chigago: The University of Chicago Press.

Helliwell, J. (1991) *Lessons from the West*. In: P. Marer and S. Zecchini (eds.) *The Transition to A Market Economy*. Paris: OECD. 115-131.

Hinds M. (1990) Issues in the Introduction of Market Forces in Eastern European Socialist Economies. Washington, D.C.: World Bank. mimeo.

Jorde, T.M. and D.J. Teece (1990) Innovation, Dynamic Competition, and Antitrust Policy. Paper prepared for the 8th International Seminar on the New Institutional Economics, June 20-22, Wallerfangen, Germany.

Klaus, V. (1990) Main Obstacles to Rapid Transformation of Eastern Europe: The Czechoslovak View. Paper prepared for the meeting of the Mont Pelerin Society, Munich, Germany, September 2-8.

Knight, F.H. (1948 [1921]) *Risk, Uncertainty, and Profit*. Boston: Houghton Mifflin.

Laird, S. and A. Yeats (1988) Trends in Nontariff Barriers of Developed Countries 1966-1986. Washington, D.C.: World Bank. mimeo.

Lindbeck, A. (1990) The Swedish Experience. Paper prepared for the OECD Conference on The Transition to a Market Economy in Central and Eastern Europe, November 28-30, Paris.

Marer, P. (1991) *Models of Successful Market Economies* In: P. Marer and S. Zecchini (eds.) *The Transition to a Market Economy*. Paris: OECD. 108-114.

Marrese, M. (1990) Entrepreneurship, Liberalization, and Social Tension. *Jahrbuch der Wirtschaft Osteuropas* 14: 101-129.

McKee, M.J., J.J.C. Visser and P.G. Saunders (1986), Marginal Tax Rates on the Use of Capital and Labour in OECD Countries. *OECD Economic Studies* 7: 45-102.

McKinnon, R.I. (1973) *Money and Capital in Economic Development.* Washington, D.C.: Brookings Institution.

McKinnon, R.I. (1988) *Financial Liberalisation in Retrospect: Interest Policies in LDCs.* In: G. Ranis and T.P. Schultz, (eds.) *The State of Development Economics: Progress and Perspectives.* New York: Basil Blackwell.

McKinnon, R.I. (1990) Financial Repression and the Productivity of Capital: Empirical Findings on Interest Rates and Exchange Rates. mimeo.

Nuti, D.M. (1991) *Privatisation of Socialist Economies: General Issues and the Polish Case.* In: H.J. Blommestein and M. Marrese (eds.) *Transformation of Planned Economies: Property Rights Reform and Macroeconomic Stability.* Paris: OECD. 51-68.

OECD (1984) *Competiton and Trade Policies: Their Interaction.* Paris.

OECD (1986) *Flexibility in the Labour Market: The Current Debate.* Paris.

OECD (1987a) *Structural Adjustment and Economic Performance.* Paris.

OECD (1987b) *Competion Policy and Joint Ventures.* Paris.

OECD (1987c) *Taxation in Developed Countries.* Paris.

OECD (1988a) *Recent Trends in Performance Appraisal and Performance-Related Pay Schemes in the Public Sector.* Paris.

OECD (1988b) *Summary of Public Management Developments.* Paris.

OECD (1988c) *International Mergers and Competition Policy.* Paris.

OECD (1988d) *The Tax/Benefit Position of Production Workers.* Paris.

OECD (1988e) *Taxing Consumption.* Paris.

OECD (1989a) *Economies in Transition.* Paris.

OECD (1989b) *Surveillance of Structural Policies.* Paris.

OECD (1989c) *Measuring Performance and Allocating Resources, OECD Public Management Studies, No. 5.* Paris.

OECD (1989d) *Economic Survey of the United Kingdom.* Paris.

OECD (1989e) *Competition Policy and Intellectual Property Rights.* Paris.

OECD (1989f) *Competition in Banking.* Paris.

OECD (1989g) *OECD Environmental Data Compendium 1989.* Paris.

OECD (1989h) *Competition Policy in OECD Countries, 1987-1988.* Paris.

OECD (1989i) *Agricultural Policies, Markets and Trade: Monitoring and Outlook.* Paris.

OECD (1990) *Financing Public Expenditure through User Charges, Public Management Service.* Paris.

Owens, J. and J. Norregaard (1990) The Role of Lower Levels of Government: the Experience of Selected OECD Countries. Paper prepared for the IIPF Conference on Public Finance with Several Levels of Government, Brussels.

Papageorgiou, D., A. Choksi and M. Michaely (1990) *Liberalising Foreign Trade.* London: Basil Blackwell.

Park, Y.C. (1990) Export-led Growth and Economic Liberalisation in South Korea. Paper prepared for the OECD Conference on The Transition to a Market Economy in Central and Eastern Europe, November 28-30, Paris.

Peltzman, S. (1971) Pricing in Public and Private Enterprises: Electric
Utilities in the United States. *Journal of Law and Economics* 14: 109-147.

Pera, A. (1989) Deregulation and Privatisation in an Economy-Wide Context. *OECD Economic Studies* 12: 159-204.

Phillips, B.J. (1990) Competition Policy and Economic Transitio Paper prepared for the OECD Conference on The Transition to a Market Economy in Central and Eastern Europe, November 28-30, Paris.

Romer, P.M. (1990) Endogenous Technological Change. *Journal of Political Economy* 98: S71-S102.

Sargent, T.J. (1986) *Rational Expectations and Inflation.* New York: Harper & Row.

Schumpeter, J. (1942) *Capitalism, Socialism and Democracy.* New York: Harper.

Sharkey, W.W. (1982) *The Theory of Natural Monopoly.* Cambridge: Cambridge University Press.

Stiglitz, J.E. (1993) Freeing Financial Markets, Paper presented at the World Bank's Annual Conference on Development Economics, held in Washington D.C. on May 3-4.

Tanzi, V. (1991) *Tax Reform and the Move to a Market Economy: Overview of the Issues.* In: *The Role of Tax Reform in Central and Eastern European Economies.* Paris: OECD.

Tanzi, V. and A.L. Bovenberg (1990) Is there a Need for Harmonising Capital Income Taxes Within EC Countries? Washington, D.C.: IMF. mimeo.

Tigrel, A. (1990) The Case of Turkey, Paper prepared for the OECD Conference on The Transition to a Market Economy in Central and Eastern Europe, November 28-30, Paris.

Vartia, P. (1990) Finland's Postwar Growth and Transformation, Paper prepared for the OECD Conference on The Transition to a Market Economy in Central and Eastern Europe, November 28-30, Paris.

Villanueva, D. and A. Mirakhor (1990) Strategies for Financial Reforms. *IMF Staff Papers* 37: 509-536.

Yang, X. and I. Wills (1990) A Model Formalizing the Theory of Property Rights. *Journal of Comparative Economics* 14: 177-198.

Yoshitumi, M. (1990) The Relevance of Japan's Post-war Economic Development for Central and Eastern Europe, Paper prepared for the OECD Conference on The Transition to a Market Economy in Central and Eastern Europe, November 28-30, Paris.

3

Democracy within Constitutional Limits

James M. Buchanan

It is not easy for Western political economists either to understand post-revolutionary developments in the former socialist countries or to proffer meaningful normative advice. The histories of these societies must evolve spontaneously, even if necessity dictates a dramatic compression of the time scale, at least in any comparative sense. At best, political economists who are external to the process can isolate and identify features of Western institutions that may be worth noting, and especially in a precautionary fashion, by those who may find themselves in positions to make critical choices during the institution building phases of transition.

In this chapter, I shall draw largely upon my own country, the United States, as a source for identifying elements of current political structure that reflect departures from the normative standards that were both expressed in our founding documents and embodied in our political history for a significantly long period. It is not an exaggeration to say that we have now, in the United States, lost our 'constitutional way.' We have lost our generalized understanding of the relationship between the two normative objectives: political equality among citizens, summarized under the rubric 'democracy,' and the liberty or independence of each citizen from the coercion of the state, an objective that was presumably to be achieved by 'constitutional' constraints on governmental authority. The American structure, as initially imagined and, to a surprising extent realized over long periods of our history, was accurately described as a 'constitutional democracy.' And I emphasize that both words are important, with 'constitutional' taking precedence over 'democracy,' if, indeed, any such ordering is desired. Unfortunately, it is the

H. J. Blommestein and B. Steunenberg (eds.), Government and Markets, 39–47.

constitutional understanding that has been largely lost from public consciousness, with consequences for all to see.

Citizens in the former socialist countries live now in the postrevolutionary moment during which there may exist opportunities to design and construct elements of political-economic orders that, once emplaced, will prove difficult to reform. The urge toward 'democratization' is surely easy to understand, and the association between nondemocratic political structures and the suppression of individual liberties leads perhaps naturally to a neglect of the potential democratic danger to individual autonomy. The institutionalization of democratic procedures of governance may produce consequences desired by no one unless these procedures are limited by constitutional boundaries.

First, I shall discuss the relationships between political democracy and the market economy, both of which are nominally listed as objectives for postrevolutionary institutional reforms in the countries that were previously organized on socialist principles. I shall then summarize briefly the distinction between 'constitutional politics' and 'ordinary politics,' and I shall discuss the relevance of this distinction for the viability of a market economy, and, indirectly, for a liberal society. Next, I shall sketch out the operation of a 'politics within rules,' and I follow this sketch by outlining specific implications for areas of policy. I conclude the chapter with a general statement of position.

Democracy and the Market

Reformers in the countries that were classified as socialist prior to the revolutions of 1989-1991 are as one in their stated twin objectives: (1) political reorganization toward introducing democracy; and (2) economic reorganization toward introducing a market economy.[1] As regards the reform leaders in the societies of Eastern and Central Europe and the republics of the former Soviet Union, it is, I think, appropriate to ask whether or not the relationships between political democracy and a market economy are well understood.

It is, of course, easy to understand why the historical experiences under the totalitarian rule of the Communist Party have generated urges toward democratic reform in politics and economic reform toward markets. Individuals seek to be able to exercise political voice, to sense that they, individually, can at least share in the decisions that shape their own lives. At the same time,

[1] China, whose authoritarian leaders crushed its incipient revolution, is identified by its difference here. China seeks to shift toward economic organization based in part on market principles while putting down pressures toward democratization of its political structure.

and for different reasons, individuals simply observe the economic failure of attempted command-control institutions to produce economic value. The system did not deliver the goods, as measured by the size, quality and content of the bundle ultimately desired, and, furthermore, the bundle was not growing larger over time.

But do the political reformers, both those who have attained positions of authority and those who might aspire to authority under fledgling democratic procedures, understand that the necessary conditions for the effective functioning of a market economy require that the range and scope of democratic authority be limited? At one level of discourse, there seems to be near universal acknowledgement that private or several ownership of productive resources must be substituted for collective or state ownership-control. But the secure ownership that is required for viability of an economy implies protection of holdings against political takings, including takings that may be orchestrated through the auspices of democratic politics. Almost by definition, a market economy both requires and itself facilitates a restricted range for the operation of government, independently of, whether or not the actions of government are subject to, the indirect controls of democratic politics. Indeed, I would suggest that this political function of the market economy is, in some evaluative sense, more important than the economic function, as measured by the size of the bundle of valued goods generated.

Properly understood, therefore, the revolutions were, and are, directed toward the devolution or decentralization of political authority, or depoliticization, which only a market organization of the economy makes possible, and, further, only within which genuinely democratic processes of decision can attain some semblance of meaning. The organizational-institutional implications of such an understanding are clear: The range and scope for political authority must be restricted, preferably by constitutional constraints that may be strategically introduced during the postrevolutionary moment and before particularized interests emerge. Explicit constitutional limits on the intrusion of politics into the market have the further advantage of providing expectational stability for persons and groups, internal and external, who might make long-term investments.

Constitutional Politics and Ordinary Politics

On many occasions, I have emphasized the necessity for a 'constitutional understanding,' by which I mean an appreciation for and an understanding of the two stages or levels of political decision making that must describe the functioning of any political order that can claim either legitimacy or tolerable efficiency. There is, first, the design, construction, implementation and maintenance of the basic rules, the fundamental law, the constitution, that defines the parameters within which what we may call 'ordinary politics' is to take place. And there is, second, the operation of such ordinary politics within these rules, so defined.

In some ultimate descriptive sense, there must always exist such a two-stage, or even perhaps a multi-stage characterization of politics as it is actually observed. But the explicit recognition of the distinction, and, more importantly, of the operational implications, is often neglected, with the result that ordinary politics is allowed to proceed as if there are no limits. It is critically important that the logic of the distinction between the stages inform thinking about politics, both during moments of constitutional choice and in the postconstitutional periods described by the workings of ordinary politics.

There are, literally, hundreds of familiar nonpolitical analogues to the two-stage structure of politics emphasized here and elsewhere. Consider word processing. The user must first choose a software program, and, secondly, choose what to write within the constraints imposed by the program. Or, consider the purchase of any durable good, say, an automobile. The capacities of the car limit to some extent the activities that may be performed in using it. Or, consider planting a fruit tree, where the initial choice is among an apple, peach, plum or pear tree. Once this choice is made, it necessarily constrains the activities involved in cultivation, and also the type of output to be expected. For economists, the Marshallian distinction between the long-run choice of a fixed facility or plant and the short-run choice concerning the level of operation of the plant, as given, is familiar, and this distinction is directly analogous to the constitutional choice-ordinary politics choice introduced here.

Constitutional politics involves setting the rules, selecting the parametric framework within which ordinary political decisions are to be made and carried out. Such politics defines the manner of selecting those who seek to govern others, the extent of the voting franchise, the timing and procedures for elections, the voting rules, the terms for eligibility for office, methods of representation and many other procedural details that are necessary for democratic processes to operate at all. These constitutional parameters for democracy will be almost universally acknowledged to be both necessary and to differ in kind from the objects upon which ordinary politics operates, even in those settings where there exists no explicit constitution, as such. But the extension of constitutional parameters to include more than these formal procedures for governance must also be recognized to be important for insuring stability of expectations. The range over which governments are allowed to act, even governments that are procedurally legitimate in the democratic features listed above, must be known, at least in terms of well-defined boundaries beyond which political intrusion shall not extend. Such constitutional limits may lay out protected spheres for personal liberties, as in bills of rights, and also for economic liberties, without which any market order remains highly vulnerable to piecemeal interferences generated by interest-motivated coalitions.

A domain for the exercise of constitutional politics may be described, but the existence of limits does not, itself, imply that there is little or no room left for the play of ordinary politics, the spaces within which the activities of governments, as we know them, may be observed. Clearly, governments may do many things, whether these qualify as 'good' or 'bad' by any criterion, that are within the constraints defined in almost any constitutional structure. But it is folly to think that governmental activities are appropriately constrained only by the feedbacks on voter attitudes that the formal procedures of democracy make possible.

Politics within Rules

Politics, as we observe it and talk about it, is, therefore, strictly a 'politics within rules,' or in the reductionist classification of the previous Section, strictly 'ordinary politics.' A well-functioning polity will, indeed, be described by stability in its basic constitutional structure, which translates into an absence of activity aimed toward continual constitutional change and discussion of such change. But the politics within rules that describe the well-functioning polity operates effectively only if the rules are themselves both understood and respected. A politics that seems to proceed as if a constraining set of rules does not and should not exist must fail in several dimensions. An imperialistic 'ordinary politics' insures the removal of stability-predictability from the whole political-legal-economic order, and thereby guarantees both economic stagnation and the loss of individual liberties.

To suggest that the constraints on the operation of ordinary politics that are embodied in a constitution, whether these constraints be formal or informal, whether they emerge through an evolutionary process or as a result of deliberative design, are not subject to continual change does not, of course, imply that genuine constitutional politics, the politics involved in changing the basic rules, is out of bounds for discussion or that genuine constitutional reform is taboo. The suggestion is only that constitutional rules should be treated as 'relatively absolute absolutes' by any comparison with the operation of within-rule politics and that these rules, if changed, be considered to be quasi-permanent, and that they be analyzed as if they are and must become elements in genuine 'political capital' (see Buchanan 1989). Politics loses meaning if every moment becomes 'constitutional' in the sense that efforts are made to modify the basic structural parameters of the system. Genuinely constitutional moments are identified in part by their singularity, by their extraordinary presence, by their intrusion of sorts into the ongoing compromises of conflicting interests that describe and define ordinary political experience.

'Democratization' may be introduced with reference either to constitutional or to ordinary politics, but it is essential that the domains be understood to be separate and apart. Democracy, defined as ultimate equality of influence over collectively determined results, may characterize procedures through which, at some appropriate moment, the structural parameters are chosen. On the other hand, and by contrast, these parameters may be imposed nondemocratically, for example, the MacArthur constitution for modern Japan. But independently of how the rules are themselves selected, these rules themselves may or may not provide for ordinary politics to operate democratically in the standard meaning. The rules may dictate that, within the boundaries specified in the constitution, individual citizens are guaranteed the exercise of equal ultimate influence over particular outcomes, with modern Japan again offering an example.

It is important to note, however, and as the discussion should have made clear, that there are limits to any 'democratization' of constitutional politics imposed by the necessary quasi-permanence of the rules. If the parameters of structure are to remain in place over a sequence of periods during which the processes of ordinary politics are expected to take place, it is necessary that citizens, acting politically in any arbitrarily chosen period, cannot expect to exercise an influence comparable to that exercised in the ordinary politics that is bound within the existing constitutional rules. In a very real sense, the electorate for an effectively democratic constitutional politics must include participants over the course of many periods. Political equality may be retained as a normative democratic ideal, but individuals must reckon that the influences exerted 'spill over' through time periods as well as among participants within any time period. That is to say, the set of participants who may claim idealized equality of influence is larger, in a temporal dimension, in constitutional than in ordinary politics.

Constitutional Misunderstanding: Examples from Modern United States

In the introduction, I stated that the United States has lost its 'constitutional way,' that constitutional understanding has been allowed to slip from public consciousness, and that modern experiences drawn from the United States may usefully serve as precautionary warnings to those who are actively engaged in constitutional design for countries that remain in a formative moment. In order to support this claim, it is necessary for me to summarize very briefly elements of the constitutional history of the American republic.

In James Madison's grand design, the central or federal government of the United States exercised extremely limited authority, but within such authority its sovereignty was unchallengeable. The separate state governments were not to restrict the free flow of commerce over the inclusive territory; the extensive internal market was to remain open, allowing for full exploitation of the specialization of labor, producing advantages that became relatively more important as technology developed. Because of this guarantee of a large internal open market, there was relatively little need for explicit and extensive constitutional constraints on the domain for ordinary politics of the several state governments. The competition, both actual and potential, among these several units within the large open market acted to insure that any excesses of ordinary politics, motivated by coalitions of conflicting interests, be kept within reasonable bounds. The competitive politics of a viable federalism can substitute for the explicit constitutional politics that would be necessary in a unitary polity.[2]

Madison and his peers overlooked the requirement for constitutional guarantees for openness in the external market, that is as between domestic and foreign traders. The central government was empowered to regulate external commerce, and the absence of explicit constraints allowed the ordinary politics of interest to generate welfare-reducing and regionally discriminatory restrictions on trade. These observable excesses of ordinary politics were at least in part responsible for the intense interregional conflict that provided the origins for the bloody Civil War in mid-nineteenth century. And the outcome of this war itself insured that the effective federalized structure of American governance would, over time, disappear. The central government, without any threat of secession on the part of states, predictably assumed increasing authority over the course of a century, with the result that modern United States is, basically, unitary in a descriptive sense. The central government is overwhelmingly dominant in any and all potential conflicts with the states.

This change in political structure was not accompanied by any recognition that the demise of the competitive politics as among the several states should have dictated the imposition of additional constitutional constraints on the powers of the central government, over and beyond those that Madison thought to be necessary at its formation. As the operation of the internal market of the United States came increasingly under the regulatory control of the ordinary politics of the single central government, there was no effective

[2] This is a simple principle that the nations of the European Union should learn and act upon. Unfortunately, the constitutional moment during which a viable federal structure might have seemed possible may already have been missed (see Buchanan 1990).

constitutional barrier to the intrusive interferences with the workings of the market, either internal or external. And the intrusion, once commenced, took on a dynamic of its own. Those interests that were successful in securing the artificially created profits or rents from politicized protection become attractors for other interests seeking, and getting, similar treatment. There were parallel extensions through the emergence of the transfer sector. The financing of genuinely collective functions from revenues raised from broad-based and general taxes was supplemented and expanded to include the financing of transfers, in money and in kind, to designated recipient groups, and taxes were deliberatively modified to insure nongenerality in liability. Many of these changes might have been tolerated without major damage to the constitutional fabric if they could have been considered as quasi-permanent. But, instead, the whole expenditure-tax structure in modern United States has been allowed to become the primary object for the machinations of ordinary politics. The fiscal system is not treated as a part of the framework within which the decisions of participants in the market sector are made. The whole budgetary process reflects little more than the continuing compromises of the conflicting interests through ordinary politics. Everything seems up for grabs, and each legislative period is marked by proposed revisions in what should be structural parameters for the economy. Modern American political leaders, regardless of party, have no understanding at all of the need for, and the potential benefits from, stability in the rules, as applied to the whole of the regulatory-fiscal framework. The quasi-stagnation of the American economy in the 1990s is directly attributable to the failure of political and intellectual leaders to recognize that a more limited politics, as reflected in stability in rules, can be a more productive politics, if productivity is measured either in economic growth or in the liberties of citizens.

Conclusion

The United States constitutional experience must be avoided if the emerging democracies and market economies are to have reasonable prospects for success, especially with the past and recent history of the failed socialist experiments, it is critically important that the private property rights, as, if and when established, be guaranteed against politicized takings, whether in the form of direct seizure, the imposition of particularized punitive legislation or indirect and onerous burdens of taxation. It is imperative that the constitutions for the formerly socialist countries contain the guarantees for procedural democracy (elections, franchise, etc.) for personal liberties (speech, press, religion, etc.) and for protections against politicized (even if democratic) invasions of private property rights. Because of the historical memories of the politicized economy, property owners can be assured on the last point only by a specific constitutional listing of the allowed scope and range for the workings of ordinary democratic politics. The 'public goods' that are to be financed by taxes must be specified, along with the basic structure of taxes to be used. A fiscal constitution is an essential element in any constitutional democracy, but it is more important in a setting where the distrust of ordinary politics and politicians is deeply imbedded in the psyche of citizens.

I am not so naive as to predict that any of the countries facing the constitutional moment of the 1990s will meet the ideal standards that I might suggest. Without a heritage of experience that embodies some understanding of the central logic of effective constitutionalism, any implementation of constitutional democracy will be difficult to achieve. But the logic remains, as does the tremendous and unique opportunity. The logic is simple, however, and appropriate leadership can influence public attitudes and opinions. And, once again, the force of potential competition cannot be overlooked. If only one of the countries in question should achieve the reforms required for a leap into genuine constitutional democracy, the exemplar offered to other countries in this age of instantaneous communication would almost guarantee generalization to other settings.

References

Buchanan, J.M. (1989) *The Relatively Absolute Absolutes*. In: *Essays on the Political Economy*. Honolulu: University of Hawaii Press. 32-46.

Buchanan, J.M. (1990) *Europe's Constitutional Opportunity*. In: *Europe's Constitutional Future*. London: Institute of Economic Affairs. 1-20.

4

Democracy, Legal State, and Constitutional Change

Huib M. de Jong and Dick W.P. Ruiter

The revolutions of 1989 have radically changed the power structures in most Eastern European countries as well as the power balances between them. The changes taking place on the European continent give rise to many economic and political debates. Economic discussions are aimed at the development of free-market economies in Eastern Europe. This kind of economic order is deemed to be the best way to provide the goods and services necessary to meet the most fundamental needs of the population. As Glenny wrote in his book on the 1989 revolutions: 'The goal of modern Western democracy may be appealing in theory to most East Europeans, but they are concerned first to ensure a basic standard of living for their children' (Glenny 1990: 183). Political debates focus on the structure of society (unionism, federalism) and the possibility of enlarging the influence of the people. In order to organize the latter, consensus on the criteria for membership in the political society is necessary. This amounts to decisions regarding the inclusion or exclusion of individuals, or even entire minority groups. In this respect actual political reality frequently shows smoke on the horizon. The collapse of the old authoritarian structures under Soviet supremacy ignited many collective outbursts of nationalistic sentiments, often ending in violence.

If we look at the ongoing debates, it is remarkable to note the lack of considerations concerning the legal orders of the countries involved and the possibilities constitutional law offers as a safeguard against undesired political or social developments. In this chapter we shall attempt to contribute to the filling in of this gap. In particular, we shall consider the basic normative structure of political societies and the demands they must meet in order to satisfy certain standards. The basic structure of political societies may be

H. J. Blommestein and B. Steunenberg (eds.), Government and Markets, 49–69.

defined as 'the way in which major social institutions distribute fundamental rights and duties and determine the division of advantages from social cooperation' (Rawls 1971: 7).

The fundamental idea underlying our analysis is that the countries in Eastern Europe are trying to evolve from a situation of dependent totalitarianism to independent liberal democracies.[1] With this assumption we shall first look at liberal-democratic political theory (the principles of freedom and equality). Subsequently, we shall deal with the transformation of political theory into legally valid norms. In this part we base our argument on the concept of a legal state. This concept refers to the institutional requirements a liberal democratic society ought to fulfil. Finally, we shall draw some conclusions and relate them to the perspective of constitutional change in Eastern Europe.

It should be clear that the different questions we raise cannot be answered fully in this chapter. We do not pretend to provide a theoretical framework to provide a kind of recipe to solve all constitutional problems in Eastern Europe. What we shall do is depict some fundamental problems that must be solved to start a rational process of constitutional design. To solve these problems it is necessary to acquire more empirical knowledge regarding the particular social systems in the countries involved, especially knowledge with regard to the choices the respective populations are prepared to make themselves. Montesquieu was right in writing that in order to be workable, constitutions must both reflect the norms and values accepted by the people and deal with the specific problems of particular countries (Montesquieu 1783).

Liberal-Democratic Political Theory

Liberal-democratic political theory is a *normative* theory (theory of justice) on the requirements the basic structure of a political society should meet. Its basis is the traditional tension resulting from the fact that human beings are both distinct individuals and part of social classes and groups. Like any other political theory, liberal-democratic theory seeks to strike a balance between the demand for social cohesion and individual liberty.

On the value level, liberal-democratic political theory focuses on individual freedom. It is plain, however, that within any political community the debate

[1] According to Finer (1970: 58-59), in totalitarian states '...regimentation is extended to its limits, the representative quality of government is all but extruded and sub-groups are all but entirely dependent.' In his view liberal democracies are states 'which rely upon the critical awareness of the population, and seek to convince them by a process of persuasion.'

Figure 4.1. Individual Freedom and Authority

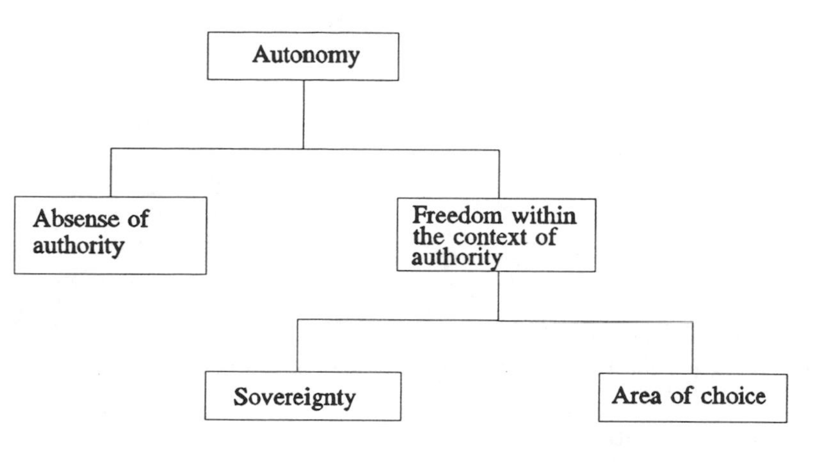

on *individual freedom* must also be a debate on *authority* (Raz 1986; Benn 1988: 306). The relation between the concepts can be interpreted from two possible perspectives (Berlin 1969). First, one can look at freedom as the absence of authority; on this way freedom implies personal autonomy, the capacity of acting in accordance with personal choice. Individual freedom is, in this perspective, part of a moral doctrine of non-intervention by any authority whatsoever. Secondly, one can look at freedom in relation to authority. Thus, freedom represents the room left for personal reasons and motives in the relationship between individuals and state authority.

This second perspective can, once again, be interpreted in two ways. On the one hand authority in political society may be understood as the sovereign supremacy of government within the state. On the other hand, it is possible to interpret society as an 'arena of choice' in which individual and organized interests, including the interests of the government, are pursued (Seidman 1978: 70).

Most modern theorists adhere to the second main perspective. Only a minority (extreme liberalism, libertarianism or anarchism) holds onto the assumption of individual freedom as the absence of authority.

Below we shall consider individual freedom in accordance with the prevailing approach in political theory. This does not mean that within this approach there are no controversies about the notion of individual freedom. The distinction between, on the one hand, government as a sovereign in the state and, on the other, political society as an 'arena of choice' provides a

Figure 4.2. The Principle of Freedom

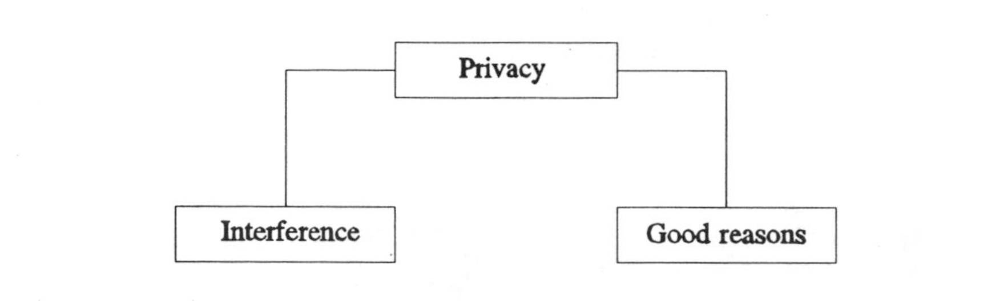

starting point for an account of the differences of opinion.

Authority and Freedom

The assumption of political authority as the internal sovereign is based on the idea that state authority is indispensable for providing or maintaining social order. In this perspective a political society without some sort of government possessing the ultimate power in the state is inconceivable. If we look at the issue of constitutional change in Eastern Europe from this angle, it leaves us with an obvious problem, for most (if not all) of the former communist regimes (e.g. Poland, Hungary) have claimed that they have always respected individual freedom within the limitations imposed by the need for effective state authority. Thus, the normative thrust of the notion of individual freedom is canceled out.

A possible way out of this dilemma is afforded by the idea of individual freedom as a *fundamental principle* of political authority. This means that political decisions may not interfere with the personal choices of citizens, unless there is a good reason for it. Any political decisions should be taken in light of the question of whether or not there are good reasons to intervene in the realm of the individual.

The problems with this line of reasoning are obvious. The concepts used (privacy, interference, good reasons) are vague. What do they stand for?

Privacy is a difficult concept. The reason is that it is hard (if not impossible) to make statements about the positions of individuals, without taking their social environment into account. Still, the concept has progressively gained in importance, especially within the realm of information technology. We shall clarify its essence with the aid of an illustrious predecessor. In his political theory John Stuart Mill used the distinction between the private and the public realm, respectively, to determine the limits of government. The object of his essay was to assert one principle:

> That principle is that the sole end for which mankind are warranted, individually or collectively, in interfering with the liberty of action of any of their number is self-protection. That the only purpose for which power can be rightfully exercised over any number of a civilized community, against his will, is to prevent harm to others (Mill 1985: 68).

At the end of his essay, which is without any doubt a jewel in the crown of political theory, it seems as if his principle would cover his whole account of political society. However, he then turns to 'cases in which the reasons against interference do not turn upon the principle of liberty: the question is not about restraining the actions of individuals, but about helping them; it is asked whether the government should do, or cause to be done, something for their benefit instead of leaving it to be done by themselves, individually or in voluntary combination' (Mill 1985: 180). His failure to provide a satisfactory analytical answer to the question of where the borderline between the private and the public lies, then becomes clear in the next quote:

> To determine the point at which evils, so formidable to human freedom and advancement, begin, or rather at which they begin to predominate over the benefits attending the collective application of the force of society, under its recognized chiefs, for the removal of the obstacles which stand in the way of its well-being; to secure as much of the advantages of centralized power and intelligence as can be had without turning into governmental channels too great a proportion of the general activity—is one of the most difficult and complicated questions in the art of government (Mill 1985: 185).

Mill's problem regards the fact that, as soon as one accepts the truth of the proposition that individual behavior cannot be explained without reference to the social context, it becomes very difficult to make clear where the line between private and public lies. The difficulty is not only theoretical in character. In the last decade—after a period of rapid growth in the amount of services rendered by governmental authorities—in nearly all countries in the Western part of the 'European house' (e.g. England, France, the Netherlands), a tendency to re-evaluate the size of the organization and the competencies of the government and its administration has emerged. Questions related to this preference for 'small government' all eventually revert to the definition of individual freedom within the context of governance. Both in theory and practice, we may conclude, to say the least, that it is, very difficult to determine a fixed line between the private and public realms.

Mill's theory not only illuminates problems concerning the privacy notion, but it also shows that it is hard to decide in concrete instances whether or not we are confronted with *interferences* of privacy. Few will be prepared to claim without reservations that any kind of aid and sustenance by public services amounts to a form of interference with individual privacy. It is important to note that in the last quote Mill shifts his line of argument from individual autonomy to individual *well-being*. This shift is a logical one as soon as individuals are seen as members of political society, but it also illustrates clearly that the meaning of any statement that the government must not interfere is, for a great part, the result of applying subjective personal criteria.

This brings us to the third concept, that of *'good reasons.'* Obviously, a political community cannot exist if all individual citizens are allowed to use their personal subjective criteria for evaluating governmental conduct.[2] Hence, other criteria must apply. If we do not accept the existence of objective values (and we do not), there is no other way but to look for socially acceptable criteria. Trial and error seems to be the only feasible mechanism. However, by accepting this mechanism we also recognize that there are no generally valid criteria for distinguishing 'bad' from 'good' reasons for the government interfering in the private realms of the citizens.

The absence of generally valid criteria does not involve the idea that freedom as a principle of governance does not hold well. Raz suggests that to deal with the problem of this vagueness we should take what he calls *'the service conception of the function of authorities'* as a point of departure, rather than the idea of individual autonomy. This means that we should agree that the primary function of government is to serve the citizens (Raz 1986: 59). For Raz this conception implies two theses:

1. *Normal-justification thesis*: 'the normal way to establish that a person has authority over another person involves showing that the alleged subject is likely better to comply with reasons which apply to him (other than the alleged authoritative directives) if he accepts the directives of the alleged authority as authoritatively binding and tries to follow them, rather than by trying to follow the reasons which apply to him directly' (Raz 1986: 53).

2. *Dependence thesis*: 'all authoritative directives should be based on reasons which already independently apply to the subjects of the

[2] See Green (1990) on this problem.

directives and are relevant to their action in the circumstances covered by the directive' (Raz 1986: 47).

If a government acts in accordance with these theses, the citizen ought to accept the rules issued by the former as reasons for conforming to them (*preemptive these*).

The solution offered by Raz is quite interesting. Both theses are grounded in 'legitimacy' as the central concept governing the relationship between individual freedom and state authority. The term 'legitimate' refers to the extent to which citizens accept governmental choices as morally justified (Green 1990: 5; Weber 1980: 16). In this conception there is room for gradations of legitimacy dependent on different issues, times and places.[3]

A second striking element in Raz's theory is the way in which he incorporates the principle of equality. His dependence thesis is no more nor less than one of the most important elements in legal philosophy: the formal principle that equal cases must be equally dealt with through judgements derived from general norms. The ideal of individual freedom, that is in this way sought after by liberal theory, cannot be reached without also accepting the *principle of equality* (Spicker 1985: 205-216). In this Raz does not stand alone. As Gutman points out equality is, in addition to the idea of rational choice, an implicit anthropological assumption of the tradition of liberalism as long as it has existed (Gutman 1980: 41).

Democracy

The acceptance of equality as a basic principle of any political society recognizing individual freedom relates liberalism to democratic theory (Held 1988; Dahl 1989). Raz conceives equality primarily as (in terms of systems theory) a feature of *the output* of political systems. Conversely, democratic theory looks at equality as a feature of their *input*. The most prominent model of democracy, coined by Rousseau, is based on the idea of a social contract, which 'establishes equality among the citizens in that they ... must all enjoy the same rights' (Rousseau 1968: 46, 76). Dahl, one of the most prominent writers on democracy of our day, calls equality one of the assumptions of a rational belief in democracy:

[3] The choice to use this conception implicitly means that we do not accept liberal-democratic theories in which liberty is intrinsically valuable, like in Hayek's 'rules of just behavior' or 'laws in the proper sense' (see Hayek 1973, 1976, 1979). The problems of Hayek's ideas on law in view of modern legal theory are discussed by Haakonssen (1988). See also Raz (1986: 7).

> With respect to all matters, all the adult members of the association (the citizens of a government) are roughly equally well qualified to decide which matters do or do not require binding collective decisions. Those who participate shall decide which matters the demos (the citizenry) is best qualified to decide for itself; which matters, in the membership's view, the demos is not qualified to decide for itself; and the terms on which the demos will delegate a contingent and recoverable authority to others (Dahl 1985: 57-58).

In Dahl's formulation of this assumption of rational belief the last part is important in light of the history of democratic theory. Rousseau adhered to the ideal of *direct* democracy. Dahl does not include this ideal in his theory. Delegation of power to representatives is an integral part of his assumptions. To justify this Dahl can refer to the examples of present-day democratic systems, but also to impressive parts of the Federalist Papers, in which a justification of the basic structure of the U.S. can be found. Madison, for instance, wrote about solving the faction problem. By a faction he understands 'a number of citizens, whether amounting to a majority or minority of the whole, who are united and actuated by some common impulse of passion or of interest, adverse to the rights of other citizens, or to the permanent and aggregate interests of the community' (Hamilton et al. 1961: 78). The threat of faction struggle renders direct democracy a fiction. Hamilton preferred a republic, by which he meant 'a government in which the scheme of representation takes place' (Hamilton et al. 1961: 81). The value of political equality is, therefore, set in the context of *representative* government.

Liberal-Democratic Values

We started this section with the assumption that liberal-democratic political theory is a *normative* theory (a theory of justice) as to the requirements the basic structure of a political society has to fulfil. Its main feature is its concern with individual freedom as a social value. Like any other political theory, however, it has to deal with the tension between *individual freedom* and *authority*. Raz suggests not using the idea of autonomy as a starting point of liberal-democratic theory, but the wider concept of 'the service conception of the function of authorities' to come to grips with the said tension. Thus he relates individual freedom to a specific interpretation of political equality: equal treatment of equal cases. In a wider sense, political equality is traditionally the core issue of democratic theory, viz. as the requirement that opportunities for influencing the country's government be equally distributed.

The conclusion of this section is that liberal-democratic theory is based on two abstract values: individual freedom and equality. In the next section we shall examine how these values are implemented in the constitution.

The Concept of a Legal State

As was mentioned in the introduction, in this part we shall attend to the concept of a legal state. This concept has become a central part of the theory of the state in the last two centuries, especially in the German tradition following Kant (in German: *Rechtstaat*).[4] The concept has evolved in interaction with liberal-democratic political theory and can, to a certain extent, be interpreted as its constitutional translation. Although all states in Western Europe present themselves as legal states, they are differently structured. A great variety of national institutions present themselves as particularly successful implementations of the values involved in the concept of the legal state. An observer is thus confronted with the puzzling problem of how so many different national arrangements can be conceived as contributing to the realization of the same concept. In order to diminish the confusion we shall attempt to isolate some features all 'legal states' have in common behind their divergent appearances.

A preliminary point deserving our attention is a current usage of the term 'legal state' in a sense opposite to its classical meaning. Even the Dutch Minister of Justice is in the habit of making statements to the effect that, in a legal state, crime shall not pay. As recent research has shown, a small minority of the members of the Dutch parliament tend to follow him in this use of the concept (De Jong and Thomassen 1992). That only a few (although prominent) political agents use the term 'legal state' in this specific way is (in a way) fortunate, because—as may be concluded from the previous section—such observations attest a serious misunderstanding. Crime contravenes the legal *order*, not the legal state. The notion of the legal state is not meant to serve the public interest, but the interests of individual citizens in receiving protection against governmental supremacy. Hence the notion of the 'legal state' is at issue not when the legal order is assailed in general, but when the government exceeds specific limits, even in the case of beneficial purposes, such as crime-prevention.

The notion of the 'legal state' is essentially a collection of requirements public authorities must fulfil in the interest of the free and equal individual citizens of the state. It is, therefore, incorrect to say that the notion of the 'legal state' requires the punishment of crime. Conversely, the statement that nobody can be involuntarily kept from the judge accorded him by law (*ius de non evocando*) is, for instance, a correct expression of one of the basic institutional requirements involved in the notion of the legal state.

[4] See Vile (1967:13) and Friedrich (1953: 209-210) on Kant's ideas about the legal state.

A second preliminary point to be made is that, rather than in the ideal circumstances of academic consensus, the legal state is especially at stake in circumstances in which its consequences are generally deemed barely acceptable. Legality is a nice notion as long as obviously innocent people are protected by it, but it becomes a nuisance when the criminal gets away on account of it. Yet, precisely cases in which well-intentioned officials are, at first sight, needlessly restrained by legal limitations in the pursuance of legitimate objectives, have time and again proven to be the litmus tests of genuine legal states. Protection from the government not only entails safeguards on behalf of the well-meaning citizenry against arbitrary power but, also, immunity for individual citizens from certain governmental measures against them, even when these measures are demanded by their outraged fellow citizens.

Institutions

It is not easy to provide a precise listing of institutional measures that make a country a 'legal state.' As we have stated, many different national arrangements can be conceived as contributing to the realization of the concept. Through the ages various authors have given different interpretations (Maus 1978). In spite of the uncertainties connected with the concept, it is possible to summarize some major features attributed to legal states.

If we accept that freedom and equality are the two basic assumptions of the legal state, this means that in the constitutional system the following general rules ought to be included:

1. All human beings shall be treated as equals.
2. Certain individual liberties shall not be affected.
3. Human beings shall have secured legal positions.
4. No public authority shall possess exclusive power.
5. Fundamental legal rules shall be established in agreement with a representation of the people.

The first four rules are related to the liberal part of liberal-democratic political theory. The last one refers to the democratic part of the system. The five rules will serve as the main themes of the following 'guidebook' to the legal state.[5]

[5] See Ermacora (1970: 92), for a different list of elements of legal states.

Equality

Article 3, sec. 1, of the German Constitution contains the following succinct provision: 'All human beings are equal before the law.' Article 1 of the Dutch Constitution provides: 'All finding themselves in the Netherlands are treated equally in equal cases.' Although these constitutional provisions are primarily addressed to the governments of the respective states, legal states generally comprise further legal rules rendering certain aspects of the principle of equality also applicable to relations between citizens.

Legal equality is formal in character. As the principle's formulation in the Dutch Constitution indicates, it does not stipulate that human beings are equal, but that they must be treated in a similar manner, once their equality in light of a pertinent criterion is established. Now the problem is how to find such criteria of equality. The notion of the legal state does not provide positive answers to this question. This led the legal theorists Kelsen and Ross to the conclusion that the principle of legal equality is identical with the principle of legal certainty insofar as it requires that legal rules be general and that particular governmental decisions be taken in accordance with general rules (Kelsen 1975: 23, 1976: 392 ff.; Ross 1974: 270 ff.). In this account, the principle entails the requirement of impartial government bound by the rule of law. In present-day legal states, the principle of equality plays an important part in the specific shape of a safeguard against discrimination on grounds of race, religion, gender or sexual proclivity. Such prohibitions of discrimination make certain factual differences between individuals legally irrelevant.

It is important to see that the principle of legal equality is not an expression of some substantive political doctrine, but an indispensable formal cornerstone of the legal state that helps to determine the borderline between governmental discretion and arbitrariness.

Secured Freedom

In legal states freedom is secured by classical basic rights. Most of these rights are also warranted by international treaties on human rights. Here we will confine ourselves to a subset of basic rights providing a comprehensive picture of the fundamental legal position accorded to individual citizens of a legal state. The rights will be presented without regard to restrictions imposed on them on account of such general interests as public order and safety.

To enhance the development of an independent, responsible and multiform national society an intricate set of basic liberties concerning the possibility of human thought and mutual communication without fear of repercussion is additionally called for. The core of these liberties consists of religious freedom, freedom of opinion, and freedom of assembly, association and demonstration. It is quite clear that these rights are essential from the perspective of the democratic process. Dahl, for example, mentions them as prerequisites of his democratic theory (Dahl 1989: 221).

A further principal basic right is the right of freedom of movement. Without this freedom open social and economic exchanges are infeasible.

Finally, a series of basic rights has the purpose of protecting the citizens' personal integrity, as well as their private and intimate social life from governmental interference: the inviolability of the human body, the inviolability of the home, protection against undue expropriation, personal privacy, confidentiality of mail, telephone and telegraph, warranted secrecy of personal data, and protection against unlawful detention.

Legal Certainty

We have already seen that the principle of legal certainty partly coincides with the principle of formal equality, inasmuch as both require that legal rules be general and that particular governmental decisions be taken in accordance with the former. However, in modern states there is more to the principle of legal certainty than is expressed by the classical ideal of 'government by rules, not by men.' No modern government is capable of acting effectively on the basis of the idea that all its decisions should result from applying general rules to particular cases. Any modern legal state is confronted with the problem of how to balance the need for governmental discretion against the requirement of individual legal protection. In general, modern legal states have sought to create suitable preconditions for solving this equilibrium problem by introducing, in addition to the regular courts, systems of specialized judiciaries charged with the judicial review of governmental decisions. These systems of administrative courts and tribunals are not only empowered to reverse governmental decisions in case the latter contravene established legal rules, but also in case they are deemed to violate general legal standards, such as the principles of administrative reliability, due care, proportionality, fairness and sufficient reason. Insight into judge-made administrative law, evolved in virtue of such general principles with regard to the relations between public authorities and individual citizens, is of the utmost importance for reaching a clear comprehension of legal certainty in West European legal states.[6]

[6] See De Moor-Van Vugt (1987), for a comparative study of the application of unwritten legal standards by administrative tribunals in Holland, Germany, France, Belgium and the European Union.

Distribution of Powers

Legal states bear witness to a profound distrust of absolute public power. They are so organized as to minimize the risk that any authority will prevail over all other authorities. This objective is pursued by distributing restricted legal powers between different public authorities so as to render them mutually dependent. The most famous theoretical design warranting a power balance between different sectors of government is the doctrine of the *separation of powers* between a legislative, administrative and judicial branch, respectively, as proposed by Montesquieu. The doctrine greatly influenced the Constitution of the United States. The legal states of Western Europe have sworn allegiance to the related, yet distinct principle of *mixed government*. It replaces the idea of a separation of powers with that of a joint exercise of powers by the legislative and administrative branches of government. Both the doctrine of the separation of powers and the doctrine of mixed government purport to warrant the state's main power balance. Legal states answering to either of the two major principles of power distribution additionally contain all sorts of designs warranting supplementary minor power equilibria on the basis of the principle of *checks and balances*. This principle requires that all public power be exercised in a formal context that provides for the respective public authority's accountability to other public authorities.[7]

Representation

The concept of accountability establishes a link with the principle of representation.

As we have earlier explained, the democratic principle has an analytic relation with the notion of the legal state, apart from its factual connection. In the first place, the analytic relation can historically be traced back to Rousseau's opinion that the bindingness of the general legal rules of a state ought to rest on popular sovereignty, that is, on voluntary self-binding acts performed by representatives of the people (la volonté générale). On this historic view, all public policymaking would amount to issuing and applying general legal rules which are legitimized by the will of the people as pronounced by its representatives. Consequently, the ultimate legitimization of the legal state would be based on the democratic origins of its normative foundations. Nowadays, this account has lost much of its cogency, since public policy no longer coincides with the creation and administration of general legal rules,

7 See Gwyn (1965) and Vile (1967) on this concept and the relation to the concept of separation of powers. On the normative value of this concept see also Buchanan and Tullock (1965) and Ostrom (1974: 77, 81, 89, and 103).

whilst the relations between the decisions of representative bodies and the will of the people are, to say the least, rather spurious. Does this mean that the modern concept of the legal state is no longer analytically related to the notion of democracy? It still is, but in a different respect. The weak spot in the idea of accountability for any exercise of public authority inherent in the principle of checks and balances is summarized in the classical problem of who will guard the guardians. *Quis custodiet custodes ipsos?* The democratic notion provides a solution to this problem, as it indicates procedures that put the democratic representatives in the position of the ultimate guardians within the government, while enabling the population to check the latter in regular general elections. As far as the notion of the legal state is concerned, the democratic principle, rather than securing the people's involvement in political life, serves as a convenient device for bringing about generally acclaimed changes of personnel and thereby as a constant threat to the sitting representatives to behave themselves. In this way, the democratic principle provides the final check on the legal state.

Results

Until now we have made two steps. First, we attended to liberal-democratic political theory. We concluded that this theory is based on two interdependent values, the principles of freedom and equality. The second step concerned the transformation of political theory into legally valid norms (the requirements a liberal democracy ought to meet). Secondly, we explained the concept of a legal state (*Rechtstaat*). It appeared that the basic structure of a 'legal state' must comprise five elements:

1. All human beings will be treated as equals. We have seen that this value primarily amounts to the requirement of *impartial* government.
2. Certain individual liberties will not be affected. We have observed that the principal liberties originate with a conception of individual humans and their societies as requiring a minimum of freedom of thought, as well as individual and collective, political, economic and social action to flourish and develop. Formal liberty thus amounts to the requirement of *restrained* government.
3. Human beings will have secured legal positions. In present-day legal states the principle of legal certainty calls for an independent judiciary that is empowered to judge the acts of government not only by the established legal rules but also by unwritten legal standards. This amounts to the requirement of *reliable and reasonable* government.
4. No public authority will possess exclusive power. The general principle of a division of public powers can be roughly translated into the

Figure 4.3. Basic Structure of a Legal State

legal equality	→	*impartial* government
secured freedom	→	*restrained* government
legal security	→	*reliable* and *reasonable* government
power distribution	→	*accountable* government
representation	→	*removable* government

requirement of *accountable* government.

5. Fundamental legal rules will be established in agreement with a representation of the people. The analytic part of the democratic principle in the legal state is that of a final check in the shape of the population's capacity of periodically changing the governmental cast. This amounts to the requirement of *removable* government.

It is clear that each of the specific requirements involved in the concept of a legal state appears to be so general as to allow for divergent implementations. In this way, particular states may possess entirely different structures and yet all fall under the category of legal states. Does this mean that the notion is too vague to provide for clear distinctions? In our opinion this is not so. The requirements are admittedly general in character, but this does not involve vagueness. They impose indeed strict limits on the kind of basic structures of states that are acceptable from a legal point of view. Therefore, they also provide general standards for evaluating constitutional change in Eastern Europe.

Constitutional Change

The main purpose of our analysis is to give some insight into the objectives that must be achieved by countries in the Eastern part of the European continent in their attempts to evolve from dependent totalitarian states to *independent liberal democracies*. What must further be done to enhance this development? We shall conclude with some general remarks on the way in which the processes of change themselves can be shaped.

At first sight, a written constitution would seem to be the first requirement from the standpoint of legal security. This requirement fits with the continental legal state tradition. The former president of the European Court of Justice, the Dutchman Donner, called a written constitution a fundamental element of a legal state:

1. A basic law or written constitution that contains binding prescriptions as to the relations between the government and the citizens;
2. in which a division of powers is guaranteed, in particular: (a) legislation in agreement with a parliament, (b) an independent judiciary power which not only decides disputes between citizens but also between government and citizens, and (c) administration in virtue of the laws;
3. and by which the civil rights of the citizens are circumscribed and secured (Donner 1983: 143).

Is the requirement that the constitution be written indeed as important as suggested? For instance, the eldest 'legal state' in Europe, the United Kingdom, has no written constitution. Moreover, it is clear that the history of countries which do have a written constitution gives evidence of many changes to their basic structures, contrary to explicit provisions in these respective documents. It follows that a written constitution is neither a prerequisite for a successful transformation process, nor a guarantee of success. In fact, we are convinced that the enactment of a written constitution can play a significant but limited part in the processes of constitutional change.

We shall now consider the concept of *constitutional change* in some more detail. In saying that the Eastern European countries attempt to evolve from dependent totalitarianism to *independent liberal democracies*, we refer to their searches for other ways of organizing the relations between governments and their citizens.

The American legal realist Llewellyn once defined three categories of agents that are involved in constitutional development: administrative specialists, interest groups and the general public. These three categories of agents might be understood as 'the interpretive community' dominating the constitutional debate and, consequently, also dominating the questions asked and the answers given. The wider audience is not unimportant. 'The audience, however, initiates neither play nor change' (Llewellyn 1962: 235). Their only effective right is the right of veto. A constitution 'can be viewed with some adequacy as the interaction of the quite different ways and attitudes of three diverse categories of people, and that of these the specialists in government stand at the focus' (Llewellyn 1962: 237). Interest groups stand in the middle, between the specialists and the public. It is unlikely for a government to be able to govern without consulting them.

Figure 4.4. The Legal State According to Donner

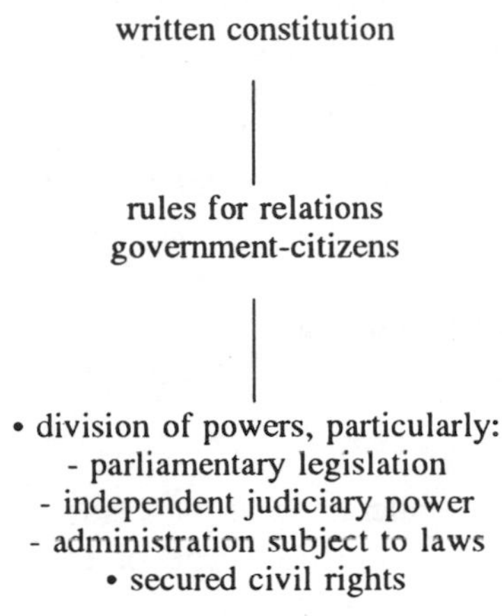

If we accept the idea of an 'interpretive community' and the different positions various agents have in it, two points should be kept in mind. The first point is the assumption of a national society. When we referred to actual developments in Eastern Europe earlier on, we also alluded to actual or threatening wars which endanger the lives of so many. It appears that certain nation states that were formed before and after the Second World War will have a hard time obtaining overall acceptance by their populations, owing to the fact that they comprise so many different ethnic groups. Governance can only be legitimate when the majority of citizens actually want to be members of the political society representing them. Here some basic tenets that were first articulated by John Locke still hold true. Locke considered consent by the citizen a necessary precondition for a legitimate exercise of political power (Locke 1984). The second point is that it is impossible to provide one and only one constitutional solution for all countries in Eastern Europe. Even in the unlikely event that one constitutional text would be enacted in all countries concerned, this would not lead to identically effective constitutions, since the constitutional practices would immediately begin to diverge (Joseph and Walker 1987: 155-181). What is needed is a program for constitutional change in every political society that exists or comes into being. For this program the following strategic 'rules of thumb' for constitutional change in Eastern Europe may be used:

1. With respect to each country an adequate analysis of its existing social and cultural structure is required.
2. With respect to each country an adequate analysis of the existing political and legal power structure is required.
3. Programs for constitutional change directed at realizing the values involved in the concept of a legal state should not be blueprints without any relation to the current social, cultural, political and legal situation.
4. The constitutional order must contain a great variety of mutually supportive mechanisms for achieving the objectives involved in the concept of the legal state (see Figure 4.3), meaning that a certain redundancy is acceptable, even if economists would be opposed on efficiency grounds.

The principles of liberal democracy and the institutions of a legal state play their most significant part in the last stage of the process of constitutional change. At this stage is may be useful to engage in designing a written constitution in order to focus the process. The same goes for the usefulness of education and training programs for politicians, civil servants, and citizens, as well as frequent exchanges of ideas with representatives of the international community.

The reason for presenting the above 'rules of thumb' for constitutional change is not their pretended novelty, for they are actually rather classical. Our only purpose was to reaffirm that changing constitutional paradigms is an even more hazardous undertaking than changing scientific paradigms. Galilei's 'and yet she moves' could eventually be proved true; the fate of a new constitutional practice does not depend on its truth, but on its being recognized as morally justified by the population. Therefore, to say that countries ought to reform themselves is one thing, to implement the transformation in terms of general agreement on values and on the nation's basic institutional structure is quite another. Before a new, stable constitutional order will exist in most of the countries involved, a long time will have passed.

Conclusion

The first step in this chapter focused on the concept of liberal democracy. Liberalism is a political theory in which individual freedom is a basic social value. Like any other political theory, however, it has to deal with the tension between *individual freedom* and *authority*. In order to deal with this tension we followed Raz's suggestion not to use the idea of autonomy as a starting point of liberal-democratic theory, but the wider concept of 'the service conception of the function of authorities.' Thus individual freedom was related to political equality. Both individual freedom and political equality are the fundamental values a liberal-democracy is built on.

The second step in this chapter aimed at transforming the liberal-democratic values into an institutional structure of given political societies. This part of our argumentation led to the following scheme:

Legal equality	→	*impartial* government
Secured freedom	→	*restrained* government
Legal security	→	*reliable* and *reasonable* government
Power distribution	→	*accountable* government
Representation	→	*removable* government

Finally, we looked at the possibility of constitutional change in Eastern Europe, which led to the following statements:

1. With respect to each country an adequate analysis of its existing social and cultural structure is required.
2. With respect to each country an adequate analysis of the existing political and legal power structure is required.
3. Programs for constitutional change directed at realizing the values involved in the concept of a legal state should not be blueprints without any relation to the current social, cultural, political and legal situation.
4. The constitutional order must come to contain a great variety of mutually supportive mechanisms for achieving the objectives involved in the concept of the legal state, meaning that a certain redundancy is acceptable, even if economists would be opposed on efficiency grounds.

The outcome of our exposé remains on a general level. This should not come as a surprise, since the aim we set at the beginning of this chapter was to try to give insight into some fundamental *problems* that must be solved to make a rational process of constitutional design possible. Such a process is, first of all, one in which the 'interpretive communities' of the respective nations of Eastern Europe must play the leading role. They must discover their own versions of the principles of liberal democracy and shape their states accordingly.

References

Benn, S.I. (1988) *A Theory of Freedom*. Cambridge: Cambridge University Press.
Berlin, I. (1969) *Four Essays on Liberty*. Oxford: Oxford University Press.
Buchanan, J.M. and G. Tullock (1965) *The Calculus of Consent*. Ann Arbor: University of Michigan Press.
Dahl, R.A. (1985) *A Preface to Economic Democracy*. Cambridge: Polity Press.
Dahl, R.A. (1989) *Democracy and Its Critics*. New Haven: Yale University Press.
De Jong, H.M. and J.J.A. Thomassen (1992) *Democratie en rechtsstaat*. In: J.J.A. Thomassen, M.P.C.M. van Schendelen and M.L. Zielonka-Goei (eds.) *De geachte afgevaardigde*. Muiderberg: Coutinho. 249-274.
Donner, A.M. (1983) *Handboek van het Nederlandse staatsrecht*. Zwolle: Tjeenk Willink.
Ermacora, F. (1970) *Allgemeine Staatslehre: Volume 1*. Berlin: Duucker und Humblot.
Finer, S.E. (1970) *Comparative government*. New York: Penguin.
Friedrich, C.J. (1953) *Der Verfassungstaat der Neuzeit*. Berlin: Springer.
Glenny, M. (1990) *The Rebirth of History*. London: Penguin.
Green, L. (1990) *The Authority of the State*. Oxford: Clarendon.
Gutman, A. (1980) *Liberal Equality*. Cambridge: Cambridge University Press.
Gwyn, W.B. (1965) *The Meaning of the Separation of Powers*. New Orleans: Tulane University.
Haakonssen, K. (1988) The Philosophy of Law in Hayek's New Constitutionalism. *Rechtstheorie* 3: 289-303.
Hamilton, A.J., J. Madison and J. Jay (1961) *The Federalist Papers*. New York: New American Library.
Hayek, F.A. (1973) *Law, Legislation, and Liberty: Volume 1, Rules and Order*. Chicago: University of Chicago Press.
Hayek, F.A. (1976) *Law, Legislation, and Liberty: Volume 2, The Mirage of Social Justice*. Chicago: University of Chicago Press.
Hayek, F.A. (1979) *Law, Legislation, and Liberty: Volume 3, The Political Order of Free People*. Chicago: University of Chicago Press.
Held, D. (1988) *Models of Democracy*. Cambridge: Polity Press.
Joseph, P.A. and G.R. Walker (1987) A Theory of Constitutional Change. *Oxford Journal of Legal Studies* 2: 155-181.
Kelsen, H. (1975 [1958]) *Was is Gerechtigkeit?* Vienna: Deuticke.
Kelsen, H. (1976 [1960]) *Reine Rechtlehre*. Vienna: Deuticke.
Llewellyn, K.N. (1962) *Jurisprudence*. Chicago: University of Chicago Press.
Locke, J. (1984) *Two Treatises of Government*. London: Dent.
Mill, J.S. (1985) *On Liberty*. London: Penguin.
Maus, I. (1978) *Entwicklung und Funktionswandel der Theorie des bürgerlichen Rechtsstaats*. In: M. Tohidipur (ed.) *Der bürgerliche Rechtsstaat*. Frankfurt a.M.: Suhrkamp.
Montesquieu, Ch. (1783) *De l'Esprit des Lois*. Amsterdam: Garnier.
Moor-Van Vugt, A.J.C. de (1987) *Algemene beginselen van behoorlijk bestuur en buitenlandse equivalenten*. Zwolle: Tjeenk Willink.

Ostrom, V. (1974) *The Intellectual Crisis in American Public Administration.* Alabama: University of Alabama Press.

Rawls, J. (1971) *A Theory of Justice.* London: Oxford University Press.

Raz, J. (1986) *The Morality of Freedom.* Oxford: Clarendon.

Ross, A. (1974 [1958]) *On Law and Justice.* Berkeley: University of California Press.

Rousseau, J.J. (1968) *The Social Contract.* London: Dent.

Seidman, R.B. (1978) *The State, Law, and Development.* London: Croom Helm.

Spicker, P. (1985) Why Freedom Implies Equality. *Journal of Applied Philosophy* 2: 205-216.

Vile, M.J.C. (1967) *Constitutionalism and the Separation of Powers* Oxford: Oxford University Press.

Weber, M. (1980) *Wirtschaft und Gesellschaft.* Tübingen: Mohr.

5

Political Culture and Political Consolidation

Max Kaase*

The mostly peaceful transitions in Central and Eastern Europe in 1989 from totalitarian rule to some kind of political order that is not yet precisely known—but may well resemble what in the language of political science is called pluralist democracy—caught Western publics as well as political scientists by surprise. As is not unusual in such instances, ex post facto explanations easily arise and, additionally, a sizable literature on regime changes exists which can serve as a starting point for analysis.

In 1970, in an influential article Dankwart Rustow characterized much of the existing work on democracies and the conditions conducive to their stability as, on the one hand, examining well-established polities and structural properties which were common among them, but, on the other hand, neglecting polities which had not achieved entry into the 'club' of democratic nations. What is so important about Rustow's approach (1970: 346) is that he emphasized that, among other factors, the causal links in the process of democratization do not always flow from social preconditions to the political sphere and, at the same time, he thought there is no single uniform road on which, step by step, a transition to democracy takes place.

Unfortunately, regime transitions are both too rare in number and too complex in structure and process to easily permit the application of standard statistical techniques for the analysis of such phenomena. It does not, there-

* The author appreciates the support from Petra Bauer-Kaase in data analysis, and from Jürgen Hofrichter, Michael Klein and Peter Schubert of ZEUS (Mannheim) for quickly and efficiently providing cumulative data files of the 1990, 1991 and 1992 Eurobarometer East.

H. J. Blommestein and B. Steunenberg (eds.), Government and Markets, 71–114.

fore, come as a surprise that the two major projects systematically approaching problems of political regime transition are following the same strategy of inquiry. The study of transitions from democratic to authoritarian rule by Linz, Stepan and their collaborators in the seventies, as well as those of transitions from authoritarian to democratic rule in the eighties, combine the development of a conceptual framework (Linz 1978; O'Donnell et al. 1986; O'Donnell and Schmitter 1986) with a series of case studies.[1,2] This specific conceptual and empirical mix enables them to overcome the fallacies of both variable-centered and case-oriented approaches (Ragin 1987).

Clearly, for the transitions from totalitarian rule the O'Donnell-Schmitter studies are particularly pertinent.[3] Basically and succinctly, they argue that an authoritarian regime becomes destabilized through a process of liberalization that grants, for whatever reason, 'certain rights that protect both individuals and social groups from arbitrary or illegal acts committed by the state or third parties' (O'Donnell and Schmitter 1986: 7). Although these rights, in principle, can be withdrawn by the ruling authoritarian elites, if not withdrawn, they spread and encourage an ever-increasing part of the population to make use of them.

Liberalization can thus be regarded as an important element in paving the way for the transition itself, although it remains a question for further research whether it *must* be present and, if yes, to what extent.[4] At the core of the transition lies the democratization phase, that is, the phase in which basic citizenship rights are institutionalized as legally binding to include every member of the polity and to set up rules which regulate contestation between competing groups. There seems to be agreement in the literature that the formulation and institutionalization of these rules for the emerging democratic polity is the most important and final phase in the transition process (see, for example, Di Palma 1990: 109-136). The move away from 'break-down games' is encouraged by the inclusion of all relevant (corporate) actors, in particular those who were previously kept out of positions of influence. Usually, the transformation to a democratic regime is symbolically as well as factually highlighted by calling a free election to a new parliament. Such elections are tremendously important because they indicate to what extent elite promises of free access to the competition game are sustained, how the newly instituted rules of the game operate and, especially, how elections result in the formation of a new government.

1 See also Diamond et al. (1991) on the topic of democracy in developing countries.

2 See Huffman and Gautier (1993) for a recent state of the art report on transition theories.

3 See also the review by Bermeo (1990).

4 Ekiert (1991: 293) too refers to the conceptual vagueness of the concept.

Among the various forms transitions can take (Karl and Schmitter 1991), transition by elite agreement has been called a pact. A pact is defined as 'an explicit, but not always publicly explicated or justified, agreement among a select set of actors which seeks to define (or better, to redefine) rules governing the exercise of power on the basis of mutual guarantees for the "vital interests" of those entering into it' (O'Donnell and Schmitter 1986: 37). In a more recent analysis carrying the systematic argument further on empirical grounds, Karl and Schmitter (1991: 280-281) maintain that it is only this particular mode of transition which seems to make for the durability of democratic regimes thus established. A pact is a change from above by elite consensus, and this notion entails two aspects to which we shall return: (1) the emphasis on the role of political elites; and (2) the concept of associability in the sense of the need of elites to mobilize and bring into the bargaining game a sufficient number of followers, be they defined on socio-structural, political or other grounds.[5]

The final phase in the process of regime change is consolidation. There are various meanings of the term, but it seems plausible to think of it as the phase which follows the establishment of the pact and its institutional democratic corollaries, in sum: the routinization of the newly acquired constitutional and institutional structure, the codification of civil rights and the operation of the democratic rules of the game for interest aggregation, representation and political decision-making (Di Palma 1990: 138-149). One need not dwell too long on the problem whether a point should also be specified at which consolidation gives way to democratic stability; experiences from the past indicate that a peaceful government change by public vote could mark such a break-even point (Dahrendorf 1990: 117; Di Palma 1990: 126, 145).

Considering the topic we want to cover in this chapter, it is particularly interesting to look at the role citizen orientations play in the literature on regime change. From Rustow (1970: 344-345) and Hirschman (1971: 323-326) to Przeworski (1986: 50-53) and Di Palma (1990: 144-152) there seems to be agreement that citizen attitudes, in particular legitimacy beliefs, are irrelevant in the transition process and for the (initial) consolidation of a democracy. This conclusion builds basically on two arguments. The first refers to two aspects of attitude theory. The assumption of a causal attitude-behavior sequence is not warranted because (1) the relationship is, in the light of intervening contextual factors, weak to start with and (2) there is a great deal of evidence for a reversed process in that, based on consistency theories,

[5] See Marks (1992) on the logic of elite behavior in strategic situations of regime transformation.

behaviors lead to later attitudinal adjustments. This consideration is well taken.

The second argument is of a more mixed nature. In theoretical terms, a major weakness of transition literature lies in its implicit or explicit emphasis on institutional arrangements (the macro level) and on the organizational infrastructure of interest groups and political parties, including their leadership (the meso level). At first sight this approach certainly makes sense for the analysis of transitions by pact, but that is not the only type of transition (Karl and Schmitter 1991), and pacts can only be stabilized if the elites—as representatives of corporate actors—can assure cooperation and support by their members or clientele. It would be desirable to avoid this macro-mesobias, which simply disregards the public at large, by developing research designs which are at least open to a more prominent role by the individual citizens (the micro level).

Given the complexity of such a micro-meso-macro design, this chapter will obviously be unable to overcome the specific weakness of transition models which concentrate on institutions and corporate actors alone. Rather, it will take the opposite path by trying to bring in the micro perspective and systematically analyze citizen orientations through survey data from representative samples in selected Central and East European Countries during the 1990-1992 transition period. Mainly, the degree of public acceptance the regime changes have found will be assessed as well as what the economic underpinnings of the respective attitudes are. The conceptual model guiding this research will be the approach of Almond and Verba (1965) in studying political culture. However, it is first necessary to take a closer look at some specifics of the political changes in Central and Eastern Europe.

Elements of Regime Change in Central and Eastern Europe

Dahl (1989: 213-308), in a seminal book, has summarized the central elements of polyarchy as well as the conditions conducive to create and maintain this type of political order. Polyarchy is defined by the extension of citizenship rights to (almost) all adults in a given political system, plus institutional structures which permit opposition to governments to the extent of voting a given government out of power. Przeworski (1991: 10) has put the essence of pluralist democracy in a nutshell: 'Beneath all the institutional diversity, one elementary feature—contestation open to participation...—is sufficient to identify a political system as democratic.'

Whereas Kielmansegg in 1988 still looked at socialism as a viable challenge and alternative to democracy, Sniderman (1981: 141), almost a decade earlier, concluded about the United States (based on empirical evidence from a survey study): 'Time has witnessed the eclipse of alternative conceptions of a political order in America. Such alternative conceptions are no longer ...live hypotheses, except in small folds of the culture.' This notion was highlighted and generalized by Fukuyama (1989: 2, 1992) who saw the end of the Cold War as a cutting point which would result in the universalization of Western liberal democracy as 'the final form of human government.'

These ideas seem to square well with Schmitter's (1992: 428-429) emphasis on the current need to study institutional variants of democracy instead of principally different concepts of the political order. The particular thrust that contemporary transition theory places on actors vis-à-vis structural conditions conducive to democratic rule should not distract from the fact that there are important factors which at least ease the way to democratic rule of formerly non-democratic polities. Vanhanen's (1990) study on democratization demonstrates that it is not just modernization or a high level of socio-economic development per se (which East European countries have already achieved), but rather the dispersion of power resources across a given society that is crucial for answering the question whether a democracy can emerge. He also refers to the fact that the Soviet Union, as a hegemonical power, was mostly responsible for the fact that the internal structural strain between relatively high socio-economic and non-material resource levels and high power concentration did not result in an earlier breakdown of totalitarian rule in Central and Eastern Europe.

Whereas these considerations all seem to point to the inevitability of becoming democracies, there is still reason enough to doubt whether the transitions in Central and Eastern Europe to quasi-democratic rule will indeed be consolidated soon or whether a return to some form of authoritarianism will be forthcoming in some countries (Wesolowski 1991: 94; Konrad 1991). In Ekiert's words (1991: 288):

> The rise of Western-type democratic regimes in the region is ...very uncertain. In my view, a transition towards another type of non-democratic political arrangement is more likely than genuine democratization, given the complexity of the current economic, political and social crisis in the region, *as well as certain aspects of its political culture and traditions.* The tasks facing new democratically elected governments are so enormous and the required shock treatment of ailing economies so drastic, that some form of coercive policies may be necessary in order to accomplish a fundamental restructuring of political and economic systems (my emphasis; M.K.).

Other than in cases of transitions from authoritarian political regimes, it is the need to completely rearrange both the political *and* the economic system *at the same time* that makes the consolidation of the new Eastern democracies so difficult (Ekiert 1991: 310-311; Frentzel-Zagorska 1991: 103-105). If one is willing to follow Przeworski's analyses (1991), then (1) there is no alternative to the kind of capitalism which has developed in the Western moderate welfare states (what, in Germany, Ludwig Erhardt, the 'father' of the *Wirtschaftswunder* (economic miracle) has called *soziale Marktwirtschaft*), and (2) that the best strategy in the long run for political leaders is a *radical* economic reform, even though this will surely create a great deal of disenchantment and dissatisfaction in the citizenry once the effects of reform begin to be felt. Here, it should be mentioned in passing, lies a major challenge for the European Union, whose support of the economic transition in Central and Eastern Europe is absolutely mandatory. While in Central and Eastern Europe there is an almost uncritical acceptance, at least in the abstract, of the need to swiftly move to market economies, the agreements in agriculture between the European Union and the CSFR, Hungary and Poland unfortunately are not an example that highlights the superiority of the market system. This, of course, reflects the nearly complete lack of market mechanisms in the agrarian sector in the European Union.

The economic dimension at present and probably for the next decade or so gives little promise to expectations of rapid consolidation. This may be different, however, with respect to claims that a mostly latent and self-organized network of individuals and groups had already developed in the late Seventies and early Eighties which began to crystallize into some sort of a political counter-culture against the hegemonical state: the civil society (Geremek 1992: 11). There was a lot of enthusiasm vis-à-vis the idea of civil society in the West (Arato 1990) and it was not by accident that there the carriers of the flame were intellectuals and scholars who had been closely involved in the debate on the legitimacy crisis in Western democracies and the ensuing prediction of the imminent breakdown of these polities. Usually (see the neo-corporatism debate), intuitively appealing concepts such as the civil society find quick and wide recognition for a while, especially in the speculative realm.[6] In the case of Central and Eastern Europe, civil society took on a more precise meaning in the sense of a network of loosely connected quasi-political organizations outside the realm of the hegemonical party state.

For democratic consolidation, prior developments towards elements of a civil society can take on two specific meanings. The first refers to the fact that, because of the willful destruction of all existing intermediary linkage structures independent of the party state in the early phases of socialist rule (Ekiert 1991: 301; Grilli di Cortona 1991: 325), civil society meant the re-creation of exactly the same structures (Frentzel-Zagorska 1991: 96) as an effort to establish a counterweight to the hegemonical state. Given the importance of associability in pluralist democracies (Dahl 1989), intermediary

[6] See Heins (1992) and Schmalz-Bruns (1992), for the German case.

organizations, developing out of the growing civil society in Central and Eastern Europe, could emerge as vital elements of a system of interest organization, which is required as part of the consolidation effort (Schmitter 1992).

The second point is that those individuals helping to develop and act out civil society were frequently members of counter-elites (Wesolowski 1991: 88-94) which played important roles in the transition process. Therefore, the political orientations of these actors are relevant for the direction into which a polity will develop after transition.

Obviously, transition itself has contributed to the ambivalence in the meaning of civil society, which derived its essence in the socialist party state as an antipode to that state and which now, in the consolidation phase, must be redefined in order to find its proper place in the emerging democratic polity. This ambivalence in meaning is probably what induced Ekiert (1991: 298-305) to introduce the analytic distinction between the domestic society, pertaining to the economic self-interests of the citizens and thereby to the private sphere, and the political society, embracing the whole array of formal and voluntary associations constituting the intermediate sector.

With the disintegration and disappearance of the hegemonical Soviet Union, a problem which has plagued Central and Eastern Europe ever since the breakdown of the Habsburg empire increasingly returns to the fore: the new nationalism. Senghaas (1992) has rightfully warned of any flat rejection of nationalism which, in its 'classical' form à la Deutsch, played a rational and important role in the nineteenth century transformations from traditional to modern societies (nation building). Senghaas also sees virtue in the nationalism of young nations after their liberation from colonial supremacy and in their quest to obtain not only political, but also economic independence.[7]

However, the nationalism now visible in some form or another in almost every Central and East European state is of a different nature. It is a reflection of the interrupted and partially frozen process of political, economic and cultural development which now re-creates historically founded cleavages. Such cleavages built on ethnocentrism are capable of demonstrating the logic of pluralist policymaking in an obvious and broadly intelligible fashion. On the other hand, their high symbolic and emotional conflict potential is very detrimental in the phase of polity seeking (Brubaker 1993). This situation is aggravated by the fact that other cleavages (such as class) are not so easily reinstituted, that there are many more 'nations' than states (Konrad 1991), and that the geopolitical distribution of those 'nations' is so complex that it cannot

[7] This perspective can be maintained independent of the fact that up to this point this 'secondary' nation-building, politically and economically, has mostly failed.

be easily transformed into ethnically homogeneous nation states without major resettlements involving large numbers of individuals (one example is the high percentage of Russians in the Baltic states). As a consequence, the chance for internal (Yugoslavia) as well as external (Moldavia) conflicts is high, and the disintegration of the CSFR into two independent nation states effected by the end of 1992 is another example of the difficulties *on these grounds* that the consolidation of the new Central and Eastern European democracies will have to overcome.

By contrast, culturally defined sub-identities in the democracies of the West are undoubtedly finding renewed and increasing support. While, as the Italian leagues exemplify, this can also lead to challenges to the unitary nation state, the large number of potential cultural cleavages—which because of their frequency enhance the probability of individuals holding multiple cultural identities—has created a situation where multi-culturality is becoming a societal and political value that is shared by a vast majority of the population.[8] Yet, this positive view of multiculturality requires an amount of intellectual sophistication and societal wealth that many countries simply cannot muster at present.

This is an empirical question however. Therefore, research into attitudes towards nationalism and, in particular, into the relationship between in-group and out-group attitudes, is important for the understanding of the consolidation process currently going on in Central and Eastern Europe. This point also serves as an excellent example to demonstrate why looking at the concept of political culture in Central and Eastern Europe bears analytical value. This section of the chapter, in looking at various problem areas in the consolidation process, was intended to help define more precisely which elements of political culture are especially worth observing.

The Concept of Political Culture: Potentials and Limitations

Although in 1956 Almond had already talked of and defined the concept of political culture, it was the five-nations-study 'The Civic Culture' (Almond and Verba 1965) which put this approach on the agenda of political science. It appears useful to allow at least one of the authors to speak authoritatively on what, in his view, political culture is: 'The political culture of a society consists of the system of empirical beliefs, expressive symbols, and values which defines the situation in which political action takes place. It provides the subjective orientation to politics' (Verba 1965: 513).

[8] See Smolicz (1991), for the example of Australia.

In a critical review of the state of research on political culture Kaase (1983) has pointed out that the concept is in constant danger of deterioratation into what Dittmer has called a 'catch-all term': a term that is so broad and encompasses almost everything political under the label of political culture. This is especially unfortunate since in 'The Civic Culture' Almond and Verba laid out a conceptual scheme (to which we shall return shortly) for the study of political cultures and then continued to demonstrate how this scheme could be put into effect as a guide to empirical research.

There is no point in dwelling on the impact the Civic Culture study and its underlying approach have had on later research.[9] What has been undoubtedly lacking since is a building on the initial Almond and Verba notions and the systematic development of instruments which are theoretically meaningful and, at the same time, can be used in comparative survey studies. What is probably most disappointing is that there has been so little truly cumulative and comparative research on political culture proper since the days of the Civic Culture study.

When thinking about political culture, a few things need to be kept in mind. First, the internal logic of the approach requires individual level data which are usually produced by the survey method. The comparative thrust of such studies makes it plausible to go for (repeated) representative cross-sections of the (usually voting-age) population, although there may always be good reasons (for instance, cultural heterogeneity) to either sample additional specific subgroups of the population or to choose such a large sample size that analyses differentiated according to region, ethnicity or similar variables are feasible.

In their study Almond and Verba sampled only national cross-sections in the five nations included (except in the Mexican case that deviated somewhat from the pattern for technical reasons). This is understandable given the novelty of the approach, the well-defined topical interest of the principal investigators and the financial resources available for the study. However, it is at least desirable, if not mandatory, in the study of political transitions, to augment mass public surveys by the systematic study of the beliefs and attitudes of strategic elites (Bermeo 1992: 276-279). This is particularly true when one thrives on an actor-oriented approach as almost all of the transition research does. In practice, however, for many reasons such research is very difficult if not entirely impossible.[10]

The initial Civic Culture study presented to readers a conceptual scheme meant to help to identify the most relevant dimensions of any given political culture. Basically, it resulted in a matrix of four political objects: (1) system;

[9] See Verba (1980) for some thoughts on the matter.

[10] Some of the reasons are spelled out in Tarrow (1991).

(2) inputs; (3) outputs; and (4) self/ego; and three modes of orientation: (1) cognitive; (2) affective; and (3) evaluative. In this conceptualization the impact of Eastonian thinking on systems theory is clearly visible. However, the scheme has never been fully developed empirically, the empirical findings are interpreted to a substantial extent in an ad hoc fashion, and there is no set of indicators which could be clearly related to each individual cell of such an object by orientation matrix.

This conceptualization was also thought to establish a micro-macro link in looking at the compatibility of (macro) structure and culture with the intention to derive conclusions about the stability of democratic political systems (Almond and Verba 1965: 20-21, 360-365; Verba 1980: 397, 402-406; see also Fuchs 1989: 5-11). This has caused scholars like Scheuch (1968) to speak of the danger of the individualistic fallacy originating from the Civic Culture study.[11] Obviously, such a conceptual problem can easily be avoided and therefore is no argument against the usefulness and need to collect micro-level data.

There is one final, important point to be addressed in the context of political culture. Early on, Almond and Verba pointed out on various occasions that they do not include behaviors as relevant elements of political culture, a point which later has been frequently neglected or overlooked by other researchers in the field. It is absolutely apparent that it is exactly the conceptual and empirical separation of attitudes and behavior which makes political culture such a useful concept for understanding parts of the political process (see also Brown 1979: 9). Only this distinction enables the researcher—provided, of course, that he or she has the appropriate data at hand—to empirically decide upon hypotheses alluded to earlier, i.e., whether democratic attitudes must precede democratic political participation or whether it is the other way around.

There have remained many open questions in the context of studies of political culture. One deals with the relationship between political culture and culture in general (Verba 1965: 521-525). This analytical distinction has not led to research which would create a reliable body of pertinent knowledge. This problem is especially relevant for the transitions under scrutiny in this chapter, where citizens in the new democracies have had no chance to become socialized into democratic political orientations. Only in passing should it be mentioned that in this context processes and agencies of political socialization, including the mass media, automatically come into the fore.

The concept of political culture is not a political theory in the narrow epistemological sense of a nomological set of premises and hypotheses which

[11] Scheuch refers to the problem of talking about macro characteristics of a given political system based on aggregated micro information from surveys.

are systematically linked to each other. It would probably have been promoted closer to that status, though, if there had been—as mentioned before—more systematic and cumulative research building on the initial concepts developed by Almond and Verba. Instead, and this also holds true for the transition literature, there is an off-and-on reference to political culture in the usual euphemistic, vague fashion but never a serious attempt to use it in an analytically precise manner (see, for example, Di Palma 1990: 144).

It is unclear whether this state of affairs is due to flaws innate in the Almond-Verba conceptualization of political culture, or to its intriguing property of being easily adaptable to almost everything political for which another concept or term is not at hand. All this, of course, cannot be remedied here. Nevertheless, at least an effort will be made to select the available evidence in a way congruent with the initial political culture concept and to interpret it in a systematic micro-macro perspective. Particular emphasis will be placed on the four political objects figuring prominently in the initial Almond-Verba scheme.

A Note on the Data Basis

The concept of political culture, as derived from the literature in the previous section, requires information on the political orientations of cross-sections of at least the voting-age population or subgroups thereof across nations. In addition, it was argued that it is also highly desirable to obtain information from elite groups in the given country.

In times of rapid socio-political change—as is typical for the situation in Central and Eastern Europe—it is particularly desirable to obtain longitudinal data, be it on a cross-sectional basis or as panel data, the latter of course enabling one, also, to study processes of individual and not only aggregate change.

Against this ideal blueprint of desirable data information, a set of real-world limitations has to be considered. First, it must be kept in mind that the logic of political culture studies requires comparative information across several countries. The organization of such studies as a collaborative effort between independent groups of national researchers can be regarded as the optimal precondition for good comparative research, because the substantive program usually will be theory-guided and each group can bring into the collaboration its specific expertise. Not only does such an arrangement need a good research infrastructure for each national group, however, it also requires substantial resources for integration and collective decision-making, and this is particularly true for the resources of time and money. As a consequence, such cooperative studies have been rare even in the West, and, while some are known to exist on the transitions in Central and Eastern Europe (see, for example, Bruszt and Simon 1992), data from those studies are not yet available (early 1994) for secondary analysis.

Fortunately, there are at least results and data at hand which stem from the safari approach in cross-national research, that is, an approach where one group has data collected on all countries it is interested in by service organizations like Gallup. Generally this approach is no longer used in the academic world, but rather in situations where government bodies and/or the mass media are interested in this information. The data and findings used in this chapter mostly originate from this kind of source.

It was mentioned above that under totalitarian rule governments were not particularly supportive of nationwide survey research. By its very nature, survey research creates potentially threatening self-observations of the attitudinal state of affairs because they may have an impact on the internal as well as external power game.[12] Unless surprising archived data later surfaces, the unfortunate situation is that no attitude data from surveys representative of the adult population in the Central and Eastern European nations will be available from the time before the transition began. Thus, one important element of political culture studies, the longitudinal analysis of the distribution of political, cultural and social orientations, and its change over time through variations in socialization structures and practices, through events and other factors, cannot easily be brought to bear on the analysis of transitions in Central and Eastern Europe.

Fortunately enough, Western interest in various academic and other institutions in this area has permitted not only the rapid creation of a reasonably operational infrastructure for conducting representative nationwide survey studies, but has also helped to generate at least some data for the crucial phase immediately following the transition from totalitarian rule. For the following analyses, five cross-national surveys will be used; for three of those—the 1990, 1991 and 1992 Eurobarometer East—the data were also available for secondary analysis for the purpose of this chapter.

Information from the following five studies will be included in this chapter:

1. The Eurobarometer East 1990 (for details see Commission of the European Communities 1991; Hofrichter and Weller 1991); fieldwork was conducted between October 20 and December 18 of 1990; countries included were Bulgaria, CSFR, GDR, Hungary, Poland, European Russia. In May and June of 1990 there were also surveys of the Greater Moscow Region and of European

[12] This is why, for instance, the politburo of the East German SED in the Seventies closed a survey research center it had itself brought into being in the Sixties.

Russia. They are not included in this analysis because questions are not comparable to those in the Eurobarometer East 1990.
2. The Eurobarometer East 1991 (for details see Commission of the European Communities 1992); fieldwork was conducted between September 27 and October 30 of 1991; countries included were Albania, Bulgaria, CSFR, Estonia, Hungary, Latvia, Lithuania, Poland, Romania, European Russia.
3. The Eurobarometer East 1992 (for details see Commission of the European Communities 1993); fieldwork was conducted between October 30 and November 17, 1992. The following countries were included: Albania, Armenia, Belarus, Bulgaria, Czech Republic, Estonia, Georgia, Hungary, Latvia, Lithuania, Macedonia, Moldova, Poland, Romania, European Russia, Slovakia, Slovenia, Ukraine.
4. The 'Neue Demokratien Barometer-NDB 1991' (for details see Haerpfer 1992; Rose and Haerpfer 1992); fieldwork was conducted between November 1991 and January 1992; countries included were Bulgaria, CSFR, Hungary, Poland and Romania, plus—to serve as a comparative yardstick—Austria.
5. The Times-Mirror-Survey (for details see Times-Mirror 1991); fieldwork was conducted in April and May of 1991; countries included were (in addition to the Western nations of France, West Germany, Italy, Spain and the United Kingdom), Bulgaria, CSFR, East Germany, Hungary, Lithuania, Poland, European Russia, Ukraine. In addition to the cross-section surveys, the study also collected information from elite interviews, focus group sessions and in-depth interviews with selected citizens.

Two notes of reservation must be introduced regarding the nations included and the questions/indicators available in those surveys. In particular in situations of rapid change it is desirable to have as much information, especially longitudinal, as possible for a given nation. This has led to the decision to bring in only these five nations, for which at least three data points from the Eurobarometer East (except European Russia, which was not included in the 1990 study) are available. Table 5.1 gives the countries and number of respondents in each of the countries for the available points in time.[13]

[13] Sample sizes for the 'Neue Demokratien Barometer' were (Haerpfer 1992: 3): Bulgaria: 1002; CSFR: 1034; Poland: 1193; Hungary: 1019; Romania: 1000; Austria: 1954. Sample sizes for the 'Times-Mirror-Survey (1991: 290-305) were:
a. In Western Europe: France: 1035; Great Britain: 1107; Italy: 1051; Spain: 1003; West Germany: 760;
b. In Central and Eastern Europe: Bulgaria: 1267; Czechoslovakia: 920; East Germany: 720; Hungary: 1000; Lithuania: 501; Poland: 1496; European Russia: 1123; Ukraine: 586.

Table 5.1. Countries and Number of Respondents in Eurobarometer East 1990-1992

Countries	Time of Survey and Number of Respondents Autumn 1990	Autumn 1991	Autumn 1992
Bulgaria	1492	989	1312
Czechoslovakia	1490	1076	1658
Hungary	989	987	1000
Poland	1014	1000	999
European Russia	-	977	1000

Source: Commission of the European Communities (1991: 9, 1992: 98, 1993: unpaginated).

The fieldwork in most countries was conducted based on some variety of a multi-stage random sample. In some instances, quota samples were applied, in some instances a precise description of the sampling procedure was not available. It should also be added that the GDR was deliberately excluded from data analysis because it ceased to exist as an independent state with German unification on October 3, 1990, and thereby constitutes what can rightfully be named a 'deviant case' in the context of transition research.

The other reservation refers to the questions asked in the various studies. First of all, since they are funded by three separate agencies, it cannot be expected that there are more than chance identities in questions raised and in question wording; the best one can hope for is a certain amount of functional equivalence across studies. Secondly, and this is particularly true for the Eurobarometer studies, the special information concerns of the funding agencies have created study emphases in areas that in many respects do not converge with those of students of political culture. This has to be kept in mind as we turn to the substantive findings.

Emergence of Democratic Political Cultures in Central and Eastern Europe?

Introduction

As the West German example amply demonstrates, a democratic political culture is not easily come by. At the time of the foundation of the Federal Republic in 1949 and for some time thereafter, there was a substantial amount of ambivalence among citizens towards democracy Western-style (Kaase 1989: 204-206). Indeed while many ways may lead to the development and stabilization of a democratic political culture, the German case speaks to the important role that economic output plays in this process (Boynton and Loewenberg 1973). Thus, it cannot come as a surprise that Almond and Verba (1965: 362-364), at the time of the Civic Culture survey (1959), observed in Germany a dominance of (economic) output orientations that was not balanced by a corresponding set of supportive input and system orientations.

What is obviously needed to inculcate the democratic creed is a stable economic and political environment, visible proof of the functioning of the democratic process—this is why in Germany the 1969 government change from the Christian Democrats to the Social Democrats was so important—and time.[14]

Given the fact that the regime changes in Central and Eastern Europe are very recent, it seems preposterous to venture any predictions regarding the extent to which democratic attitudes may develop there or how long such developments might take. Of course, notwithstanding a long period of totalitarian indoctrination it is an altogether different question whether attitudes favorable to democracy already existed before the transition; supportive evidence to that effect is available (Gray 1979: 265). Nevertheless, the co-occurrence of political and economic regime changes puts a tremendous strain on the consolidation of the new Central and Eastern European democracies. It seems therefore warranted to begin the expedition into political culture in Central and Eastern Europe with a look at the output dimension and especially at the way the economic transformation and its consequences are viewed by the mass populations in the five countries chosen for analysis.

The Market System and the Output Dimension

It is difficult to assess how far the structure of the economic system has already been changed by 1993 to correspond to the logic of a social market economy without a detailed study of the developments in each individual country. At present such a study does not exist and obviously cannot be achieved in the context of this chapter. However, it is at least possible to consider the subjective perceptions of how the respective countries have been changing economically and generally over the last three years. To do this, the following questions in the Eurobarometer East surveys and the Times-Mirror-Survey (for one point in time; 1991) will be analyzed.

1. *Evaluation of General Development of Country*
   Q.: In general, do you feel things in (our country) are going in the right or in the wrong direction?

[14] See Fuchs (1989) and Westle (1989), for a detailed analysis of the emergence of a democratic political culture in West Germany.

2. *Approval of the Creation of a Market Economy*
   Q.: Do you personally feel that the creation of a free market economy, that is one largely free of state control, is right or wrong for (our country's) future?
3. *Speed of Economic Reforms*
   Q.: The way things are going, do you feel that (our country's) economic reforms are going too fast, too slow or about the right speed?

The Times-Mirror-Survey included one question which is functionally equivalent to the second question in the above set from the Eurobarometer East:

4. *Approval of the Creation of a Market Economy*
   Q.: Overall, do you strongly approve, approve, disapprove or strongly disapprove of efforts to establish a free market economy in (our country)?

Talking first about the general sentiment that things were going in the right direction, whatever optimism that existed in 1990, and less so in 1991, seems to have been replaced by—to phrase it mildly—a sense of skepticism. Only in the former CSFR is the outlook less gloomy and this is due mostly to the Czechs who, in the late autumn of 1992, might have already been looking forward to separation from the Slovaks, a feeling which was not reciprocated at the same level by the Slovaks. With the distinct exception of European Russia, the concept of a market economy is still widely accepted, although with a generally decreasing level of enthusiasm. Yet, dissatisfaction with the general state of affairs persists and one reason may rest with the sharply rising (since 1991) opinion that the economic changes simply take too much time to take effect (again with the exception of the Czech Republic and Slovakia).

Obviously, the basic understanding still prevails that radical reforms are mandatory and that fast-paced change is necessary because only then will there be a chance to see the light at the end of the tunnel; per aspera ad astra. But the important question to be raised is how long this supportive attitude will remain when people are no longer convinced that better circumstances will entail.

This should also be kept in mind because there is a lot of ambivalence and ambiguity in attitudes toward economic reform. Surprisingly, in 1991, citizens in all five nations were, at least in the abstract, willing to accept unemployment as a price to be paid for a better economic future. The same was true with respect to a major flaw in the previous system of planned economy, but with an even wider margin: about three-quarters of the people accepted personal accomplishment as the basis for individual salaries. It is understandable that many are unwilling to give up on the state completely as the institu-

Table 5.2. Assessment of Perceived Political and Economic Changes 1990-1992 (in %).[1]

Assessment of perceived political and economic changes		Countries				
		Bulgaria %	CSFR %	Hungary %	Poland %	European Russia %
(1) *Evaluation of General Development*						
Things are going in the ...						
right direction	1990	53.2	67.7	-	59.0	-
	1991	74.0	53.1	40.1	26.0	45.8
	1992	50.4	57.6	23.0	33.6	39.2
wrong direction	1990	46.8	32.3	-	41.0	-
	1991	26.0	46.9	59.9	74.0	54.2
	1992	49.6	42.4	77.0	66.4	60.8
(2,4) *Creation of a Market Economy*						
Market economy is...						
right	1990	65.4	82.2	83.1	81.6	-
	1991	79.5	75.3	85.5	73.7	58.8
	1992	73.4	60.4	75.6	69.6	49.4
approve[2]	1991	83	89	89	88	62
wrong	1990	34.6	17.8	16.9	18.4	-
	1991	20.5	24.7	14.5	26.3	41.2
	1992	26.6	39.6	24.4	30.4	50.6
disapprove[3]	1991	17	11	11	12	38
(3) *Speed of Economic Reforms*[3]						
Reforms are going...						
too fast	1990	1.9	25.2	-	32.4	-
	1991	6.3	25.0	15.7	33.8	6.8
	1992	4.5	20.4	17.5	18.9	30.2
at the right speed	1990	13.7	36.1	-	32.9	-
	1991	60.8	38.6	59.0	51.9	87.7
	1992	23.9	45.0	19.9	12.8	12.5
too slow	1990	84.4	38.6	-	34.7	-
	1991	32.9	36.4	25.3	14.3	5.5
	1992	71.6	34.6	62.6	68.3	57.3

[1] Eurobarometer East (1990, 1991, 1992). The average share of valid responses on these questions is about 80%, with a considerable variance across countries. The missing data were excluded before calculating percentages.

[2] Times-Mirror (1991: 42, tabular appendix). For this table the two 'approve' and the two 'disapprove' categories were collapsed. There was an average of 10% missing data which were excluded before calculating percentages.

[3] In 1992, a sizable number of respondents volunteered the reaction that no reforms were taking place at all: 10% in Bulgaria, 4% in the CSFR, 7% in Hungary, 9% in Poland and 19% in European Russia.

tion responsible for easing the strains of the economic transition process, but here too, the Czechoslovakians and particularly the Russians are against a large role for the state when this role impinges on individual freedom. These data also indicate that in 1991 there was, with the partial exception of European Russia, a widely felt need for economic reform and a willingness to support this reform even at high personal cost. Unfortunately, data for 1993 that could answer the question whether these orientations still exist after two years of economic reshuffling and turmoil are not yet at hand.

In East Germany, with the July, 1990, currency union, the most abrupt change conceivable, from a planned to a market economy, happened. This transition has since resulted in an almost complete breakdown of industrial production structures and an ensuing high rate of temporary and permanent unemployment. Were it not for the enormous transfer payments from West Germany, it would have been likely that a state of political and social anomie followed the transition. There are interesting lessons to learn from this case.

Even before the formal unification of the two Germanies on October 3, 1990, a lot of the enthusiasm in East Germany which had made unification possible had been replaced by the sorrows and grim outlook for the country's economic future (Kaase 1993). The 1991 Times-Mirror survey indicated that, when asked about the most important problems facing their country, also the people in Central and Eastern Europe were almost exclusively concerned with the economic implications of the regime change- understandably so. As the same source shows, this concern did not impair the feeling that basic rights and freedom of political and social expression were gained in exchange. Nevertheless, talking about such matters in the abstract in an interview and being personally confronted with the consequences of political and economic transition are two entirely different stories.

When people are asked in surveys how they assess their personal economic situation and that of the country they live in, the usual finding for Western democracies is one of great discrepancy between the two: the individual situation is usually evaluated much better and much more stable than that of the country. This, of course, reflects the high level of individual economic achievement in modern democracies as well as the ongoing emphasis on economics and on the need of individual citizens to base judgments regarding public matters almost exclusively on mass media reports.

In 1990, 1991 and 1992, the following questions regarding the assessment of the country's *economic* and personal *financial* situation were asked in the Eurobarometer East:

a. *Economic Situation of the Country*
   1. Compared to 12 months ago, do you think the general economic situation in (our country) has got a lot better, got a little better, stayed the same, got a little worse, or got a lot worse?

Table 5.3. Attitudes Towards Market Economy 1991 (in %).

		Countries				
		Bulgaria	CSFR	Hungary	Poland	European Russia
		%	%	%	%	%
Q1. *Unemployment*	No unemployment	41	22	36	42	31
	Accept some unemployment	59	78	64	58	69
Q2. *Price control*	Price control	62	53	73	38	40
	Free prices	38	47	27	62	60
Q3. *Profit seeking*	As much as they can	61	37	48	43	46
	Limit it	39	63	52	57	54
Q4. *Personal liberty*	Freedom	66	45	70	76	38
	Nobody in need	34	55	30	24	62
Q5. *Salary*	Fixed salary	26	25	21	32	26
	Salary on accomplishment	74	75	79	68	74

Note: In the survey, the following questions were used:

Q1.: Some people feel that there should be no unemployment in (our country) even if it means that (our country's) economy will not be improved and modernized in the near future. Others feel some unemployment in (our country) is acceptable if that's what it takes to improve and modernize the economy. Generally, which position comes closer to your point of view?

Q2.: Some people feel that prices should be allowed to rise so that products will be available even if everyone can't afford them. Others feel that prices should be kept low, even if it means that products are not available. Which opinion generally comes closer to your point of view?

Q3.: Do you think that people who start privately owned business should be allowed to make as much profit as they can or should the government limit how much profit they can make?

Q4.: What's more important in (our) society: that everyone is free to pursue their life's goals without interference from the state or that the state play an active role in society so as to guarantee that nobody is in need?

Q5.: In general, how would you most prefer to be paid—on a fixed salary basis so that you always know how much you will earn—or mostly on an incentive basis which will allow you to earn more if you accomplish a lot, but may result in less earnings if you don't accomplish enough?

Source: Times-Mirror (1991: 90 (1,2), 91 (3), 96 (4), 98 (5), tabular appendix). The average percentage of missing data is 5% (1), 12% (2), 7% (3), 9% (4) and 8% (5). Missing data were excluded before calculating percentages.

2. And over the next 12 months, do you think the general economic situation in (our country) will get a lot better, get a little better, stay the same, get a little worse, or get a lot worse?

b. *Financial Situation of Household*

3. Compared to 12 months ago, do you think that the financial situation of your household has got a lot better, got a little better, stayed the same, got a little worse, or got a lot worse?
4. And over the next 12 months, do you expect that the financial situation of your household will get a lot better, get a little better, stay the same, get a little worse, or get a lot worse?

Similar questions were also asked in the Neue Demokratien Barometer in 1991:

a. *Past, Present and Future Economic (Financial) Situation of Household*

5. All in all: how do you rate the *economic* situation of your family today: very satisfactory, fairly satisfactory, not very satisfactory or very unsatisfactory?
6. And when you compare your overall household *financial* situation today with five years ago, would you say it was then much better, a little better, much the same, a little worse, or a lot worse?
7. What do you think the economic situation of your household will be in five years time, will it be much better, a little better, much the same, a little worse, or a lot worse?

b. *Fear of Unemployment (Only Asked of Those With Regular Job)*

8. Are you worried about unemployment?

The results from these questions are displayed (as means) in Table 5.3. These data give precious little reason for enthusiasm. Comparing 1990 and 1991, there is almost always, both on the collective ('our country') and individual dimension, a trace of hope, but it is ever so slight. In addition, contrary to the general wisdom derived from studies in Western democracies, in the five Eastern nations citizens more frequently anticipate that their own economic slump will continue rather than their country's economic fate. There is no major change in this structure for 1992 except that the citizens' outlook for 1993, regarding their household's financial situation, is now much closer to the outlook for the country than in preceding years. And the overriding result, which is also buffered by correlational analyses (data not shown), remains that a syndrome exists which closely links economic orientations towards the country at large with those held toward one's own situation. The most threatening element in this syndrome is probably the overriding fear of unemployment.

These cognitions and fears have an obvious impact on the way citizens in Central and Eastern Europe look upon their life in general. In the Times-

Table 5.4. Assessment of General and Personal Economic/Financial Situation of Country and of Respondent's Household 1990-1992 (mean values).[1]

Change of economic/financial situation of ... compared to ...		Bulgaria	CSFR	Hungary	Poland	European Russia
Country/Economy						
1. 12 months ago:	1990	4.54	3.91	-	2.80	-
	1991	3.54	3.62	3.69	3.84	4.37
	1992	3.46	3.68	4.06	3.58	4.14
2. in 12 months:	1990	3.48	3.30	4.09	2.66	-
	1991	2.63	3.10	3.08	3.20	3.53
	1992	2.89	3.34	3.67	3.22	3.51
Household/Finances						
3. 12 months ago:	1990	3.76	3.83	-	3.42	-
	1991	3.90	3.79	3.88	3.84	3.73
	1992	3.62	3.58	3.99	3.76	3.75
4. in 12 months:	1990	3.54	3.68	4.08	3.06	-
	1991	2.96	3.23	3.37	3.32	3.66
	1992	3.07	3.39	3.65	3.31	3.43
6. Five years ago:	1991[2]	2.26	2.36	2.23	2.41	-
5. Today:	1991[2]	2.89[3]	2.53	2.98	3.07	-
7. Five years from now:	1991[2]	2.58	2.58	2.74	2.97	-
Job						
8. Fear of unemployment:	1991[4]	69	70	71	62	-

[1] Eurobarometer East (1990, 1991, 1992). Missing data on both future-oriented questions averaged 12%, whereas for the past-oriented questions they were 4% (country) and 2% (household). Response categories were: (1) a lot better; (2) a little better; (3) the same; (4) a little worse; (5) a lot worse.

[2] Rose/Haerpfer (1992: 87-89). When calculating the means, response categories were coded as in the previous note. Missing data averaged around one to 2% and were excluded before calculating the means.

[3] Rose/Haerpfer (1992: 87). When calculating the means, response categories were coded as (1) very satisfactory; (2) fairly satisfactory; (3) not very satisfactory; (4) very unsatisfactory.

[4] Rose/Haerpfer (1992: 89). Entries are valid percentages of those employed respondents who are very or somewhat concerned about losing their job. With the exception of Bulgaria and Romania where there were practically no missing data, missing data averaged 10%.

Mirror study, a Cantril-type eleven-point ladder was used to allow respondents to assess where on that 'ladder of life' they were standing five years ago, today, and five years from now, and, with the same procedure, where they saw their country standing:

Q.: 1. Here is a (eleven-point) ladder representing the 'ladder of life.' Let's suppose the top of the ladder represents the *best* possible life for you; and the bottom, the *worst* possible life for you. On which step of the ladder do you feel you personally stand at the present time?
2. On which step would you say you stood *five years ago*?
3. Just as your best guess, on which step do you think you will stand in the future, say about *five years from now*?
4. Looking at the ladder again, suppose the top represents the *best* possible situation for our country; and the bottom, the *worst* possible situation. Please tell me on which step of the ladder you think our country is at the present time?
5. On which step would you say our country was about *five years ago*?
6. Just as your best guess, if things go pretty much as you now expect, where do you think our country will be on the ladder, let us say, about *five years from now*?

In this instance it is particularly rewarding that the Times-Mirror Survey permits a comparison of West and East European countries, (including separate data for the Western and Eastern part of Germany), thereby offering some kind of a 'normality' yardstick.

Since data are presented for ten countries (East and West Germany are counted here as one country), only the most general observations can be discussed. On the dimension of *personal* progress/decline and optimism/pessimism, in 1991 the most obvious cleavage was—as it should be—between the Western and Eastern nations. While even in the West there is a feeling of decline among about one-fourth of the people, this can in no way match the pervasive feeling of personal decline in the East—East Germany being an interesting and plausible exception. This West-East schism also exists when looking into the future, although optimism clearly outweighs pessimism with the exception of Hungary (some attribute this to the noteworthy negativistic Hungarian character). In this respect sizable numbers of people in Central and Eastern Europe in 1991 still believed that they would indeed find the light at the end of the tunnel. But, in toto, even over a span of five years skepticism prevails—again with the notable exception of the East Germans.

Looking now at the collective, country-related orientations, one observation for the West corroborates what was noted above: there is a wide gap between personal orientations and those directed at society in general. Regarding the latter, feelings of decline and stagnation dominate. In the East, the perception of an enormous decline in the last five years is counteracted by an almost breathtaking sense of optimism in Bulgaria and Czechoslovakia, and, also, on

Table 5.5. Sense of Personal and Country-related Optimism/Pessimism (Cantril 0-10 Ladder Scale) in Western and Eastern Nations 1991 (Row Percentages).

	Personal Optimism/Pessimism						Country related Optimism/Pessimism					
	Progress[1] %	Neither %	Decline %	Optimism[2] %	Neither %	Pessimism %	Progress %	Neither %	Decline %	Optimism %	Neither %	Pessimism %
United Kingdom	43	28	29	51	37	12	16	27	57	49	33	18
France	36	34	30	42	39	19	15	44	41	30	39	31
Spain	34	43	23	39	48	13	38	40	22	43	44	13
Italy	41	34	25	51	32	17	16	33	51	43	27	30
West Germany	45	38	17	42	46	12	27	28	45	38	31	31
East Germany	34	33	33	62	29	9	45	25	30	76	19	5
Bulgaria	16	24	60	56	20	24	8	13	79	82	12	6
Czechoslovakia	29	22	49	41	33	26	29	20	51	69	22	9
Hungary	18	25	57	26	40	34	11	21	68	48	36	16
Poland	27	21	52	36	40	24	44	19	37	56	32	12
European Russia	21	22	57	40	36	24	4	10	86	48	31	21

1 Progress/Decline is based on a comparison of five years ago/today.
2 Optimism/Pessimism is based on a comparison of today/five years from now.

Source: Times-Mirror (1991: 21-23, tabular appendix). On the personal dimension, missing data for the past and present averaged 1 to 2%, for the country 3 to 4%. On both dimensions, the future was not assessed by an average of 20%. Cases with missing data were excluded from this calculation.

a lower level, in the remaining countries.

The findings presented in this section indicate that people in the five Central and East European countries discussed here have a clear awareness of the problems ahead, problems they locate especially in the realm of economic transitions. A sense of optimism still seems to prevail which is buffered by the fact that people do not expect instant improvements in their lot. The 1992 Eurobarometer East, though, begins to convey a distinct sense of irritation and impatience that things are not going (and improving) faster.

Many of the responses volunteered by the citizens reflect opinions which are derived in large numbers from mass media information and which therefore can turn out to be quite fragile. This may be a problem or a blessing, depending on the circumstances. Probably the gravest blow to the willingness of Central and East Europeans to support the transition process will come from the extent to which individuals will face personal unemployment. This fear is pervasive, and much will depend on the number of people who will suffer extended unemployment and who, for lack of resources, cannot be properly supported by the state or other agencies (like trade unions or churches).

The Times-Mirror data, as was pointed out before, show an ambivalence in attitudes towards unemployment which may soften its impact. But an empirical analysis for Poland testifies not just to the fact that employment supersedes all other economic variables in effect. What is essential in the context of political consolidation is the Przeworski (1993: 174) finding that unemployment has a direct and vast impact on trust in democratic institutions. An analysis by Bauer (1991a: 446-451) has also shown for East Germany that a substantial relationship exists between the assessment of the economic situation and prospects on the one hand, and satisfaction with democracy on the other. The same findings were also obtained in the Eurobarometers East 1991 and 1992. Positive expectations regarding the development of the personal financial and the country's economic situation (altogether four indicators; see Table 5.4) consistently positively correlated with the degree of satisfaction regarding the way democracy is developing.[15] All of this testifies to the old wisdom: in democracies, (economic) output matters.

Political Involvement: the Input Dimension

For Almond and Verba it was self-evident that the willingness and capability of citizens to get actively involved in the democratic process was a core

[15] The average correlations—Pearson's r—for each country in 1991 (1992) are: Bulgaria:.32 (.44); Czechoslovakia: .31 (.35); Hungary: .32 (.33); Poland: .35 (.35); European Russia: .25 (.33).

element of a mature, democratic political culture. This is true notwithstanding the fact that their ideal 'civic culture' constitutes a mix of subject and participatory orientations, in the sense that in a given polity only a basic level of participation is needed, provided that an additional participation potential exists which would make itself known in the democratic process if proven to be necessary. Later studies have revealed that Western democracies have, during the past three decades, moved toward an extended repertory of political action that embraces a variety of institutionalized and non-institutionalized modes of participation (Kaase 1992).

Elections in 'normal' established democracies are important mechanisms for legitimating the allocation of political power for a constitutionally limited term and by virtue of this command a lot of public attention. Thus, it is not surprising, that in all of the transition literature, elections are regarded as central vantage points on the road to democratic consolidation (as one example see O'Donnell and Schmitter 1986). This is true despite the fact that precisely because the transitions in Central and Eastern Europe came about mostly through pacts, citizens may have felt quite ambivalent about those initial elections.

In general, it is believed that these elections were a step in the direction of democratic consolidation.[16] At the same time, turnout for at least some of these elections was quite low; this may have been a repercussion of the transitional pact which was preponderantly elite-manufactured and was not based on broad, active citizen participation. Thus, the degree of participation in these founding elections is probably not the most reliable indicator for political involvement.

Data from the Times-Mirror study show that in Central and Eastern Europe mass populations are about evenly split in their agreement and disagreement on the opinion that they are quickly losing interest in political matters (substantive interpretation of this finding is difficult because a clear reference point is missing). For lack of better comparative indicators on political involvement, one has to rely on two Eurobarometer questions about (1) subjective interest in politics and (2) the frequency with which one tries to persuade friends, relatives or co-workers in political matters important to him or her. Both indicators produce fairly even results across time and the five nations, and the level of involvement visible in the data is not blatantly lower than that found in Western mass populations. The conservative interpretation of these findings is that the people of Central and Eastern Europe are neither outrageously politicized nor completely alienated from politics. It is interesting to observe but difficult to interpret that in 1992, in all five countries, the

[16] See Bogdanor (1990: 292). On the elections in general, see Butler and Särlvik (1990) and East (1992)

Table 5.6. Political Involvement 1990-1992 (mean values).[1]

Modes of political involvement	Countries				
	Bulgaria	CSFR	Hungary	Poland	European Russia
Participation in political discussions					
(1) When you get together with friends, would you say you discuss political matters frequently (1), occasionally (2) or never (3)?					
1990	1.78	1.70	-	1.97	-
1991	1.81	1.79	1.90	1.94	1.68
1992	1.89	1.86	2.00	1.93	1.79
Persuade others in political matters					
(2) When you hold a strong opinion, do you ever find yourself persuading your friends, relatives or fellow workers to share your views? Does it happen often (1), from time to time (2), rarely (3) or never (4)?					
1990	2.43	2.27	-	2.29	-
1991	2.06	2.00	2.28	1.97	2.06
1992	2.30	2.45	2.70	2.33	2.33
(3a) If there were a parliamentary election next Sunday (May 1991), would you go out to vote?					
Yes[2]	65	63	53	49	-
(3b) If there were a general election today (Oct. 91/Nov. 92), would you go and vote in the next general election?					
Yes[3]	84	74	61	51	56
	84	84	70	60	67

[1] Eurobarometer East (1990, 1991, 1992). Missing data on (1) averaged 2%, on (2) 5% and on (3) 6%. They were excluded before calculating the means, but were *not* excluded with (3).

[2] Times-Mirror (1991: 98, tabular appendix).

[3] Commission of the European Communities (1992: Annex, Figure 9); Commission of the European Communities (1993: Annex, Figure 10).

efforts to convince others of one's own political opinion had noticeably decreased. It looks like people were beginning to withdraw from political discourse, but not yet necessarily turning away from the vote.

In Western polities, political involvement is consistently and substantially related to high formal education (Kaase 1992) and to other individual resources. Education in this context plays a double role of raising levels of cognition and indoctrinating the democratic creed. In totalitarian systems, it can be assumed that this first role is more or less equally performed while, of course, the second points exactly in the opposite direction. This ambiguity cannot be resolved on empirical grounds unless the content of socialization is brought into the picture, which is impossible here. So far, no clear a priori hypothesis can be developed for the data available for analysis here. However, if one remembers Gray's (1979) conclusions on the study of political culture in Communist states which are very skeptical regarding the successes of communist indoctrination, then the minimal expectation should be that people with a higher level of education are more likely to get politically involved. This is indeed what the Eurobarometers show, although the correlations are only moderate in magnitude (ranging from a low 0.18 in Czechoslovakia to a high of 0.39 in Bulgaria). As in the West, men are more politically involved than women, but the political impetus of the Western youth is not at all visible in the East.[17] In sum, political involvement in Eastern Europe at present lacks clear structural contours. However, this may also be due to an unsatisfactory data situation because a survey study with greater differentiation conducted in May of 1990 in European Russia, concludes that the emerging structure of political participation, in principle, bears many resemblances to that in the West (Duch and Gibson 1992). Also, in terms of level and modes of participation, Russians did not fall into the trap of withdrawal into private life which is so typical for transitions from authoritarian rule.

The Times-Mirror study sheds some additional light on the matter because it contains two indicators each on the dimensions of internal efficacy (subjective sense of ability to influence political outcomes) and external efficacy (belief in the responsiveness of political authorities to citizen demands). Again, as in the case of the 'ladder of life,' the availability of the same data for six Western democracies, this time including the U.S., can serve as a reference point to assess the results in the East.

Regarding internal efficacy, and especially the impact of voting, Western and Eastern nations are not so far apart as one might expect. Surely, the frustration of the Italians with the lack of government-opposition exchange is easy to understand, and the same is true for the skepticism of Britons, in the

[17] See Kaase (1992), especially in the field of unconventional politics.

Table 5.7. Internal and External Political Efficacy in Western and Eastern Nations 1991 (Row Percentages).

	Internal Efficacy				External Efficacy			
	People like me don't have any say about what the government does.		Voting gives people like me some say about how the government runs things.		Generally speaking, elected officials lose touch with the people pretty quickly.		Most elected officials care what people like me think.	
Countries:	Agree %	Disagree %	Agree %	Disagree %	Agree %	Disagree %	Agree %	Disagree %
United States	58	42	75	25	80	20	45	55
United Kingdom	62	38	56	44	86	14	36	64
France	38	62	78	22	86	14	28	72
Spain	53	47	78	22	84	16	28	72
Italy	-	-	51	49	90	10	15	85
West Germany	68	32	61	39	88	12	33	67
East Germany	84	16	46	54	91	9	32	68
Bulgaria	78	22	86	14	88	12	24	76
Czechoslovakia	78	22	61	39	87	13	31	69
Hungary	86	14	53	47	86	14	33	67
Poland	90	10	44	56	91	9	25	75
European Russia	-	-	52	48	92	8	20	80

Source: Times-Mirror (1991: 116, tabular appendix). Respondents were asked whether they completely agreed, mostly agreed, mostly disagreed or completely disagreed with these statements. Both 'agree' categories and both 'disagree' categories were collapsed for the purposes of this tabular display, missing data being excluded before calculating percentages. The missing data for these data averaged between 2 and 3%, with the exception of Bulgaria where they averaged 13%.

light of their majoritarian electoral system which regularly denies about one-fourth of British voters parliamentary representation. In the East, one must expect split sentiments toward the vote because of the long history of elections without choice and of the recent political transitions by pact which probably did not create the general impression of true choices through voting. With this legacy, the positive attitude of the majority of citizens toward the vote in all Eastern countries except Poland is all the more remarkable.

The widespread skepticism regarding the impact one can have on political outcomes is well understood, given the complexity of decision-making in modern area states. Therefore, the even smaller sense of efficacy in the East than in the West does not come as a surprise.

As for external efficacy, West and East meet in their belief that there is precious little willingness by political authorities to respond to citizen demands. The point here is not whether this estimate is justified or not nor what conditions might be conducive to altering it (which is, of course, desirable). In terms of democratic consolidation it seems that this specific posture has not endangered the survival of democratic regimes in the West. Rather, it appears to belong to the worldwide political folklore stemming from the distance the average citizen feels from the world of politics. In this sense, the new Central and East European democracies are already sharing the folklore. Still, it may make quite a difference whether such orientations exist in a firmly established democratic polity or in one that is just beginning to seek public support.

Summing up this part of the analysis, findings on the input structures into politics have not given rise to principal doubts regarding the ability of the Central and East European citizens to participate meaningfully in the democratic political process. Of course, this does not alter the concern voiced in previous sections of the chapter, that beyond a connection via a liberal and pluralist system of mass communication, it is important for the new democracies to develop linkage structures through intermediary interest organizations, including political parties. These linkages should give the political process a stable underpinning beyond the voluntary elements of the civil society and provide citizens with regular channels to get involved, beyond the vote, in politics and make their voices heard.

The Political System—Attitudes Towards Democracy

The past decades have seen substantial increases in sophistication in research on support for the democratic political system.[18] Most of the relevant re-

[18] A good summary of the literature can be found in Westle (1989).

search in some way or other has been based on the Eastonian differentiation into objects and modes of political support, particularly on the distinction between the political authorities and political regime.

For the analysis of system orientations in Central and Eastern Europe a major problem arises, but also an opportunity. The questions to be addressed are (1) whether the amount of time elapsed between 1989 and 1993 has been sufficient to permit at least some common idea of the new political regime to grow, and (2) what role do perceptions and recollections of the 'old' regime play in shaping orientations towards the 'new' system.

One can speculate that the transitions by pact and the ongoing rule setting have not particularly helped to create the feeling of a clear-cut regime break or images of the 'new' political system. An additional problem arises from the fact that the incongruences between nations and states resulting from seventy years of state-building 'from above' in Central and Eastern Europe have led to ethnical, religious and cultural strains within states which are anything but conducive to the creation of political communities with a sense of state identity.

The 'highest' object in the Eastonian hierarchy of political objects—the political community—is very difficult to operationalize and has sparked only limited interest in empirical research (McDonough et al. 1986: 737-738). Political community refers to a shared orientation toward a particular level of the political system, in the case here, the level of national policy making (see also Westle 1989: 52-55). Whereas in a federalized political system a citizen can adhere to more than one political community (national, state, local), to speak of a nation-state as one operative political community a sense of national political community must exist.

There are no data at hand which could address this question directly. Yugoslavia and Czechoslovakia are two obvious examples of a situation where no common national object of orientation exists. The Times-Mirror study permits at least some clues as to what the magnitude of the problem is, regarding a lack of political community in the five Eastern European countries. Respondents were asked how favorably or unfavorably they felt towards certain ethnic and other groups (these groups varied in part across countries because not all groups are equally pertinent to all nations). Table 5.8 gives the results from this question.

With the exception of Poland, in all other nations, there is a degree of sizable ethnic antagonism toward out-groups, which, in all likelihood, will constitute a major obstacle in creating a unified political community and a sense of identification with that community. While it is difficult to assess the meaning of the data on the Gypsies and the Jews, the conclusion seems at least warranted that there is a widespread resentment against ethnic out-groups formally belonging to the same state in these countries. Some of that

Table 5.8. Disliked Groups 1991 (in %).

I'd like you to rate some different groups of people in (our country) according to how you feel about them. For each group, please tell me whether your opinion is very favorable, mostly favorable, mostly unfavorable or very unfavorable.	Countries					
	Bulgaria %	CSFR %	Hungary %	Poland %	European Russia %	
Mostly unfavorable/very unfavorable						
Ethnic groups						
Arabs	36 (36)[1]	*[2]	60 (29)	*	37 (14)	(Asian Russians)
Bulgarians	21[3] (17)	*	*	*	46 (9)	(Georgians)
Czechs	*	9 (1)	*	*	27 (12)	(Lithuanians)
Germans	*	20 (14)	4 (23)	45 (16)	46 (11)	(Armenians)
Hungarians	*	49 (19)	40[4] (15)	*	47 (12)	(Azerbaijanis)
Romanians	*	*	30 (22)	*	7 (9)	(Ukrainians)
Slovaks	*	23 (1)	11 (28)	*	*	
Other groups						
Gypsies	71 (8)	91 (3)	79 (7)	*	*	
Jews	9 (28)	20 (31)	12 (21)	34 (26)	26 (16)	

1 Percentages in brackets refer to those who do not know the group in question. These percentages refer to the full samples.
2 Group not asked about.
3 Muslim Bulgarians.
4 Hungarians from Romania who settled in Transylvania.
Source: Times-Mirror (1991: 74-78, tabular appendix). Percentages refer to full samples.

resentment, for instance, against the Germans in Czechoslovakia and particularly in Poland, has obvious historical roots. Yet, there is more behind this problem, as indicated by the 73% (!) of Poles, 31% of Czechoslovakians and 27% of Hungarians who agree with the statement that they have little in common with other ethnic groups or races.

To be fair, it must be added that in the Western democracies an average of 40% also agrees with this statement. But the difference is that the feeling expressed in that statement in the West is directed much less toward groups who are themselves already part of the polity.

The data on Russia are especially revealing. They convey an impression of the range of negative feelings towards ethnically defined out-groups which makes the difficulties in the former Soviet Union in trying to maintain a unified state understandable. But there is, again, more to those data. In the previously mentioned study on (European) Russia by Duch and Gibson, these authors document in detail how Russians can be characterized by a high level of *general* intolerance, that is, intolerance also directed at groups such as homosexuals. It is no wonder that they conclude from these data that intolerance may be a serious impediment for democratic development (Gibson and Duch 1993: 88-89).

Turning now to the Eastonian category of the political regime as the set of values, norms and political institutions in a given polity, again the situation is that the appropriate empirical basis is lacking for an adequate assessment of pertinent citizen orientations in these five nations. From the Times-Mirror study one can at least draw the conclusion that, in principle, the majority of citizens favors the transition to democracy because it has led to a codex of civil rights that did not previously exist. However, there is little doubt, that in the thinking of Central and Eastern Europeans, democracy is the shorthand term for everything positive they expected from the regime transition away from socialism. Only when the democratic rules and institutions take on their final form and people have had time to become familiar with them is a first and basic condition for the development of regime orientations met. It is an altogether different question how these democratic procedures and institutions will be evaluated, and here the output dimension will undoubtedly play a decisive role.

The longitudinal analysis of system orientations in Spain by McDonough et al. (1986) has shown that the transition from the authoritarian Franco regime to a pluralist democracy was eased by the fact that people clearly distinguished between the two regimes, they saw a great deal of virtue in the transition, and, also, shortly after the transition had already experienced a peaceful government change. The question in Central and Eastern Europe will be to what extent will the regime change by pact be clearly recognized as such and, if so, to what extent will the old regime serve as a point of negative reference, in the sense that the difficulties following the transition will be attributed to the 'old' regime. This problem will be aggravated as the basic reservoir of goodwill toward the political and economic transition will increasingly be strained when dissatisfaction with the consequences of the transition grows.[19]

1990/91 data from the Ten Nations Political Culture Study (Bruszt and Simon 1992: 124) show that the effects of regime change, particularly in Bulgaria (better: 7%; worse: 41%), Czechoslovakia (11%; 36%) and Hungary (7%; 43%) have been regarded as a mixed blessing, to say the least. These figures should not be overinterpreted because the reference points of the previous and present regimes cannot automatically be read as referring to a totalitarian system on the one side and a democratic system on the other. This implication could only be justified if the 'new' system was clearly identified by the respondents as a 'democracy' and if the concrete ideas people have about the concept of democracy were known. Nevertheless, more recent data from the 1992 Eurobarometer East reinforce the above findings (although, again, as in the case of the Ten Nation Political Culture Study, the wording of the question is not on the theoretically desirable target):

> Q.: Taking everything into account, do you feel things are better for you now under the present political system, or do you think things were better for you under the previous political system? (A spontaneous reaction 'neither' occurred frequently and was properly recorded.)

Whatever the 'new' and the 'old' system means for the respondents, there can be no question—and this is particularly true for European Russia—that friendly recollections of an earlier system of political order linger. Unfortunately, this most interesting question was not asked in the 1990 and 1991 Eurobarometer East, so results are difficult to interpret. Yet, distinct traces of such a phenomenon have emerged which Westle (1992) also discovered in East Germany, and which could be regarded as the 'socialist myth.' Under such circumstances, attitudes toward democratic governance are especially worthwhile studying.

Whereas there can be no doubt that (institutionally and organizationally enforced) democratic behavior (like voting in competitive elections, membership in democratic political parties) can help to develop democratic attitudes over time, it is equally clear, that at least in a consolidated democracy, stable democratic attitudes can serve as a buffer against short-term disappointments resulting from output deficiencies of the political process. The data at hand

[19] There is some sketchy evidence from Russia that economic problems do not undermine the support for politico-institutional reform; see Duch (1992).

Table 5.9. Preference for Old or Present Political System 1992 (in %).

	Countries				
preferred political system	Bulgaria	CSFR	Hungary	Poland	European Russia
new system	40.3	53.4	21.7	38.7	21.4
neither	18.0	15.1	21.4	14.7	19.1
old system	41.7	31.5	56.9	46.6	59.5

Source: Eurobarometer East (1992: Annex, Figure 13). Missing data across countries averaged 8% and were excluded before calculating percentages.

unfortunately only convey a vague notion as to what the structure and distribution of democratic attitudes in Central and Eastern Europe is.

The Times-Mirror study contains information on two elements of democratic beliefs: attitudes toward the admission of non-democratic parties and attitudes toward restrains on the mass media. Both indicators are flawed in some respects (for example, the unwillingness to permit non-democratic parties in Germany and Italy reflects both countries' fascist past, and conditions are not specified under which constraints on the mass media should be applied), but if one is willing to accept them as valid measures, the findings do not reveal any broadly based anti-democratic attitudes.

In some ways this result, after decades of totalitarian indoctrination, may be surprising. There are, however, two reasons why such an outcome should have been expected. The first refers to diffusion. The 'iron curtain' for many years has not been so 'iron' after all; the level of tourism, worker mobility from the East and access in Central and Eastern Europe to Western mass media has been constantly rising over the last two decades with the Cold War coming to an end, not to speak of the internationalization of the intelligentsia and *nomenklatura* in these countries. It is true that no reliable information on the impact of these linkages exists. Still, various studies have uniformly testified to the surprisingly well-developed level of democratic attitudes in East Germany and they have attributed this, in part, to the fact that for a long time East Germans have 'virtually' participated in the democratic process in West Germany through watching West German television (Bauer 1991a, 1991b; Bauer-Kaase 1994; Weil 1993).

The second consideration refers to what Bermeo (1992) calls political learning and what was alluded to earlier in the chapter. It may well be that the Sniderman (1981) claim of the eclipse of alternative notions to democracy had quietly made an inroad into Central and Eastern Europe, with an obvious

Table 5.10. Attitudes Towards Pluralism in Western and Eastern Nations 1991 (Row Percentages).

	Q1: political parties		Q2: newspapers	
	allow all	outlaw some	approve	disapprove
Countries	%	%	%	%
United States	64	36	-	-
United Kingdom	52	48	58	42
France	70	30	48	52
Spain	55	45	28	72
Italy	41	59	56	44
West Germany	33	67	29	71
East Germany	22	78	50	50
Bulgaria	57	43	32	68
Czechoslovakia	57	43	19	81
Hungary	37	63	30	70
Poland	61	39	24	76
European Russia	36	64	27	73

Note: The questions are:

Q1: Some people feel that in a democracy all political parties should be allowed, even those that don't believe in the democratic system. Others feel that even in a democracy certain political parties should be outlawed. Which comes closer to your view?

Q2: Would you approve or disapprove of placing greater constraints and controls on what newspapers print?

Source: Times-Mirror (1991: 96, Tabular Appendix). Missing data on Q1 and Q2 averaged 11%; there were excluded before calculating percentages.

impact on the counter-elites of the emerging civil society as well as on the reigning elites (this may in part account for their willingness to engage in a pact for the peaceful regime transition).

All in all, the two questions raised at the beginning of this section —whether the elapsed time since the 1989 transition has sufficed to create clear contours of democratic beliefs and what role images of the 'old' regime have played in this process—could not be satisfactorily answered. The available survey data cover only three years 'into' the transition, and there is simply too much missing information to reliably assess what the structure and content of attitudes towards the democratic system are. What is available warrants the conclusion that, on the one hand, some elements of democratic beliefs exist. On the other hand, the data also reveal strong ambivalence towards the present political systems and also certain orientations which are clearly not conducive to democracy. The real difficulty lies, of course, in the analysis of what impact these attitudes have on the ongoing process of consolidation.

The Self Dimension

Of the four initial Almond-Verba objects of orientation, the dimension of self—the democratic citizen—has received hardly any attention in research. This is probably due to the fact that efforts to identify special personality traits conducive or detrimental to democracy (like the authoritarian personality, the dogmatic personality, and so on) have not provided reliable evidence to contribute to a better understanding of the democratic political process.[20] As a consequence, this dimension of the political culture concept will not be dealt with here as well.

Conclusions

The study of political culture as defined in the Almond-Verba tradition is an established component of political science studies in Western democracies. The lack of serious concern with citizen political attitudes in transition research reflects both theoretical and empirical shortcomings. One theoretical problem lies in the fact that totalitarian and authoritarian regimes either seek to completely control by mobilization or to depoliticize the citizenry. This situation is principally different from the one in democratic polities which are legitimated only by the citizens of those polities and therefore, on a priori grounds alone, cannot be understood without the study of political culture. At least scholarly parsimony might justify the present emphasis in transition research on institutions and actors. This chapter was also written to stimulate thinking on the micro perspective. An additional theoretical problem is of a more general nature. As long as political theories are missing which simultaneously look at micro, meso and macro phenomena and try to systematically link these three levels in concrete research designs, it is impossible to empirically assess the relative explanatory weight of the various factors.

The neglect of citizens' political orientations is aggravated by the fact that the pertinent empirical information is difficult to obtain and is acquired only at high financial cost. Micro social research needs theoretical and methodological expertise as well as a developed infrastructure. These conditions are not easily met.

Studies on the political culture of nations as an integral element will require a level of conceptual sophistication and richness of data that at present

[20] See Schumann (1990), for an effort to move in this direction.

only rudimentarily exist for the countries studied in this chapter. The evidence at hand paints a picture of nations under severe strain, but equipped with some attitudinal elements which are conducive to the emergence of a democratic political culture. However, the political and economic problems as well as the attitudinal ambiguities discussed above are numerous enough to justify Ekiert's (1991) doubt as to whether transitions will indeed lead to consolidated democratic polities in Central and Eastern Europe.

When asked about the way they feel democracy is developing in their countries, by 1992 citizens everywhere struck a mostly skeptical chord. Unfortunately, the question's wording contains an ambiguity which does not permit one to discern whether a negative answer refers to the fact that there is not enough or good enough democracy, or whether the respondent was dissatisfied with his exposure to whatever democracy existed in the given country. Whatever the correct interpretation of the responses is: a strong sense of discontent comes through.

Finally, it also seems worthwhile to put together a picture from the pieces of the various findings that permits us to look at the individual countries in a composite fashion. Bulgaria is the country which shows the most dramatic mood swings, especially regarding the pace of economic change. This impatience is accompanied by an increasing political and economic skepticism, but the data indicate that people in 1992 still have not definitely made up their minds against the 'new' political system.

In the case of Czechoslovakia, the analysis is hampered by the fact that in 1993 the country changed into two independent republics. When looking at the 1992 data separately for the two parts of the country, it appears that especially the Czech population, in anticipation of the separation, was striking a more optimistic chord than the Slovaks in all areas studied. It almost seems as if the Czechs regarded the upcoming separation as an antidote to the ailments that existed in Czechoslovakia at that time. Of course, it remains to be seen whether these expectations will be fulfilled in the future and how the Slovaks will experience this fundamental change.

In Hungary, the pervasive sentiment seems to be dissatisfaction. Reforms are not going fast enough, economic expectations regarding the country and individual households are low and falling, political apathy spreads, and political discontent is on the rise. Positive recollections of the Kadar regime loom large, and the present government faces the very difficult task of convincing the Hungarians that the 'new' political system is on the right track.

Of the five Central and Eastern European nations studied in this chapter, Poland appears to be the most stable. Given the overall situation, it should surprise no one that skepticism still prevails, but it may well be that the quick and deep-reaching economic reforms will pay off in the long run. Still, there

Table 5.11. Satisfaction with the Way Democracy is Developing 1990-1992 (in % and mean values).

On the whole: are you very satisfied, fairly satisfied, not very satisfied, or not at all satisfied with the way democracy is developing in (our country)?	Countries				
	Bulgaria	CSFR	Hungary	Poland	European Russia
very satisfied					
1990	2.2	22.5	2.4	5.6	-
1991	5.7	1.7	2.6	3.7	1.5
1992	4.4	2.0	1.7	2.5	1.0
fairly satisfied					
1990	32.8	39.3	18.5	44.8	-
1991	40.0	27.7	31.1	31.0	16.8
1992	35.5	30.7	22.4	33.6	12.0
not very satisfied					
1990	41.0	30.1	46.7	42.0	-
1991	37.2	54.6	43.2	44.7	48.7
1992	35.5	53.5	46.4	43.6	47.9
not at all satisfied					
1990	24.0	8.1	32.4	8.1	-
1991	17.1	16.0	23.1	20.7	33.0
1992	24.6	13.8	29.5	20.3	39.1
mean satisfaction/dissatisfaction					
1990	2.87	2.24	3.09	2.52	-
1991	2.66	2.85	2.87	2.82	3.13
1992	2.80	2.79	3.04	2.82	3.25

Note: To compute mean values the response categories were coded as follows: (1) very satisfied; (2) fairly satisfied; (3) not very satisfied; (4) not at all satisfied.
Source: Eurobarometer East (1990, 1991, 1992). The average share of missing data for this question in 1990 and 1991 was 15% and in 1992 10%. These missing data were excluded before calculating percentages.

is a lot of ambivalence vis-à-vis the 'new' political system.

European Russia certainly is the one country where the transition has run into the most difficulties. Support for a market economy is lower than in the other four countries, personal and country-related expectations are negative, and it is here where the 'old' system finds the most support; dissatisfaction with the way democracy is developing here is correspondingly high. This instability is heightened by the fact that the surrounding newly independent nations originating from the former Soviet Union are also very shaky in citizen attitudes and institutional arrangements. One-third of European

Russians by late 1992 expected a political coup within the next 12 months; this clearly speaks to the precarious political situation in European Russia.

One more point deserves special mention. A factor analysis for the five countries in the 1992 Eurobarometer East which included variables for the three dimensions of economic satisfaction (Table 5.4), political satisfaction (Tables 5.2, 5.9 and 5.11) and political involvement (Table 5.6) produced two factors with a poignant structure in all countries except European Russia: the involvement dimension (with two variables) as the smaller of the two, and a strong satisfaction/dissatisfaction factor on which all economic and political variables loaded equally high. This is a clear indication that, in 1992, the future of democracy in the thinking of the population in Bulgaria, Czechoslovakia, Hungary and Poland was inextricably wedded to the way the personal economic well-being and that of the country were developing. The gloomier the future is seen by people, the likelier it is that they feel things are going in the wrong direction, that they look back positively to the 'old' political system and are dissatisfied with the way democracy is developing in their respective country. In this game the concept of a market economy plays a vital role. The positive correlation between support for a market economy and the feeling that the pace of economic reforms is not fast enough points to the fact that people's hope in these difficult times rests on the idea that a market economy—and not the political system as such—is the carrier of the flame. The beliefs discussed above have configurated into a densely organized belief system which will not easily be disentangled. This is the chance or pitfall of democracy in Central and Eastern Europe at least as far as citizen orientations are concerned.

In this analysis European Russia is special in the sense that economic satisfaction and concepts of the political order are separated. This points to the fact that positive evaluations of the past political system lead a life of their own, thereby dividing the polity and making the transition to democratic rule even more challenging.

In sum, the survey data on five Central and Eastern European countries indicate that the road to democracy is not one easily traveled. As with a half-filled glass, some will say it is half full, and some that it is half empty. The findings speak loudly to the problems accompanying the transition, but they still permit some ever-so-fragile optimism for the future. Democracy just barely remains a card on which the Central and East European peoples bet as they become increasingly skeptical about their present political systems which, at least formally, figure as democracies. This widespread skepticism raises the question whether the transition by elite pact will really turn out to be such a stabilizing factor in the long run as the transition literature claims it should. In this context, the Spanish example comes to mind, where a peaceful transition through elite pact was built on an already well-functioning market economy and an experienced economic elite, thereby paving the way for an increasingly reduced role for the old elites. However, this is exactly the condition absent in Central and Eastern Europe. Therefore, it might well be argued that under such circumstances it is precisely the lack of a clear-cut regime change in institutional as well as in elite personnel terms which nurtures the doubts regarding the prospects for democracy in Central and Eastern Europe in the minds of the population.

The findings presented in this chapter, in the context of the political culture approach, indicate that the study of political culture in the Almond-Verba tradition is an important element in the analysis of all phases of regime change: liberalization, democratization and consolidation. These findings speak to the fact that the democratic consolidation in Central and Eastern Europe did not come about automatically as institutional changes were put into force. Rather, it is the interaction of institutions and people, based on economic recovery and growth, which will finally determine the outcome of this process, also, in regime terms.

References

Almond, G. A. and S. Verba (1965 [1963]) *The Civic Culture*. Boston: Little Brown.

Arato, A. (1990) Revolution, Civil Society und Demokratie, Transit. *Europäische Revue* 1: 110-126.

Bauer, P. (1991a) Politische Orientierungen im Übergang. Eine Analyse politischer Einstellungen der Bürger in West- und Ostdeutschland 1990/91. *Kölner Zeitschrift für Soziologie und Sozialpsychologie* 43: 433-455.

Bauer, P. (1991b) *Freiheit und Demokratie in der Wahrnehmung der Bürger in der Bundesrepublik und der ehemaligen DDR*. In: R. Wildenmann (ed.) *Nation und Demokratie. Politisch-strukturelle Gestaltungsprobleme im neuen Deutschland.* Baden-Baden: Nomos Verlagsgesellschaft. 99-124.

Bauer-Kaase, P. (1994) *Die Entwicklung politischer Orientierungen in Ost- und Westdeutschland seit der deutschen Vereinigung*. In: O. Niedermayer and R. Stöß (eds.) *Parteien und Wähler im Umbruch*. Opladen: Westdeutscher Verlag. 226-297.

Bermeo, N. (1990) Rethinking Regime Change. *Comparative Politics* 22: 359-377.

Bermeo, N. (1992) Democracy and the Lessons of Dictatorship. *Comparative Politics* 24: 273-291.

Bogdanor, V. (1990) Founding Elections and Regime Change. *Electoral Studies* 9: 288-294.

Boynton, G.R. and G. Loewenberg (1973) Der Bundestag im Bewußtsein der Öffentlichkeit. *Politische Vierteljahresschrift* 14: 3-25.

Brown, A. (1979) *Introduction* In: A. Brown and J. Gray (eds.) *Political Culture and Political Change in Communist States*. New York: Holmes and Meier. 1-24.

Brubaker, R. (1993) *East European and Soviet, and Post-Soviet Nationalism: A Framework for Analysis.* In: F.D. Weil, J. Huffman and M. Gautier (eds.) *Democratization in Eastern and Western Europe.* Greenwich: JAI Press. 353-378.

Bruszt, L. and J. Simon (1992) *Political Culture, Political and Economic Orientations in Central and Eastern Europe during the Transition to Democracy. The Codebook of the International Survey of 10 Countries.* Budapest: Institute for Political Science of the Hungarian Academy of Sciences.

Butler, D. and B. Särlvik (eds.) (1990) Special Issue 'Elections in Eastern Europe.' *Electoral Studies* 9: 277-366.

Commission of the European Communities (1991) *Eurobarometer. Results of Polls in Bulgaria, Czechoslovakia, Hungary, Poland. April 1991.* Brussels.

Commission of the European Communities (1992) *Central and Eastern Eurobarometer. Public Opinion About the European Community; No. 2: Ten Countries Survey. Autumn 1991.* Brussels.

Commission of the European Communities (1993) *Central and Eastern Eurobarometer. Public Opinion About the European Community, No. 3, Eighteen Countries Survey. Autumn 1992.* Brussels.

Dahl, R.A. (1989) *Democracy and its Critics.* New Haven: Yale University Press.

Dahrendorf, R. (1990) *Betrachtungen über die Revolution in Europa in einem Brief, der an einen Herren in Warschau gerichtet ist.* Stuttgart: Deutsche Verlags-Anstalt.

Diamond, L., J.J. Linz and S.M. Lipset (eds.) (1991) *Democracy in Developing Countries. Volume 1: Persistence, Failure, and Renewal.* Boulder: Lynne Rienner.

Di Palma, G. (1990) *To Craft Democracies. An Essay on Democratic Transitions.* Berkeley: University of California Press.

Duch, R.M. (1991) Tolerating Economic Reform: Popular Support for Transition to a Free Market in Republics of the Former Soviet Union, Houston: University of Houston. mimeo.

Duch, R.M. (1992) Economic Chaos and the Fragility of Soviet Democracy. Paper presented at the 1992 ECPR Joint Workshop Sessions, Limerick.

Duch, R.M. and J.L. Gibson (1993) Democratization and the Rise of New Soviet Political Participants. Houston: University of Houston. mimeo.

East, R. (1992) *Revolutions in Eastern Europe.* London: Pinter.

Ekiert, G. (1991) Democratic Processes in East Central Europe: A Theoretical Reconsideration. *British Journal of Political Science* 21: 285-313.

Frentzel-Zagorska, J. (1991) Two Phases of Transition from Communism to Democracy. *Sisyphus* 7: 95-114.

Fuchs D. (1989) *Die Unterstützung des politischen Systems der Bundesrepublik Deutschland.* Opladen: Westdeutscher Verlag.

Fukuyama, F. (1989) The End of History? *The National Interest* 16 (Summer Supplement): 1-14.

Fukuyama, F. (1992) *The End of History and the Last Man.* New York: The Free Press.

Geremek, B. (1992) *Civil Society and the Present Age.* In: *The Idea of a Civil Society.* Research Triangle Park: National Humanities Center. 11-18.

Gibson, J.L. and R.M. Duch (1993) *Emerging Democratic Values in Soviet Political Culture.* In: A.H. Miller, W.M. Reisinger, V.L. Mesli (eds.) *Public Opinion and*

Regime Change. The New Politics of Post-Soviet Societies. Boulder: Westview Press. 69-94.

Gray, J. (1979) *Conclusions.* In: A. Brown and J. Gray (eds.) *Political Culture in Communist States.* New York: Holmes and Meier. 253-272.

Grilli di Cortona, P. (1991) From communism to democracy: rethinking regime change in Hungary and Czechoslovakia. *International Social Science Journal* 128: 315-330.

Haerpfer, C. (1992) Neue Demokratien Barometer (NDB 1991). Fünf neue Demokratien (Bulgarien, CSFR, Polen, Rumänien und Ungarn) im Vergleich mit Österreich. Vienna: Institut für Konfliktforschung. mimeo.

Heins, V. (1992) Ambivalenzen der Zivilgesellschaft. *Politische Vierteljahresschrift* 33: 235-242.

Hirschman, A.O. (1971) *A Bias For Hope. Essays on Development and Latin America.* New Haven: Yale University Press.

Hofrichter, J. and I. Weller (1991) Central and Eastern Eurobarometer, No. 1. The Evolution of Public Opinion in Central and Eastern Europe-1990, Second Draft. Mannheim: Zentrum für Europäische Umfrageanalysen und Studien (ZEUS). mimeo.

Huffman, J. and M. Gautier (1993) *Continuity in Transitions Theory.* In: F.D. Weil, J. Huffman and M. Gautier (eds.) *Democratization in Eastern and Western Europe.* Greenwich: JAI Press. 5-24.

Kaase M. (1983) *Sinn oder Unsinn des Konzepts 'Politische Kultur' für die vergleichende Politikforschung oder auch: Der Versuch, einen Pudding an die Wand zu nageln.* In: M. Kaase and H.-D. Klingemann (eds.) *Wahlen und politisches System-Analysen aus Anlaß der Bundestagswahl 1980.* Opladen: Westdeutscher Verlag. 144-171.

Kaase, M. (1989) *Bewußtseinslagen und Leitbilder in der Bundesrepublik Deutschland.* In: W. Weidenfeld and H. Zimmermann (eds.) *Deutschland-Handbuch. Eine doppelte Bilanz 1949-1989.* München: Hanser-Verlag. 203-220.

Kaase, M. (1992) *Direct Political Participation in the EC Countries in the Late Eighties.* In: P. Gundelach and Karen Siune (eds.) *From Voters to Participants. Essays in Honour of Ole Borre.* Aarhus: Politica. 75-90.

Kaase, M. (1993) *Electoral Politics in the New Germany.* In: C. Andersen, K. Kaltenthaler and W. Luthard (eds.) *The Domestic Politics of German Unification.* Boulder: Lynne Rienner Publishers. 37-59.

Karl, T.L. and P.C. Schmitter (1991) Modes of transition in Latin America, Southern and Eastern Europe. *International Social Science Journal* 128: 269-284.

Kielmansegg, P.G. (1988) *Das Experiment der Freiheit.* Stuttgart: Klett-Cotta.

Konrad, G. (1991) Sondermeinungen eines Urlaubers. *Frankfurter Allgemeine Zeitung* 238 (14 Oktober): 12.

Linz, J. (1978) *Crisis, Breakdown & Reequilibration, Vol. 1 of The Breakdown of Democratic Regimes.* Baltimore: Johns Hopkins University Press.

Los Angeles Times (1991) World Report. Special Edition: Pulse Europe. September 17.

Marks, G. (1992) Rational Sources of Chaos in Democratic Transition. *American Behavioral Scientist* 35: 397-421.

McDonough, P.B., S.H. Barnes and A. Lopez-Pina (1986) The Growth of Democratic Legitimacy in Spain. *American Political Science Review* 80: 735-760.

O'Donnell, G. and P.C. Schmitter (1986) *Transitions from Authoritarian Rule. Tentative Conclusions about Uncertain Democracies.* Baltimore: Johns Hopkins University Press.

O'Donnell, G., P.C. Schmitter and L. Whitehead (eds.) (1986) *Transitions from Authoritarian Rule: Comparative Perspectives.* Baltimore: Johns Hopkins University Press.

Przeworski, A. (1986) *Some Problems in the Study of Transition to Democracy.* In: G. O'Donnell, P.C. Schmitter and L. Whitehead (eds.) *Transitions from Autoritarian Rule: Comparative Perspectives.* Baltimore: Johns Hopkins University Press. 47-63.

Przeworski, A. (1991) *Democracy and the market. Political and economic reforms in Eastern Europe and Latin America.* Cambridge: Cambridge University Press.

Przeworski, A. (1993) *Economic Reforms, Public Opinion, and Political Institutions: Poland in the Eastern European Perspective.* In: L. Pereira, J.M. Maravall and A. Przeworski (eds.) *Economic Reforms in New Democracies.* Cambridge: Cambridge University Press. 132-198.

Ragin, C.C. (1987) *The Comparative Method. Moving Beyond Qualitative and Quantitative Strategies.* Berkeley: University of California Press.

Rose, R. and C. Haerpfer (1992) New Democracies Between State and Market. A Baseline Report of Public Opinion. Glasgow: Centre for the Study of Public Policy, University of Strathclyde. mimeo.

Rustow, D.A. (1970), Transitions to Democracy. Toward a Dynamic Model. *Comparative Politics* 2: 337-363.

Scheuch, E.K. (1968) *The Cross-Cultural Use of Sample Surveys: Problems of Comparability.* In: S. Rokkan (ed.) *Comparative Research across Cultures and Nations.* Paris: Mouton. 176-209.

Schmalz-Bruns, R. (1992) Civil Society—ein postmodernes Kunstprodukt? Eine Antwort auf Volker Heins. *Politische Vierteljahresschrift* 33: 243-255.

Schmitter, P.C. (1992) The Consolidation of Democracy and Representation of Social Groups. *American Behavioral Scientist* 35: 422-449.

Schumann, S. (1990) *Wahlverhalten und Persönlichkeit.* Opladen: Westdeutscher Verlag.

Senghaas, D. (1992) Vom Nutzen und Elend der Nationalismen im Leben von Völkern. *Beilage zur Wochenzeitung Das Parlament.* 31-32 (24. Juli): 23-32.

Smolicz, J.J. (1991), Cultural Diversity and Ethnic Pluralism: an Australian Perspective. *Sisyphus* 7: 133-149.

Sniderman, P.M. (1981) *A Question of Loyalty.* Berkeley: University of California Press.

Tarrow, S. (1991) Aiming at a Moving Target: Social Science and the Recent Rebellions in Eastern Europe. *PS: Political Science and Politics* 24: 12-20.

Times-Mirror (1991) *The Pulse of Europe: A Survey of Political and Social Values and Attitudes.* Washington, D.C.: Center for The People & The Press.

Vanhanen, T. (1990) *The Process of Democratization. A Comparative Study of 147 States.* New York: Crane Russak.

Verba, S. (1965) *Comparative Political Culture.* In: L.W. Pye and S. Verba (eds.) *Political Culture and Political Development.* Princeton: Princeton University Press. 512-560.

Verba, S. (1980) *On Revisiting the Civic Culture: A Personal Postcript.* In: G.A. Almond and S. Verba (eds.) *The Civic Culture Revisited.* Boston: Little Brown. 394-410.

Weil, F.D. (1993) *The Development of Democratic Attitudes in Eastern and Western Germany in a Comparative Perspective.* In: F.D. Weil, J. Huffman and M. Gautier (eds.) *Democratization in Eastern and Western Europe.* Greenwich: JAI Press. 195-225.

Wesolowski, W. (1991) Transition to Democracy: The Role of Social and Political Pluralism. *Sisyphus* 7: 79-94.

Westle, B. (1989) *Politische Legitimität—Theorien, Konzepte, empirische Befunde.* Baden-Baden: Nomos.

Westle, B. (1992) Strukturen nationaler Identität in Ost- und Westdeutschland. *Kölner Zeitschrift für Soziologie und Sozialpsychologie* 44: 461-488.

6

The Economic Role of Government

Rolf Alter[*]

A few years ago the role of the government in the transition process appeared to be a non-issue: Aspiring to a market-based economic system, Central and East European countries would just reduce the government to a bare minimum, while the private sector flourished free from half a century or more of oppression. Sequencing of reforms—an issue where the role of the government could have been a crucial point of discussion—was primarily a technical debate on the order of implementing the individual elements of the reform; the 'implementing agency' was generally not subject to further considerations.

Today, the enthusiasm of the early days after the Big Bang has waned. The process of transformation is taking longer than anticipated; it is turning out to be more costly, and not only in money terms. Despite tremendous work in a number of areas, results are unsatisfactory—rising unemployment, high inflation, declining output. There is growing concern that the initial social consensus for radical change has become more fragile or may already be lost.

Under these circumstances renewed interest in the economic role of the government cannot come as a big surprise.[1] Basically, two schools of economic thinking can be identified: On the one hand, the 'reformers,' who would like to see more reliance on market forces, blaming slow economic progress on the reluctance of the government to withdraw; on the other hand,

[*] The views expressed are the sole responsibility of the author and do not necessarily reflect those of OECD.

[1] The emphasis of the discussion is put on the economic role of the government. There are, however, important linkages between the economic role and the institutional and administrative requirements and capacity for government.

H. J. Blommestein and B. Steunenberg (eds.), Government and Markets, 115–128.

the 'interventionists,' who favor greater involvement of the government, claiming that its withdrawal was too radical and fast.

Indications are that neither interventionists nor reformers could actually provide adequate guidance for determining the economic role of the government.[2] Focusing primarily on two distinct categories of economic policy instruments, both schools tend to overlook the importance of economic objectives.[3] Also, they do not reflect sufficiently the experience of the last few years. Traditional policy instruments work differently in transition economies; some have failed, and new ones had to be created that cannot be categorized easily.

Reconsidering the responsibilities of governments in transition economies and the constraints economic policies are facing—not as a theoretical exercise, but in light of transition experience—a case is made for replacing primarily instrument-driven approaches for an 'objective-driven' approach. The role of the government needs to be defined on the basis of a comprehensive target function—including objectives for the systemic change and for the economic aggregates—or, in reference to Buchanan's distinction, 'constitutional' and 'ordinary' policy objectives.[4] Instruments will then be selected because of their technical efficiency, not due to ideological consistency.

Introducing a framework for determining the government's role in general is, of course, not an exhaustive treatment of the issues of transition—there remains ample room for debate of individual policy domains. It does also not aim at comprehensively defining the role of the government once and for all—the role will change with progress in transition because of changes and shifts in the target function; in fact, it may even be difficult to separate transition from the role of the government because defining its role is characterizing the transition itself. During transition, 'constitutional' and 'ordinary' economic politics overlap.

[2] Government is understood in a comprehensive sense as the political authority both setting the rules for the economic agents in a market economy and conducting public economic policies within this framework. No distinction is made with respect to individual elements of government, such as, the legislative and executive branch.

[3] Economic policy instruments include in a wider sense the allocation mechanism.

[4] See Buchanan (1994). Constitutional decision-making is defined as the design, construction, implementation and maintenance of basic rules, the fundamental law that defines the parameters within which 'ordinary politics' are to take place. Ordinary politics are operating within the rules so defined.

What are the Responsibilities of the Government in the Present Stage of Transition?

Advancing the reform process, designing the market system for the country, and exercising effective management control are distinctive features that reflect currently the responsibilities of the government in most Central and East European countries. The multiplicity of tasks and their scope give the government a far greater importance than in developed economies.

The Government is Still the Engine of the Economic Reform Process

Transition means first of all that the government is organizing its own withdrawal in order to create room for a market-based coordination between independent economic agents. This assignment reflects both the initial omnipresence of the government in planned economies and the nature of the peaceful revolution in Eastern Europe. The process is not facilitated by the fact that it implies releasing functions that granted power, recognition and 'rents.'

The fact that today the emergence of private initiatives still depends to a large extent on public initiative is a clear indication that the responsibility of the government as an agent for the reform has not yet diminished. Privatization and hard budget constraint policies are prominent examples for the priority of government action for private initiative to develop.

Privatization is in most countries based on government programs. It has been placed at the heart of the transformation process, and bold and courageous concepts have been invented. However, implementation is far behind schedule, and conceptual and technical doubts have emerged. Regarding the participation of foreign capital in privatization, policies in many Central and East European countries have not yet cleared sufficiently its economic and legal status.

Hard budget constraints and bankruptcy policies have not yet met the test. Admittedly, implementing these rules is probably the most important economic conflict in the transition period. Closure of capacities is, however, a necessary condition for factors to reallocate in the private sector—under pressure and in expectation of profits.

The Government is Still in Search of its Role as the Regulatory Power as in Developed Market Economies

Transition also means that the government defines rules and institutions of the new economic system based on the market as primary allocation and distribution mechanism, with important and very direct implications for its role during and after transition. This process could be best characterized as creating the 'economic constitution' of a country.

A typical question asked in the early days of transition was, whether East European countries would, for example, be moving towards the 'Swedish' social-democratic model or the 'Thatcherite' model, implying quite different economic constitutions and, consequently, different roles for the government. It seems fair to say that if ever there was clarity in Central and East European countries about the 'model' it has not been refined. The fact that Central and East European countries are in transition to a market economy is not a description of the final stage, it gives only the direction of the process.

Some have argued that the question about the ultimate economic constitution is not yet ripe and may even be the wrong one (Roland). I do not agree that the question is unripe. Yes, the initial situation and shocks occurring during the transition period will influence the final outcome, perhaps more than initial ideological choices, but the vision of the end result has considerable impact on transition policies. A number of 'ordinary' government policies and reforms will depend on the final objective: If state monopolies are to be maintained, privatization is not an issue here; where income distribution is of no concern, there is no need for redistribution schemes, etc. Less uncertainty about the objectives of the reform will also make private initiatives more likely, which could facilitate the role of the government considerably (Genberg 1991).

I would admit, though, that the question could be wrong to the extent that it would be asking for a static answer. A market economy is not a steady state but, rather, should be regarded as a process of continuous adjustments—by the private sector and the government. Recent developments in the model economies mentioned above or the present discussions of the role of the government in the U.S. clearly prove the point. Consequently, transition may be more of a process with a moving target, although the requirement of adjustment does not necessarily translate in all cases into changes of the economic constitution.

The Government is Still Looking for an Entrepreneurial Strategy

Transition means finally that the government must assume the role of ownership in a market environment—an element quite distinct from constitutional and ordinary economic politics. There are few indications that the new function is already adequately met; converting state-owned enterprises into legally independent entities is at most the first step of the reform. Where the government as shareholder has not yet defined the objectives of its enterprises, where no effective control nor incentives for management exist and where the management of state-owned enterprises do not know how to act in a market environment, maintaining the status-quo and 'muddling through' are rational attitudes for managers; their initiative will not be encouraged if privatization could sweep them out of office tomorrow.

As the direct or indirect owner of production facilities, the government has maintained not only substantial influence on microeconomic decision making, but has a substantial impact on the macroeconomic performance. In most countries of transition, state-owned enterprises still account for the greater part of national output—and in view of the progress in privatization it is not an unlikely statement to say that it will stay like that for quite some time.

A complicating factor for assuming its new role could be the inherent tendency for the government to become increasingly the owner of only bad assets. In a way, governments are facing the 'paradox of privatization': Without privatization, there is no relief for the government, including the budget, but with privatization, the burden of bad assets is increasing.

What are the Constraints for the Role of the Government?

Any approach a government wants to follow for assuming its considerable responsibilities in and for transition has to take into account three major constraints: The need to maintain the social consensus for the transition process, the limited knowledge of and experience with the economics of transition, and the bottleneck of administrative capacities. All have proven to be important elements for the design of transition policies.

Social Consensus

Economic policymakers are realizing that the transition process is more than a technical matter of changing the coordination mechanism between economic agents from 'plan' to 'market.' People in the countries of transition knew that economic hardship would come with the political changes, but after three years of economic decline patience starts waning—election results and political events in Poland, Czechoslovakia, East Germany and Lithuania are clear indications for growing concern in the population. Previously, the return to democracy and building a market economy were inseparable, equally supported by the elites and the people; now, a rupture between the leading political class and the population can no longer be excluded.

Meeting the requirements of political and social sustainability should not be confused with trying to minimize transition costs. Acknowledging the existence of political and social constraints means that they may jeopardize the transition process when overlooked or incorrectly analyzed. Transition is therefore not a period when policy objectives can be neglected or simply reduced to 'exchange of coordination mechanisms.' On the contrary, the relationship between expected economic gains of the transition and current losses requires policy management on the basis of a target function, including the main economic aggregates.

What is technically feasible or desirable must also be acceptable for people who have experienced for a considerable amount of time a very different rationality, particularly in economics, but also in other areas, such as formation. A social security system may help reduce the financial consequences of unemployment, but what about the psychological effects for those who never had to think about employment? The replacement of the previous social relationship of bureaucratic subordination and paternalism by a social relationship based on formal equality and freedom, implying individual choices and uncertainty, needs time and cannot be carried out 'at all costs' or it might eventually fail.

The need for social consensus may include respecting political-historical experiences in economic policies, even if this implies a sub-optimal economic solution. Examples exist: Worker councils in Poland are regarded as an important element in the privatization process due to their contribution in bringing about the political changes in the first place, although in economic terms and particularly in privatization they may be more of an obstacle. Voucher privatization has been frequently justified on political grounds to have the population participate in the redistribution of the national wealth. Has 'employment' not similar characteristics—beyond the pure economic meaning?

Transition: A New Economic Phenomenon

At the outset of the transformation process, much had been said about the lack of economic understanding of the transformation of a centrally-planned economy to a market-based system. However, this basic insight did not prevent many from attacking the problems radically—contributing to high expectations for a quick turn-around. By now, policymakers and advisors have come to understand that exchanging one allocation and distribution mechanism for another is not just a question of introducing new rules or a legal framework. The legacy of the previous system weighs heavily not only on the economic performance during transition but also on the way the coordination through the market does or does not function.

An important aspect of the lack of market-based interaction between economic agents and aggregates in transition economies is that the instruments of economic policies do not necessarily work in the same way as in developed economies. For some transition problems completely new policy approaches have to be developed. At some point, the well-known relationship between the quantity of changes that lead to a new quality is still a valid consideration.

A few examples may demonstrate the point. How to conduct restrictive monetary policies where the banks have weak balance sheets, only limited experience in risk analysis, hardly face competition, etc., and where the customers of the banking sector, for the most part, make use of their own monetary world of inter-enterprise credits or simply do not pay their taxes? How to fight inflation, when big bang price liberalization enables state-owned enterprises to exercise monopoly power—cutting output and raising prices? Should inflation stabilization be postponed as long as there is no progress in enterprise reform?

Must the fall in output beyond any expectation be regarded as 'unavoidable'? Should monetary policies be loosened to reduce the credit crunch or is the decline in output to be blamed on the monopolies? Has the supply response to the withdrawal of the government in form of price liberalization or the cuts in subsidies been overestimated? The two elements of restructuring—destruction and construction—have a different time frame: Withdrawal tends to translate into the closure of capacities more or less immediately, while production and new jobs are only created with delay. But the delay will be extended when the allocation mechanism does not work properly!

Privatization is a new game altogether—measured by size as well as by intended speed. Can mass privatization schemes work when information about enterprises is relatively incomplete? How will the initial dilution of ownership impact corporate management behavior? Can owners of equity without savings or access to capital provide the basis for investment and restructuring? What about the asymmetry of risks and profits in the auction à la Czechoslovakia that a market does not know of: Limiting the individual investor's maximal loss to the cost of the vouchers, while there is no restriction for private profits, could be interpreted as a sale of assets, where risks and liabilities are to remain with the government. Even more fundamental: Are privatization programs perhaps slowing down true, i.e. spontaneous privatization?

Providing answers to these questions is not facilitated by the fact that there are not many references available for the economic issues of transition. One may find comparable situations in Western economies for specific markets or sectors. However, in most examples there does exist, even if fragmentary, an economic framework, while in East European countries it is its creation that counts for a considerable part of transition policies. The inherent risk of only partially valid comparisons is that they may lead to incorrect policy decisions in a different environment.

Comparisons and lessons are increasingly emerging from within the group of Central and East European countries. As a few countries have started their reform process earlier than others, there could in fact be some sharing of each other's experience. Lessons from other transition economies are very likely to be accepted more easily as relevant points of reference, while Western experience is increasingly rejected. I would, however, urge including all reforming countries in the analysis, i.e. Eastern Germany also. Too often it is disqualified as an example, because of the 'rich cousin' argument; for the question of the role of the government it provides rich insights.

The lack of reference and comparability is, by the way, also one of the difficulties in designing and implementing foreign assistance. To the extent that it is based on the experience in the West it is not necessarily valid in the specific circumstance of East European countries. A prominent example is the frequent reference to the Marshall Plan; a thorough analysis would not reveal too many similarities between post-war Europe with the present situation in Eastern Europe.

And finally, analysis and policymaking have been complicated by the fact that the internal shock of transition is compounded by external shocks. Primarily, the collapse of the Council for Mutual Economic Assistance (CMEA), but also the global economic downturn have increased the difficulties in coming to a better understanding of the economic interrelationships in transition economies.

Institutions and Administrative Systems

There should be no doubt about the need for constitutional economic politics to clarify the rules of the new game—whether in such diverse domains as banking, international trade, social security, intellectual property rights or the commercial code. But no matter how well government policies or laws may have been designed, they need to pass at least two 'obstacles' that will influence their contribution to the transition.

First, today laws are discussed and voted upon by Central and East European countries' parliaments—reflecting the weaknesses and strong points of democratic decisionmaking in parliaments that have overcrowded agendas (Alter and Wehrle 1992). Passing a law, however is, only part of the problem. Implementing and enforcing it can be an even more constraining bottleneck. The way in which a government wishes to play its role must take into account administrative capacities. For institutions and administrative systems strong and efficient enough to exercise their supervisory and regulatory power, people must be found and trained for the new functions, and there is always an initial period of learning and inexperience. For example, simulating the market for state-owned enterprises in the voucher privatization of the CSFR is a very sophisticated and ambitious undertaking from a technical point of view; it remains to be seen whether it has respected the constraints of the country's administrative capacities.

Reformers vs. Interventionists: The Wrong Alternative

Against the background of the responsibilities of the government and the social, technical, and administrative constraints, discussions on 'instrument-driven' policies—as they are reflected in reformers vs. interventionists—suggest an alternative role for the government that does not really exist. In times of systemic change it perhaps should not be surprising that the categories of economic policy instruments may receive greater attention than the discussion of the objectives of economic policies. Can it be explained by the reluctance to withdraw and the mistrust in the market forces by former planners—and with the total belief in market forces by the new and occasionally uncritically pro-capitalistic political class (Laski 1991)? The economic role of the government must be determined as a function of the economic constitution and the objectives of ordinary politics. Moreover, even if the issue of the policy objectives were put aside, reformers and interventionists tend to miss the technical dimension of their policy advice.

Reformers should not forget that there must be a functioning market where there is no government—otherwise liberalization will very likely result in greater instability and fragility. Undeveloped or underdeveloped financial markets, a lack of functioning labor markets, especially with respect to the determination and differentiation of salaries, monopolistic/monopsonistic markets, state ownership, or uncertainties due to restitution imply the persistence of structures and rigidities unsuitable for market signals to emerge or to be received and responded to effectively. The regional dimension of sectoral adjustment problems adds another complication. The challenges of internal adjustment have been aggravated by the complete collapse of the external trading system.

Providing no enforceable rules and no room for the government in order to speed up the process and to have a maximum of market forces at work also reflects a misperception of the market system. Even in very liberal market economies, fair and beneficial competition is based on a transparent and solid framework under the surveillance of the government. Where markets are not working efficiently, unconditional withdrawal will very likely violate the social consensus constraint.

A qualitative aspect of a quick and radical withdrawal needs to be stressed because of its long-term consequences for the functioning of the market system (Blommestein 1993). Where, for example, investment funds in the process of privatization are allowed to operate without regulation or supervision, conflicts of interest will arise; more importantly, however, the whole new economic system may be discredited if first-time investors find out that fraud seems to be an acceptable part of the new game.

Interventionists must know that there will never be a market where individual risks are minimized and private initiatives are not allowed to exploit opportunities. Following the interventionist path has frequently meant governments intervening on a discretionary basis when problems and pressures are mounting. However, no functioning market and no functioning government is definitely the worst combination. Bailing out companies or granting specific incentives to large foreign investors does not only result in distortions, but it creates moral hazards. Why adjust to the new economic environment, when in the end there is the government that will take care of the problems without negative sanctions for the state-owned enterprise management? Why invest now, instead of waiting until the government is eventually ready to grant even higher subsidies to the foreign investor—who will in addition benefit from the further decline in the value of the intended acquisition because of the wait-and-see attitude of current management.

It would be a great mistake to put discretionary interventionism in the perspective of helping to meet the social consensus constraint. On the contrary, individual measures will only reduce resources that could be available for general policies. Moreover, it creates uncertainty for potential investors who do not know whether the economic policy conditions they take as a basis for their decision will persist.

For an Objective-Driven Approach

The objective-driven approach to determining the role of the government implies four central elements.

First, governments must operate on the basis of a comprehensive target function including objectives for the constitution of the market system and for economic aggregates. Maintaining the social consensus is a key determinant for the selection and ranking of constitutional and ordinary objectives of economic politics.

Second, governments must not limit themselves in the use of economic policy instruments, particularly not for reasons of ideological consistency. Leaving the vicious circle of decline to embark on the virtuous circle of growth is not an ideological issue. The government will have to draw on instruments from both policy camps of reformers and interventionists. In addition, creativity and flexibility will be necessary to develop new instruments that can cope with transition-specific problems; the bad loan issue is a prominent example. The administrative capacities will be an important constraint for the design of instruments.

Third, economic policies need to be organized horizontally, integrating all relevant policy domains. Contrary to the impression that was created by the debate on sequencing, transition must be tackled on a horizontal basis where different aspects of the economic interaction need to be taken into account.

Fourth, government policies require policy concepts—for predictability of policies instead of perfectionism of rules and regulations. Concepts will help to create transparency and credibility, and to minimize political bargaining. Concepts do not mean a commitment in details—which would exceed the administrative capacities anyway; they have to be a commitment to predictability. Investors do not need nor want too much 'fine print' in economic policies. However, there must be a reasonable probability to be able to predict government positions in areas that are not (yet) fully specified.

In the current situation the objective-driven policy approach could be interpreted primarily as a call for policies to consolidate the social consensus. Indications are that present employment would especially have to figure more prominently in the target function. At the instrument level, measures to improve and support the functioning of the market mechanism are needed. Reducing the deficit in structural policies in comparison with the emphasis so far on macroeconomic policies should be the major consequence (Alter 1992; Bouin and Coquet 1991).

A better balance between macroeconomic and structural policies would reflect the interdependence between the two policy domains. Note that the reform process in all Central and East European countries has been initiated by price liberalization, the ultimate structural policy instrument—but with considerable differences in sequencing and implementing from country to country, which may help explain the different inflation performances. The introduction of a safety net was regarded as essential everywhere, beyond its direct income support effect, because it could strengthen the commitment to a hard budget constraint.

There is no reason why the positive relationship between the two policy domains could not be exploited in other cases as well. Why, for example, should active trade policies or 'priority industry' policies be ruled out, as long as they are designed along market principles and not motivated by protectionism and redistribution? Does the infant industry not provide a valid argument where the previous administratively organized exchange of goods within the CMEA is now expected to follow global competitiveness and the comparative advantage? What about the role of a tax-cum-subsidy policy to reduce output losses (Fanizza 1992)? East Germany represents an interesting example for a macro-, structural, and microeconomic policy mix; although the legal and institutional framework—more or less complete, in any case well experienced—was available literally over night and macroeconomic stability does not pose any problem, a whole range of transitional structural policies have been discussed or implemented—not all of them available due only to the tremendous transfers of resources (Kantzenbach 1992).

A balance and integration of macroeconomic and structural policies has sometimes been doubted because of the difference in the timeframe of the two categories. The possibilities for better-coordinated policies have improved. It seems to now become clear that the macroeconomic stabilization is taking much longer than anticipated, not only, but also due to the lack of structural policies.

A particular aspect of the objective-driven approach is the separation of the economic policy role of the government from its entrepreneurial obligations. Based on the assumption that appears realistic, that state-owned enterprises will remain in government hands for quite some time, the government has to assume clearly the responsibilities of a shareholder for improving the performance of state-owned enterprises in a market environment, to prevent such enterprises from becoming an obstacle for the emergence of the private sector. As the owner, the government has to determine the target function for the enterprises and to exercise effective management control, including an incentive system for managers based on performance and training to overcome, as quickly as possible, the lack of experience in operating in a market environment. The argument that internal reforms have never worked before in Central and East European countries does not hold because of the systemic change in the economic environment. In addition, if managers of state-owned enterprises cannot adjust to new incentives and training, how can transition work anyway?

Assuming the entrepreneurial role should, of course, not lead to a slowdown in privatization efforts. On the contrary, it could help make state-owned enterprises a more interesting object for investors, including foreigners. It would be the role of the government to moderate the fears of the population of being 'bought up'. Xenophobia could best be avoided by foreign investors behaving as agents of civilized capitalism bringing in new technology and paying reasonable wages in return for productivity, and not acting as speculators.

Conclusions

In the initial enthusiasm for the switch from 'plan to market' there seemed to be no role for the government, other than withdrawal from interfering in the coordination among economic agents. Three years down the winding road of transformation, a reassessment is warranted. In fact, managing transition implies considerable responsibilities for the government: Advancing the economic reforms, defining the market system for the country and exercising effective management control are three distinct challenges, where withdrawal is only part of the process. Moreover, it has by now become clear, that these challenges have to met against a background of serious social, technical, and administrative constraints of policymaking.

Reassessing the role of the government on the basis of primarily instrument-driven approaches—as represented by 'reformers' on the one hand and 'interventionists' on the other—suggests, however, an alternative that actually does not exist. Focusing on categories of instruments misses the importance of policy objectives for the role of the government, and it does not reflect the lack of technical efficiency of traditional instruments during transition.

Leaving, therefore, the controversy between interventionists and reformers behind, the role of the government should be defined on the basis of an objective-driven approach presenting itself as the natural correspondent to the process of transition, particularly now that in many Central and East European countries the initial reform shock has already taken place.

In reviewing the policy objectives during transition, exchanging the allocation and distribution mechanism can only be one element of the target function; it must include a comprehensive list of entries for 'ordinary' economic politics and 'constitutional' economic politics—also in order to respond to the growing concern over the sustainability of the social consensus. Those who would dismiss such re-orientation of policy objectives may remember that without social and political stability there will very likely be no reform at all.

According to the experience of the last three years, replacing the plan as an allocation mechanism implies that traditional policy instruments may temporarily be inadequate or may fail altogether—where there is not (yet) a market, market-based instruments cannot work, while direct interventions no longer work. Instruments, therefore, need to be selected not on the basis of ideological consistency, but for their technical efficiency. In addition, there is clearly a case for policies of different domains to be integrated into policy concepts to manage transition more effectively.

Against the background of this analysis, the argument is made for a better balance of structural and macroeconomic policies. At present, this implies mainly reducing the deficit of structural policies—in support of the market mechanism—to facilitate adjustment and improve macroeconomic performance. A particular aspect is for the government to assume its function effectively as owner of production facilities in a market environment.

References

Alter, R. (1992) The New Challenge in Eastern Europe: Investment and Restructuring. *Intereconomics* 27: 16-19.

Alter, R. and F. Wehrle (1992) Foreign Direct Investment (FDI) in the Six Eastern European Economies in Transition (Poland, CSFR, Hungary, Romania, Bulgaria and Albania). *International Business Law Journal* 5: 491-553.

Blommestein H.J. (1993) *Financial Sector Reform and Monetary Management in Central and Eastern Europe.* In: D.E. Fair and J. Raymond (eds.) *The New Europe: Evolving Economic and Financial Systems in East en West.* Dordrecht: Kluwer.

Bouin, O. and B. Coquet (1991) La réforme des structures économiques dans les pays de l'Europe de l'Est. *Observations et Diagnostics Économiques* 38: 207-226.

Bruno, M. (1992) Stabilization and Reform in Eastern Europe: A Preliminary Evaluation. *IMF Staff Papers* 39: 741-777.

Buchanan, J.M. (1994) *Democracy within Constitutional Limits.* In this volume.

Fanizza, D. (1992) Price Liberalization in a Reforming Socialist Economy: A Search Equilibrium Approach. Washington, D.C.: IMF. mimeo.

Genberg, H. (1991) The Sequencing of Reforms in Eastern Europe. Washington, D.C.: IMF. mimeo.

Kantzenbach, E. (1992) Thesen zur deutschen Wirtschaftspolitik. *Wirtschaftsdienst* 5: 239-246.

Laski, K. (1991) Transition from Command to Market Economies in Central and Eastern Europe: First Experiences and Questions. Vienna: Vienna Institute for Comparative Economic Studies. mimeo.

Roland, G. (n.d.) Political Constraints in the Transition from Socialist Economies in Disequilibrium to Market Economies. Brussels: Université Libre de Bruxelles. mimeo.

7

The Role of Government Institutions in the Process of Privatization

Paul G. Hare, Anna Canning and Timothy Ash*

Throughout the former centrally planned economies, the economic programs which have been adopted, or which in some instances are still being debated, have two important features in common. The first is the aim of bringing about a transition from central planning to some form of market-type economy. The second is the recognition that such an economy cannot be expected to function effectively while the bulk of each country's productive assets remains in state hands. A market economy requires private agents able to make economic decisions in the light of the market signals they perceive, supplemented by their own judgements. Accordingly, there is general agreement in former centrally planned economies that a key component of a viable transition program must be a privatization program.

Privatization broadly defined refers to the transfer of state-owned productive assets to new, private owners. It can be accomplished in many different ways, and different countries in the region have already indicated that a variety of approaches is likely to be pursued. In detail, these depend on the type of asset being transferred, the price at which transfers occur, characteristics of the new owners, the legal and fiscal framework in effect, and the overall speed of the process. On the last point, it is important to stress that the programs now under way in several former centrally planned economies, even if not executed as rapidly as initially planned, are likely to proceed many times faster than the rates of privatization achieved in any Western

* Some of the research for this paper was carried out with the help of an ESRC grant under the East-West Program.

H. J. Blommestein and B. Steunenberg (eds.), Government and Markets, 129–157.

programs, such as that carried out in the U.K. during the 1980s (and still continuing). This desire to build up a large private sector quickly has important implications for the conduct of the privatization process, as we explain below.

Aside from its speed, there is a second respect in which privatization in the former centrally planned economies differs sharply from Western experience. This is the fact that many of the candidates for privatization are enterprises which either have no hope of being transformed into competitive entities, or must undergo drastic restructuring in order to do so. Such restructuring is not absent from Western programs, but in its scale, urgency and difficulty the former centrally planned economies region is unique. Inevitably, therefore, this issue interacts with privatization itself in quite complex ways, influencing the priorities, the methods of privatization, the likely revenues, and the ultimate ownership structure of the firms concerned. Moreover, arguments arise concerning the timing of restructuring, specifically whether it should precede, accompany or follow privatization. The treatment of these issues also bears on the role of state agencies in the whole process, because these remarks imply that such agencies could fulfil a number of different roles:

- preparing firms for privatization;
- supervising/regulating the privatization process;
- dealing with financial aspects of the privatization process (including bank reform and/or privatization);
- organizing enterprise restructuring to restore/maintain viability;
- managing those firms which will not be privatized early.

No single agency could be expected to take on all these functions and execute them effectively, since there are some clear conflicts of interest between them. This is already reflected in practice in former centrally planned economies, in that several countries have already adopted relatively complex institutional arrangements to cope with their privatization programs, assigning different functions to distinct bodies. At the same time, all countries in the region have to contend with a situation in which there is widespread mistrust of *any* government agency, whatever it is supposed to be doing, which means that any new privatization agencies must anticipate great problems in establishing their credibility and effectiveness, quite aside from the inherent difficulties of their allotted tasks.

Not only that, but in parts of the region, governments themselves are highly unstable or at best weak, and, despite valiant efforts to break away from the past decades of communist rule, the new governments frequently find themselves adopting patterns of behavior which are much more in accord with the patterns established under communism than with Western democratic practice. This is strikingly evident in the case of privatization, since such vital interests are at stake in the re-distribution of each society's productive assets.

It is never easy to escape from the shackles of the past, but it is orders of magnitude harder when new and old interest groups benefit from long established practices.

In what follows, we start by discussing some of the more critical theoretical issues concerning the role of new state agencies in the former centrally planned economies concerned with privatization, which entails a re-examination of the nature of the 'state' itself in these economies. This is followed by a brief examination of the Hungarian experience, treated as a case study. Even though Hungary's chosen method of privatization is unique in excluding (so far) any form of voucher privatization (i.e. free, or almost free distribution of shares to the population), its experience thus far is of great interest, and offers important insights related to our broader theme. Then we sketch the experience of new state agencies in other former centrally planned economies, before summarizing the more significant conclusions at the end of the chapter.

Government Agencies and Privatization

Definitions

The definition of the *state* depends on what society we are describing. In liberal, Western market economies the state can generally be seen to encompass the government, the civil service, the judiciary, the army and the police. The crucial difference between this definition and that which describes the state in centrally planned economics is that in the latter the state also takes the place of the market in managing the economy. Thus, whereas in market economies the state has a limited economic role in setting the framework in which markets operate, in centrally planned economies the state assumes the dominant role in the economy. Hence in centrally planned economies, the state economic bureaucracy is large, extending right down to the micro-level of enterprise management.

In addition, whereas in democratic market economies the state would incorporate the government of the day, i.e. the political party or parties commanding majority support in parliament and forming the government, in centrally planned economies the political dominance of the ruling party ensured that the leading party apparatus permanently merged into the state, becoming almost indistinguishable and inseparable from it.[1]

This merging of the political, economic and state apparatus, traditional even in some Western market economies, has so far proved enormously difficult for the former centrally planned economies to disentangle as these

[1] Encompassed in Article 6 of the former Soviet constitution, and in corresponding articles in the constitutions of all other former centrally planned economies.

countries embark on the transition to democratic market economies. Thus in Hungary there has been continued concern that the ruling coalition government led by the MDF (Hungarian Democratic Forum) has tended to assume the role formerly held by the Communist Party, by placing its party officials in positions of power within the state apparatus, as well as in nominally independent agencies. In most of the former centrally planned economies it is proving difficult to separate out the economic and political over-centralization of the state and to redefine a new role for the state more in line with the functions of the state in developed market economies.

In what follows the *state* is taken to include both the government and the state apparatus or bureaucracy.

As indicated in the introduction, the most commonly used definition of privatization regards it as the transfer of state assets into private ownership. To clarify this, it is useful to examine the objectives set for privatization, which are:

1. To improve the efficiency of state-owned enterprises and, by so doing, of the economy at large;
2. To improve government finances through the receipts from the sale of state assets and hence to help secure the wider governmental objective of macro-economic stabilization; and
3. To develop wider share ownership and hence political support for the government and for the concept of 'the market.'

In the case of the last, acutely political, motive for privatization the most obvious solution would appear to be to simply give away, *gratis*, shares in state assets. Unfortunately this is obviously at odds with the second objective, the desire to earn revenue from privatization, and numerous studies have revealed that a large number of owners, i.e. the dissipation of ownership rights, is not conducive to enterprise efficiency (see Winiecki 1991). Even with purely political motives in mind, giving away shares may not be the most politically appropriate policy to pursue. As the Thatcher government in the U.K. has proved, the sale of shares to the lower-middle classes, admittedly at favorable prices, can prove to be a most effective means of ensuring political support. In fact this strategy has proved to be optimal both from the political and economic perspective, although not perhaps in terms of social equality.

In practice, privatization in the majority of cases to date has actually involved the sale of property rights from the state to the private sector, rather than any truly free transfers. Even the so-called 'voucher' privatization program currently being implemented in the CSFR is firmly grounded upon a market process. Thus, all citizens wishing to participate in the program had to first register their interest by means of the payment of a small fee of approximately \$ 35, whereupon they were then allocated 1,000 investment points. This initial all-but-free allocation of bidding rights has then been used in a market bidding process to purchase shares in state assets.

This use of sales as the principal means of disposal of state-owned assets can be defended on the grounds of economic efficiency. Thus by disposing of an asset by sale it is ensured that the purchaser is the one who can get the greatest net return from the asset. Identifying the new owner(s) becomes, then, a process of efficient self-selection.

Since, then, we regard *privatization* not just as the transfer, but as the sale of state assets to the private sector, and hence as a market-driven process, it seems entirely logical that it should be left in the hands of private institutions. The fact that the sale of these assets has, in Western market economies, typically been implemented by market institutions, e.g. merchant banks, represents an acknowledgement by the governments concerned that private firms responding to market forces are better equipped to market (value) state-owned enterprises than is the state through its bureaucracy.

The State's Role in Privatization

Despite the need for market involvement in the actual sale of state assets, i.e. in the implementation of a privatization program, the role of government and hence also of the state bureaucracy in the privatization process cannot be underestimated. The government, in line with its own political objectives, establishes both the extent of the privatization program and the legislative and administrative framework in which it is to be implemented. Then the state administration has to formulate how the privatization is to proceed in detail, and to supervise it in accordance with government policy.

In developed market economies, the regulatory role of the state apparatus has proved to be crucial in ensuring that the objectives set for privatization by governments are met. Thus, for example, if the overall objective of privatization is to improve the efficiency of state-owned enterprises then it is important to note, as emphasized in Vickers and Yarrow (1988), that privatization, and therefore ownership, is not the crucial determinant of enterprise efficiency: instead, competition is. Thus, even after the privatization of state-owned enterprises the state's role is to regulate the environment in which the privatized enterprises operate to ensure that competition prevails. This promotes efficiency both of the former state-owned enterprises and within the economy at large. The state has, therefore, an important role to play through the provision and implementation of anti-trust policy, and in other measures which promote competition.

Drawing a clear distinction between the respective roles in the privatization process for government, the state bureaucracy and market institutions can, however, be quite difficult. For, even in developed market economies like the U.K., the state can become quite involved in what should strictly be a market process. For example, establishing a market price for assets to be privatized in the U.K. involved both market and political decision-making processes. Western experience points therefore to a very sophisticated role for the state in privatization. The government of the day broadly defines the level of state intervention in the privatization process and, as has been seen in the U.K. experience, this has been significant. But the state bureaucracy then has to implement and operationalize the concrete forms of state intervention as determined in outline by the government. It is the state bureaucracy which is ultimately left to determine the extent of its own intervention in the day-to-day administration of privatization.

Fine tuning of state intervention is difficult to achieve, as there is an agency problem between those in the government and those in the state administration. This problem is solved to some extent in developed market economies by the overlapping of the state bureaucracy and government, associated with the development of think-tanks within government and political appointments into the bureaucracy (e.g. the appointment of state-owned enterprise management by government on the understanding that the management understand, support and are committed to implementing the government's privatization strategy).

So Western experience suggests that privatization, while theoretically a market process, also involves considerable state intervention due to the sheer complexity of implementing governmental decisions and due to the potential for market failure, and in particular the need to ensure competitive markets. It also implies an efficient, pragmatic and responsive state apparatus, which is able to transmit government directives into practice.

Implications for Former Centrally Planned Economies

In market economies some of the burden of privatization is, as already observed, sub-contracted out to private institutions, e.g. merchant banks. In addition, the valuation and placing of shares in state-owned enterprises is eased by the presence of market institutions, such as well developed financial markets (including stock markets) and a generally well-functioning and reasonably well understood price mechanism. Clearly, in the majority of the former centrally planned economies these institutions of the market are not well enough developed to allow the state to share the burden of privatization to the same extent. In effect this suggests that the state bureaucracy will have to assume the bulk of the workload of privatization. But if the institutions of the market are not yet developed enough in the former centrally planned economies to assume the dominant role in privatization, they might only develop—or their development could at least be assisted—by being involved in the privatization process. Thus the more the state takes over the role of these institutions the less likely they are to develop. Perhaps the state should refrain from intervention in the hope that these institutions can somehow quickly evolve to fill the institutional gap. However, we doubt whether this could happen rapidly enough. Consequently, an enlarged role for the state in the former centrally planned economies in connection with the implementation of privatization programs seems to be unavoidable. Hence the capability and flexibility of the state bureaucracy in these countries requires further study.

Since it is now generally accepted that the former centrally planned economies were highly inefficient, and since the state apparatus was in effect the central planning apparatus, one must conclude that in a sense the state apparatus itself operated inefficiently. If so, this would imply that the state apparatus in these economies would be wholly unable to implement such a complex, market-determined program as privatization. However, while there is little doubting the inefficiencies of the centrally planned economies, the fact that the state apparatus was able to formulate and implement a central plan at all is something to admire, in view of the vast computational and organizational problems involved. Given the ability of the state apparatus to implement a remarkably complex central plan, why could the same state apparatus not plan and implement a privatization program which would appear no more complicated than the problem of central planning of an entire economy?

Quite obviously, however, there is a great difference between the role of the state apparatus under central planning and that required to implement privatization. The role of the state in central planning evolved over time, hence bureaucrats in the planning apparatus had time to adjust to the rules of the central planning game. The system was rigid, and had to be to ensure the plan was achievable, hence the rules of central planning changed little, and were not designed to be subtle and dynamic. In developed market economies the role of the state bureaucracy has again evolved over a period of time. However, the state bureaucracy has learnt that its role is to complement and improve the market process not to replace it. It is thus far more flexible and responsive to the need for change, because it has had to change and adapt itself as market conditions have themselves changed. Thus when comparing the state bureaucracy under central planning and in developed market economies it is almost like comparing the hands of a bricklayer with those of a concert pianist.

Although the rough and ready state apparatus in the former centrally planned economies was simply not suited to carry out the complex privatization processes initiated at the outset of reform in the late 1980s, it could be argued that if the process had been set out as a detailed plan for state bureaucrats to follow then, in theory, the state apparatus could have implemented it. But it would probably have taken a number of years for the state apparatus to learn how the privatization plan operated. Also no such privatization plan was available. Indeed this lack of a plan may have served to delay the process in several countries as the state apparatus, unable to take a pragmatic approach to privatization because they were used to having a blueprint to follow, spent an inordinate amount of time trying to develop such a privatization plan. Unfortunately, it is probably impossible to devise a simplified plan for privatization. It requires a state bureaucracy which is able to adapt the concept of privatization to individual country-specific, sector-specific and enterprise-specific conditions. The result of this planning vacuum, in effect, was chaos and delay in the privatization process.

The view that the state apparatus was not up to the task of privatization played some part in the introduction of the so-called 'shock therapy' reform strategy in a number of former centrally planned economies. The state bureaucracy was seen as an obstacle to the privatization process, and hence it needed to be side-tracked in the privatization drive or else shocked into becoming responsive to market forces. Thus in Poland privatization initially occurred in a largely uncontrolled manner, i.e. through spontaneous privatization. While this form of privatization did produce an initial burst of activity, it was unsustainable in the longer term as it produced a backlash of popular claims of *nomenklatura* profiteering. Managers and well-connected members of the bureaucracy were able to benefit enormously through such privatization. This produced a popular reaction against privatization and a concerted call for increased state regulation of the whole privatization process.

Now, if the state bureaucracy was ill-equipped to carry out the delicate process of privatization even prior to 1989, the situation subsequently became much worse. For one consequence of the political and economic revolutions which spread throughout the former centrally planned economies was that what little cohesion and bureaucratic ability the former state apparatus possessed under the previous central planning regimes was swept away. Previously, the central planning bureaucracy worked as it did only with the help of the transmission mechanism of communist ideology. The power of the communist party and the threat of its repression had forced bureaucrats to go along with the game of central planning. Indeed, playing along with the game could produce lucrative economic rewards for capable bureaucrats, and hence the more competent and ambitious people in the former centrally planned economy societies were drawn into the state administrative apparatus as the main route to personal advancement.

But once the ideological underpinnings were removed, the oil in the central planning machine quickly ran dry. In the new market environment, capable individuals could now earn large rewards in the expanding market sector. As a result, the state bureaucracy lost some of its best staff, which undermined its effectiveness. At the same time, other staff who remained in the bureaucracy also took on outside jobs, most frequently part-time commercial activity. In effect their loyalty and commitment to the state apparatus were reduced, and increasingly they saw their role in the state apparatus as a means to further their own commercial objectives.

The state machine itself was caught in an ideological vacuum. The governments of these newly democratic countries were strongly oriented towards the free market and encouraged entrepreneurial activity. For those in the state sector it must have been difficult for them to distinguish between this new market ideology emphasizing personal gain, and the Western concept of a state bureaucracy of even-handed, mostly incorruptible state officials carrying out the will of the people as expressed by the government. The result was the development of an extremely corrupt state bureaucracy desiring a share of the spoils from the new market conditions.[2]

This destruction of the old conception of the bureaucracy under central planning and then the movement back towards increased state regulation in connection with the privatization process was unfortunate. For the demise of the old-style bureaucracy prevented it from acting like the conscientious state apparatus of a developed market economy, while the privatization process itself offered plentiful opportunities for corrupt self-enrichment.

The state bureaucracy has at its disposal the tools to profit from privatization. Thus, in the old central planning mechanism bureaucrats enhanced their own economic position by intervening in the activities of enterprises. Many of the bureaucrats had a large web of personal inter-relationships and hence a micro-economic sub-culture had developed of bureaucratic interdependence. This 'old boy' network could be used to good effect by the bureaucrats to claim various property rights over enterprises being privatized.

Intense debates developed concerning the proper role for the state and the means by which privatization should be implemented. Frequently, the debate was conducted in terms of a trade-off between the need for efficiency versus social equality. Within the ensuing process of negotiation various vested interests appeared. In Poland, for instance, the idea of the 'Bermuda Triangle' has been evoked, i.e. that the triangle of enterprise managers, trade unions

[2] While the authors acknowledge that corruption was a serious problem even under the former centrally planned regimes, the sheer value of assets currently being privatized mean that the opportunities and hence temptation for corruption are far greater now than in the former period.

and worker collectives hijacked the discussion of privatization. Each had an incentive to ensure that the official 'large' privatization programs were delayed. Workers feared that privatization would lose them their jobs, trade unions feared a loss in members and enterprise managers feared a loss of their own influence (Bienkowski 1992). Bolton and Roland (1992) have similarly seen the process as a battle for the economic rent derived for the sale of state assets, a battle which has served to confuse and hence delay the privatization process.

For the former centrally planned economies the need for a strong government in setting the legislative framework for privatization is even more acute than in Western countries, as the state apparatus is not used to implementing policy independently. Without clearly-defined limits on the power of the state apparatus, that apparatus is liable either to be confused by the privatization process or else, in the newly created environment of personal gain, to abuse the privatization program for its own advantage. But in the former centrally planned economies, governments are typically weak.

Weak governments have proved unable to overcome one of the most serious problems which has unexpectedly paralysed the entire privatization process, the problem of establishing clearly defined ownership rights over former state property prior to privatization. Intense battles have often been fought between regions and levels of government with regard to the ownership of 'state' assets. The problem has been exacerbated as various levels of government have seen their revenue sources eroded in the course of economic reforms. These legal (and political) battles over pre-privatization ownership have often caused as much disruption and debate as the actual process of privatization.

That privatization is a lucrative business, there is no doubt. It involves the sale of assets worth billions of dollars. Since many deals have been negotiated with foreign multi-national companies, for bureaucrats participating in the negotiation process these have provided extensive opportunities for self-enrichment, including accepting bribes, and opportunities for career advancement through being head-hunted by international corporations. The result has been to over-bureaucratize and complicate the privatization process. Every bureaucrat has wanted to be involved in the privatization process in some way. Being seen as important and hence being able to influence a particular privatization has given an individual an ability to earn a return from the privatization process. The problem is made worse by the inability of government to provide clear directives to the state apparatus regarding both the current ownership, and the means of privatization, of state assets. As a result a twilight zone between the state and market has developed under which enterprise management and the state bureaucracy have been able to profit greatly.

Large privatizations have been delayed. On the other hand lots of small, local-level shady deals have been negotiated. Thus, state-owned enterprise management have frequently privatized parts of enterprises for self-enrichment under the eyes and tacit approval of the state bureaucracy, whose officials were then rewarded for looking the other way. Thus state enterprises have often become shells for a whole host of private economic activity.

The result of this process has been to produce a dual-level process of privatization. On the one hand bureaucratic competition has delayed the privatization of large and medium sized enterprises. But in the meantime the small privatization has proceeded apace. Often the small privatization has resulted in the further development of the black economy. For the state itself the result has been disastrous. The state sector has gradually become more inefficient, with the back-door sale of many of its best assets, while the emerging private sector has increasingly been driven underground. In most countries, official state revenues from privatization have been minimal. Hence taxes on 'official' enterprises have had to be increased to maintain overall revenues. Not surprisingly, this has increased the incentives for business to go 'underground' or operate in the 'grey' or 'black' markets, with the result that a dual economy has developed.

In the former centrally planned economies, there is apparently only a limited possibility to choose positions between the extremes of comprehensive state control and no state control. Such conflicts have arisen for example in connection with the Hungarian privatization process. Thus, as demands for increased state regulation of privatization to avoid *nomenklatura* privatization intensify, complaints about the excessive dominance of the old state apparatus are also widespread. This dominance, extending into new areas, is seen as increasingly stifling initiative and as presenting a possible threat to nascent democracy itself.

In effect, the response to criticism of spontaneous privatization has been to delay the implementation of the official privatization programs and the political arena has become immersed in intense and protracted debate as to the future course and underlying philosophy of privatization. In the meantime the process of spontaneous privatization has continued, but perhaps in a worse form, with the same elite strata of state and former state officials benefiting enormously.

The main argument against *nomenklatura* or spontaneous privatization has been that it enables former communists and those who have made their money in the black market to dominate the privatization process. The desire to avoid this and to bring about a fairer, more socially just privatization process has pushed the state into increased intervention in the privatization process, as mentioned earlier. But determining what might be socially just is not easy, and it is not clear that privatization should be the principal means of securing social justice. Also, whatever privatization strategy is pursued in the former centrally planned economies, whether state-administered, spontaneous privatization or else a voucher-type program allowing for the widest possible participation in the process, the same elite group in society will come out on top. In the former CSFR privatization scheme it is already becoming clear that those with inside information as to the best enterprises being sold are at a distinct advantage. These people are typically the same individuals who were or are part of the state apparatus and who were formerly criticized for being part of the spontaneous privatization strategy. So the result of attempts to curb the so-called wild privatizations may well simply be to delay the whole privatization program, without changing its end result.

The process of spontaneous privatization, which the state is powerless to stop, can also be seen in terms of the elites engaging in a process of primitive capital accumulation. In this case the accumulation is the appropriation of former state assets at very favorable prices. While, for the long-term development of these economies, such capital accumulation is essential, what is important is how that currently taking place is being used. Unfortunately, given the very unstable economic and political conditions in the former centrally planned economies, these primitive accumulators are typically investing in the non-productive sphere of these economies. The result can probably best be described as a process of asset-stripping of the state sector for non-productive investment. As evidence of this point one has only to look at the emerging structure of private business in the former centrally planned economies, which is primarily based in the services, trade and retail sectors, with very little in manufacturing as yet.

This suggests that governments, far from trying to ensure a more equitable distribution of assets in the privatization process, an honorable aim which is proving difficult to organize and implement—and which in any case will still result in the elites acquiring the majority of assets—should concentrate instead on stabilizing the economic and political environment in these economies. This would then ensure that more of the primitive capital accumulation that is occurring is directed towards productive investment.

This conception of the state's role, both allowing spontaneous privatization and intervening in the macro-management of the economy rather as Western governments regulate the market environment, could be considered rather naive. As the state is unable to intervene to regulate privatization effectively, because of its inflexibility and the predominance of private interests which corrupt the process, the same questions should be raised about its ability to manage macro-policy, too. However, there is an important difference between privatization policy and macroeconomic policy. This is that the latter is not directed at specific economic agents, but is concerned with wider issues of tax rates, interest rates, the exchange rate and so on, which are intended to apply equally to all agents in the economy. This being so, there is neither the incentive nor the opportunity for firms to lobby government for special treatment, and the scope for corruption is relatively limited (though not, unfortunately, entirely absent, since old habits die hard and some firms do still act as if they regarded macroeconomic policy as a personal attack on them, and seek special dispensations from tax rules).

Already, in a number of former centrally planned economies, governments are realizing that the state apparatus, through the various privatization agencies, is not proving effective in the implementation of privatization. However, it remains to be seen how far the state can truly step back from the privatization program and allow such spontaneous privatization when it comes to large and medium-sized enterprises and those which, if privatized, would undoubtedly face bankruptcy. In a recent paper Bolton and Roland (1992) argue that the most efficient and optimal means of disposal of state assets in the former centrally planned economies is through the sale of assets to the highest bidder. This is qualified in that to facilitate a more equitable distribution of state property, i.e. to reduce the tendency to *nomenklatura* privatization, and also to maximize the long-run stream of state income the state should encourage non-cash bids for state assets. Thus the state, through a state privatization agency, would offer an asset for sale and the tender offering the highest discounted stream of future income to the state for that asset would win the right to purchase the asset. Self-selection would ensure that those bidding for assets would be those most able to manage them efficiently, and not necessarily those able to pay immediately. The role of the state apparatus in this process would be to act as the arbiter in the process of bidding.

However, while theoretically appealing, the above argument ignores the reality of the state apparatus in the former centrally planned economies. It assumes that the state apparatus is largely incorruptible and that the government seeks to maximize the long-term returns to the state exchequer. On the first point, given the current chaos in the state apparatus, the ability of that apparatus to administer such a program in the even-handed pragmatic manner it requires could be questioned. The tendency would be for the process to become over-bureaucratized and corrupt. On the second point, in the case of the currently weak governments in the former centrally planned economies, with state revenues dwindling and political futures in the balance, governments can be assumed to have a very high discount rate on future earnings from privatization. In this situation their objectives will be to maximize the current earnings from privatization. Hence they can be expected to prefer bids for state assets which offer immediate or short-term returns.

Case Studies: Hungary, the CSFR, Poland and Russia

Hungary

In the case of Hungary, several factors determined—and to some extent limited—the specific options open to the first post-communist government with regard to the privatization of state-owned assets.

A major consideration was Hungary's commitment to service its substantial inherited external debt (the highest per capita in the region) and thus, it was hoped, retain and build on its already considerable standing in the international financial and business community as a comparatively stable and welcoming destination for foreign investment. This commitment meant that the option of a voucher-style free distribution of shares in former state assets was not so readily available to Hungary. In the former Czechoslovakia, in contrast, where foreign debt was minimal, the pressure to maximize revenue from privatization was considerably lower.

Revenue-centered privatization had wider implications also with respect to the role of the government and to the development of the types of institutions and transaction mechanisms which would be required to administer it. On the one hand it effectively tied the government and its administration into the privatization process, thus leaving it exposed to accusations of political manipulation and making it potentially more difficult for the government to reform the public-sector budget. In fact the long-awaited and necessary budget reform measures have so far failed to materialize. At the same time, given the administrative requirements of this form of privatization, the process could easily tend to become over-bureaucratic and lacking in transparency—as indeed happened in the case of Hungary, although measures allowing decentralization of the privatization process have since been put in place ('self-privatization') and appear to have eased the situation somewhat.

Another factor which had a major influence on the way in which Hungary's privatization developed was the legacy of 20 years of economic reform, a process which had begun in 1968 with the introduction of the New Economic Mechanism. The New Economic Mechanism and subsequent reforms, although in terms of their original aims only partially successful, had done much to change the patterns of economic organization and behavior in Hungary, and to change the forms of involvement of the government and the state apparatus in the microeconomic sphere.

In the mid- to late 1980s Hungary set up enterprise councils in all but the largest firms and then passed a new Company Law and Transformation Law to govern conversions of state-owned firms to Western-type company forms. Both liberal economists and the government itself regarded the introduction of the Company Law as a logical and necessary continuation of the on-going process of reform, the process of moving away from centralized planning towards a devolution of power from state apparatus to enterprises, and as a means of ensuring that the limited results of the earlier devolution of control would be improved upon by forcing the enterprises into new patterns of behavior. However, the ownership rights of the state and the enterprises were left unclarified at this stage, and this was to cause problems later as the wave of enterprise transformations quickly became immersed in controversy and was dubbed 'spontaneous privatization.' Fears grew that the old, party-appointed enterprise managers were exploiting their positions and connections to perpetuate their power and secure an income for themselves.

Enterprises under the direct control of the state administration were bound by law to seek ministerial approval of their transformation plans. In general, however, the ministries simply approved the plans submitted, occasionally setting conditions on the transformation, although these tended to be general rather than specific to each case, e.g. that the transformation should not affect export and other contractual commitments. The government administration also had the option of placing an enterprise council-run firm under ministerial control; this procedure was required by law in the cases where the enterprise's assets were to be sold to a foreign investor in their entirety.

Interventions of this type, for example in the case of the Nagykanizsa Brewery (Havas 1990), and that of the Ganz Electricity Measuring Factory, failed to result in a successful sale transaction, and the transformed companies' shares were eventually handed over to the State Property Agency. Such interventions, even where a sale was completed, were also criticized on the grounds that the approach taken by government bodies was scarcely different from to that of the enterprises: publicity was avoided, prospective investors were not invited to compete, and the selling price tended to be undervalued or at least questionable.

In addition, there were numerous cases of enterprises facing bankruptcy or liquidation, where transformation was managed directly by government institutions (the Rehabilitation Organization (Szanáló Szervezet), Finance Ministry and branch ministries). However, even in these cases the role of the enterprises was important, while that of the state institutions seems to have been either relatively passive or extremely ineffectual.

Thus, although the state was neither absent nor simply a passive onlooker in the process of enterprise transformation, it is clear that attitudes on the part of state representatives to intervening in the process were ambivalent and that, in cases where the state did intervene, this had little impact on the decisions or actions of the enterprise management. In practice, this gave enterprise managers immense power and enabled them to devise ways of acquiring large stakes in formerly state-owned firms, sometimes resulting in major public scandals.

The resulting outcry reinforced the idea of establishing a body to manage state assets. Draft legislation on the State Property Fund, on the management of state assets, and also for the privatization of retail, catering and consumer services outlets, was ready in November 1989, bearing the title 'Ownership Reform and Privatization Program.' The new body came into being on March 1, 1990, with the somewhat altered title of State Property Agency, under the chairmanship of István Tömpe, who had been the government's Privatization Commissioner. Its primary task was to supervise the transformation of state enterprises and to safeguard state assets from plundering through 'spontaneous' privatization. As the new coalition government under József Antall developed its strategy on privatization and the State Property Agency began its 'active' privatization programs in summer 1990, the debate flared up again regarding the role of the state and the accountability of its agent, the State Property Agency, in its dealings with enterprise management and investors. There were accusations of shady deals; some were certainly badly managed by the still inexperienced State Property Agency, while the lack of consolidated government strategy and legislation made matters even more difficult. There were calls for the 'privatization of privatization'; for leaving privatization to market forces, for encouraging competition in the privatization process, for increasing the role of financial intermediaries such as commercial banks in managing privatization transactions and reducing that of the various departments of the State Property Agency, which in the meantime was consolidating its internal structure and refining its methods of operation. Others continued to argue that until real owners and real investors appeared on the scene, and until the legislation and institutions of a market economy were in place and operational, some degree of supervision and planned, 'active' privatization on the part of the government, via the State Property Agency, were needed.

The State Property Agency managed to fend off most of its critics, but the progress of privatization through the State Property Agency's programs remained slow, hampered by the difficulties in valuing assets and by bureaucracy, as well as by the lack of investors, especially on the domestic market. In summer 1991 the State Property Agency announced its intention to initiate a program of 'self-privatization,' making it compulsory for small and medium-sized enterprises to transform and privatize by the end of March 1993 with the assistance of independent consultants selected by the State Property Agency, but without close supervision. The State Property Agency had recognized early on that 'the role of enterprise-initiated self privatization—or so-called spontaneous privatization—has been the most significant.' The same report, detailing the activities of the State Property Agency during its first six months of operation, described at some length the problems of 'administratively prescribed and enforced privatization' and advocated giving priority to finding means of 'making the process of spontaneous privatization smoother and better organised.' There was clearly a need to harness the momentum of spontaneous privatization, and the use of decentralized methods, regulating the activities of the intermediaries in the process by means of a contract and offering financial incentives for rapid conclusion of the privatization deal, seemed the most logical solution. The fact that 'market' intermediaries were involved meant that privatization would itself be privatized, i.e. self-regulating, supervised by a government agency but avoiding the need for heavy-handed state intervention. The Hungarian public would be reassured that abuses of power by former *nomenklatura* managers had been brought under control, the political opposition would be appeased by the 'market-oriented' rather than state-run solution, since they had long feared the centralizing tendencies of the Antall government, and it was hoped that this de-bureaucratization would speed up the process of privatization and halt the rapid decline in value of state assets caused by the delay.

It is possible that this decentralizing drive was also a response to the acrimonious criticism to which the State Property Agency was subjected at the time. Thus the Finance Minister, Mihály Kupa, in a supplement to his 4-year economic program, anticipated the direction of the government's privatization strategy (Karsai 1992), including the setting up of a separate government body, the State Ownership Institute, which would divest the State Property Agency of decision-making powers over some state assets (Figyelö 1991, 28: 13). The concept of the State Ownership Institute gave rise to heated debate; the State Property Agency published a report (Figyelö 1991, 28: 14) defending its activities, disputing the logic of the Finance Ministry and warning of the danger that setting up a new and all-powerful institution would mean not a devolution or redistribution of power, but an even greater centralization or stratification of the privatization process than the State Property Agency had often been accused of. The Finance Minister now came under attack from many quarters, suspected of attempting to bring privatization under his direct control and thus build up a dangerous concentration of power (Kocsis 1991a).

After a period of uncomfortable silence on the issue of privatization in early autumn, the Finance Ministry finally published its draft 'Government Strategy on Ownership and Privatization' in September 1991. The preamble of this document stated that 'privatization cannot be based on centralized considerations ...the power-base of the state supervisory system set up eighteen months ago has already become too broad...,' and the bill outlined proposals for establishing a State Ownership body to separate institutionally 'the task of exercising state ownership and that of executing privatization,' as well as stressing the need for a simplified privatization process. Rounds of ministerial bargaining then ensued to reach agreement on the nature and status of the proposed State Ownership Institute, and it was finally agreed that the new body should have responsibility for managing assets which are to remain in state ownership in the longer term. A list of these was to be drawn up by the various ministries for government approval. Meanwhile the State Property Agency, in somewhat modified form, would continue as a separate entity, alongside rather than responsible to the State Ownership Institute, taking responsibility for privatization.

The next stage of the debate was concerned with two main issues:

1. The organizational framework of the State Ownership Institute; whether it should be a traditional budget-funded government institution, or whether, following the model of some Western countries, it should be a commercial holding company. Under a barrage of objections to the first alternative, mainly on the grounds that it would provide the government administration with too many opportunities to influence the State Ownership Institute, and therefore also the sectors of the economy under its management, the government opted for the latter (Kocsis 1991b). Many economists in Hungary had reservations, however, since the leadership of the new State Ownership Company was to be selected by the Prime Minister, and although it would be more difficult to dictate from above the economic factors of the individual firms, there appeared to be little safeguard against politically-influenced redistribution of revenue from these companies. Despite these reservations, however, legislation on the new organization was passed by Parliament in summer, 1992, and the 'giant holding company' began operations in October under the name of the State Asset Management Company.

2. The second bone of contention was the reasoning behind the proposals from the ministries regarding which enterprises or 'strategic' sectors to retain in state ownership, the problem of the extent to which political and personal interests may influence the drafting of the list, rather than 'strategic' considerations—if such could be said to exist at the time—and the problem of the likely effect and possible dangers for the economy of long term state ownership in general (Karsai 1992). This latter issue was settled in late 1992, with the decision to assign to State Asset Management Company 160 companies, including some of the largest energy conglomerates and public utilities, with assets worth almost half of the total estimated to belong to the state sector.

While the State Asset Management Company has the right to privatize firms under its management and the list of corporate assets to be retained by the state in the longer term is to be reviewed every two years, it is now clear that a substantial proportion of state-owned assets are unlikely to be privatized for some time. Despite uncertainties regarding how the new organization will operate and how efficiently it will interact with the State Property Agency, the establishment of the State Asset Management Company represents a significant change in perception of the privatization process; in effect, it is a recognition of the fact that many original assumptions concerning the speed and sequencing of privatization were over-optimistic, even naive. It is now accepted that many firms will remain wholly or partly in state ownership for some time, and that the issue of how to manage these assets should be addressed separately from that of privatization.

Politically, the establishment of the State Asset Management Company in the form of a single giant holding company with the state as its exclusive shareholder met with a less than favorable response. It was seen, even by many economists, as a manifestation of the Antall government's ambivalence towards market-oriented reform, and of its reluctance to disengage itself and the state apparatus from economic life. Coming when it did, with the public sector budget deficit set to soar to three times that planned for 1992, and revenue from the State Asset Management Company to the budget pinned in advance at HUF 34bn for its first year of operation, the government could certainly expect to gain more than simply a pragmatic solution to the problem of longer-term asset management.

Compared with the situation a year previously, it now seemed to be the State Property Agency which was most consistently supporting and encouraging 'market' privatization, and trying to resist attempts on the part of the coalition government to bring the process under greater state control. The State Property Agency appeared to be reconsidering its own privatization programs in a self-critical manner, and announced ambitious plans to extend its 'self-privatization' program to around half of all state enterprises. It countered demands from the government for increased property protection measures with the argument that the most effective way to ensure this was to increase competition among the potential buyers on the privatization market; the only way to do this, Csepi argued, was to foster demand, both within Hungary and among foreign investors. The State Property Agency advocated pumping more of the revenue from privatization back into the economy rather than siphoning it off to fund state debts. It proposed using some of the revenue to create the funds needed to provide guarantees and collateral for privatization loans, to create reorganization funds to enable old enterprises to restructure, and to set up a fund to support activities aimed at environmental protection and job creation.

It was also felt that one of the reasons for renewed demands for a return to state-controlled asset management might be the lack of success in attracting domestic investors to purchase former state assets; this in turn was due at least in part to the nature of the credit schemes set up with the intention of promoting domestic demand on the privatization market. The conditions imposed on these loans generally proved too severe for the potential Hungarian investors and business-persons, who had very little capital and were extremely cautious, often preferring to set up new businesses rather than to buy former state assets.

The CSFR

In the former centrally planned economies, identifying an optimal privatization program has been seen as an almost mythical promised land. Of all the former centrally planned economies in transition, the greatest hopes for finding this optimal path have recently rested with the former CSFR and now, since the breakup of that country, with the Czech republic and its voucher privatization program. In the second section we argued that the state was responsible for setting the legislative and regulatory framework for privatization but that market institutions should be used to sell state assets. The former CSFR voucher privatization scheme comes closest to this model. Thus the state has established the legal and administrative framework surrounding the voucher scheme, including who is entitled to vouchers, the form of their distribution, their value and so on.[3] While in theory market driven, the bidding procedure entails a very sophisticated role for the state in deciding which bids for individual state assets should be accepted and at what price.

To avoid excessive informational asymmetry as between the firms being 'sold' and the 8,5 million individual voucher holders, the former CSFR, and now the Czech republic, has allowed private investment funds or trusts to be established. So far, over 450 have been registered and some 430 are actively operating. Thus individual citizens can entrust their vouchers to these funds in exchange for a pre-specified rate of return. Investment funds then use their accumulated stock of vouchers to bid for shares in the firms being privatized. This decentralized approach contrasts with that adopted in Poland, where it was envisaged that there would only be a few investment funds, set up at government initiative.

Some 2,523 companies were to be sold via the voucher privatization method with a book value of capital of 260 billion Koruna ($ 9,2 billion) (Havel and Kukla 1992). In theory, the advantage of the scheme is that it will allow the rapid transfer of a large number of state enterprises into the private sector. Thus, in the longer term the state's role in the management of enter-

[3] To facilitate the privatization process the state has established, as have other former Centrally Planned Economies, a state agency to administer privatization, the National Property Fund.

prise activity should be limited. But it remains to be seen how successful the scheme will be. On paper it appears to offer voucher holders large returns from their initial small outlay. Thus with 260 billion Koruna of assets to be sold by voucher privatization to 8,5 million voucher holders, this suggests a return of over 30,500 Koruna ($ 1,089) per voucher book from an initial outlay of only 1,035 Koruna ($ 36); it is, of course, highly uncertain how much of this value can be realized.

There is concern that many of the new investment trusts are aiming to purchase state enterprises with the intention of carrying out asset-stripping activities. Such concern is strengthened by the quite unreasonable promises made to investors by some trusts. The best known investment trust, the Harvard Investment Fund, offered to pay voucher holders ten times the initial cost of voucher books within one year. Such claims would be difficult to meet without selling off privatized assets, and buyers might not be easy to find. If, as a result of the current recession in the former CSFR, a large number of the enterprises sold through the voucher scheme go bankrupt then large sections of the population stand to lose, or feel that they have lost from the scheme. This could undermine popular support for privatization in the former CSFR. Moreover, if investment funds fail to meet their pledges, there would be considerable pressure on the state effectively to re-nationalize at least some former state enterprises and bail out loss-making investment funds, both to avoid disenchantment on the part of voucher holders and to avoid the large increases in unemployment which would otherwise follow.[4]

The former CSFR faced strong pressure to regulate the activities of the new Investment Funds as concerns grew over their ability to meet their pledged returns to voucher holders. Such regulation would represent a role for the state very much in line with that which occupies the state in developed market economies and cannot be used as ammunition against the privatization process. Indeed, by summer 1992 regulations were introduced under which the more obviously fraudulent funds, such as the Harvard Fund noted above, quickly disappeared from the scene or changed the way they operated.

By December 1992 about 93% of the shares of the 1,500 enterprises sold in the first wave of voucher privatization had been allocated to individuals and investment funds and almost all voucher points had been spent. However, the break-up of the former CSFR into separate Czech and Slovak republics has caused some considerable disruption to the whole voucher program and underlines the importance of the point made earlier in this chapter of the need for a stable and strong government actively supporting privatization. Due to

[4] Bolton and Roland (1992) cite the example of the Chilean privatization program in the 1980s where the state was forced to bail out loss-making banking groups owning stakes in privatized state assets.

the more profitable nature of enterprises in the Czech republic, more Slovak citizens have invested voucher points in the Czech republic than vice-versa and, as a result of this, the Czech republic has demanded compensation from Slovakia. Both republics are now formulating their own separate privatization programs, with Slovakia looking set to abandon voucher privatization completely. For its part the Czech republic has announced plans for a second round of voucher privatization.

Poland

Although initial targets set for privatization in Poland were ambitious, the actual implementation of privatization thus far has been disappointing, with the exception of the so-called 'small privatization' of shops and small-scale service establishments. Thus the initial objective of the Mazowiecki government, which was subsequently accepted by both the Bielecki and Olszewski governments, was to privatize half of the state sector by 1993 (Slay 1992).

In many ways Poland reflects the model of the privatization process sketched earlier. Initially privatization followed the spontaneous path which resulted in popular demands for increased state regulation over the privatization process. The government reacted in August 1990 with the creation of the Ministry for Ownership Transformation, set up to oversee the entire privatization process. A number of privatization strategies were outlined, including plans for a former CSFR-style voucher privatization but with an expanded role for investment funds. In the meantime privatization proceeded both with a British-style series of showcase sales of enterprises by public offering and through privatization through liquidation. However, in the event, the state apparatus has proved unable or unwilling to carry out a large scale program of public offerings and only a score or so state enterprises of the 157 initially identified for sale by this means had been sold.

In order to speed up the privatization process the Bielecki government announced details of the Polish voucher-style program in June 1991. 400 of the largest Polish companies were to be transformed into joint stock companies and then 60% of the shares in these enterprises were to be allocated between 20 or so investment trusts. Shares in these investment trusts would then be allocated to 28 million Polish adults free of charge. These relatively large trusts were expected to exert ownership control over privatized enterprises, so encouraging their efficient performance. Of the remaining 40% of shares in these enterprises, 30% would be retained by the state for sale at a future date and the other 10% was earmarked for allocation, free of charge, to each enterprise's workforce.

In the event the Polish voucher scheme has failed to get off the ground for a number of reasons. The deteriorating condition of the state budget caused by the recession increased the pressure on the government to move away from the free distribution of shares towards their sale. Additionally, as the recession deepened, many of the enterprises identified for the voucher privatization scheme were close to bankruptcy and hardly presented sound financial investments for potential buyers. There was also concern about the inflationary effects of giving away vouchers which in theory could then be redeemed for cash. Subsequently the Polish parliament rejected the program on March 18, 1993.

The inability of the state apparatus to handle the privatization of large and medium sized enterprises, given the problem of valuing enterprises without the benefit of well-functioning stock markets, led to the formulation of a sector-orientated privatization policy from July 1991 onwards. Here foreign consultancy firms were to be employed to establish privatization strategies for particular sectors of the economy. By December 1991, 250 firms had been identified for privatization by this means with the possibility of a further 342 others at a later stage (Slay 1992). In the event the sectoral privatization program has failed to live up to expectations and few enterprises have been privatized by this means. The main reason explaining the demise of sector privatization was the failure of the Ministry of Ownership Transformation and the Ministry of Industry and Trade to agree on its implementation (Slay 1993).

Privatization through the sectoral approach has been closely linked with industrial policy and the desire to restructure enterprises prior to privatization. In many respects this reflects the changing ideology within the Polish economic reform strategy. Initially, under the so-called Balcerowicz 'shock therapy' approach to economic reform, there was a belief that only by fully opening the economy to market forces could reforms be pushed through against the delaying tactics of the bureaucratic state apparatus. However, as the economic recession deepened in Poland, it was realized that this strategy could produce the catastrophic bankruptcy of large sections of Polish industry. As a result of the new emphasis on the need for restructuring prior to privatization a new strategy of so-called 'restructuring privatization' has been developed (Slay 1993). Here managers bid for the right to manage an enterprise over the transition period prior to privatization by proposing restructuring plans for enterprises. The successful bid is the plan seen to provide the optimal restructuring path for the particular enterprise as determined by the Ministry of Transformation. The winning management bid must put a downpayment of 5% of the book value of the enterprise prior to restructuring the enterprise, but this is redeemable should the restructuring plan be successful in meeting its targets. The management group receives a share of the increase in the value of the enterprise as a result of the implementation of the restructuring program.

Restructuring privatization suggests a combination of state and private sector involvement in the privatization process but still places a relatively large burden on the Ministry of Ownership Transformation in successfully evaluating management bids. In the event few bids for this form of privatization have been received, possibly due to the absence of high-quality Polish management able to implement such restructuring programs (Slay 1993).

At the time of writing, it remains unclear what form of privatization strategy will emerge in Poland, following the apparent failure of the policies pursued in the last two years. The latest privatization 'craze' in Poland appears to be based upon a social contract between workers, management and government for determining the form of privatization for state-owned enterprises. Here the inability of the Polish government to obtain majority support in parliament for economic reform proposals has ensured that the privatization strategy being pursued is based on this kind of compromise. The success of such a policy remains seriously in doubt, however, as the objectives of the different groups engaged in deciding on the form of privatization are likely to differ and hence obtaining agreement on the form of privatization could prove to be a long drawn-out process.

Russia

While we stressed the importance of clear government priorities and strong guidance from government in the conduct of privatization, in the states of the former Soviet Union this strong political direction has been woefully lacking. In Russia, for example, one only has to observe the recent conflict for political power between the Russian parliament, led by Ivan Khasbulatov, and the embattled government of the President Boris Yeltsin. The privatization program of Russia, as with economic reform in general, is being thrown into confusion by the war of laws between these two institutions of the state.[5] This confusion can be resolved only by a clear differentiation of power between the two bodies, and yet despite numerous presidential decrees and the April 1993 referendum this problem remains seemingly intractable. The only light on the horizon remains that the parliament will accept, given the moral victory of Yeltsin in the April referendum, a compromise constitution proposed by the President, in which the power of parliament vis-à-vis the government would be much reduced.

[5] This new war of laws has replaced the earlier war of laws between the Union government led by Gorbachev and the Russian government led by President Yeltsin. This earlier battle served to delay the process of reform and privatization in Russia for the first 8 months of 1991.

Privatization policy has also proved more contentious in the former Soviet Union than elsewhere because of conflicts between the regions and newly independent republics themselves. In particular the question of ownership rights over state assets formerly belonging to the Union level government has proved difficult to resolve. Under Soviet rule many enterprises under the jurisdiction of Union level ministries had assets spread over a number of republics. With the disintegration of the Soviet Union the newly independent republics claimed ownership rights over all assets located in their republics. Privatizing enterprises in this situation has proved difficult, although with the acceptance by the Russian Federation of responsibility for the external hard currency debt of the former Soviet Union in exchange for ownership rights over Soviet assets, this problem has been mitigated somewhat.

The state structure in the former Soviet Union is not capable of carrying out a set-piece privatization program on the model of the U.K. experience. The lack of a clearly defined legislative framework for privatization means that much of the privatization thus far has been of the *nomenklatura* type (Tedstrom 1992). Corruption is rife and large-scale *nomenklatura* profiteering can hardly be avoided. Numerous large-scale corruption cases have recently come to light.

The basic law governing privatization in the Russian Federation stems from the *Law on the Privatization of State and Municipal Enterprises in Russia* of July 1991. This has since been substantially amended by the document, *Fundamental Provisions of the Russian Federation's Program for the Privatization of State and Municipal Property in 1992*, signed by President Yeltsin on December 31, 1991, and by the decree signed by Yeltsin a month later *On the Acceleration of the Privatization of State and Municipal Enterprises*, and a much updated law on privatization in the Russian Federation was approved by the Russian Federation parliament on June 5, 1992.[6] This hotchpotch of legislation makes the Federal State Assets Management Committee responsible for the development and implementation of the privatization program as well as for preparing assets for privatization. The actual disposal of state assets is handled by the Russian Federation State Asset Fund and its local agents. Local privatization programs are developed and implemented by city and regional administrations within the Russian Federation through the creation of Federal State Assets Management Committees and Russian Federation State Asset Funds at the Autonomous republic, Krai, Oblast, Raion, city and local levels.

Federal and Regional State Assets Management Committees are jointly responsible for identifying state assets to be privatized and for deciding the

[6] See Ash and Lewis (1992), for a review.

means of privatization. However, it is also possible for foreign and Russian individuals and enterprises to initiate privatizations of Russian Federation state property by applying to the relevant Federal State Assets Management Committee. There are, however, quite stringent rules concerning the scope of foreign participation in the privatization process.

Once an asset has been identified as being subject to privatization, a privatization committee is established to oversee the privatization process and present a privatization plan to the relevant level of the Federal State Assets Management Committee. Enterprise privatization committees are composed of representatives of the relevant level Federal State Assets Management Committees, workers' councils, local authorities, representatives of the anti-monopoly commission and other appointed 'experts'(sic). Given the relatively low rates of pay in the state administration responsible for privatization compared to the private sector, the inducement to corruption faced by officials would appear to be high.

It is the duty of the Federal State Assets Management Committees to determine how individual enterprises should be sold within the framework established in the basic law on the privatization of state and municipal enterprises. However, numerous means of sale are available depending upon the size and type of enterprise concerned. These include: sale by auction, tender, share flotations and a new innovation of a competitive tender where the winning tender is not necessarily that offering the best price but that which meets a number of conditions attached to the sale, e.g. the maintenance of employment rates, investment, etc. Numerous schemes are available allowing preferential share purchases by current and former employees.

The actual implementation of privatization plans for individual enterprises is to be the responsibility of the Russian Federation State Asset Fund. Where the preferred means of sale is through a share issue after the transformation of the state enterprise into a joint stock company, the Russian Federation State Asset Funds for each particular enterprise are allocated a tranche of shares in the newly formed joint stock company. Through this controlling share issue, the Russian Federation State Asset Funds initially run the joint stock company until control is divested to new shareholders.

Income received from the privatization of enterprises is allocated to municipal, oblast and federal budgets depending upon which of these levels is deemed to have formerly owned the enterprises concerned. For example, of the income received from the privatization of enterprises formerly owned by municipal bodies, 50% is to be allocated to municipal budgets, 10% each to the oblast and federal budgets and also 10% to the workers' collective of the privatized enterprise. The largest share, 50%, is thus to go to the budget of the administration formerly owning the enterprise; where this is the republican government the share is to be 60%. Monies distributed to work collectives are allocated to workers in accordance with the collectives' wishes. The Russian Federation State Asset Funds are financed through a levy on the income received from the privatization of enterprises. The Federal State Assets Management Committee itself is financed through the state budget.

There is obviously potential for conflict between different administrative levels which will compete for the ownership rights and therefore revenue earned from the privatization of enterprises. The Federal State Assets Management Committee is responsible for identifying the 'owners' of the state assets to be privatized but the process is likely to be complex and time-consuming. There is also great confusion over the roles of the Federal State Assets Management Committees and the Russian Federation State Asset Funds, with the two sets of bodies expected to negotiate about the division of responsibilities between them (Commersant 23, 1992: 25).

Following the perceived success of the voucher privatization in the former CSFR, the Russian Federation introduced its own version of mass privatization in the Autumn of 1992. All 148 million citizens of the Russian Federation, upon registration, received a book of vouchers with a nominal value of 10,000 rubles, which could then be used to bid for shares in enterprises subject to privatization. Vouchers are freely tradable and can be used in various ways to purchase shares in enterprises subject to privatization. For example, voucher holders can bid for shares in a series of voucher auctions where shares in some 5,000 medium and large enterprises are currently being put up for sale. Workers in enterprises subject to sale can also use vouchers as part payment for shares in their enterprises. Thus far the results of voucher privatization are difficult to measure. 97% of the eligible population have registered and received vouchers. The first voucher auctions were held in December 1992 and by May 1993 the plan was for a total of more than 700 such auctions to be held.

The future of voucher privatization has however been thrown into some confusion as a result of the political power battle between the parliament and the government. The parliament opposes a mass privatization program, preferring worker/management buyouts, and in a number of legislative acts passed prior to the April 25, 1993, referendum, instructed the Federal State Assets Management Committee to halt the mass voucher privatization.

It is however interesting to note that even the current Yeltsin-approved privatization program allows for significant worker/management participation in privatization. In practice, of the state enterprises that are currently being sold through a share flotation, most appear to have chosen a privatization path which firmly places the management and workforce in a dominant ownership position, owning a majority of shares. The implications of this, given the experience of worker self-management in former Yugoslavia, are that enterprise efficiency will improve only gradually, if at all.

In conclusion, given the sheer number of state enterprises to be privatized in the Russian Federation and the political and legislative complexities which have arisen, first with the fragmentation of the Soviet Union and possibly in the future of the Russian Federation itself, and finally with the battle between the legislative and executive organs of power, the privatization process is certain to be difficult, confused and prolonged. The scope for *nomenklatura* corruption is immense, for although the legislative framework for privatization is being formulated surprisingly quickly, the 'hands on' experience of working with that legislation is limited. And even with the proper legislation in place, it is still uncertain whether the Russian Federation possesses either the political consensus or the administrative capacity to implement a successful former CSFR-style voucher privatization.

Conclusions

Here we briefly draw together some of the threads from the above argument, and consider them in the light of the actual institutions which are being established in former centrally planned economies to carry out their privatization programs.

This chapter has argued that the state apparatus in the former centrally planned economies is generally not up to the task of exerting a leading role in the privatization process on the lines of a planned privatization program. However, equally under-developed are the market institutions which have allowed the state apparatus in developed market economies to step back from large scale intervention in the privatization process. Whereas this might suggest that the state should intervene to take the place of the market in the former centrally planned economies, this option is not appropriate as the state apparatus has become largely inept and corrupt. The bureaucracy in effect is only interested in the privatization process as a means to generating additional private income.

Consequently, the second best option is to avoid excessive state intervention in the privatization process, while encouraging a largely marketized implementation.[7] This will then stimulate a healthy evolution of market institutions. Overall, therefore, we favor the continuation of spontaneous privatization but with the approval and hence within the regulatory framework of the state. Thus the role of the state apparatus should be a simplified one of regulating the environment in which spontaneous privatization proceeds. This we believe to be feasible, and capable of functioning in a way which limits

[7] As reflected in different ways in Hungary and the former CSFR, less so in Poland, and scarcely at all in the Russian Federation so far.

both the extent of corruption and the possibility of interest groups to block privatization.

References

Ash, T.N. and R.A. Lewis (1992) Recent Developments in Russian Privatization. *Survey of East European Law* 3: 3-13.

Bienkowski, W. (1992) Poland's Bermuda Triangle. *RFE/RL Research Report* 1(17): 22-24.

Bolton, P. and G. Roland (1992) The Economics of Mass Privatization: Czechoslovakia, East Germany, Hungary and Poland, paper prepared for the 15th Panel Meeting of Economic Policy in Lisbon on 2-3 April.

Havas, A. (1990) Keserü szájízzel. *Heti Világgazdaság* 6 (February 10): 67.

Havel, J. and E. Kukla (1992) Privatization and Investment Funds in Czechoslovakia. *RFE/RL Research Report* 1(17): 37-41.

Karsai, G. (1992) Törvényjavaslatok az állami vagyonról. *Figyelö* 36 (March 12): 1,4.

Kocsis, G. (1991a) Privatizációs kormánystratégia—A legnagyobb közös megosztó. *Heti Világgazdaság* 39 (September 28): 78.

Kocsis, G. (1991b) Allami Tulajdonosi Intézet—Vagyonkezelö központ. *Heti Világgazdaság* 48 (November 30): 78.

Kocsis, G. (1992) Allam és tulajdon—Poszt-kommunizmus. *Heti Világgazdaság* 5 (February 1): 7.

Slay, B. (1992) Poland: an Overview. *RFE/RL Research Report* 1(17): 15-21.

Slay, B. (1993) Evolution of Industrial Policy in Poland since 1989. *RFE/RL Research Report* 2(2): 21-28.

Tedstrom, J. (1992) Russia: Progress Report on Industrial Privatization. *RFE/RL Research Report* 1(17): 46-50.

Vickers, J. and G. Yarrow (1988) *Privatization: An Economic Analysis.* London: MIT Press.

Winiecki, J. (1991) Theoretical Underpinnings of the Privatization of State-owned Enterprises in Post-Soviet-type Economies. *Communist Economies and Economic Transformation* 3: 397-416.

8

Property Rights, Institutions, and Market Reform

Holger Schmieding

The debate on the appropriate role of the state in the transformation from socialism to a democratic and market-based society has three major facets. The first concerns the desirable endpoint of the transformation process, i.e. the role which should finally be assigned to the state in the new economic and political order that an ex-socialist country is trying to establish. The second facet concerns the possible role that a competent, determined and powerful government could and should play to ease the pains of transformation. The third facet transcends narrow economic theory; it focuses on the question whether and to what extent policy recommendations should be different for countries that, for the time being, have weak governments with largely incompetent bureaucracies.

Although the choice of the endpoint is indeed highly relevant for the discussion of how to get there, the first facet is not taken up in this chapter. In line with my classical liberal *Weltanschauung*, I simply assume that this role should be very limited indeed. I constrain myself to some notes on the second and third facets. To set the stage for the discussion, I start with a brief enquiry into the causes of the transformation crisis. The subsequent discussion puts particular emphasis on the role of the state in one of the most essential and controversial aspects of the transformation process, namely, the privatization of state-owned enterprises.

On the Nature of the Transformation Crisis

In stark contrast to initial expectations, the demise of socialism has so far caused a considerable slump in Europe's emerging market economies. Many

H. J. Blommestein and B. Steunenberg (eds.), Government and Markets, 159–173.

authors discussing this feature refer vaguely to some traditional arguments which are routinely employed to account for recessions in the West or the Third World, notably surprise disinflation, insufficient aggregate demand and the need for large-scale structural change. Other oft-mentioned suspects include the dismal legacy which socialism has left behind and the terms-of-trade shock delivered by the transition to world market prices in trade between emerging market economies in Europe. Institutional explanations, which also advanced at an early stage (see Murrell 1990; Schmieding 1991; Frydman and Rapaczynski 1991) have only recently received more attention.

The discussion on the sources of the transition crisis is often clouded by imprecise verbiage. Many authors fail to make sufficiently clear whether they are dealing with an issue of statistics, namely, the causes of a substantial fall in officially recorded output and GDP, or whether they are dealing with an issue of substance, namely, the causes of a genuine drop in aggregate value added, correctly measured at world market prices. Numerous authors (see, for instance, Lipton and Sachs 1990, Winiecki 1991) have pointed out that the official statistics are grossly misleading. To a considerable extent, the recorded fall in output and GDP mirrors the demise of those types of production which never possessed any positive value added if evaluated at world market prices. This fall in production actually leaves the economy, as a whole, better off than before. However, these arguments do not shed light on the theoretically far more fascinating question why the transition from inferior socialism to superior capitalism should go along with a temporary drop in correctly measured aggregate value added, i.e. with a transformation crisis. My subsequent discussion deals solely with possible causes for a genuine decline in aggregate value added (which would have to be measured at world market prices), and not with statistical oddities.[1]

[1] In the following exposition, I assume that the emerging market economies are engulfed in a genuine transformation crisis. Although the official statistics are grossly misleading, it is taken for granted that at least the negative sign of change as recorded in the statistics in the immediate aftermath of the collapse of socialism tends to indicate the direction in which genuine GDP has evolved. Even if this assumption turns out to be wrong, at least the institutional arguments presented below would not need to be discarded. The same arguments could still be employed to explain why opportunities for faster growth have not been exploited, despite the incentives that the sweeping liberalization has provided. The discussion in the following paragraphs draws on Schmieding (1993).

Some standard explanations for the transformation crisis can be dismissed almost out of hand:

1. The *legacy of socialism*, dismal as it may be, explains the low starting level of GDP and perhaps also a trend decline that may have set in before the regime switch. It cannot be employed, though, to account for the observation that the abolition of socialism seems to cause a fall in GDP.
2. The need for large-scale restructuring, great as it may be, also cannot account for a fall in GDP. Although *internal relative prices* (including non-monetary incentives and constraints) have changed dramatically to become more in line with world market relative prices, the *world market prices* have not. An emerging market economy could thus continue to produce whatever it produced before and attain the same level of real GDP as before without any structural change. Any supply response to the new and improved incentive system increases GDP.
3. My above argument implicitly assumes that factor prices are flexible. If *factor prices* were rigid, the adjustment of internal relative prices to unchanged world market prices could indeed cause a fall in GDP. The economy could no longer produce what it did before because some factors, resisting a detrimental change in relative factor prices within the country, would become unemployed. However, the most important factor price in this respect, the real wage, has been surprisingly flexible downwards in the emerging market economies in the initial phase of the transformation period (Schmieding 1993). Although factor price rigidity may play a residual role, it does not qualify as a major cause of the transformation crisis.
4. For the same reason, the slump in the emerging market economies can hardly be attributed to a *surprise disinflation*. The way in which a shock stabilization is usually perceived to affect output, namely, an unwarranted rise in real wages caused by backward-looking indexation or by inflationary expectations that the surprise disinflation renders excessive, is belied by the actual degree of real wage flexibility.

Other arguments need to be taken more seriously. The terms-of-trade shock, notably the rapid rise in the effective price for Russian energy exports, has indeed contributed considerably to the economic difficulties of individual countries. However, the fact that both the energy importers and the energy exporters (such as Russia) among the emerging market economies have plunged into a roughly comparable crisis after the demise of socialism proves that this argument, relevant as it may be for the specific experiences of individual countries, cannot be employed to account for the overall crisis in post-socialist Europe.

Standard Keynesian arguments about a shortfall in aggregate demand, as well as more refined arguments about a squeeze in enterprise liquidity (Calvo and Coricelli 1992), may account for some features of the exact time profile of the fall in production, However, they cannot explain the fall itself. Poland's abortive attempt at reflation in the summer and fall 1990, which led to a re-acceleration of inflation and loss of government credibility but not to any lasting output gain, underscores this point.

This leaves institutional arguments. Institutions serve to reduce transaction costs (for a recent exposition, see North 1991). Traditional neoclassical and Keynesian theories largely abstract from the institutions for the coordination of individual activities; they are simply taken for granted. In Central and Eastern Europe, the socialist bureaucracies and firm managers have steered a highly complex division of labor in time and space, both within and between the socialist countries. Albeit inefficient by the standards of capitalism, it worked in its own way. The institutions were geared towards their peculiar tasks in the socialist political and economic order. The human capital embodied in these institutions was specific to these tasks. Although state administrations, banks, management structures and other institutions existed, they had little in common with their capitalist namesakes.

After the collapse of the institutional arrangements of socialism, the emerging market economies are now lacking—for the time being—the fundamental institutional devices for a reliable coordination of an extended division of labor. Until the ultimately far superior institutions of capitalism have evolved, until both the people running the institutions and the people operating under the new institutions have acquired sufficient institution-specific human capital, and until economic agents place sufficient trust in the new institutions, the additional transaction costs can overcompensate the positive incentive effects resulting from the abolition of socialism. In addition, temporal inconsistencies in the transformation process, notably an insufficient definition of property rights after the devolution of decision-making powers to the enterprise level, may systematically distort individual incentives and exacerbate the transformation crisis.[2]

The institutional perspective also helps to explain the far superior performance of post-socialist China. The transformation from developed socialism to developed capitalism in Europe differs fundamentally from the liberalization of markets in less developed economies such as China and Vietnam. The latter countries started their reform process with a prevalence of labor-inten-

[2] On property rights issues, see also Blommestein (1994).

sive agriculture and a low degree of specialization in space and time. The less elaborate and sophisticated the previous institutions were and the less they needed to coordinate an extended division of labor, the less an institutional revolution could disrupt the inherited pattern of the division of labor and the more it could contribute to an immediate rise in output.

The Role of the State in Reshaping the Institutional Order

As the transformation crisis at least partly reflects the institutional semi-void that the demise of socialism has left behind, an enquiry into the proper role of government in the transformation to capitalism needs to put institutional issues into focus. Institutions as defined in this chapter go far beyond state bureaucracies and administrations. They encompass the entire body of formal laws, rules and regulations as well as the informal conventions and patterns of behavior that constitute the non-budget constraints under which economic agents can pursue their own ends. The state plays a tantamount role in shaping the institutional order. Formal laws, rules and regulations, and the way they are implemented and enforced effectively define the leeway for non-state institutions, including private behavioral patterns.

After the collapse of socialism, the resulting institutional semi-void could be filled in two very different ways: either by conscious efforts of a public authority, that is, by design, or by the spontaneous emergence of institutions out of repeated private interactions, constrained only by a few minimal laws and regulations. At first glance, the case for an activist approach, i.e. for a prevalence of design over spontaneous evolution, appears to be strong. As capitalist institutions exist and work in the West, albeit in rather different varieties, a competent and benevolent emerging market economy government can make rational and well-informed decisions about what institutions would serve it best. The spontaneous evolution of institutions would be much slower and could hardly yield better results. Strong arguments can thus be employed for assigning the state an important and powerful role, going well beyond a mere liberalization. Frydman and Rapaczynski (1991: 15) explicitly argued that

> ...paradoxically, the most important aspect of the transition to a spontaneously functioning market economy cannot be initiated by the market forces themselves. Indeed, the only force powerful enough to set the market forces in motion is the very state which is supposed to remove itself from the picture.

They thus advocated, as I also did back in 1990 and 1991, an activist approach to property rights reform that goes far beyond the mere definition and protection of private property rights and a few basic rules for privatization. In this vein, they presented a detailed blueprint for mass privatization via intermediaries, to be implemented by the state even against the resistance of enterprise insiders such as workers and managers.[3]

This assignment of tasks takes for granted that a sufficiently powerful entity called 'the state' has survived the demise of socialism. However, socialism was a political as much as an economic system. Its collapse has impaired the effectiveness of the state as the sole and resourceful wielder of coercive power, as much as it has disrupted the accustomed ways of coordinating the division of labor. Although the state administrations still exist, they have never performed the tasks which they are now supposed to perform. Even if they had not been all that bad at their old job, they now appear disoriented and incompetent. In addition, large organizations everywhere in the world have extreme difficulties in adjusting to a totally new environment. And there has hardly been an organization anywhere larger and more rigid than a socialist bureaucracy. Of course, existing bureaucracies can be dismantled or bypassed. However, the shortage of competent people to staff a new administration puts severe limits on the ambitions of reformist governments.

Most importantly, the accustomed mechanism for enforcing political decisions, the communist party, has de facto withered away. The weakness of the post-socialist state, as well as the shortage of competent staff, leads to one major normative conclusion: Despite whatever theoretical merits state activism may have—and I have sincere doubts that the reasons given for many discretionary state interventions would hold up to scrutiny—the emerging market economies should adopt as liberal a transformation approach as possible (see also Aslund 1993). Wholesale liberalization does not immediately yield textbook results because of a panoply of gross market imperfections. However, the state is ill-suited to take such imperfections explicitly into account and to design, implement and enforce an activist approach designed to deal with the imperfections. If for no other reason, the state needs to concentrate its limited resources and weak enforcement powers on the most vital tasks and leave the remainder to the spontaneous forces of the market. This renders most discussions obsolete whether the emerging market economies could, for instance, learn something from the interventionist policies which Japan, South Korea and Taiwan have allegedly pursued in earlier decades.

With respect to the emergence and establishment of market-conformable institutions, the weakness of the state in the transformation period implies that the state should: (1) keep laws, formal rules and regulations to a minimum; (2) opt for simple and self-enforcing solutions; (3) let spontaneous evolution

[3] Similar proposals, presupposing a powerful state, can be found i.a. in Kostrzewa (1989), Gomulka (1989), Blanchard and Layard (1990, 1991), Schmieding and Koop (1991), Steinherr and Perée (1991).

and competition prevail even in areas where theoretical arguments may be found for substantial state intervention (such as anti-monopoly policy); and, (4) let well-established external institutions perform some of the tasks which would usually be performed by home-grown ones.

As the starting conditions differ from country to country, the above considerations matter more for some emerging market economies than for others. In some Central European emerging market economies, for instance the Czech Republic, the state has remained comparatively strong. In some successor states of the Soviet Union such as Russia, a state in the Western sense of the word hardly exists anymore. In some parts of the Russian Federation, regional entities chose almost at will whether or not to comply with whatever Moscow wants. Instead of contesting the autonomy that Russian regions or even municipalities have de facto acquired after the collapse of the Soviet state apparatus and the communist party, Russia's central authorities should concentrate their residual enforcement capabilities on a few essential tasks, notably the maintenance of internal and external peace, the formulation of a few essential property rights rules, the protection of these rights and the provision of a sound money. Ideally, this sound money should be, via a currency board-type arrangement, a well-reputed foreign currency rather than the discredited ruble. A currency board is one of the major ways in which an emerging market economy can draw on the well-established credibility of an external institution, namely, on a foreign central bank such as the German Bundesbank that has a long track record of monetary rectitude.

Privatization

Privatization Priorities

The limited capability of the state to effectively design, implement and enforce complex policies makes it mandatory for the state to think in terms of priorities, even with respect to privatization, one of the central elements of the transformation to capitalism.[4]

First, the foremost priority in privatization is the definition and protection of tradable property rights, not the design of schemes to disburse specific firms to private owners.

Second, a clear distinction should be drawn between: (1) *the privatization of an economy*, that is, the growth of the private sector relative to the state

[4] The following paragraphs draw heavily on Schmieding (1992).

sector; and (2) *the privatization of firms*, that is, the transfer of ownership titles in existing firms into private hands.

Given the dismal state of many present firms and the time which their privatization will inevitably consume, this *top-down establishment of capitalism* is likely to be of rather limited importance. The experience of post-socialist Europe so far supports the hypothesis that the growth of the private sector and hence the economic reemergence of the post-socialist countries will have to come about to a considerable extent via the establishment of new private enterprises and the growth of existing small units (*bottom-up emergence of capitalism*). The priority task of any privatization policy should thus be to remove all de jure and de facto obstacles to the establishment and expansion of small or new private firms. This involves a liberalization rather than an activist design.

Third, private ownership is not the major difference between a Soviet-type and a capitalist economy. Rather, it is one of the ways in which the major difference between the two economic orders manifests itself, namely, the difference in the devices and procedures for the coordination of a complex division of labor in time and space. In the liberalization and privatization of former command economies, priority should thus be given to those sectors which are most essential for the new pattern of a decentralized and spontaneous coordination of individual activities and the allocation of resources, notably trade, transport and information.

Most importantly, I would suggest starting with financial intermediaries, the institutions which ought to provide for a coordination of the activities of local and foreign savers and investors. Many privatization problems—as well as the more serious arguments for transitory protection of domestic industry—are based on the notion that potential owners and viable firms may have insufficient access to credit. Hence, the European emerging market economies would be well advised

- to clean the balance sheets of existing state banks from the inherited burden of old loans (which are mainly to state firms anyway and which are often not being served),
- to adopt the regulatory framework which governs the financial sector in the European Union (EU),
- to copy those aspects of the financial system from one EU member which will remain subject to host-country control even in the single market 1992 (preferably from a system which provides for universal banking),
- to ask the regulatory body of the respective EU member to establish a branch and to regulate the nascent banking system in the emerging market economy as well, and

- to invite all foreign banks to acquire existing banks, to establish branches and subsidiaries and to become active in the emerging market economies subject to the just-adopted EU system of regulation and prudential supervision.

This involves a sweeping liberalization, in this case, the radical opening of the domestic financial system to the world, and an import of institutions rather than activist domestic design. The principle of home country regulation for foreign banks would also help to economize on the ultra-scarce regulatory expertise in the emerging market economy itself.

Together with: (1) a swift small privatization which seems to be comparatively easy; (2) a device to force the most unprofitable firms into bankruptcy so that at least the remaining assets can be sold off in pieces; and (3) a rudimentary social policy, the proposals for which are outlined above, should solve the better part of the privatization problem.

The Voucher Debate

Let me now turn to privatization in the narrow sense of a transfer of ownership titles in big, existing state firms into private hands. I first assume that the state is strong enough to actually implement a first-best privatization approach. Thereafter, I address modifications which a weak state may need to adopt in order to actually get a privatization policy implemented.

The privatization of substantial state property is, of course, political dynamite. Its core is the grand scale redistribution of property rights, wealth and opportunities at a time of general economic turbulence—and a time at which the new democratic institutions may yet be untested. Such a process is necessarily corruption-prone. And even if all those who handle privatization were genuine angels, the fluctuations in asset values, to be expected initially because of the high ratio of noise to meaningful information, will give rise to popular allegations of errors, incompetence and corruption. Hence, it seems essential to foster public support for the privatization process, for instance, by issuing vouchers or other variants of give-away schemes.

Give-away schemes are seen as introducing an element of fairness and equity and of giving domestic citizens without substantial savings the opportunity to become property owners. The case for give-away schemes however is less clearcut than may appear at first glance. The oft-mentioned lack of domestic financial assets need not be an impediment to privatization that ought to be cured by creating a specific investment-money (vouchers). Consider the financial consequences of sales instead of give-aways. At given levels of state expenditures, the population would reap the financial benefits of privatization either via direct distribution of proceeds or correspondingly lower taxes. The tax cuts and direct handouts would imply a substantial increase in net incomes of the domestic citizens which they could use to purchase state property. The famous lack of financial resources to buy state property could thus take care of itself in the emerging market economies even without vouchers.

If domestic citizens can afford to buy ownership titles in firms and how their net wealth may change are not matters of sales versus give-away schemes. These schemes are mainly different devices for distributing the same amount of wealth. Whether the net wealth of the citizenry as a whole is affected, depends on two issues:

1. If the state keeps and wastes some or all of the privatization revenues which it gets, the net effect of privatization on the wealth of citizens is less positive than if all proceeds had been distributed. This hazard constitutes a proper argument for giving away ownership titles in state firms—and for abolishing taxes, for that matter.
2. If foreign capital is allowed to participate in the privatization process from the very beginning, the profitability of firms will be enhanced and their values will rise. Regardless of the way in which the financial advantages will be distributed to the population, the admission of foreign capital and the corresponding inflow of ideas and expertise amounts to a net addition to domestic wealth.

Hence, the real political argument for give-away schemes is not that they increase the financial or overall wealth of citizens. Give-aways merely make the financial gains from privatization much more visible—and more directly identifiable with privatization—than in the case of property sales cum tax reductions.

The distribution of vouchers is not the only possible variant of a give-away scheme. A distribution of sales revenues offers almost the same advantages as the voucher scheme while avoiding its major drawbacks. If state property is sold and if a considerable percentage of the privatization proceeds is then distributed directly among the population on a regular basis and on equal terms, this could help to foster political support for the privatization process. Citizens wanting to buy ownership titles could use the revenues they are accruing for this purpose. The financial assets of the population would be replenished regularly so that privatization is not hampered by a persistent lack or a supposedly undesirable distribution of domestic savings.

In the case of sales with a distribution of revenues, ownership titles would at least be acquired by those who want to hold them and perhaps even exercise corporate control; the hazard of an excessive spread of ownership would be minimized. Most importantly, the distribution of proceeds could help to weaken opposition against the participation of foreign capital. The more foreigners are allowed to bid for ownership titles in state firms, the higher prices will be—and hence the privatization proceeds to be distributed to the citizens. The citizens would thus experience a direct and positive link between foreign capital and their own material well-being. Some voucher schemes, on the other hand, are explicitly designed to artificially restrict the role of foreign capital in the first stages of the privatization process.

Foreigners are not the only group of prospective owners which many people in the emerging market economies would like to exclude. If the ex-socialist countries really wanted to keep former black-marketeers and members of the discredited *nomenklatura* out of the privatization process, the wealth of these people would have to be confiscated outright. It would be rather useless to restrict their portfolio choices. If they retain their wealth and want to become shareholders or owners of small firms or shops, they will find ways to convert financial assets into real assets, either legally once trading restrictions for the original purchasers of property are lifted or illegally via front men. Trying to impose some devices to prevent this would be almost fruitless—and give rise to a damaging property rights uncertainty.

For the same reasons, attempts to keep foreigners out would be largely futile as well, at least in the medium and long run. Worse, if such attempts succeeded for some time, the recovery of the economy would be delayed. A few years later, when foreigners are admitted, they could still buy on the cheap from the state or local private owners.

The proponents of vouchers need to be explicit about the purpose that vouchers are intended to serve. If they are meant to popularize the privatization process, they should be used for the best state firms and for the comparatively attractive small privatization to minimize the danger of disappointment and political discontent. If vouchers are to be employed for cases in which other privatization methods are supposed to fail, for instance, for less attractive firms whose future prospects are very uncertain, vouchers may be a helpful technical device to some extent. Unfortunately, they may turn out to be quite unpopular once a sizable number of firms—or some mutual funds—in which people have acquired shares via vouchers has gone bankrupt.

If the political support argument for give-aways is serious, I would prefer the way which is most visible and interferes least with efficiency, the regular distribution of at least part of the privatization proceeds. Unfortunately, the overall value of state assets may be so low that there may not be all that many privatization revenues to be distributed in the first place.

The Merits of Insider Privatization

The above debate about the usefulness of give-away schemes presupposes that the state actually possesses substantial property which can be given away. De jure, this is of course the case as most enterprises—and in most ex-socialist countries also the better part of land and city flats—formally belong to the state or para-state type institutions. De facto, this is no longer the case. Control over enterprises has largely devolved to the enterprises themselves. In many countries, including the ex-Soviet Union, this process started long before the final abolition of central planning. Enterprise insiders, notably managers and workers and, to some extent, local bureaucrats make the relevant decisions. However, the combination of formal state ownership with decentralized control is not incentive-compatible. Because insiders cannot sell their claims, these de facto property rights are incomplete. The insiders thus have an incentive to take the short view and maximize their current income rather than the capital value of the firm.

The activist approach to this problem would be to try to override the claims of insiders and to implement whatever privatization program the government has chosen. However, the fate of the Polish mass privatization program illustrates the possible consequences of this approach. Because of stiff resistance from insiders, it took three years until parliament finally adopted the program in Spring 1993. In the process, many important modifications were inserted that, in the end, awarded a much greater role to insiders than originally envisaged.

In my view, the weakness of the state has a most relevant implication for the design of feasible privatization programs: Being ill-suited to quickly crush resistance of the old *nomenklatura* elite and the workers in the major, formally state-owned enterprises, the reformers need to co-opt rather than confront them. In practice this means letting part of the old ruling stratum (notably managers) turn its erstwhile political power into formal property rights to some extent—and thus to turn members of the communist elite into defenders of private property rights. In a similar vein, this means largely recognizing the customary rights of workers who have become used to a substantial say in enterprise affairs in the last phases of socialism and the subsequent interregnum period.

Unfortunately, much of the privatization debate has focused on a distributional issue, i.e. how to prevent or crack down on *nomenklatura* (or 'spontaneous') privatization, rather than on how to establish secure, legally protected and tradable private property rights. Although I understand the moral outrage against co-opting the old managerial elite in this way[5], I am afraid that strategies which do not offer considerable sweeteners to the relevant insiders (notably the old managerial elite and workers) will not be sustainable

[5] Aslund (1993) uses the terms 'theft and embezzlement' with respect to *nomenklatura* privatization.

if the state is weak. If the property rights awarded to workers and managers are made tradable, the usual drawbacks of employee-ownership would be avoided. The insiders would then have a financial incentive to safeguard the capital value of their firms.

Legitimate and democratically elected governments may, of course, be able to override the customary rights of insiders to some extent. Although democratic elections are important as a source of legitimacy, the Polish difficulties in getting mass privatization started illustrate that democratic legitimacy alone hardly suffices to effectively overcome insider resistance against privatization attempts which do not take their claims (or, in the words of Naishul (1991), the customary rights) sufficiently into account (see also Heinrich 1993). Even in the Czech republic, where the state is much stronger than in almost all other emerging market economies, the successfully implemented voucher program has been tailored to meet many demands from enterprise insiders, who have a substantial influence on the details of the privatization method and the share of property rights to be disbursed by vouchers.

These arguments are most relevant for major successor states of the Soviet Union, such as Russia and Ukraine, where the state is in a particularly weak position vis-à-vis both regional bodies and organized interest groups. Fortunately, the Russian program of mass privatization goes quite some way in this direction without compromising the program too much in the eyes of the general public. Enterprises themselves were asked to choose between three different privatization variants. Each of the variants gave insiders preferential access to a substantial part of formal property rights titles, under one variants to more than 50%. Regions have considerable leeway in the actual implementation. Although the Russian mass privatization program involves vouchers that were distributed to the adult population for a notional fee, this device to popularize the process does not play the predominant role. It thus does not invite the dogged resistance of the enterprise insiders. Although the insiders may actually lose some of their customary ownership rights, they still strike an attractive bargain because the privatization program formally codifies their hitherto uncertain rights to a considerable extent.[6]

Conclusions

Strong arguments can be found for assigning the state a pivotal and activist role in the institutional transformation that is a crucial part of the overall transition from plan to market. However, the state is ill-suited to play such a role. After the collapse of socialism, the state tends to be extremely weak. It

6 For details on the Russian program, see Heinrich (1993).

lacks the expertise to design and implement ambitious, activist and discretionary policies which may, theoretically, help to mitigate the panoply of market imperfections in the transformation period. The state has little power to effectively enforce ambitious designs. Instead, the weak state should concentrate on a few essential tasks and leave ample room for the spontaneous evolution of institutions and the import of institutions from the West.

With respect to the privatization of existing firms, the state needs to recognize that these firms have long escaped tight central control. Privatization approaches thus need to take the de facto ownership rights of enterprise insiders sufficiently into account. Otherwise, the resistance of insiders may lead to a protracted political struggle, that because it increases uncertainty about the present and future distribution of property rights, impairs the incentives of the present enterprise insiders to safeguard the capital value of the firms.

The essential task of privatization policy is to define and protect tradable property rights, even if a substantial share of such rights are first awarded to managers and workers. The distribution of such rights is of secondary importance. To some extent, give-away schemes benefitting the population at large may be helpful to foster popular support for the privatization process. Give-aways should, however, not extend to such a substantial fraction of ownership rights in enterprises as to invite the stiff resistance of the insiders.

References

Aslund, A. (1993) The Nature of the Transformation Crisis in the Former Soviet Countries. Paper presented to the conference 'Overcoming the Transformation Crisis,' April 22-23, at the Kiel Institute of World Economics.

Blanchard, O. and R. Layard (1990) Privatising Eastern Europe: Making it Safe for Capitalism. *The Financial Times* 11 July.

Blanchard, O. and R. Layard (1991) How to Privatize. Paper presented at the Kiel Week Conference on 'The Transformation of Socialist Economies,' Kiel Institute of World Economics, 26-28 June.

Blommestein, H.J. (1994) *Markets and Government in Advanced Market Economies: Experience and Lessons.* In this volume.

Calvo, G.A. and F. Coricelli (1992) Stagflationary Effects of Stabilization Programs in Reforming Socialist Countries: Enterprise-Side and Household-Side Factors. *Economics of Planning* 25: 21-35.

Frydman, R. and A. Rapaczynski (1990) Privatization in Poland. New York: Columbia University. mimeo.

Frydman, R. and A. Rapaczynski (1991) Evolution and Design in the East European Transition. New York: Columbia University. mimeo.

Gomulka, S. (1989) How to Create a Capital Market in a Socialist Country and How to Use it for the Purpose of Changing the System of Ownership. London: London School of Economics. mimeo.

Heinrich, R. (1993) The Merits of Spontaneous Privatization: What Russia can learn from East-Central Europe. Kiel: Kiel Institute of World Economics. mimeo.

Kostrzewa, W. (1989) Exakte Definitionen und abgestimmte Schritte für ein Privatisierungsprogramm. *Handelsblatt* 15 December.

Lipton, D. and J. Sachs (1990) *Privatization in Eastern Europe: the Case of Poland.* In: *Brookings Papers on Economic Activity.* Washington, D.C.: Brookings Institution. 293-333.

Murrell, P. (1990) 'Big Bang' versus Evolution: East European Economic Reforms in the Light of Recent Economic History. Washington, D.C.: PlanEcon. Report no. 26.

Naishul, V.A. (1991) Liberalism, Customary Rights, and Economic Reforms. Moscow. mimeo.

North, D.C. (1991) *Institutions, Institutional Change and Economic Performance.* Cambridge: Cambridge University Press.

Schmieding, H. (1991) From Socialism to an Institutional Void: Notes on the Nature of the Transformation Crisis. Kiel: Kiel Institute of World Economics. mimeo.

Schmieding, H. (1992) *Alternative Approaches to Privatization: Some Notes on the Debate.* In: *Privatization Symposium in Honor of Herbert Giersch.* Kiel: Kiel Institute of World Economics. 97-108.

Schmieding, H. (1993) From Plan to Market: On the Nature of the Transformation Crisis. *Weltwirtschaftliches Archiv* 129: 216-253.

Schmieding, H. and M. Koop (1991) Privatisierung in Mittel- und Osteuropa: Konzepte für den Hindernislauf zur Marktwirtschaft. Kiel: Kiel Institute of World Economics. mimeo.

Steinherr, A. and E. Perée, (1991) Prometheus Unbound: Policy Proposals for Restructuring in Eastern Europe. Paper presented at the Kiel Week Conference on 'The Transformation of Socialist Economies,' Kiel Institute of World Economics, 26-28 June.

Winiecki, J. (1991) The Inevitability of a Fall in Output in Early Stages of Transition to the Market: Theoretical Underpinnings. *Soviet Studies* 43: 669-676.

9

Privatization in Hungary: Implementation Issues and Local Government Complications

Laurence J. O'Toole, Jr.

As recent experiences easily demonstrate, the challenges of executing transformations to democratic governments and market-based economies are enormous. Much more than good intentions is needed. Preceding chapters have analyzed developments in Central and Eastern Europe during this turbulent period. This chapter adds to the foregoing investigations by examining the privatization process during 1989-1993 in Hungary, with an emphasis on 'implementation': the issue of what happens between the pronouncement of public policy and its impact on the world of action.

Studies of policy implementation in Western Europe and the United States now amount to a sizable literature. How well does this implementation research clarify the developments currently underway? The argument developed below is that events in Hungary pose challenges to the perspectives available from Western-oriented scholarship.

This is so, it can be argued, because in the Hungarian case and in parallel cases elsewhere in the region many issues cannot be neatly classified as 'merely' implementation matters. There are indeed manifold problems in the Hungarian effort to carry out privatization. However, many of these are derivative of tensions inherent in the Hungarian policy approach and reflective of complex sets of values being pursued. And these policy strains are themselves also a manifestation of even more deep-seated and currently-unresolved questions regarding the principles on which the regime is based. Thus, despite the putative importance of 'top-down' and 'bottom-up' variables in explaining implementation results, at least as explicated in the literature on policy implementation in Western settings, the Hungarian difficulties appear

H. J. Blommestein and B. Steunenberg (eds.), Government and Markets, 175–194.

to stem primarily from other forces, which have been generally ignored in the study of the field.

The chapter begins with a brief overview of some basic elements of Hungarian privatization policy and then introduces ideas from the field of implementation research. Findings on the implementation of Hungarian privatization, especially via the national State Property Agency, are then reported. Special emphasis is given in this report to coverage of the role of local governments in the emerging developments, since other features are covered elsewhere in this volume and the local government issue complicates the overall picture. The findings are compared with the dominant sets of ideas in the field of policy implementation, and implications are sketched.[1]

Privatization, Hungarian-Style

The Hungarian decision to privatize a substantial portion of state assets commits the government to a challenging course of action. It can be argued, however, that conditions in Hungary should be more promising for implementation than is the case in much of the remainder of the region.

The Challenge

The task the government has committed itself to is large and complex. New 'greenfield' investments, the development of a domestic capital market, the creation of a legal and regulatory structure within which private activity can develop, even the development of a procedure for bankruptcies—all these must be part of the effort. The attention here is concentrated on the move to transfer the central government's assets into other hands.

[1] Beyond literature sources and government reports, the findings in this study derive primarily from 32 interviews conducted during summer 1992 in Budapest and six other Hungarian municipalities. Included were respondents from university and research institutes, business executives and management consultants, officials with the national government, especially the State Property Agency and the Ministry of Interior Affairs, one elected former member of Parliament, and local officials. Additional data and documentation were sought where appropriate.

Support was provided through the Netherlands Center for Economics and Interdisciplinary Studies in Europe, at Twente University; the Moret Fund; and the Ministry of the Interior of the Netherlands. Additional financial assistance was rendered by Auburn University in the United States. Acknowledgement must be offered as well to Peter Boorsma, Vera Hanekamp, Gábor Péteri, Peter Wulms, Anneriëtte Rulkens, Dan Durning, and the interview respondents. None of these individuals or institutions is responsible for the interpretations reported here.

This aspect of privatization policy in Hungary can be summarized briefly. The central government has committed itself to encourage rapid development of a private market economy. State-owned enterprises are to be sold (with some exceptions) at fair prices. Investment and purchase by Hungarians is to be encouraged. But because of the lack of capital and capital markets in Hungary, foreign investment has been encouraged, even to the point of subsidization through tax policy. Oversight is handled by a central State Property Agency, which now manages the government firms and is charged with facilitating the sale of state properties and monitoring transactions to ensure fair prices and processes. And the new local governments are to receive some kinds of state property and have considerable discretion over its disposal. Recently, the market-based Hungarian approach has been rendered more complex by additional policy efforts aimed at speeding the process and stimulating more activity. However, over the longer period these broad features have distinguished the Hungarian method.

Supportive Features of the Hungarian Context

While the privatization challenge in Hungary is substantial, there are reasons to suggest that implementation might be eased by some particularly favorable features of the Hungarian context.

First, the state of the Hungarian economy was not nearly so desperate at the initial period of transformation as in several other post-socialist settings. Consequently, and despite the traumas of the collapse of COMECON, the nation has been able to develop substantial foreign markets, attract significant levels of investment from abroad, and reduce relative foreign indebtedness. These achievements have eased the shocks of transition and provided opportunity for both institution building and implementation support.

Second, the Hungarian effort comes after many years of experimentation with quasi-market institutional forms. While these earlier experiences have contributed to some complications, as explained below, they also provided valuable experience for many Hungarians. The nation reached the transition period with a set of experienced entrepreneurs and some general support for markets and their functioning.

Third, and relatedly, the privatization effort in Hungary enjoys broad favor among the populace and the major political parties, at least by comparison with many neighboring countries. Although there are important differences among parties with respect to form and timing of the privatization initiatives, and increasingly with the high level of foreign participation, there is little of the deep division that marks the privatization debates in Poland and numerous other contexts.

All in all, then, Hungary has moved into the privatization process with some special advantages, from the point of view of those supporting liberalization. Yet the actual process in Hungary has been very complicated and, in several respects, disappointing. Accordingly, the discussion shifts now to a consideration of important lessons developed in the Western-oriented scholarship on policy implementation.

Implementation Lessons, Western-Style

Since the publication of Pressman and Wildavsky's (1984) now-classic case study of policy implementation, hundreds of investigations have been undertaken. Early work was marked primarily by single case studies of notable 'failures.' As the research effort on implementation has matured, the focus on single case investigations has given way to cross-case comparative inquiry (for instance Browning et al. 1984). Innovative analyses of the complexities of intergovernmental implementation have been developed (for instance Stoker 1991), and some researchers have examined the implementation of privatization, albeit for smaller-scale programs in the United States (see O'Toole 1993). These studies suggest complications in practice, even in modest privatization efforts.

Amidst this outpouring, numerous theoretical contributions have also appeared. Most of these can be classified as either 'top-down' or 'bottom-up' in perspective. While these labels have been used somewhat ambiguously in debate, the most significant distinction for present purposes centers on a basic question of empirical theory. Top-down approaches emphasize the importance of factors that are under the putative control of central policy officials in a regime. Thus top-down implementation theory emphasizes such variables as clarity and consistency of formal mandates, sanctions, and monitoring and enforcement in explanations of implementation success or failure (see, for instance, Mazmanian and Sabatier 1990). Bottom-up criticisms of such analyses argue, variously, the futility of the notion of central control, the importance of contextual or field-centered variables, and the advantages of discretion at the bottom for encouraging better matches between policy intention and action (Hull with Hjern 1987).

Recent years have seen efforts to close the gap dividing these approaches, especially by developing perspectives that build on the strengths while avoiding the weaknesses of each (Sabatier 1986). While some of these approaches offer promise, no implementation theory commands general acceptance. One way of developing increasingly general approaches is to conduct comparative, especially cross-national investigations. A topic of particular importance is how well the theories that have been developed to explain implementation results—top-down, bottom-up, or combined—can be extended to settings like today's Central and Eastern Europe.

Implementation Experience in Hungarian Privatization

Many interesting developments can be observed in the Hungarian privatization experience of the past several years. The present coverage is selective. The information here has been chosen to address the implementation issue, particularly with respect to complications stemming from the emergence of new local governments. The section begins with a broad outline of the implementation approach. Some measures of achievement and summary discussion of obstacles are then reviewed.

Implementation Approach

The October 1988 Law on Economic Association allowed state firms to convert themselves, 'spontaneously,' into joint stock companies. The results included insider abuses (see Kazár 1991: 31-33). The creation of the State Property Agency in March 1990 and some features of the Hungarian approach developed since the regime change were reactions to these 'early' practices. Implementation efforts have often been marked by emphases on aboveboard processes and enhanced legitimacy for the overall effort.

The State Property Agency has served as the administrative center for the transfer of state assets. During its brief life, the emphasis on regulation has also been supplemented by several additional programs. The rulebound aspects of Hungarian policy remain important, however, as the government seeks to administer the development of market-based activity. Tensions in the mission of the State Property Agency during implementation can be seen by considering its dual obligations to reach optimal deals for the state, on the one hand, and to privatize speedily, on the other.

Nor is the tradeoff even this simple. The State Property Agency explains that

> the main criteria for judging offers is (*sic*) the opportunities the prospective venture will create regarding the asset in question and the economy as a whole... (including questions like) financial stability, the introduction of modern technology and securing long term market prospects. An understanding to undertake employment obligations or a willingness to engage in new activities are further advantages in this respect (State Property Agency 1991: 5).

At best, then, this policy requires the execution of an excruciating balancing act.

This walk along the policy tightrope has been executed through a process that generally begins with the 'transformation' of a state enterprise into a recognizable corporate form. This procedure includes a valuation of the company's assets in preparation for the effort to sell. Transformations also give the State Property Agency leverage in reasserting central government control over the often semi-autonomous companies—an ironic point, since the weakened control by the state stemmed in part from the earlier quasi-market experiments—and may include substantial internal restructuring of the firm and investment of additional capital. Then, the State Property Agency and its government-appointed governing board approve or reject a deal.

This general description is misleading in that it implies a single privatization program, whereas several now operate. Among the most important have been the preprivatization (small company) privatization program, involving a simplified procedure; the 'active' privatization programs designed to encourage sales of groups of highly-visible state firms; and 'self-privatization,' a track by which many state enterprises select private consulting companies to help them fulfill the requirements of the privatization process and then arrange a sale with reduced State Property Agency review. In late 1992, the government also began to experiment with sales of shares of a couple of state-owned firms on the Budapest stock exchange. And most recently, the government has decided—under pressure from the national elections scheduled for 1994—to initiate its first mass privatization program, one based on interest-free credits. Implementation is scheduled to begin in 1994. The overall objective of the privatization effort had been to complete the shifts within approximately two or three years from the 1989 shift in regimes. Needless to say, that goal has not been met.

Implementation Results

It is helpful to consider the implementation of privatization in terms of process (activities undertaken), outputs (cases decided, units privatized), and outcomes (movements toward a mixed economy).

Implementation Process. The legal structure now requires market-based valuations, foreign investment is encouraged, questions of compensation and ownership are being addressed, potential liabilities for investors are being reduced, firms are being restructured, and State Property Agency operations have been routinized. While by no means complete, the construction of a legal basis for market operations is a considerable accomplishment (see, for instance, Kazár 1991; Ministry of Finance 1991b; State Property Agency 1991, 1992).

Implementation Output. In its own reporting, the State Property Agency has emphasized transformations. The steps of that process can be meaningful, but transformations themselves may signify relatively little regarding privatization *per se*. And no information distributed by the government provides adequate measures of privatization. Official records must be studied, one firm at a time, to reach conclusions about disposition. Monitoring the actual extent of privatization in Hungary is thus impossible at present. One private organization estimates that as of mid-1993 approximately 17% of state property has been privatized (see *New York Times*, May 6, 1993). The state-owned portion of the transformed companies continues at almost exactly the proportion of the first year: roughly two-thirds.

The programs of 'active' privatization experienced the most difficulties. The First Program, through which efforts were made during 1990 to market a score of the largest and most visible firms, produced no buyers. The Second Program, the following year, was more successful in terms of sales. In several cases, however, these entities had already had most of their valuable assets emptied out via spontaneous privatization. The more recent self-privatization efforts followed in part from such setbacks.

And what of the effort to privatize small shops? As of mid-1992 3,303 shops had been privatized of the total of more than 10,000 (*Privinfo* 1, 6: 39). This rate was substantially below that found in neighboring nations pursuing somewhat different approaches. Among the complications has been the fact that only leasing rights to the physical location of shops were included in the scheme. Sales were not completed by January 1993, as called for in the original law.

One other output measure has to do with foreign investment. As of mid-1992, the share of foreign capital in companies is approximately 35% projected to each company in percentage weighted with capital (*Privinfo* 1, 6: 40). Hungary has attracted much more foreign capital, on a proportional basis, than its neighbors. This result has itself generated some political backlash.

Implementation Outcome. Estimates are at present that approximately 30% of the Hungarian GDP is produced privately, although these figures must be viewed as very tentative. This proportion is approximately the same as for other recent years. Overall outcome to this point, then, must be judged as modest. Indeed, this issue is likely to be a central one in the new round of national elections scheduled for 1994, as the liberals critique the relatively slow pace of overall privatization.

Especially interesting for an analyst of implementation in the Hungarian setting is that explanations for the relatively limited overall success do not seem to lie primarily with either the top-down or the bottom-up perspectives, nor even in some combination. This theme is developed below. First, some of the complications visible in the Hungarian implementation experience are summarized. Special attention is devoted to the interactions of the privatization and local government institution building initiatives.

Complications of the Effort

The discussion above demonstrates that the Hungarian implementation effort has encountered significant obstacles. Why? The answer can be understood by noting that the current context is one in which the implementation of privatization policy must proceed apace, even as that effort is developed in tension with other contemporaneous policy initiatives, indeed even—in some respects—with itself. Furthermore, and more fundamentally, implementation now proceeds as the basic characteristics of the new regime are undergoing definition. Small wonder, then, that complications ensue. A sampling of the difficulties encountered in this initiative can be summarized.

A starting point is the basic design of the Hungarian approach. In reaction to early abuses a highly-administered structure was put into place. While the government has recently sought to create channels for facilitated privatization, the process continues to be marked by administrative complexity. The full scope of Hungarian law on the subject is confusing, somewhat contradictory, and sometimes vague. Many private consultants operate now as necessary participants. While it is obvious that the top officials of the State Property Agency are under significant political and public pressure to complete deals, they are also reluctant to move too quickly in their complex regulatory setting. Legal constraints are important on such matters as competition, property management, company reorganization, safeguards of employees and local councils, and the role of foreign investment.

The point can be put more broadly, in terms of the design principle undergirding the policy. The State Property Agency is expected to encourage privatization via market-based standards in a setting in which many elements of 'standard' markets are not yet firmly in place: 'There is essentially no capital market to speak of, there is substantial internal and external debt to contend with, and there are still important political changes to be considered' (State Property Agency 1991: 3, 1992: 1). The Hungarian approach is a program to regulate a massive process of deregulation. This point explains many of the twists and turns of the implementation.

More specific instances of the tensions in policy can be documented. Although the general norm for the implementation process is the market and its assessments, policy makers and implementers are well aware of the dislocations that markets can trigger; and the State Property Agency is charged with minimizing their negative impacts. The most obvious instance is unemployment. The State Property Agency is under pressure to assist with this problem via negotiations over employment guarantees during bargaining for privatization. So too with other goals like updating Hungarian-based industrial competitiveness and dealing with the potentially-explosive issue of foreign investment. The circumstances under which liabilities might be claimed for environmental damage, for example, remain unclear. So too with ownership challenges by those desiring redress of state seizures under the previous regime. It is also yet unclear how fully the courts will enforce the government's policy on property rights. Some potentially-salable state assets must await these determinations.

The multiple levels and directions of 'implementation,' then, really reflect much more than the typical complications of assembling instrumental action for public programs. They mirror the complications of policy and regime development as these ramify into the world of action. As a way of demonstrating how some of these difficulties can entangle the privatization effort, the chapter now turns to the relationship between this initiative and the emergence of new local governments in Hungary.

Local Governments and the Privatization Process

A complication of the privatization process is that this effort is occurring in conjunction with numerous other important social and institutional shifts. The interrelations among such changes can serve to confound important details of the implementation process.

One such development is the establishment of new local governments in Hungary (see Boross 1992; Government of Hungary 1990; Ministry of Finance 1991a; Péteri 1991; Takács 1991). While Hungary has had a centuries-old tradition of considerable local autonomy, the several decades of communist rule replaced functioning local units with a system largely structured to serve one-party central control. Following the important changes at the central level a few years ago came major local shifts as well. The local soviets (councils) were dismantled and in their place opportunities for actively functioning governments—or local 'self governments,' in the Hungarian usage—were created. Currently more than 3,000 units operate.

In October 1990 the first free elections in more than 40 years were held for mayors and members of local representative bodies. Generally speaking, these elections brought into office leaders who were either politically independent of party (though a number held office during the previous regime) or members of the national government's opposition.

The new local entities have been given significant policy and fiscal responsibilities, but must operate within important practical constraints. These units have been assigned numerous responsibilities and have also been granted authority, within limits, to develop local schemes of taxation on persons and property, including businesses (see the Local Self-Government Act of 1990; the Act on Local Taxes 1990; the annual Act on the Budget; as well as Péteri 1991; Bird and Wallich 1991; Boross 1992). The general arrangement involves substantial local duties in such sectors as health, housing, transportation, social services, and public works. Localities are given large discretion. Indeed, in sectors like housing and social services, the central government now provides virtually no regulation. Localities are monitored only with respect to the legality of their conduct. The structure of local government revenue, in turn, involves heavy but declining transfers from the center; these currently amount to 82% of total local revenue (see Bird and Wallich 1992: 4). Local taxation is likely to prove inadequate for a number of reasons, including: increasing local problems like unemployment, combined with heavy local spending needs; reluctance of new elected local political leaders to tax local populations that already receive burdensome levies from the center; inadequacy of local systems for administering tax schemes; and, in many communities, small and relatively fragile entrepreneurial and industrial sectors. Currently, most local units levy no taxes. However, changes are underway due to the substantial fiscal pressures.

An examination of some aspects of local operations demonstrates complications inherent in the privatization strategy.

Property Transfers to Local Governments

As a part of the national effort to redistribute state property, but in a program independent of the State Property Agency and the various sales schemes, the Hungarian government has embarked on an effort to give property to the local governments. Parliament enacted the broad outlines of the program, and implementation is being handled by regional committees. For some local governments, property transfers have now been completed. For others, the precise decisions regarding who will own which properties has not yet been decided. Needless to say, this implementation task itself is substantial.

For the most part, the property transfers do not consist of the provision of potentially revenue-producing assets to the local level. Notably, for instance, the local units are receiving title to the public housing within their jurisdictions. Most of these structures are in exceedingly bad repair and are occupied by impoverished people. The rents are nominal and thus provide virtually no revenue; the investments needed to render them suitable would be substantial. Local governments have full discretion to keep them, sell them, or give them away. However, none of these courses of action seems attractive. The housing is being handled in very different ways in different communities.[2] Much of the new property, nevertheless, constitutes a fiscal burden and thus complicates budgeting at the local level.

There are, however, some exceptions. The results of the negotiations at the committee level regarding local property have yielded some potentially valuable assets, in revenue terms.[3] In one city of 27,000 visited during July 1992, the locality had been granted a substantial equity position in a factory. Depending on the fate of this firm in the new market context, this asset may or may not prove valuable for the city. In either case, of course, intergovernmental transfer is a form of 'state' divestment that does not constitute privatization, and local partial ownership of state firms adds actors to the bargaining table and complicates the privatization prospects.

In other localities, the governments had entered as partial or full owners of firms, even prior to the political changes of the late 1980s. And, as discussed below, some communities also became effective owners of local public utilities in earlier years and have had these properties fully transferred to them under the new structure.

Overall, however, the general result of the property transfer to localities has been to create fiscal burdens along with discretion, and to sow the seeds of potential complications in the new market environment.

Property Transfers to Churches

Although the basic Hungarian policy on property transfer calls for compensation rather than restitution, a partial exception has been made for certain private institutions, especially churches. Decades earlier the state seized much church property, and current policy allows for a return of the assets that the churches actually need to perform their function. What is 'needed,' of course is a matter of judgment; in Hungary, these rulings are now being made by committees comprised of state and church appointees. Approximately 6,000 church-based claims are being considered.

A reason why this issue matters, in the context of the current discussion, is that a considerable portion of this contested property is now in the hands of

[2] Comments on local government assets, decisions, and complications are based on interviews with local officials in, and data gathering from, seven localities, including Budapest, one village, and five smaller cities. Additional interviews and analysis of supplementary data suggest that these generalizations apply across many other localities.

[3] This circumstance is not likely to develop for most local governments. The guidelines from Parliament generally retain most potentially income-producing property for the central government.

the local government, where the property is in use as schools, health care centers, and other public functions. Transfers of such assets, while arguably justified on grounds of fairness, puts yet another constraint on local government action, and in some cases clearly signals new budgetary needs as substitutes are developed. In one small locality visited for the current research, a former church property is now being used as the elementary school. Plans now involve some as yet unspecified sharing of the structure between locality and church. The nation's Constitutional Court ruled in February 1993 that such transfers to churches would be honored even in small villages where no nonreligious alternative institution would be available. Opposition parties are displeased and may seek a reversal in policy. Even where satisfactory resolutions are eventually likely to develop, the current setting is often clouded with uncertainty, which in turn affects local decision making and the possibilities for private investment.

Local Government Choices and Their Links to Privatization and Economic Development

In this complex and evolving context, then, the new local governments in Hungary must adapt and make choices. Yet the interdependence of local choices with the nascent market setting also offers the potential for complications and unanticipated consequences.

Local Taxation. While most local governments have not yet implemented tax policies, the larger locales have been active. Numerous others have plans to move in this direction. However, given the relatively heavy tax burdens currently imposed on enterprises from the central government, local business taxation is likely to be problematic. Indeed, firms can be expected to seek reductions or exemptions. And this form of taxation in the current environment of widespread tax evasion and lax enforcement could be a source of corruption.[4]

Corruption. In the prevailing context of extensively pluralized governmental structure, new and often inexperienced local officials, and relatively slight oversight by the central government, it is not excessively cynical to anticipate some corruption. There have been some publicly-reported cases from the local level; furthermore, in field work for the current project two obvious cases of conflict of interest were documented in smaller Hungarian cities. Additional

[4] One insider in Budapest city government estimates that only one third of businesses now operating within the city pay their legally-obligated taxes to the city.

hearsay reports were also provided. Each involved local officials' seeking to use ties with firms to advance their own fortunes.

Local Governments as Entrepreneurs. Local governments have come under increasing budget pressure. Their expenses, and the demands being placed upon them, are escalating; the trend is likely to continue as infrastructure problems become more apparent and the local social service burden escalates under market-generated unemployment. At the same time, the central government faces its own serious budgetary problems. Indeed, any central desire to assist the locals in their plight may be rendered even more unlikely by the fact of some political party competition between the different levels. Finally, as indicated earlier, current local taxing possibilities are likely to prove inadequate. One of the few possibilities now available in Hungary is for local governments to go into business as entrepreneurs, competing in effect with the private sector.

Some of the difficulties of such a local strategy have been outlined in a recent analysis, which deserves quotation at length. The World Bank cautioned strongly against

> the even less desirable path which localities (in Hungary) appear to be pursuing of real estate development and business entrepreneurship. There is considerable danger that the soon to be made decisions on property transfer will give full scope to the entrepreneurial ambitions in the local governments, and that, exploring their new-found property rights, driven by the pressure to 'activate' idle property, and faced with the difficulties of selling property or businesses in the present environment, the country will soon be awash with many local government owned businesses undercutting both private competitors and their own tax base, while falling prey to the 'developmental' opportunities and projects that will undoubtedly be offered to them.
>
> It is important to recall that in the market economies, the rate of small business failure is high: statistically only 20% ...of such businesses survive their first three years, and there is no reason to expect that localities in Hungary can successfully defy these odds. Pressures will arise once again to subsidize local business, to maintain employment, and the role of the government in the economy will not have diminished.
>
> Most importantly, this entrepreneurial activity by localities is *fundamentally inconsistent with the privatization* drive, and represents a bottleneck to true decentralization... (Bird and Wallich 1992: 27; emphasis in original).

One might quarrel with the assessment regarding 'true decentralization,' but the issue outlined is clear enough. The property transfer rules adopted after this report was completed do not allow full expression for the entrepreneurial possibilities and incentives at the local level. However, they do allow certain initiatives. Of the seven localities visited in the field work for this study, five currently have financial interests in businesses; two or three of these, at least, intend expansions. There are similar plans elsewhere. The issues here are the risk of scarce public capital on relatively peripheral activities, and the conflicting policy directions across levels of government on the roles of public and private economic activity.

Local Governments' Interests in Utility and Related Entities. As was alluded to earlier, one form of property transferred to local governments is public utilities and related enterprises. In a small city visited for this study, all local utilities plus assorted other functions were transferred to the unit by the regional committee for property transfer. All had been run by state-owned firms organized at the county level prior to nationalization. In some senses, this set of transfers returns the property distribution to the *status quo ante*.

Simultaneously, however, there has been progress in developing interest in privatizing certain types of utilities from the central level. For instance, some elements of the gas industry have been seeking private investment from foreign sources. With portions of the utility ownership newly returned to local government hands, the process of privatization becomes more complex. Ownership rights have been decentralized and the privatization process, should it proceed, will develop in a somewhat more complex fashion, and possibly at greater cost to private investors. Some local governments, at least, may seek to gain significant revenues in the negotiations. Fairness considerations, among other reasons, give pause to any substantial criticism of this arrangement. The point here is to draw attention to another way in which the institutional development of the new self-governments carries implications for privatization.

The Special Case of Budapest. In many ways, developments in Budapest deserve particular consideration. One fifth of the nation's people live in the capital city. And, while some economic challenges may seem less severe in Budapest, other difficulties are especially serious there. The infrastructural needs of Budapest currently are staggering, and substantial development effort can be expected to be necessary not only for serving the current Hungarian population, but also for stimulating economic development and privatization.

Only one feature of the developing local government in Budapest is discussed here: the formal structure of local government in the capital. Under the new framework, Budapest consists of 23 formally separate local self governments: 22 representing each of the city's districts, and one for the city overall. The latter cannot take action on many matters without majority consent of the former, an unlikely circumstance for important matters. Therefore, for the past three years, many aspects of local policy and development have been stymied. Numerous significant local policy (for instance, housing) decisions are entirely in the hands of the district authorities, which are currently pursuing radically divergent policies. Coordinated city-wide action, planning, or even application for financial assistance from potential donor authorities are stymied in this context. Although political party might be expected to be a coordinating force, thus far no such lines of concertation have developed. Whereas the new institutional arrangement may over time lead to genuine political dialogue and mutual problem solving across the city, thus far the major consequence has been inaction. The implications for the development of solutions—public *and* private—to social problems are obvious.[5]

In a variety of ways, therefore, the development of the Hungarian privatization effort and the movement toward genuine local government are interdependent. The review in the preceding pages is meant to show through this one dimension of Hungarian development how complex and challenging are the circumstances confronting the current privatization effort.

Lessons from the Hungarian Experience

As but one case, the findings chronicled here cannot resolve the general issues of privatization or policy implementation. However, the results are suggestive for both subjects, and each is addressed in this concluding section.

The Hungarian instance demonstrates that even in apparently-propitious circumstances, the challenges of privatization on the scale envisioned for Central and Eastern Europe are exceedingly daunting. This point is supported by the various elements of the privatization experience recounted above, and especially in the detailed coverage of the local government developments. The fact that the Hungarian approach was designed with sensitivity to the complexities of institution building and market creation could not finesse the convolutions and even contradictions of such an effort. The initiative to shift state property into private hands can certainly not be counted a failure. However, when viewed by the multiple measures applicable to implementation ventures, the subtle difficulties become apparent. Even under favorable circumstances, the task is technically complex, requires significant investments of resources and the presence of quality public management, and demands the continual exercise of skill and judicious action.

But that is not all. The challenges are likely to be amplified in circumstances, like those in Hungary, when policy makers opt to deal with, rather than ignore, the potentially destabilizing forces unleashed with the introduction of markets. It has long been known that the ramifications of such a shift

[5] Indeed, a point worth emphasizing is that success on privatization over the longer haul is likely to depend on adequate development of skilled, capable, and appropriately-motivated *public* administration, as well as on the development of political leadership and the emergence of genuine political dialogue.

can be highly disruptive (Polanyi 1944). The lessons from the onset of capitalism in the West are available to the Hungarians, who now must deal with rather fundamental issues.

The point is brought into bold relief by the very structure of the Hungarian approach, which amounts to a carefully administered process for reducing administrative presence, an effort to protect the state's interest in a massive shift aimed ultimately at reducing the state's stake. As broad strategy, and over the long haul, this approach can be rendered both consistent and plausible. In the specifics of the implementation effort, however, the incongruities and ironies are regularly apparent. They appear repeatedly in the predicaments of social welfare, property rights, church-state relations, foreign investment, institution building and the role of government, environmental protection, and the need for a more effective but less officious public administration.

In similar (one hesitates in the present context to say dialectical) fashion, the creation of autonomy for new local self-governments and the attendant fragmentation of policy and structure may indeed reduce the centralization of power in Budapest. But the resulting—intended—lack of coordination threatens from another direction policy coherence on such issues as privatization. The manifold simultaneous developments now underway challenge the clarity and reach of any pristine policy, including one of thoroughgoing privatization. But the multiple considerations and accents may all be requisite priorities.

The sobering reality of the Hungarian privatization effort is that it reflects not merely imperatives in tension. The stresses in policy in turn mirror the reality of a broader society in transition. In this circumstance, and although much has been achieved in the current setting, the most basic choices about the size and scope of government and market, and about the nature of their relationship, have not yet been clarified. However, as the analysis demonstrates, the imperatives of implementation cannot patiently wait for a neat resolution of even such elemental questions. Indeed the causal arrows run in both directions.

To mention this subject helps also to make a central point about policy implementation. For those who seek privatization, as in Hungary, there is simply no choice but to stake a course and to begin the many practical steps that move institutions and economies into transformation. Beginning the 'implementation' process, in turn, forces the context-specific consideration and reconsideration of the complicated tradeoffs that emerge as institutions take shape, shift, and meet contrary tendencies that are in turn catalyzed by the dynamics of the change itself. The pragmatic experimentation through implementation, a hallmark of Hungarian adaptation even before the change in regimes, in turn generates the knowledge that can be utilized not only in the development of policy but even in the continued crafting of the regime.

There is some danger of caricature in this interpretation. It is certainly not as if the Hungarian setting provides unlimited room for maneuver. Policies have been debated and developed, and some of the most important values of the new regime have achieved consensus status. Hungary in transition is a far cry from anarchy. Rather, the point is to emphasize that the implementation effort does not, and fundamentally cannot, flow instrumentally from prior efforts to circumscribe the action via 'policy.'

The point can perhaps be put most clearly by using the public-choice notion of arenas or 'levels' of action. Following Kiser and Ostrom (1982), one can consider social action as taking place at multiple levels: the realm of practical effort, or the operating level; the arena in which rules about operations are determined—collective choice or 'policy'; and the level at which rules about rule-making are determined: the world of constitutional choice. Specific actors, or events, may involve moves at multiple levels, sometimes simultaneously.

Collective choices are clearly more 'basic' than operations; and constitutional action is the most fundamental. Standard perspectives suggest that the more basic realms structure the action which develops at less basic levels. Sometimes this conceptualization is made explicitly normative, as, for instance, Buchanan (1994) does. That formulation incorporates two levels of action rather than three, but the issues are the same: the nations of Central and Eastern Europe are encouraged not to make constitutional changes for the sake of immediate, partisan, or short-term interests; the constitutional realm is to be protected from the efforts of politics as usual.

Both constitutional custom and public choice perspectives suggest considerable wisdom in such a view, especially regarding the dangers of majoritarian threats to liberty. However, the Hungarian experience highlights the impracticalities of a wholehearted embrace of this viewpoint. In Hungary, and likely elsewhere in the post-socialist region as well, all three levels of choice are and must be simultaneously in flux. When each set of rules is dynamically altering, and when even constitutional choices need to be informed by the experience of implementation, it may prove unrealistic to expect straightforward execution. What is more, the moves at each level influence the clarity and relative attractiveness of possible choices at other levels, and the flow is by no means solely one-way. The apparent details of implementation provide clarifying and enlightening experience that is being put to use in Hungary, not only on the resolution of policy issues but also on such very basic questions as the nature and scope of the government, local autonomy, property rights, the economy, and the most desirable course of transition.

What, then, does this interpretation suggest about the study of policy implementation as it has developed in the U.S. and Western Europe? It is certainly no surprise to find that in Hungary, as with so many cases in the research literature, implementation is far from a *fait accompli*. In this respect, at least, the efforts to privatize in Hungary are generally consistent with experiences elsewhere. However, beyond this generalization, the findings are more complex and more interesting.

The evidence in Hungary suggests that it is *neither* variables at the 'top' of the policy system that can be considered the main bottlenecks, nor is it the field-contextual elements at the 'bottom' that really control. This is so despite the many complications in the field, as illustrated most clearly in the interaction between local government developments and privatization processes. Instead, it is the dynamics of the concurrent shifts in the three different worlds of action, elements of which develop at both top and bottom. Thus, while some parts of the Hungarian experience reflect 'implementation' complications, others follow quite directly from the contradictory tendencies of the Hungarian policy itself, and even from the still-developing constitutional choices about the character of the regime. The role and autonomy of local governments in the new order, the structure of property relations, and the institutional loci for enforcing and interpreting the new ideals—all these fundamental matters remain in flux, and they entangle the shifts in property currently underway.

Scholars of policy implementation have largely neglected to see this way in which their findings have been limited by the contexts in which systematic research has typically been undertaken. In long-stable regimes, with constitutional issues well-settled or, at most, shifting deliberately, implementation can be investigated without a multi-levelled sensitivity. While some students of implementation have taken care to emphasize that implementation causes (eventual) shifts in policy and not merely the reverse, a basic operating assumption has been the relative dynamism of the 'implementation' (operating) action and the relative stability of policy. Privatization in Hungary offers a different base of experience.

A lesson for students of the transition from plan to market, then, would seem to be that the practical requirements of democratic governance may have to allow for more interpenetrations among the worlds of action than is suggested in the standard analyses of constitutional choice. Indeed, the design of constitutions in a broad sense, in Hungary and elsewhere in the region, must attend to the lessons of implementation directly—just at the converse is also true. Transition might even be served best by some institutionalization of the processes by which practice can inform policy and even regime design, as well as the other way around.

A lesson to specialists in policy implementation is that this specialty has relied implicitly on assumptions that become readily visible, and questionable, in empirical settings like contemporary Hungary. Further careful comparative analysis, then, especially in non-Western settings and in societies in transition, would seem to be important for scholarly advance. In particular, investigations of the subtle relationships among the levels of action involved in policy efforts should be an important focus for sustained attention. Under certain circumstances, at least, such considerations may be the most important of all.

References

Bird, R., and Ch. Wallich (1992) Financing Local Government in Hungary. Washington, D.C.: The World Bank. Policy Research Working Paper WPS 869.

Boross, P. (1992) Central Public Administration and Local Governments in Hungary. Lecture given in Wageningen, The Netherlands, May 25.

Browning, R., D.R. Marshall and D.H. Tabb (1984) *Protest Is Not Enough*. Berkeley: University of California Press.

Buchanan, J.M. (1994) *Democracy within Constitutional Limits*. In this volume.

Government of Hungary (1990) *Fundamental Acts on Local Self-Government in Hungary*. Budapest: Ministry of the Interior.

Hull, Ch.J., with B. Hjern (1987) *Helping Small Firms Grow: An Implementation Approach*. London: Croom Helm.

Kazár, P. (1991) *Privatisation Guide with a Focus on Hungary and the State Property Agency*. Budapest: Coopers & Lybrand.

Kiser, L.L. and E. Ostrom (1982) *The Three Worlds of Action: A Metatheoretical Synthesis of Institutional Approaches*. In: E. Ostrom (ed.) *Strategies of Political Inquiry*. Beverly Hills: Sage. 179-222.

Mazmanian, D. and P. Sabatier (1990) *Implementation and Public Policy: With a New Postscript*. Latham: University Press of America.

Ministry of Finance [Hungary] (1991a) *Public Finance in Hungary: Volume 77, Finances of Local Self Governments—Local Taxes*. Budapest.

Ministry of Finance [Hungary] (1991b) *Public Finance in Hungary: Volume 81, Privatization Process in Hungary*. Budapest.

O'Toole, L.J., Jr. (1993) Interorganizational Policy Studies: Lessons Drawn from Implementation Research. *Journal of Public Administration Research and Theory* 3: 232-251.

Péteri, G. (ed.) (1991) *Events and Changes: The First Steps of Local Transition in East-Central Europe*. Budapest: Local Democracy and Innovation Project.

Polanyi, K. (1944) *The Great Transformation*. New York: Rinehart.

Pressman, J. and A. Wildavsky (1984 [1973]) *Implementation*. Berkeley: University of California Press.

Sabatier, P. (1986) Top-down and Bottom-up Approaches to Implementation Research: A Critical Analysis and Suggested Synthesis. *Journal of Public Policy* 6: 21-48.

State Property Agency, Government of Hungary (1991) *Annual Report, 1990*. Budapest.

State Property Agency, Government of Hungary (1992) Report on Privatisation Trends and Developments. Paper presented at OECD meeting, Warsaw, Poland.

Stoker, R.P. (1991) *Reluctant Partners: Implementing Federal Policy*. Pittsburgh: University of Pittsburgh Press.

Takács, K. (ed.) (1991) *The Reform of Hungarian Public Administration*. Budapest: Hungarian Institute of Public Administration.

10

Competition Policy and Privatization: An Organizational Perspective

James Langenfeld and Dennis A. Yao*

Competition (antitrust) policies in Central and Eastern Europe need to address both short-term problems associated with the transition to a market economy as well as the development of institutions suitable for a mature market economy. In this paper we employ an organizational perspective to explain some recent decisions by competition agencies in those countries and examine how those decisions may affect the competition agencies' abilities to carry out their longer-term missions. The theme of the paper is that events and responses during transition will have important effects on 'permanent' policy, that the transition period problems are different from the long-term problems, and that choices made today should, to the extent possible, be cognizant of the problems such choices might present for future choices.

We begin with a brief introduction to the goals and nature of competition policy and then discuss competition policy as an 'organizational/legal technology' through which antitrust policy is implemented and note that, while there is a relatively limited amount of controversy over whether the technology works in mature economies, the same technology may not work for transitioning economies. This discussion is followed by a brief review of privatization and its relationship to competition policy. We then address some of the transition issues faced by these emerging institutions and from a Selz-

* The authors wish to thank Phyllis Altrogge for her comments and contributions to this paper and participants at the 1992 Strategic Management Society Conference for their comments. The opinions expressed and arguments employed in this paper are the sole responsibility of the authors and do not necessarily reflect those of Phyllis or of the Federal Trade Commission.

H. J. Blommestein and B. Steunenberg (eds.), Government and Markets, 195–218.

nickian (1957) perspective argue that many of these issues are critical events that will shape the long-term goals and capabilities of the agencies. Throughout our discussion we will refer to the privatization process and the privatization institutions because of their salience within the competition agency's transition environment.

The Western View of Competition and the Technology of Competition Policy

While Western economies differ somewhat in their approaches to competition policy, the bulk of the analysis and its implementation is relatively similar. There is a reasonably well-established economic and legal basis for antitrust analysis that is largely shared by enforcers in mature market economies. For example, the U.S., European Union, German, and most other Western antitrust systems share many common objectives (Langenfeld and Blitzer 1991: 354). They seek to protect consumers and promote the free flow of goods and services in a competitive market economy.

In general, these laws seek to present buyers with a free choice of goods and services from independently acting suppliers. Monopolists can restrict output and raise prices above cost if buyers have no alternative choices. However if sufficient choice is available to buyers, they can choose the most desirable products at the most attractive prices, forcing the suppliers to reduce their prices to their costs (including a return on capital invested) and also inducing suppliers to reduce their costs to the lowest possible level. In this way, the market eliminates the need for price controls by offering a flexible system that can rapidly adjust to changes in costs and consumer demand.

Anticompetitive behavior can take place when a dominant firm undertakes actions that prevent entry by new firms or raises the costs of its smaller competitors without offering a better or cheaper product, thus disadvantaging its competitors and reducing the effective choices of buyers. Similarly, if competitors agree to raise price and restrict output, buyers again do not have adequate choice because they are not being presented with independently offered products and prices, resulting in an outcome much like buyers facing a single monopoly supplier.

The specific business practices challengeable under most Western laws are similar, if not identical. Most Western laws condemn abusing dominant positions in a market to establish or maintain supracompetitive pricing, establish some form of merger review, and condemn price fixing and territorial allocations among competitors as illegal unless some overwhelming efficiency justification can be shown.[1, 2] Additional goals of European integration and realization of economies of scale, plus the legal construction of the Treaty of Rome and continental law systems, have led to some differences in Western enforcement policies.[3] However, these differences have narrowed over time, and indications are that this process will continue to converge.

Most countries of Eastern and Central Europe have passed competition laws and have operating antimonopoly offices. These laws are often modeled on competition laws of the European Union, in particular focusing on Articles 85 and 86 of the Treaty of Rome, but are influenced by U.S. antitrust laws and crafted to meet the locally perceived needs of each country. Although laws differ from country to country it is doubtful that any country seriously questions the principles underlying antitrust laws in a free-market economy.

In Central and Eastern Europe, including the Russia and the former Soviet Republics, additional policy goals may lead to differences in enforcement of competition policy from the U.S. and Western Europe. One important difference between Eastern Europe and the West is that in the East competitive markets did not already exist when a competition law was adopted. An end to central planning does not create real markets or the benefits from these markets until competition is allowed to develop. This is particularly true in Central and Eastern Europe and the former Soviet Union where state-owned enterprises were either monopolies or organized into cartels by government

[1] Such practices may include, under certain circumstances, exclusive distributorships or tying arrangements that force the purchase of certain unwanted goods from the same supplier.

[2] Mergers are reviewed and prohibited to prevent a competitor from buying its chief rivals when the merger would create a dominant firm or significantly enhance the ability of the remaining firms in the market to collude.

[3] Traditionally, the competition policy of the European Union has also been used to help create a single market within the Community. For example, certain distribution policies—such as exclusive distributorships—are seen as ways for firms traditionally dominant in their home markets to delay the expansion of competing firms from other countries, even after trade barriers have been eliminated. Accordingly, they are generally viewed with more suspicion than in the U.S., although many in the European Union expect this extra vigilance to be phased out as the markets grow closer. Similarly, European Union merger policy has tended to favor larger firms that supposedly could compete more effectively in international markets, allowing European firms to overcome a loss in economies of scale that could result from firms limited to relatively small home markets. Competition policies in countries such as Germany and France have tended more to encourage larger, more internationally competitive firms at the expense of domestic competition, with an antitrust accent on preventing dominant firms from engaging in monopolistic practices designed to eliminate actual and smaller potential competitors (Fox 1986).

ministries. One goal of competition law in these countries is therefore to nurture the development of competitive markets.

In addition, the prevention of monopoly pricing through competition policy may be particularly important in formerly centrally planned economies, since only a portion of the benefits of a market economy will be passed on to the population at large if the transformation to the market merely creates privately-owned monopolies. Accordingly, Eastern and Central European competition policy may be pro-active in the sense that it encourages the restructuring of industries and helps to introduce firms to competition.[4]

Moreover, certain buyer and seller arrangements may be more problematic than in the U.S. With capital scarce and entry potentially more difficult than in the U.S., these business arrangements (such as exclusive contracts or refusals to deal) may limit the opportunities for new entry without offering a better product or service. Breaking old links that reflect inefficient business relationships may be needed, even if the attendant dislocation costs make structural remodeling undesirable.

Finally, monopoly pricing and output reduction are illegal in virtually all of the laws, similar to Western Europe. Remedies such as price controls are available, and antimonopoly agencies, such as the Polish Antimonopoly Office, have attempted to use them.[5] If competition will take a long time to develop, it has been argued that interim price limits could be the best way to prevent incumbent monopoly abuses.

Western competition analysis of many Central and Eastern European situations often consists of projecting experiences in relatively mature market economies onto an economic setting with which the world has had little experience. Overlay the political issues and the prospects that any one government will stay in power long enough to exert a consistent economic policy, and it becomes very hard to argue that the exact technology for competition policy in a transitioning economy is truly known.

Despite these concerns, there are at least four reasons to think that the Western models of competition policy may be desirable and useful for a country with a developing market economy. First, the Western approach is likely to be economically sensible since Western laws and institutions appear to function reasonably well in achieving the common goals of competition policy. We expect in many—if not most—situations, competition policy that

[4] Such a goal may be tempered, however, with other concerns usually not under the direct purview of the competition agencies, such as allowing arrangements that foster exports.

[5] U.S. competition policy has tended to stay away from such determinations because it is difficult to know when a price or output has been set at the monopoly level, and U.S. antitrust law does not permit competition agencies to fix prices.

encourages and protects the key elements of competitive markets, as discussed above, will significantly benefit consumers.

Second, to the extent competition laws and enforcement in developing market economies are similar to those in Western countries, private firms in Western countries will be better able to predict government actions. This reduced uncertainty will tend to encourage private investment in these transitional economies.

Third, most Central and Eastern European countries wish to become part of the European Union, so it may be politically practical for these countries to adopt laws and organizations based at least loosely on Western models. Harmonious laws should help facilitate that goal, as we have been told by both European Union and Eastern and Central European officials.

Fourth, the existence of these institutions in the West and the desire of Eastern and Central European countries to establish closer ties with the West can also be useful in resisting transitional pressures to delay the development of competitive markets and well-functioning competition agencies. Even with the uncertainty associated with the applicability of the Western 'technology' of antitrust to transitioning economies, it would not be surprising either if the mirroring of Western institutions also served the purpose of providing external (and internal) legitimacy to these institutions. In these circumstances it is difficult to assess the effectiveness of antitrust policy. The outcomes that occur from these policies—if you can accurately observe them—cannot be compared with alternative outcomes from alternative decisions.[6] The inability for assessments based on outcomes leads, as suggested by Meyer and Rowan's (1977) institutionalization theory of organizations, to evaluations that are based on visible manifestations of the organizations such as the type of laws, procedures, personnel, or organization structure associated with the agency.

All of these countries depend heavily on the West for financial support, sources of investment capital or investment, and other resources. Thus it matters for the Central and Eastern European countries that outsiders such as the World Bank, IMF, and Western businessmen believe that these countries have an appropriate competition policy. While such entities cannot evaluate outcomes other than by comparison to Western solutions to (possibly) similar problems, these entities can observe and be troubled with laws, structures, or procedures that appear unorthodox. Thus, even if a Central and Eastern European competition agency knew that adopting a Western form might be

[6] It is also not easy to measure the impact of competition policy in market economies that have existed for many years. The U.S. Federal Trade Commission has attempted to evaluate the impact of certain mergers that it did not challenge (Schumann et al. 1992).

inappropriate, it might still be inclined to adopt such a form to legitimate itself with the critical outside sources of resources. If such resources were inappropriate, they might be decoupled in practice from the actual operations of the organization.

The Contrasting Development of Privatization Goals and Laws

The development of the privatization agencies provides an interesting contrast to that of the competition agencies. Privatization is an essential aspect of the transition to a free market economy, together with such steps as the adoption of a transparent and just system of public and private law, price liberalization, open trade and convertible currencies. Privatization creates a set of incentives for investors and workers to develop products that they can sell to reap the rewards of their efforts and investments.

Not only does privatization develop investment and more responsive management within a country, it can also stimulate foreign investment in existing enterprises and help reduce a government's budget deficit during the transition. Given the budgetary conditions of a country in transition, these aspects of privatization can also be very important.[7]

The goals of the privatization process, however, usually contain elements other than creating a well-functioning market system. Privatization can also be used to redistribute wealth. There is the question of how to deal with claims of those from whom state-owned property may have been confiscated, handle the sale of privatized enterprises to people who may have benefitted 'unfairly' under the previous regime, and handle workers' and managers' claims on the business. Most efforts at privatization have some element of income redistribution, if only to prevent government employees from disposing of government assets at low prices in order to receive 'kick-backs' from private purchasers of assets. Accordingly, the goals of privatization are often more diverse than those of competition agencies.

Privatization agencies also differ from competition agencies because of the absence of a 'correct' or consensus Western model for privatization. The technology of privatization is relatively unknown and the goals of privatization agencies differ. Thus, we see a number of different types of privatizations and structures for privatization agencies. In most of the countries there has been massive 'spontaneous' privatization, where managers have taken control

[7] Foreign investment in terms of money, technology, and expertise may be critical for successful long run growth of the economies in question, while the revenues from the sales can be of at least some assistance paying off foreign debt, creating a social safety net, and financing domestic entrepreneurs.

of their enterprises. In the case of small retail and distribution enterprises, many have been subsequently sold to managers or in auctions without excessive interference of the privatization agencies (Sachs and Lipton 1990; Johnson and Kroll 1991). This process led to complaints that the *nomenklatura*, the former communist elite, and black marketeers were the only one who could afford to buy state property (see Hare et al. 1994). Concerns of impropriety resulted in the creation of the State Property Agency in Hungary, slowed the speed of privatization in Poland, and resulted in a careful auction process in the Czech and Slovak Republics.

In the Czech Republic and Slovakia, the process follows three general steps.[8]

1. Management or a competing group work out privatization plans for an enterprise, often with the help of consultants. The plans are submitted to the Ministry of Economy, and the Privatization Ministry and the Antimonopoly Department review and make recommendations on the plans. If the competition and privatization agencies disagree, then the plan is appealed to the Legislature in session.
2. After the approval, the assets are transferred to the Fund for National Property. The Fund determines whether the enterprises should be sold to a private firm or individual, offered for voucher privatization, kept in state ownership, put into bankruptcy, or should adopt some mixture of these alternatives.
3. Auctions compose the third stage of privatization. To the extent that the enterprise being privatized is subject to the voucher system, vouchers sold to the public at a low price can be used by the public to buy stock in specific voucher firms once a stock market has been set up.

As can be seen, the Privatization Ministry's main task is to approve a privatization plan, subject to concurrence and review by other government bodies. Management and other groups usually initiate the plans, and The Fund for National Property decides the form of ownership and control.

Poland's system is similar, except the Ministry of Ownership Transformation and the Parliament appear to be much more involved in determining which enterprises that wish to go private should be allowed to. Despite

[8] Information from Andre Juris, Official in the Slovak Antimonopoly Office. This system was established by the former Czechoslovakian government. As of May 1993, the Czechs were proceeding with the program as planned. The direction and speed of the Slovak privatization program was somewhat less certain.

starting their reform process earlier, Poland has not made as significant strides as the Czech and Slovak Republics.[9]

Hungary is so far the leading example of a privatization system that does not use any voucher system.[10] In some other ways the process has been similar to the systems in other countries. It was primarily designed to prevent spontaneous privatizations, where the state did not get adequate compensation from the purchasers of the assets. Hungary's medium and large scale privatization seems to be proceeding faster than in the other countries. In part this may be due to the variety of methods employed in Hungary to privatize and the relative lack of intragovernmental review of the State Property Agency's decisions.[11]

The politics of privatization appears to have created these idiosyncratic organizational responses, not only because of the diversity of goals and the lack of a clear model from the West, but because privatization may be more salient in the short run than competition policy to both the citizenry and to interested (and important) foreign parties. Privatization approaches also may be more idiosyncratic because they are, at least in theory, transitory processes that need to be done with some haste. The institutions created to effect privatization, at least in theory, should fade away and do not need to be viable beyond the transition period. Agencies, such as those responsible for competition policy, are being created during the transition period and presumably will last into the indefinite future. Accordingly, idiosyncratic forms of (say) competition policy and institutions could present long run problems if such policies and institutions are not effective beyond the transition and if such institutions become entrenched.

Beyond the long run nature of competition policy, competition policy would seem to have at least four advantages compared to privatization and many other newly created institutions in Eastern Europe. The consensus on

[9] On 30 April 1993 the Polish Parliament approved a long-awaited plan for mass privatization of 600 large enterprises after defeating an earlier version in March (Slay 1993).

[10] At this writing (May 1993), the Hungarian government has indicated it may introduce a voucher-type privatization program to supplement the existing system. The program will give citizens access to long-term, low-rate credit to purchase equity in privatizing enterprises (Okolicsanyi 1993).

[11] The State Property Agency in Hungary is a quasi-governmental agency involved in at least four types of privatization programs. One commentor characterizes the alternatives as: (1) sector-specific programs, in the fields of wine production, construction, and firms heavily affected by the collapse of COMECON; (2) small company privatization through a simplified procedure; (3) investor-induced privatization; and (4) so-called 'self privatization', a track in which state enterprises below a certain size can select private consulting companies to help them arrange a sale (O'Toole 1994).

the relatively narrowly focused goals of competition policy and potentially anticompetitive acts has led to relatively consistent policies to date whereas agencies such as those responsible for privatization, appear to have diffuse goals. Second there has been a great deal of management turnover in other types of agencies. The management and general direction of many competition agencies have been very stable.[12] This is particularly true in Poland, which has seen several governments come and go, but its competition office has not been significantly affected by the changes. Third, the competition agencies do not appear to have been subject to as much special interest pressure as many other government agencies. Fourth, competition agencies have a clear counterpart in developed market economies, whereas organizations such as privatization agencies either do not exist or have had relatively short tenures in the West.

Transition Problems and Organizational Development

We now move from these global organization choice considerations to look directly at some transition problems that are faced by the Central and Eastern European competition agencies. The perspective that we adopt is one which suggests that organizational change is not easy, that organizations become institutionalized as discussed by Selznick (1957), and therefore that early decisions will indirectly affect later decisions. This approach contrasts with a more 'economic' approach that starts from a premise that organizations can be continually optimized to fit changing conditions.[13]

Selznick describes organizations as developing distinctive characteristics and competencies over time in response to critical challenges posed to the organization from within and from without. These characteristics and competencies as imbued in the structure, procedures, and personnel of the organiza-

[12] The Hungarian competition law went into effect on January 1, 1991, with the creation of the Economic Competition Office. The former head of the Price Control Board, Dr. Vissi, and a significant portion of his old staff comprised the initial staff. He continues as the President of the competition office. Dr. Anna Fornalczyk, a professor at the University of Lodz, has headed the Polish Antimonopoly Office since it became an independent agency under a new competition law in April 1990. However, the Federal Competition Office in Czechoslovakia was abolished on October 15, 1992, and the existing Czech and Slovak competition offices replaced its functions. Such changes reflect the potential for politically motivated changes.

[13] The theory of regulation as an optimal expression of the public interest was articulated in Hotelling (1938). More recently, economists have offered theories that regulators optimize various private interests. For a synthesis of those views, see Becker (1983).

tion can both be benefits and liabilities; while well-tailored to some needs, they may restrict an organization's ability to meet other needs. Not only are organizational capabilities developed over the natural history of the organization, so too are the goals.

Selznick's classic study of the U.S. Tennessee Valley Authority (1949) illustrates these ideas. President Roosevelt pushed for the Tennessee Valley Authority (TVA) as

> a corporation clothed with the power of government but possessed of the flexibility and initiative of private enterprise. It should be charged with the broadest duty of planning for the proper use, conservation, and development of the natural resources of the Tennessee River drainage basin... (Selznick (1949: 5).

After the TVA was created by Congress in the early 1930s, it faced the difficult challenge of developing and administering a whole-scale federal program to a region suspicious of the federal government. To do this, the TVA coopted a number of local leaders, trading broader participation in decision-making for local political support. The result was that TVA pursued a number of goals that were goals of the coopted local officials and not of the program as originally designed. For example, the Agricultural Relations Department within TVA became a proponent of the land-grant college system and

> ...under the pressure of its [coopted] agriculturists, the Authority did not recognize Farm Security Administration and sought to exclude Soil Conservation Service from operation within the Valley area. This resulted in the politically paradoxical situation that the eminently New Deal TVA failed to support agencies with which it shared a political communion, and aligned itself with the enemies of those agencies (Selznick 1949: 263).

While the TVA experience may be an extreme example of what Selznick calls institutionalization, some of the broad themes of his argument seem relevant to understanding the development of the competition and privatization agencies in Central and Eastern Europe. In what follows we will sketch out some possibilities that are suggested by the theory and what we know about competition agencies and their relationships to privatization agencies and other parts of the government. Similar considerations could be applied to privatization agencies.

A basic premise of this approach is that an organization's ability to change its policies and its underlying capabilities diminishes over time; organizations become rigid. Amongst other causes, rigidity may result from development of distinctive competencies which are 'more efficient' to pursue than developing new competencies, changes in organizational goals, and information production systems that are geared to traditional needs.[14] To the extent that development of rigidity occurs, it poses a severe management challenge to agency administrators and policymakers, especially if the organization's environment is expected to undergo substantial but unpredictable change.

Competition agencies in Central and Eastern Europe are new organizations existing in rapidly changing economic and political systems. An important question in this regard is whether responses to current external considerations and constraints will create structures and procedures that may prove somewhat unfortunate in the intermediate future.[15]

In what follows we look at five transition problems that the competition offices have faced, their solutions to the problems, and how those solutions may create problems for the future. We focus on 'transition' problems: currently salient problems that will become considerably less salient in ten or so years, because transition problems are more likely to introduce organizational institutions that are ill-suited for the agencies' long-term missions. These problems include: finding appropriately-trained management and staff (the human resource problem), the interrelationship between privatization goals and competition goals (the privatization emphasis problem), the lack of a full set of regulatory laws and institutions (the incomplete institutions problem), the lack of a culture of competition within the economy (the nonmarket culture problem), and lack of available economic information about firms and industries (the information availability problem).

Human Resource Problem

One of the most difficult problems for the young enforcement agencies stems from the absence of a pool of potential hires trained in the law or in Western economics. This shortage has a direct effect on the nature of analysis done in

[14] To the extent that organizations compete against each other, poorer performers can be expected to be replaced by better performers. Focus on the current environment—the selection mechanism—would appear to be very important in the analysis of organizations facing competitive pressure. Where organizations face very weak competitive pressure, such as is usually the case with respect to governmental organizations, focus on the historical relationship between the organization and its environment may well be of greater value for understanding the current organization than would focus on the current environment.

[15] Western competition agencies, too, carry the burden of their past histories. However, this is not the subject of this paper, and is really only a warning that adopting the Western models without considering how history shaped these models may provide an incomplete understanding of the agencies themselves and what they offer in terms of models to the transitioning economies of Central and Eastern Europe.

the agencies and has an indirect effect in that the agencies lose skilled personnel to the private sector after they have been trained. In addition, there may be an equally powerful, but more invidious, effect on organizational structure and decision-making. We focus primarily on the latter concern.

The importance of the background of the staff and leadership on its organizational structures and on its development has been noted by observers studying Western agencies. For example, with respect to staffing issues in the U.S. antitrust agencies, Katzmann (1980) and Weaver (1980) note that professional training has an influence on the types of cases that are supported. Antitrust lawyers are seen as preferring simpler cases involving conduct explicitly prohibited by law whereas economists prefer complex structural cases based on arguably shakier legal precedent.

The implications for Central and Eastern European enforcement agencies of staffing are likely to be more severe. There, not only is professional training an issue, there is also the problem of experience with a central planning perspective on enforcement and potential remedies.

Staffing considerations can also impact the organizational structure chosen by the agency. For example, agencies whose staff have more 'generalist' professional training such as from law and economics may find generalist departments such as merger shops or investigation departments more congenial whereas agencies employing industry specialists (engineers or production managers) are more likely to have departments based on industry type.

Staffing by types of background varies widely across the various agencies. This outcome is a partial reflection of the talent available and, where less-constrained choices can be made, on the preferences of the initial leadership group. We have been told by officials from almost all of the competition offices in Central and Eastern Europe that there is a shortage of trained attorneys, in part because the former Communist system usually did not use a transparent court system to resolve disputes. Moreover, most economists trained under the Communist system did not study market economics, but learned Marxist doctrine. We have also been told that the emerging private sector (particularly foreign companies) has been able to pay two or three times the existing government wage to attract the best individuals out of government service.

The result of these shortages, and the relative abundance of 'engineers' (technically trained professionals usually specializing in a given industry such as petrochemicals) has lead to a mix of staff at these agencies that differs from most Western competition agencies. For example, the former CSFR Federal Competition Office had more engineers than lawyers and economists and therefore had departments based on industry groups. In contrast, the Bulgarian Committee for the Protection of Competition is composed largely of lawyers and has a structure built around data collection and investigation groups and ad hoc case investigation teams drawn from the departments.

The nucleus of the Hungarian Economic Competition Office was composed of socialist-trained economics and industry experts but, to its credit, now has a number of new employees with experience in business enterprises. It has divided its staff into a Competition Council (a group that acts as judges of competition and consumer protection cases) and a Directorate of Experts (staff that investigates and prosecutes cases). The Directorate is divided into offices that concentrate on different areas of the economy—industrial, commercial, services, and food processing—which takes advantage of the areas of expertise of its staff (Hungarian GVH (Competition Agency) 1992).

The Polish Antimonopoly Office, which has a plurality of economists and engineers, has been organized around two major departments, one that examines the structure of industries (unlike other agencies the Polish Antimonopoly Office can order divestitures) and a legal department. Monopolistic practices cases are developed and prosecuted by the legal department, composed primarily of lawyers and some industry experts, and the regional offices. The other major enforcement department deals with industry structure. Although headed by an attorney, that department is made up of industry experts and economists.[16]

The heads of these offices have varied backgrounds as well. Some of the heads have professional training in economics or law, some are politicians, others have been judges. The President of the Polish Antimonopoly Office and her vice president are formerly academic economists, another possible reason why the Polish Antimonopoly Office has so many economists. In Hungary the President is an economist, but his vice president is a lawyer. In Bulgaria, the committee is composed largely of politicians and judges. In the Czech Republic, the head is a politician and a former enterprise manager.[17]

There are some potential problems that could arise from the current mix of experience of these staffs. For example, engineers with industry expertise gained from the pre-transition period could be expected to focus much of their analysis on production cost considerations and to weigh heavily arguments that duplication of facilities would raise costs. In a market economy,

[16] Its function is to identify parts of the economy where monopoly and monopsonies are likely to exist. This information is used in two ways, (1) with the legal bureau to identify parts of the economy that should be investigated for monopolistic practices, and (2) to decide which privatization or transformation plans should be rejected as strengthening monopolies.

[17] It is also possible that the leadership in these organizations may weigh the maintenance of the ruling groups power in decisions that affect the organization. See, for example, Michels (1949) discussion of the 'iron law of oligarchy.'

this type of duplication (e.g., two firms have two accounting offices, but one firm needs to employ only one accounting office) will always exist. However, competition induces efficiencies that usually outweigh these additional costs, and have the added benefit of forcing prices down to their lowest possibly level. If too much weight is given to technical efficiency arguments by the industry experts employed by these agencies and too little given to competitive concerns, then these agencies may not be sufficiently aggressive in pursuing cases that facilitate maintenance or development of competitive markets.

Although reorganizations can fix these transitional staffing considerations, the task will be difficult. First, those currently in management and in staff will become interest groups that are likely to resist shifts that reduce their influence (Pfeffer 1978). Second, the organization will develop 'knowledge' through operating procedures and culture that will be built around the existing human resources, and these elements of organizations generally persist through reorganizations (Cyert and March 1963). Third, because these agencies are law enforcers, they will be influenced by the precedent of their previous decisions. Although the legal systems in these countries are based on a continental system of laws, past cases cannot but influence how these agencies analyze future cases. Moreover, almost all of the agencies are developing rules to flesh out their statutes, which will tend to solidify current thinking. Thus, we would expect that each competition agency will, on the basis of their initial staffing alone, develop in different directions than their sister agencies. Because these agencies were formed in 1990 or later, it is too early to be sure what directions are being taken.

The type of previous professional experience that leadership and staff has had can also make a difference. The Hungarian Competition Office was formed out of the former Hungarian Price Office. While that office did oversee price liberalization, it will be interesting to see if that background influences the degree to which the office is willing to engage in regulatory (price or quality) approaches. To date, the policy of the Hungarian Competition Office has been to avoid price regulation, although it has the ability to force prices it believes monopolistic down to lower levels. The temptation of using explicit 'command-and-control' regulation, however, is likely to pervade almost all of the competition agencies because staff and management experience has been that of central planning.

The use of outside technical assistance by these countries may also influence their early development. These agencies have received help from the European Union, OECD, the German Cartel Office, the U.S. antitrust agencies, and others.[18] In general, this advice has accented the importance of focusing on anticompetitive behavior and structural relief (e.g. facilitating new entry), rather than on price and output controls. The latter controls, it is generally believed, would move the economy back towards central planning and away from developing a free market economy.

Privatization Emphasis Problem

Privatization has progressed at different rates and in different directions in each Central and Eastern European country. The extent and nature of privatization has a direct effect on the types of cases that will be faced by competition agencies. For example, where the privatization agencies are not concerned with competition issues, many state monopolies could become private monopolies. Such a policy, if accompanied by a protectionist trade policy, would present numerous monopoly pricing problems for the competition agency. Privatization plans that encouraged foreign investment lead to different issues than privatizations that are focused on internal investment or voucher programs.

Poland, for example, prior to its most recent elections (1993), planned to have some twenty investment funds own the shares of 600 large privatized firms. Such a scheme could introduce politically explosive issues relating to potential antitrust problems caused by the investment fund managers. One fund might own large blocks of shares in competing companies. Such issues may also prove troublesome in the Czech Republic where investment funds have obtained (through market means) a substantial fraction of ownership vouchers to be used in privatization.

Competition policy concerns may not be welcomed by heads of privatization agencies because such concerns are likely to interfere in the attainment of a swift and profitable sale: the goal of most privatization agencies.

> To put it simply, the (mostly) foreign buyers want to purchase good market positions...and the Hungarian companies themselves are also interested in selling themselves in one unit, because a strong market position ensures their future prosperity. Caught in the middle the AVU (State Property Agency) is unable to overcome these interests...The concrete dilemma quite often looks like this: the AVU has an immediately realizable and financially promising business deal on its hands, but it is expected

[18] Interaction with these groups can also be a source of legitimacy both inside and outside the country. The fact that similar cases were brought by Western agencies is an important argument used to justify an agency's enforcement decisions. The Eastern and Central European agencies also interact with sister agencies in other Eastern and Central Europe.

to opt for a financially worse, lengthy and perhaps also divided privatization deal which promises to create competition (Hungarian GVH 1992: 16-17).

This statement captures the feelings that were expressed in our own conversations with officials of the privatization agencies in Bulgaria and Hungary where competition considerations seem secondary to other goals. In addition, privatizations may sometime be negotiated under conditions that reduce competition. This presents interesting policy dilemmas for the competition agency.

One would suspect that large privatizations will occur in industries where anticompetitive concerns are most likely to surface. This being the case, the possibility of conflict is clear. However, given the political salience of privatizations and the greater importance given to privatization over competition issues, competition agencies may well be faced with cases that are resolved with politics playing an important, if not dominant, role.

The situation would appear to be different in Poland and the former CSFR where the competition agencies have had a 'veto' over privatization plans. Because of the high political profile of privatization efforts, however, agencies in these countries have been reluctant to exercise this veto, and so one wonders about the ultimate effect this formal power gives to the competition agencies. Poland, for example, has only vetoed two privatizations directly; the primary influence the agency has had is through the clever use of conditional approvals (60 during this time) that forces later actions on the part of the privatized firm to accommodate some competition concerns. Confrontations between privatization agencies and competition agencies can affect more than just the outcome of a case. For example, the Slovak Antimonopoly office head resigned after a battle over a privatization that led to the former CSFR Parliament siding with the privatization agency.[19] However, even in Poland, the Czech Republic, and Slovakia the impact of the competition offices is limited, because privatization is the responsibility of a 'ministry' and the competition agencies are 'offices' with politically less clout.

Because of privatization's effect on the structure of domestic industry, privatization choices by the government (as well as foreign trade choices) will determine to a great extent the types of anticompetitive conduct most likely to emerge. Thus, to the extent that the competition agencies are able to influence the privatization process, they have an opportunity to change their long-run environment, or conversely, if they are unable to influence privatization, their environment will be given to them.

[19] Ironically, he (Dolgos) later emerged as the head of Slovak privatization agency, before recently leaving the government.

If, for example, competitive concerns result in privatization into smaller units, less antimonopoly (but possibly more merger) oriented enforcement actions would occur relative to a policy of privatizing large multiplant enterprises as single dominant firms. In addition, if privatization does not include restructuring of enterprises that takes into account competitive concerns, then subsequent antimonopoly cases against these firms could inhibit later privatization attempts. Unless purchasers clearly understand the future policies of a competition office, the purchasers could perceive the 'rules of the game' changed after the purchase, reducing expected profits, increasing business uncertainty in an already somewhat uncertain economy, and thus discouraging future investors.[20] Moreover, purchasers of privatized companies may believe that they have an implicit understanding with the government regarding competition constraints and could bring to bear political pressure in an attempt to prevent competition agencies from taking actions against these companies. Accordingly, it appears critically important for competition agencies to work closely with the privatization ministries, either to fix potential competitive problems during the process or (at least) to make investors aware of the future constraints to which these companies may be subject.

Incomplete Institutions Problem

In countries such as Bulgaria and Poland, the lack of preexisting regulatory agencies creates a vacuum for competition agencies to get into the regulatory (or sometimes consumer protection) game. In addition to the problems discussed above with respect to the central planning background of many of the staff members, there is a general problem associated with mixing price or quality regulation and antitrust functions in the same agency.

Antitrust regulation begins with the premise that markets work. The job of antitrust officials is to ensure conditions under which this will happen, for example, by preventing mergers that would reduce the number of competitors in an industry. Price regulation (in its most polar form) especially with respect

[20] That is, the sale price of a company reflects the purchaser's belief about government's future interference in the industry and about the constraints the government will place on a privatized company. If the purchaser believes he is buying a monopoly position in the domestic market for some period of time, but the competition agency prevents this from happening, then the investor will not get his anticipated returns. Future investors will be discouraged because, once some investors have been 'fooled,' others will fear more unanticipated government actions that too would reduce anticipated profits.

to natural monopolies, begins with the opposite premise: markets do not work and the market mechanism needs to be replaced with government regulation of prices. Because of the differences in starting points, these approaches are not fully compatible and an antitrust organization that also does price regulation may be inclined to interfere in the workings of the market more than it should.

Because of the size of the national economies, the state monopoly starting point, and the slowness of privatization efforts, a primary area of enforcement activity for these agencies is policing abuse of dominant position. Oftentimes this abuse amounts to an evaluation of whether the price is in fact a competitive price. For example, in 1991, 48 of the 114 cases investigated in Hungary involved abuse of dominant power. While most of these cases were found to be unsubstantiated, in many the office was forced to 'judge prices by the terms of the competition law' and the office in some rare cases was able to determine 'which part of a concrete price increase was justified and which was not' (Hungarian GVH 1992: 12) despite the concern that 'the Competition Law must not be allowed to reintroduce the quasi-official pricing of goods.'[21]

While competition agencies may rightfully feel compelled to engage in some price regulation because of the lack of other institutions, such actions by Western standards are more interventionist than is considered to be appropriate for a competition agency. Intervention (in terms of prices or standards) can lead the agency to treat anticompetitive problems at least in part as a price-oriented (or quality-oriented) regulatory agency would do—assessing what the proper level is—arguably undermining the underpinnings of the antitrust approach to correcting potential market problems. Where, for example, contracts are violated because of monopoly abuse, the development of confidence in contracts is undermined. Similarly, agencies that have made direct regulatory interventions may also get involved for better or for worse with more interventionist remedies for anticompetitive mergers or conduct, because they feel more comfortable with such actions. Such interventions will also create some bureaucratic inertia favoring future interventions that may potentially be counterproductive to ensuring a freely operating market economy.

[21] There is also the problem of the general court system, capital market infrastructure, property rights, and other issues such that fall broadly under unfair competition statutes.

Nonmarket Culture Problem

A primary concern of the competition agencies is the extent to which the managers and consumers in the transitioning economies understand how to compete (Fornalczyk 1992). While it may be true in the long run that those who do not will either learn or be driven from the market, in the short run nonmarket behavior can lead to problems.[22] A common anecdote told about competition is that managers of recently demonopolized industries are often at a loss in deciding what price to charge and then call the other competitors and determine the market price. Such a mentality could mean that many price-fixing cases will occur during the transition.

One bureaucratic tendency is for organizations to 'find' and 'solve' the same kinds of problems that they have previously dealt with (Cohen et al. 1972). If this tendency persists and the types of cases that emerge as a result of nonmarket culture are cases less likely to be a problem within a market culture, there may be undue emphasis on 'nonmarket' culture types of cases such as monopolist practices, buyer and seller agreements cases, and perhaps explicit price-fixing cases.[23] Of course, one expects that the market culture is

[22] As a pragmatic response along related lines, President Fornalczyk of the Polish Antimonopoly Office has suggested that an appropriate industry structure in a transitioning economy might be less concentrated than in a mature economy because of the potential benefits that a transitioning economy would get from putting more managers 'on line.' Any problem posed by this approach could be remedied later through an appropriate merger policy.

[23] Of 158 cases that were resolved by the Slovak Antimonopoly Office in 1991, 79 involved abuse of market dominance. Most of the abuse of dominance cases involved tying, which in the transforming Slovak economy is used as a means of rationing scarce commodities and of evading price regulation. These types of cases are rare in the U.S., where few products are price regulated.

At the Hungarian Office of Economic Competition during 1992 102 decisions were handed down, of which 32 involved abuse of dominance, 24 involved consumer fraud, 8 were mergers, and 6 were price notification violations. Many of the dominance cases were commercial disputes involving contractual provisions. Most of the disputes were resolved through negotiation, and in only 11 of the 32 dominance cases was actual abuse found. The office noted that the small proportion of actual abuse found was evidence that market participants were still uncertain about what constitutes a competition problem.

Price fixing cases present evidentiary problems in many transitional economies because it may be very difficult to obtain documents showing an agreement due to the ability of like-minded managers to verbally agree to fix prices and due to imperfect legal methods of obtaining information from companies. Of the 102 Hungarian decisions in 1992, only three involved cartel agreements (price-fixing) (Hungarian

likely to change gradually, so that agencies may be able to adapt successfully as their environment changes.

One role of competition agencies in Western countries has been to advocate competition both within the government and to explain the role of competition to the public in general. The U.S. Federal Trade Commission, for example, does not only publicly comment on the effect of proposed laws and regulations, but also produces public staff reports on important competition issues. Commissioners and staff members also give many speeches explaining the importance of competition, what is expected from both businesses and consumers in a market economy, and the appropriate role of the Commission in ensuring that competition is maintained. Such activities would seem to be even more important in an economy where people are less familiar with the workings of an market economy.

Information Availability Problem

Enforcement agencies depend heavily on information provided by the subjects of their investigations and by other parties. Without relevant information the analytical basis (especially that of the Western agencies) for enforcement decisions is greatly weakened. The agencies have two major problems with information. First, the information they desire may not exist, partly because firms may not have developed market competition oriented cost accounting data that they need for their own internal purpose. Second, much general industry information is not collected.[24] Agencies, such as the Polish Antimonopoly Office, have attempted to collect economy-wide data on industries that better reflect relevant antitrust markets, and the Hungarian Competition Office has a separate division of data collection. However, for relatively small agencies to gather this information can be difficult, especially when so much of the historic information is now completely outdated and based primarily on production considerations without taking into account the demand side of markets. Moreover, even in an investigation, the agencies appear to lack the legal power to obtain as much information as Western agencies can from the enterprises that are the target of an inquiry (e.g., CSFR Volkswagen-Skoda joint venture investigation, where the agency stated it did not receive suffi-

GVH 1992). Of 168 cases investigated by the Slovak Antimonopoly Office in 1991, 12 involved cartel agreements (Slovak Antimonopoly Office 1991).

[24] In addition, because these agencies will often need to determine information from foreign sources (to determine potential entrants, the extent of a market, etc.), this information is also difficult to obtain across borders. Western agencies face similar problems in this regard.

cient information from the parties and was considering challenging the joint venture to block it until sufficient information was received).

Lacking information, heuristics and short cuts may need to be applied. For example, the agencies may rely heavily on documents of intent and testimony, eschewing more sophisticated economic analyses, and may also rely heavily on rough industry concentration statistics. A question in this regard is whether such transitional short cuts will become longer term policy. For example, the past very heavy reliance on concentration numbers for U.S. antitrust decisions has to many observers continued to greatly influence antitrust analysis despite a changed understanding of the importance of such numbers and the existence of additional relevant information (Easterbrook 1984).[25]

To the extent that the system can evolve to reflect information availability, more sophisticated analysis, etc, the initial responses to a general dearth of information will not pose a long-term problem. But such responses could still pose a significant management challenge in the future.

Conclusion

Competition agencies in Central and Eastern Europe are new organizations that are in the process of developing their structures, policies, and procedures. They also face an environment that is rapidly changing and is not the environment that they will confront in the long run. To the extent that organizations do become constrained in their capabilities and goals as a result of their responses to critical events during their history, the types of responses developed in response to a transitioning economy may limit the ability of these agencies when they face a more mature economy.[26]

The short-run environment has put considerable pressures on these agencies to prevent 'high' prices that fall under the competition laws as possible abuses of dominant power. Lacking full trade liberalization and agencies that are developed specifically for regulatory purposes, competition offices have been forced or have voluntarily decided to solve these problems. We believe that cultivation of this regulatory approach to competition may cause these agencies difficulty as they attempt to meet the needs of a mature market economy.

[25] See U.S. vs. Philadelphia National Bank, 374 U.S. 321 (1963).

[26] The transformation of goals may be more immediately evident for privatization agencies that are in theory supposed to have limited lifespans. Some observers (Slay 1993) have suggested that the slowness of the privatization process might be partly due the agencies' interests in extending its life and influence in addition to the normal reasons.

Despite these pressures, the normal work of an antitrust agency leads to an agency whose staff and management are firm believers in market solutions to economic problems. As a result, such agencies (e.g., U.S. Federal Trade Commission and U.S. Department of Justice) have been primary advocates within the government for market-based approaches to policy problems. The Polish Antimonopoly Office has served this role already and we suspect that the other agencies will do so also.

Finally, one interesting prediction that comes of this analysis is that if functions that are not normally the province of competition agencies (e.g., consumer protection) are placed within these agencies, the implementation of these functions is likely to be different than the implementation had the functions been located in a non-competition agency. It could be argued, for example, that the consumer protection functions of the U.S. Federal Trade Commission might have been more interventionist (e.g. quality standard setting) if the functions had not been placed with an agency that also had a competition mission.[27] Many of the offices in Eastern and Central Europe have such consumer protection responsibilities (Hungary, Bulgaria and Poland). We expect that these dual responsibilities will have a long term impact on the evolution of competition and consumer protection in the respective countries. A consumer protection agency that mandated minimum quality standards could interfere with the market, because it could mandate rigid standards that would prevent innovative new firms from entering the market and could facilitate collusion among competitors. Accordingly, both the short and long term evolution toward a market economy can be shaped by the range of responsibilities given to a competition institution.

[27] The U.S. Federal Trade Commission, for example, focuses its consumer protection responsibilities on making sure consumers are adequately informed, without requiring minimum product quality standards. The belief is that fully informed consumers can best make the decision about the quality of products they desire, and that a competition market will then respond by providing those products. In this way, the approach of the agency in these two areas of law enforcement complement one another, and many of the investigational techniques and industry expertise can be used in both.

References

Becker, G.S. (1983) A Theory of Competition Among Pressure Groups for Political Influence. *Quarterly Journal of Economics* 98: 371-400.

Cohen, M.D., J.G. March and J.P. Olsen (1972) A Garbage Can Model of Organizational Choice. *Administrative Science Quarterly* 17: 1-25.

Cyert, R.M. and J.G. March (1963) *A Behavioral Theory of the Firm.* Englewood Cliffs: Prentice-Hall.

Easterbrook, F. (1984) Limits of Antitrust. *Texas Law Review* 63: 1-40.

Fornalczyk, A. (1992) Competition Law and Policy in Poland, Speech before International Bar Association, Budapest, Hungary, June 21.

Fox, E. (1986) Monopolization and Dominance in the United States and the European Community: Efficiency, Opportunity and Fairness. *Notre Dame Law Review* 61: 984.

Hare, P.G., A. Canning and T. Ash (1994) *The Role of Government Institutions in the Process of Privatization.* In this volume.

Hotelling, H. (1938) The General Welfare in Relation to Problems of Taxation and Railway and Utility Rates. *Econometrica* 6: 242-269.

Hungarian GVII (1991) *Report to Parliament.* Budapest.

Hungarian GVH (1992) *Report to Parliament.* Budapest.

Johnson, S. and H. Kroll (1991) Managerial Strategies for Spontaneous Privatization. *Soviet Economy* 7: 281-314.

Katzmann, R. (1980) *Federal Trade Commission.* In: J.Q. Wilson (ed.) *The Politics of Regulation.* New York: Basic Books. 152-187.

Langenfeld, J. and M.W. Blitzer (1991) Is Competition Policy the Last thing Central and Eastern Europe Need? *American University Journal of International Law and Policy* 6: 347-398.

Meyer, J.W. and B. Rowan (1977) Institutionalized Organizations: Formal Structure as Myth and Ceremony. *American Journal of Sociology* 83: 340-363.

Michels, R. (1949 [1915]) *Political Parties.* Glencoe: Free Press.

Okolicsanyi, K. (1993) Hungary Plans to Introduce Voucher-Type Privatization. *RFE/RL Research Report* 2(17): 37-40.

O'Toole, L.J., Jr. (1994) *Privatization in Hungary: Implementation Issues and Local Government Complications.* In this volume.

Pfeffer, J. (1978) *The Micropolitics of Organizations.* In: M. Meyer (ed.) *Environments and Organizations.* San Francisco: Jossey-Bass.

Sachs, J. and D. Lipton (1990) Privatization in Eastern Europe: The Case of Poland. *Brookings Papers on Economic Activity* 2: 293-333.

Schumann, L., J. Reitzes and R. Rogers (1992) Case Studies of the Price Effects of Horizontal Mergers. Washington: U.S. Federal Trade Commission. mimeo.

Selznick, P. (1949) *TVA and the Grass Roots.* Berkeley: University of California Press.

Selznick, P. (1957) *Leadership in Administration: A Sociological Interpretation.* Berkely: University of California Press.

Slay, B. (1993) Poland: The Role of Managers in Privatization. *RFE/RL Research Report* 2(12): 52-56.

Slovak Antimonopoly Office (1991) *Annual Report*. Bratislava.

Weaver, S. (1980) *Antitrust Division of the Department of Justice*. In: J.Q. Wilson (ed.) *The Politics of Regulation*. New York: Basic Books. 123-151.

11

The Role of Banks and Financial Markets in the Process of Privatization

Tad M. Rybczynski

Privatization and the role played in this process by the financial system is now—belated in my view—among the top items on the political, economic and social agenda of ex-Communist countries, in Central and Eastern Europe. Many conferences, papers and books provide a testimony that policymakers and those in the world of letters are already fully aware of that this problem is urgent and of the utmost significance if the process of transformation is to proceed at a satisfactory pace.

The aim of this chapter is to examine the major issues involved in the process of privatization, focusing on the part played by the financial system. Looked at in a wider perspective, this process embraces the creation of an entirely new and different institutional framework, based on the principle of individual freedom and choice in place of the coercion that is at the heart of all arrangements governing the working of all planned economies. The way the new institutional arrangements are put in place will bear directly on the cost and duration of the transitional period. Here the role of government and its adopted approach is of crucial importance. It is of crucial importance regarding the nature, timing, efficacy and equity impact of the measures it introduces and, also, their consistency with the longer term aims of the reform.

To see the interaction of the main elements, I will first comment briefly on property rights and their importance in market economies. Then I will discuss the relationship between fund providers and fund users and the functions performed by this link in the market economies in the West, described nowadays 'as corporate governance.' Next, I will look at the problems of transfering property rights in ex-command economies from the state to private

H. J. Blommestein and B. Steunenberg (eds.), Government and Markets, 219–229.

ownership, the mechanisms which can be employed for this purpose, and the implications of using them. The merits and demerits they have are described in the following section, emphasizing their impact on the financial system. Concluding observations, relating to the link between privatization and the restructuring of the financial system and the macroeconomic policy of stabilization and liberalization, are contained in the final section.

Private Property in Market Economies

Private property is at the heart of a modern capital-based economy which depends on investment and capital accumulation and modernization for increases in productivity. Without property rights a market economy could not function in a satisfactory manner nor deliver high and rising standards of living. Private property, which is a necessary but insufficient condition for steady advance, also reduces the power and dominance of the state. It reduces its patronage, it is a shield against political coercion, it results in dispersion of power and influence and leads to decentralization of decisions and consequent diversification of risk.

Private property imparts almost a natural dynamism to an economy by providing on the one side incentives to save and on the other incentives to invest. Incentives to save are incentives to defer present consumption in favor of future consumption. They offer those wishing to do so either an immediate remuneration in the form of interest payable on relatively low risk type of financial asset or a relatively higher remuneration in the form of interest on a higher risk financial asset. Or they offer higher remuneration in the form of a dividend on a financial asset representing real asset-carrying risk (i.e. shares) or a relatively low immediate remuneration on similar assets but with the promise of a rapid future increase in income such assets generate and linked to that, increase in capital values.

Incentives to invest are incentives to use savings for the purpose of innovation and improving methods in an optimal manner, with the view of increasing future income (for the benefit of those who have provided the necessary financing in the first place).

Any decision to invest—and this applies both to funds used to acquire real assets and financial assets—involves risk. The bridge which links the process of savings (i.e. the deferment of consumption with the view of increasing it later) and the process of investment is the financial system. It is the financial system which transforms decisions to save into property rights or claims to income and assets which generate them, and enables those using the resources released by savers to create assets and property rights in them through the process of investment. Thus, in market economies the financial system is of crucial significance, first, in the creation of property rights through the process of collection and allocation on newly generated savings; second, in providing the payments system indispensable in facilitating the division of labor without which the modern economy could not function; third, in providing the mechanism for monitoring and disciplining the users of old savings as embodied and represented in the financial and real estates.

Financial System and Corporate Governance

The way the financial system in market economies performs the third function mentioned above, i.e. monitoring and disciplining the use of old savings, and linked to that, the first function it discharges, collection and allocation of new savings, depends on the phase of development of the real economy, i.e. per capita income and wealth and the stage of evolution of the financial system.

The monitoring and disciplining of the users of old savings obtained from others through the financial system—now debated intensely in the West under the heading of 'Corporate Governance'—can be done predominantly by banks and, to a smaller extent, by other depository institutions and various savings collecting institutions; or it can by done mainly by capital markets.

Bank monitoring and disciplining of those having property rights in financial and real assets is done by the banks being the main providers of loan and risk capital to other financial and non-financial enterprises. This is effected either by the banks having first claim to the income from service loans made by them or through holdings of equities, i.e. having direct property rights in such assets as generated income. Acting as creditors, owners, or representatives of the owners, banks effectively supervise the functioning of various enterprises. If they consider the functioning inadequate, on the basis of information they obtain directly from the enterprise, they are able cause changes in management and, sometimes, also in ownership, either through bankruptcy and liquidation, or amalgamation or takeover.

Alternatively, the exercise of monitoring and disciplining users of past savings by banks can also assume the form of creating financial-cum-industrial groupings. This involves a bank acting as the central point of a group of companies with cross-holdings among the members of the group. The bank (also having holdings in some or all of the enterprises) exercises effective control and maintains intimate links designed to ensure that each member uses effectively the resources at its disposal while cooperating with other members of the group. Corporate governance centered on banks tends to be characteristic of the so-called 'bank-oriented' financial systems, where banks are the main suppliers of external funds to non-financial enterprises and where capital markets play a relatively modest role. Bank-oriented financial systems are normally associated economies in an early stage of development with three types of economies: (1) with relatively low per capital income and wealth; (2) with developed countries which have specialized financial systems in which the provision of various types of external funds is closely regulated by the state, but which are characterized by virtual absence or unimportance of funded pension schemes as well as collective saving schemes using capital markets to place the savings they collect; or (3) with developed economies dominated by universal banks providing equity funds and acting as centers of financial-cum-industrial groupings but, also, accompanied by virtual absence of funded pension schemes and unimportance of savings collecting organizations as above (e.g. open-ended and closed trusts).

Corporate governance can also be centered on capital markets. This tends to be characteristic of countries with the so-called market-oriented and security-oriented financial system, where the bulk of external funds used by non-financial enterprises is obtained through the medium of capital markets, ultimately provided by savings collecting institutions other than banks. These comprise, above all, pension funds but also insurance companies and, to a modest degree, wealthy private individuals.

The process of monitoring and disciplining in countries with such systems is basically done first by closely observing the performance in terms of profitability, earning and dividends with reference to published information as required by stock exchanges and unpublished information, and by evaluating the ability of individual units to service debt and pay dividends now and in the future; and second by valuing each company's debt and risk capital in the light of its performance, present and future, i.e. according it an appropriate price/earning ratio and dividend yield with regard to the current interest rate and valuation of all other securities. This valuation can be either favorable, unfavorable or highly unfavorable. In the latter two cases, what happens is that the unfavorable valuation tends to attract a prospective buyer who perceives the opportunities of improving performance by changes in management and disposal of assets and who then produces a threat of takeover, merger or amalgamation.

Market-oriented and security-oriented financial systems tend to thrive predominantly in countries where there is a separation of management and ownership, and where there may be conflicts of interest between these two parties. As a rule they do not exist in countries where ownership and management are in the same hands—something which is true of countries with low per capita income and wealth, countries dominated by small and medium-size enterprises and countries with financial-cum-industrial groupings and without significant institutional shareholding.

The Problems Associated with Transfering Property Rights in Ex-Communist Economies—Non-Viable Debts

In transforming into market economies, the former command economies must transfer property rights to specific assets of individuals and transform their financial systems so they perform the functions carried out by financial systems in the market economies in the West. The problems they face include deciding what methods are best employed, what the optimum mixture of methods should be, what type of financial system and, accompanying it, what system of corporate governance they wish to create, and what the best way is to remove the obstacles they face in embarking on this task.

The principal difficulty arises from the now well-known feature of the command economies having had a financial system comprising only one bank (mono-bank). This bank was used by the planners, first, merely as a channel of transmission for new savings extracted from the population by means of taxes and, to a limited extent, voluntary savings, for investment in projects decided upon by the planners without any reference to profitability or risk; and second, for controlling wages. This has resulted in the banks in command having no skills to assess risks and allocate savings according to their relative profitability, and having a substantial part of their assets in loans to non-viable companies which are unable to service their debt, let alone earn an adequate rate of return on the capital they employ.

I will not discuss here the basic problems of establishing a legal system with property rights at its center; commercializing all companies (including banks and other financial and non-financial companies) and providing them with a proper capital structure to facilitate the evaluation of their performance; educating those engaged in banks and other financial institutions to assess risk; and, creating a small but well-functioning and properly structured capital market. These are the necessary preconditions which those concerned with the transformation are by now fully aware, but which are not easy to satisfy.

The primary and fundamental problem is how to deal with non-viable debt on banks' books which represent liabilities of either non-viable or temporarily ill enterprises. While it is correct to say that if all enterprises and banks are state-owned simply writing off non-viable bank loans and corresponding them to liabilities of enterprises could resolve this problem—since it would not make any difference to a consolidated balance sheet and could be done by a stroke of a pen—this is neither possible nor practical. It is not practical because this view completely disregards the fact that having collected household savings, the state is also a debtor and, therefore, such a step would inflict considerable damage on households who have saved in the past. Write-offs of debts and assets without affecting the consolidated balance sheet is only feasible if they are within the same sector. In fact this was done in the U.K. where nationalized industries were cleaned in the first instance, i.e. their debt to the state was written-off before privatization. One can also mention in passing the rescue operation of the Savings and Loan Association in the U.S., at the cost of nearly $500 billion, and the wholesale bailout of virtually all banks in Sweden and Norway, all of which had to be financed by the state.

If one accepts that it would be neither desirable nor feasible to close a large number of banks and enterprises owing debt to them, then the question is how non-viable loans should be dealt with. The problem is how to decide which loans and enterprises are viable and which are not. I will refer to this later. What I want to stress here is the fact that even if one assumes that all viable enterprises are sold, there is reason to believe that the proceeds obtained will not be adequate to cover bank loans extended to non-viable enterprises.

This in fact is the position of Treuhand, the East German Agency which has been created as the only body charged with the task of selling all state owned East German enterprises, bringing to health those which can be cured, and closing the remaining ones. According to recent estimates, by the mid-1990's—the time by which most of the enterprises will be disposed of—Treuhand will have accumulated a deficit conservatively estimated at between DM 250 and 300 billion, tantamount to some 8% of the GNP, which will increase further in the following 5 to 10 years. A similar lesson is being learned by Hungary, which, having adopted until recently the policy of only selling the state assets, has discovered that some of the large state-owned banks will have to be liquidated unless they are supported.

For post-Communist countries which freely distribute state-owned assets, the relative size of non-viable debt will be even larger than in East Germany and will impose a much greater burden of servicing unless defaulted through inflation with a negative real interest. This problem has important implications for the process of privatization and for foreign help providers, in that it bears on both the process of restructuring and stabilization, to which I will return later.

The Mechanisms of Privatization and Their Implications

In essence there are two basic methods of privatization that involve the transfer of property rights to specific assets and income they will generate from the state to individuals as well as the assumption by the latter of risk attaching to such rights embodied in equity shares. The first method is to offer property rights for sale. The second method is to distribute them free. Each method has a number of variations. It is possible to sell the same shares at different prices to different buyers. It is possible to distribute property rights to different groups in different proportions. It is possible to combine these methods in various ways. Which methods are most conducive to efficiency by ensuring the most effective type of corporate governance? Which create a level playing field as far as various companies and industries are concerned and are fair, reasonable and equitable from the point of view of citizens, and which are most conducive to macroeconomic stability?

Whatever method is used, there is no doubt that the balance sheets of the banks and the balance sheets of various corporations must first be cleaned. In former Eastern Germany, Treuhand approached this matter by trying to classify various companies—after they had been examined and subdivided into smaller units if necessary or re-organized—into three groups, those viable, those which had to be put into intensive care to reach viability, and those non-viable which would have to be closed. In essence, similar approaches have been adopted in Hungary, the Czech and Slovak Republics, and Poland, with certain variations.

There is no problem selling fully viable companies capable of servicing their debt and offering adequate return, with regard to risk on their equity shares to prospective owners at home or abroad. In this case, there is no problem for banks which have, in the past, advanced loans to such enterprises because they are serviceable. Such sales can be made for cash to foreign and domestic buyers. They can be made partly for cash and partly by employing leasing arrangements to be set up by the state. Or they can be made by using the method of Management Buy-Out or Leveraged Buy-Out, using banks for necessary funds, or a combination of both. Such methods, of course, can also be combined with offering shares at special prices to workers and managers. The main criticism of this method is that it is tantamount to what is described as 'cherry picking,' i.e. selecting the best units and offering them by way of negotiation to selected classes of buyers, but only with indirect and largely subjectively estimated references to possible market prices. To the extent that banks are willing to provide loan financing, on a micro level this method tends to result in a system of corporate governance linked to a bank-oriented financial system, placing the burden of monitoring and disciplining on banks. Excluding small privatization, where there is no problem of separation of management and ownership, this approach has been employed by Hungary, where all disposals of state property have been by way of sales only. Under this approach the state and banks are still left with enterprises which require curing and those which have to be closed, the loans from the banks being either doubtful or non-viable.

The free distribution of property rights to the population at large employs the method of distributing vouchers that entitle those who obtain them to a holding in a unit trust controlling a number of companies (as is the case in Poland), or individual companies, or holding companies (as is the case in the

Czech and Slovak Republics). Transferability of holding so obtained may be restricted for a certain period or fully permitted. The main feature of this approach is that it attempts to create a financial system centered on capital markets that will monitor and discipline the performance of individual industrial units through marketability of their holdings in various unit trusts and holding companies. The main question to be asked in this connection—apart from the 'cherry picking' aspect—is if the creation of a capital market-centered financial system is feasible, to what extent it creates a level playing field for the investors and enterprises (original receivers of vouchers), and to what extent it may have to be modified.

Merits and Demerits of Different Methods of Privatization

There are two main criticisms of free distribution. First, that it is unfair and inequitable, in that it suffers from what is known as asymmetric information which favors some individuals at the expense of others. Because capital markets are very narrow and restricted, and information about the merits and demerits of various holdings and industrial companies is likely to be very limited, those in possession of it will be able to benefit unduly by buying shares at prices that bear no relation to the present and prospective earnings and dividends.

The second criticism is, that in view of a low per capita income and wealth, holders of vouchers and/or holdings in various groups will wish to sell them immediately or shortly after receiving them and use the proceeds to invest in property and highly liquid assets. Such an action would depress prices, bring the whole approach and capital markets into disrepute and might require some rescue operation. Such a rescue would have to be undertaken by the state, involving the state directly or central banks or a specially created bank buying such shares with profound consequences for money supply and stabilization policy. The absence of deep, well-functioning and mature capital markets and the relative unimportance of pension funds and other institutional investors would mean that the takeover mechanism, the ultimate threat and weapon in the market-oriented and security-oriented financial system, might not work or might work in a feeble and very painful manner.

Neither the sales method nor the free distribution method deals with the sick companies which must be kept in an intensive care unit, some of which may be terminally ill, nor with those with incurable weaknesses and where the question of employment becomes important. This of course raises the question of how to best deal with them and the cost of doing so. Treatment in an intensive care unit may last a good few years; it would call for financing and would have to rely on new expertise, initiative and restructuring. This would be costly and must, to a certain extent, be financed directly or indirectly by the state although schemes can be devised supporting a joint approach by the relevant bank and industrial unit involving incentives in the form of options, convertible shares, and other means designed to motivate management to embark on the right treatment, and to diagnose those loans and assets which can earn an adequate rate of return and those which cannot.

Another important difference between the two approaches to privatization (sales and free distribution) bearing on macro-stability is that the former (sales) has a positive impact on governmental receipt while the latter does not; the former tends to assist the evolution of the bank-oriented financial system while the latter makes a jump toward a market-based and security-oriented financial system which may prove to be difficult to achieve, encountering significant difficulties.

The Problem of Non-viable Loans and Non-viable Enterprises

It has already been mentioned that the process of privatization will result in the discovery of non-viable loans and, correspondingly, non-viable enterprises whose assets will be unable to earn an adequate rate of return to service the funds they have obtained in the past. What is the best way of dealing with them from the point of view of the viability of the financial system and above all the banks, from the point of view of the industrial enterprises, and from the point of view macroeconomic policy especially that concerned with stabilization?

Assuming that such loans can be agreed upon, the best way to deal with them from the financial system's point of view would be to transfer them to the state or special organization set up specifically for this purpose, in exchange for long-term government securities carrying a low interest rate or indexed long-term zero coupon bonds, thus enabling banks to behave in a commercial manner, though possibly restricting the use of such securities somewhat. This is, in fact, a technical problem which I will not go into, though I am prepared to discuss it if necessary. What is important is that such an action would require the government to service such loans, consequently adding to its spending and possibly deficit. To that extent, the problem of containing total (not primary) deficit becomes more difficult. In so far as stabilization policy requires holding the deficit at a very low level, it can be argued that the restructuring policy and stabilization policy would be assisted if foreign aid were used for the specific purpose of reducing such debt issued by the central government.

One additional implication of the need for the state to relieve banks of non-viable debt by transferring it to its own books is that it also tends to favor the sales method rather than free distribution. This is because the sales method is likely to provide better incentives to make better use of resources and help contain deficit and assist stabilization. By so doing, it can be expected to accelerate the rate of growth and spread its benefits to the population at large. Free distribution, while it may have a favorable impact on corporate governance, has a number of dangers attached to it and is likely to result in a higher deficit than would prevail with the sales method.

Concluding Remarks

This contribution has tried to survey in a very compressed manner the issues concerning privatization and restructuring of the financial system. These two elements of the transformation of command economies to market economies work at the micro level but are closely linked to the policy of stabilization and liberalization on the macro level. Privatization can be implemented by the sale of various enterprises after they have been commercialized or by the free distribution of shares in them through the medium of vouchers to the population at large. Whichever method is used, non-viable loans and correspondingly, non-viable enterprises will remain on the books of banks and will have to be taken over by the state, in one way or another. These represent to a certain degree past voluntary savings of the population as well as dead-weight debt that will have to be serviced by the taxpayers at large. To the extent that this burden could be reduced by using foreign help, it would help macroeconomic stabilization policy.

The use of the sales method is likely to result in lower dead-weight debt, can be expected to lead to the development of a bank-oriented financial system and, linked to that, a bank-based method of corporate governance. The free distribution method can be expected to result in high dead-weight debt and a greater burden of taxation to service it, and a move of the economy towards a market-oriented financial system, relying principally on capital markets with a corporate governance arrangement to monitor and discipline the users of past savings. The transformation of the financial system in this direction may prove difficult and carries certain dangers that in fact, may require the intervention of the state, which would be contrary to the original aims. For these reasons it would appear that the sales method has certain advantages, both on grounds of efficiency and equity, as well as grounds of assisting the stabilization policy. A judicious mix of the two methods, with initial emphasis on the former, appears to have some advantages because it provides time to restructure banks and to assist healthy growth of capital markets.

References

Buchanan, J.M. and R.D. Tollison (eds.) (1972) *The Theory of Public Choice*. Ann Arbor: University of Michigan Press.

Furubotn, E. and S. Pejovich (1972) Property Rights and Economic Theory: A Survey of Recent Literature. *Journal of Economic Literature* 10: 1137-1162.

Hayek, F.A. (1976 [1949]) *Individualism and Economic Order*. London: Routledge and Kegan Paul.

Hayek, F.A. (1960) *The Constitution of Liberty*. London: Routledge and Kegan Paul.

Pejovich, S. (1990) *The Economics of Property Rights: Towards a Theory of Comparative Systems*. Dordrecht: Kluwer.

Lane, T.D. (1994) *Financial Sector Reforms: Banking, Securities, and Payments*. In this volume.

Kornai, J. (1986) The Hungarian Reform Process: Visions, Hopes and Reality. *Journal of Economic Literature* 24: 1687-1737.

Pelikan, P. (1989) Evolution, Economic Competence, and the Market for Corporate-Control. *Journal of Economic Behaviour and Organization* 12: 279-303.

12

Monetary and Fiscal Management During the Transformation

George Kopits*

The purpose of this chapter is to provide a broad assessment of the use of monetary and fiscal policies for macroeconomic stabilization during the transformation from socialist central planning to market-based institutions. Structural reform in the areas of money and banking, taxation, and budgetary practices, is dealt with only insofar as it pertains to the stabilization goal. While drawing heavily on experience accumulated in a number of Central and East European countries as well as the new independent states of former Soviet Union, the discussion does not focus on any particular country. Instead, it seeks to develop some insights of more or less general application mainly in the early stages of transformation, encompassing institution-building as well as the role of government.

Following a few remarks about the analytical mindset of policymakers in these economies and of their Western advisors or counterparts, the chapter proceeds with an overview of the institutional and technical impediments to monetary and fiscal management during the transformation. Specifically, it surveys the dysfunctional institutional arrangements found in the state enterprise sector and in its nexus with the banking system and the consolidated state budget. In addition, the technical difficulties in determining the macroeconomic policy stance are examined. Subsequently, the discussion turns to the choice of monetary and fiscal instruments in the evolving institu-

* The author is grateful to Guillermo Calvo, Manuel Guitián, Vito Tanzi, and the editors of this volume for useful comments on an earlier version. The views expressed are those of the author and do not necessarily reflect the position of the International Monetary Fund.

H. J. Blommestein and B. Steunenberg (eds.), Government and Markets, 231–246.

tional framework. Lastly, the chapter examines the interaction between macroeconomic management and democratic institutions.

Dialogue of the Deaf

The formulation and implementation of monetary and fiscal policies in countries in transition are handicapped by the shortage of macroeconomists who have a background in the analysis and application of indirect market-based policy tools or who trust in the effectiveness of such tools. This limitation stems from continued reliance on direct quantitative signals to—and on negotiating their implementation with—economic agents during at least four, if not nearly seven, decades of central planning. Above all, macroeconomic analysis was conducted almost exclusively in real terms, largely in a rigid interindustry input-output framework, with only incidental attention paid to financial flows. There was little use for neoclassical marginal analysis that characterizes much of Western economic thinking and underpins the application of indirect policy tools. As a consequence, there is a remarkable absence of fiscal and monetary literacy among economists trained in the socialist economic tradition.[1] And even among those who, in principle, favor market-oriented reforms, there seems to be a deep-rooted mistrust in the effectiveness of price signals—through which indirect financial policies are meant to act—in influencing the decisions of enterprises and households.

Prior to the transformation, financial policies were entirely subservient to the annual economic plan; stated differently, fiscal and monetary instruments did not have a distinct function but were passive components of the plan. Operationally, the central bank was simply appended to the ministry of finance, and in turn, the ministry of finance was totally dependent on the planning agency and the industrial branch ministries.[2] Policymaking was concentrated in the planning agency directly under the authority of the highest state-party organ (usually the central committee of the party). Not surprisingly, at present, many key policymakers in central banks and finance ministries

[1] The exceptions, who previously found refuge in abstract mathematical institutes or so-called laboratories, are now in some cases in policymaking positions and by necessity rely on practical advice from the holdover staff.

[2] The economic policy structure could be depicted as a set of *matryoshka* dolls, with the largest doll symbolizing the Gosplan, the smallest one the Gosbank, and the Ministry of Finance between them.

are officials who have been conditioned under the plan to intervene with quantitative tools in a discretionary manner.[3]

The difficulty in applying financial policy tools—for instance, with regard to formulating and implementing the budget, designing and administering parametric taxes, conducting monetary, credit, or foreign exchange operations—is nowhere more evident than in the new independent states of the former Soviet Union. There, until very recently, economic authorities simply acted as a transmission belt between the center and the periphery, that is, conveying orders from the union-level Gosplan and branch ministries, through republic-level counterparts, to administrative offices and enterprises at the local level.

In sharp contrast with the approach inherited from the past and still prevailing in a number of economies in transition, Western macroeconomists —academicians and policy analysts alike—who are called upon to provide technical assistance or to negotiate financial arrangements with these countries, often couch their prescriptions in the monetary and fiscal fields on the basis of conceptual constructs and of institutional arrangements found in industrial or developing countries. The prescriptions take for granted relatively well-functioning commodity and factor markets, including a fairly integrated process of financial intermediation. But perhaps more important, many of these economists assume the applicability of marginal analysis without being fully aware of its limitations and tend to indulge in elasticity optimism, in an environment that in many cases has been atrophied and devoid of key technological, institutional, and behavioral elements. These limitations are particularly evident in the state enterprise sector.

The State Enterprise Sector—A Monkey Wrench?

Broadly speaking, the post-socialist economy can be viewed as consisting of four sectors: the government, state-owned enterprises, private enterprises, and households. Whereas households and private enterprises tend to respond fully to price signals and to abide by a hard budget constraint, state-owned enterprises have been isolated from such signals and have been operating under a soft budget constraint for too long. Lack of a well-defined objective function—such as profit maximization and risk minimization—easy access to bank credit and subsidies, and no effective exposure to market forces, including

[3] With their penchant for case-by-case intervention rather than rules, former central planners are likely to feel less constrained by their previous policy announcements than Western policymakers. Also, the former are more disposed to reneging on past promises if, as expected, reform brings about sharp changes in income or wealth distribution and in job security.

absence of bankruptcy risk, all characterized the operations of state-owned enterprises.[4] Neither the management nor the workforce was concerned with the profitability of the enterprise. On the contrary, managers and employees sought their own individual gain—in terms of bonuses, benefits in kind, and indiscriminate wage increases—without regard to the enterprise ownership which by default was increasingly assumed by the employees—through enterprise councils and workers' councils in Hungary and Poland, respectively. For decades, enterprises were required to satisfy, in volume terms, merit wants assigned by the planning office and branch ministries, rather than to meet, both in quantity and quality, market demand; at the same time, they were not required to economize in the use of factor inputs in terms of relative input prices determined by market conditions. The state-owned enterprises' isolation from product markets had led to a virtual absence of marketing skills, on the one hand, and their isolation from input markets resulted in the ignorance of cost accounting, on the other.

The state-owned enterprises' lack of contact with market-determined price signals is understandable. Under central planning, state-owned enterprises were supposed to meet quantitative targets without any regard for effective demand for their products; equally, access to factor inputs was subject primarily to quantitative supply constraints and rationing, rather than to the availability and price of financial resources. Against this background, it is unrealistic to expect that the behavioral response of state-owned enterprises to variations in output and input prices, interest rates, the exchange rate, and tax rates, would change overnight as the market-oriented transformation gets under way.

The limited autonomy provided to state-owned enterprises during market-oriented reforms in Hungary, Poland, and under *perestroika* in the former Soviet Union, in the 1980s, for the most part did not sensitize state-owned enterprise behavior in any radical way. Instead, it unleashed wage demands by the workforce, induced inventory accumulation and enhanced case-by-case bargaining between enterprises and the planning office or branch ministries to obtain ad hoc tax preferences and subsidies.[5] Meanwhile, to balance the state

[4] The lack of a hard budget constraint for state-owned enterprises was the object of the well-known analysis by Kornai (1980).

[5] In addition, until its collapse, in the Soviet Union a large number of industry-specific branch ministries continued to allocate substantial financial resources from profitable to loss-making enterprises. In 1990, at the time of the enactment of the enterprise income tax legislation and announcement of reduced *ad hoc* budgetary intervention among state-owned enterprises, transfers through the centralized funds under the direct control of branch ministries are estimated to have amounted to some 5% of GDP.

budget and to reduce the monetary overhang, from time to time state-owned enterprise were subject to discretionary confiscation of profits and to forced savings schemes—including compulsory holdings of government securities.[6] The state enterprise sector was somewhat more amenable to indirect financial instruments after these reform experiments than in countries which adhered more rigidly to central planning prior to the transformation.

In the early stages of the transformation, especially in the new independent states, the state-owned enterprise constituted a major institutional impediment to fiscal and monetary restraint. This impediment resulted from a complex interaction among the state-owned enterprises, the banking system, and the fiscal and monetary authorities. The enterprises through their representatives in the legislature could exercise strong influence on the central bank and the government to extend credits and budget transfers, respectively, without regard to macroeconomic consequences. Thus, the monetary and fiscal institutions, which abdicate their roles in domestic and external stabilization, and the state enterprise sector, which operates implicitly a host of quasi-fiscal activities—mainly public employment, income maintenance, and various social security schemes—all exhibit a dysfunctional behavior, at far less than an arm's-length distance from each other. Therefore, clearly, a fundamental requirement not only for improving allocative efficiency but equally for stabilization purposes consists of the redefinition of the objectives and behavior of enterprises as well as the redefinition of the role of the government in the economy.[7]

A Major Imponderable: Determining the Appropriate Policy Stance

The initial adjustment task faced by most economies in transition, including the new independent states, was the need to absorb the monetary overhang, which has been largely accomplished with one or several rounds of relative price adjustments. In the wake of these adjustments and without sufficient market discipline on the state enterprise sector—from within or from abroad—a wage-price spiral was fueled by mounting inflation expectations. At the same time, an extraordinary output contraction was inevitable as state-owned enterprises were no longer bound by the economic plan to satisfy merit wants. Externally, the contraction was compounded by the spectacular collapse of the Council for Mutual Economic Assistance (CMEA) and of

[6] Even in Hungary, in many respects at the forefront of the market-oriented reforms, there was confiscation of state-owned enterprise profits in 1985; in Bulgaria state-owned enterprise profits were confiscated as recently as 1991.

[7] For a discussion of the role of government during the transition in Hungary, see Kornai (1992).

inter-republican trade within the former Soviet Union. In addition, the reorientation of production from rigid (and often technologically obsolete) input-output relations among highly concentrated industrial enterprises toward market-oriented activities has been evidenced by an output implosion within each economy. The extent of this implosion depends on the degree of industrial concentration, openness toward market economies, previous supply or demand dependence on other centrally planned economies, and enforcement of the hard budget constraint on state-owned enterprises.

There is broad agreement among observers and practitioners that the macroeconomic policy stance, supported by structural reform, must be geared simultaneously to arrest, or eventually to reverse, the sharp fall in output and to extinguish high and variable inflation expectations—a very difficult double goal, especially in view of the technical impediments to the formulation of monetary and fiscal policies.[8] The first step toward this goal consists of setting realistic objectives for both performance variables. In principle, the inflation target would call for approximation of price stability over a limited period of, possibly, one or two years, while a broadly consistent growth target should be predicated mainly on structural reform measures aimed at improving the allocation of resources. However, in the initial years of the transition, the output target seems elusive; neither the level of market-determined potential output nor the feasible path of adjustment to that level is known. As a corollary, and in view of greater risk of high inflation, priority should be assigned to reducing significantly the rate of inflation; deceleration in inflation would pave the way for sustainable growth over the medium term (see Bruno 1992).

More specifically, the monetary stance has to be formulated on the basis of incomplete and largely unreliable information. Neither the necessary parameter estimates—lacking relevant historical experience—nor the expected value of the determinants—especially output and interest yields—are available to calculate even approximately the demand for money during the transformation. Instead, the desired rate of monetary expansion—often expressed in terms of a broad measure of liquidity—is typically predicated on a constant income velocity, pegged to past measured nominal GDP, with a wide margin of uncertainty.[9] Ex post, from a practical standpoint, it is sometimes argued that any shortfall in activity is broadly compensated with an excess of the price level above target, thereby approximating projected nominal GDP, while

[8] On the external front, most of these countries faced limited access to foreign financing (especially in the event of debt restructuring), which prevented the emergence of large current account imbalances.

[9] See Bredenkamp (1993), for reasons for targeting, instead, a narrow monetary aggregate.

money demand is implicitly assumed to remain inelastic with respect to inflation expectations, interest rates, or the exchange rate. Partly owing to these shortcomings in determining the appropriate monetary growth rate, it is worth considering the alternative of fixing the nominal exchange rate in terms of a hard currency—as done for example by Poland in 1990, following a brief period of floating. Such an approach usually needs to be supported by a restrictive fiscal stance.

In general, determination of the appropriate fiscal stance during the transition is also subject to limitations. The first involves the virtual impossibility of fine-tuning a neutral stance through the removal of the cyclical impact, as this would require a measure of potential output. As an alternative, it is tempting to simply compensate for the fall in output, due to market-oriented restructuring, with an injection of public expenditure, an accommodated revenue shortfall, or both, to support aggregate demand, with little regard for the resulting budget deficit. A second consideration, which to some extent helps address the first one, concerns the sources of financing the budget deficit. In the event that the deficit is fully monetized, as it is likely to be the case during much of the transition—absent financial markets for government securities—there is a serious risk of exacerbating inflation. Later in the transition, as the deficit can be financed from nonbank sources, there is a risk of crowding out private activity—as interest rates must be sufficiently high to attract such financing—at the very moment when there is an acute need to promote such activity. As a third consideration, it is necessary to define the budget balance as broadly as possible, and, in particular, the domestic borrowing requirement of the consolidated public sector, including any deficit on account of quasi-fiscal operations of nonfinancial state-owned enterprises and public financial institutions.

Thus far, the authorities in several countries in transition have correctly attempted to eliminate, or at least limit, bank-financed budget deficits to contain inflation pressures. By contrast, other countries have given in to the temptation of injecting purchasing power into the economy, particularly by continuing to subsidize loss-making state-owned enterprises through the budget or indirectly through bank lending.

Choice of Monetary Instruments

There are numerous impediments to the use of market-based monetary instruments of control in post-socialist economies: at the enterprise level, at the level of banking sector, and at the policymaking level. Only by taking full account of these impediments, is it possible to design and use instruments that are both effective for stabilization and least damaging to the efficient allocation of financial resources. Furthermore, in identifying the appropriate instruments, it is necessary to bear in mind the timeframe and manner in which eventually a given country can use successfully indirect market-based instruments. And, all along, there should be room for experimenting—albeit on a limited scale—as the more advanced economies in transition already do, with bank repurchase agreements, open market operations, auctions of government paper, development of money markets, and other innovations. So far, Hungary has made the greatest progress in adopting such instruments.

Economies in transition suffer from a number of structural deficiencies in the financial sector in general and the banking sector in particular.[10] The poor quality of the initial balance sheets, the inability of commercial banks to assess the creditworthiness of borrowers, and prevalence of moral hazard, are just some deficiencies that are likely to entail a long learning curve and a series of financial crises (see Harberger et al. 1992). Nevertheless, certain market-based instruments, notably an active interest rate policy—that is, sufficiently high deposit and lending rates, in excess of inflation expectations—can be effective in stimulating the demand for money and restraining the demand for credit early in the transition. In this manner, interest rate policy can also contribute to efficient financial intermediation in the private sector, consisting mostly of households and small- and medium-size enterprises.

In contrast to private enterprises and households, as discussed above, state-owned enterprises are more prone to respond to quantitative limits on bank credit than to interest rates. Not only the obvious lack of developed and integrated financial markets in post-socialist economies, but more important, the inability of privatizing or changing rapidly the behavior of a critical mass of state-owned enterprises, which will continue to dominate for a while these economies, limit the scope for using indirect instruments of monetary control. However, as experienced since 1990, rationing of bank credit has not been all that effective either. Indeed, as commercial banks restrict credit, either to stay within limits prescribed by the central bank or to abide by newly-adopted capital adequacy ratios and other prudential regulations, state-owned enterprises accumulate payment arrears vis-à-vis each other. The buildup of inter-enterprise arrears has been met already in some countries by specific regulations, including initiation of bankruptcy proceedings. At any rate, the accumulation of interenterprise arrears can be viewed as a substitute for previous easy access to transfers from the budget or from extrabudgetary funds controlled by branch ministries, and to bank credit.

At the policymaking level, successful imposition of limits on refinancing credits in the first place and then—as the commercial banks' position im-

[10] For a survey of the necessary structural reform measures in this area, see Sundararajan (1991), Blommestein (1994), and Lane (1994).

proves—on bank credit to state-owned enterprises, presupposes information and experience that in many economies in transition are patently lacking. First, it requires ability to determine the appropriate path of monetary expansion and to project capital inflows, and flexibility to adjust domestic credit ceilings in the face of large unanticipated changes in key macro aggregates—a tall order even for experienced Western central bankers. The difficulty in gauging the appropriate credit limits lies in the fact that the monetary authority must thread a thin line between responding in a timely fashion to an exogenous decline in output or jump in capital inflows, and avoiding a liquidity crunch given the vulnerability to financial crisis under excessive segmentation of financial markets.[11]

The second and in some respects even more demanding requirement involves the allocation of credit under the aggregate ceiling. The standard approach followed for example by Western European countries that have resorted until the 1980s to various forms of credit ceilings (for instance, under France's *encadrement du crédit* or Italy's *massimale*) as the main instrument of control, has been to allocate credit in terms of a uniform percentage increment in reference to a past base period for all commercial banks. During the transition this would be tantamount to freezing the industrial or enterprise structure of the economy according to the implementation of a central plan formulated under a defunct and obsolete regime; arguably, such an approach is inconsistent with the very essence of market-oriented transformation.

An alternative method apparently applied in some economies in transition has been for the central bank to ration refinancing credits or bank credits according to some desired profile of industrial development, which is risky in view of the propensity of planners-turned-macroeconomic policymakers to pick 'winners' and 'losers' and allocate bank credit accordingly. Another option that avoids such misallocation of credit would simply consist of a prohibition on any new bank credit for state-owned enterprises.[12] Despite its attractiveness for supporting price stability at an early stage, if binding, this option could also lead to allocative inefficiencies. Apart from a potential buildup of interenterprise arrears, the availability of internal equity funds to a given state-owned enterprise, or to state-owned enterprises in a given sector, could be an unintended windfall gain resulting from the sequence and profile of price adjustments, or from the monopoly power enjoyed by that enterprise or sector, rather than a reflection of the present value of its profits in open markets over a longer time horizon. Thus, from an allocative standpoint, a no-credit rule (equivalent to a 100% reserve requirement) is not necessarily more

[11] For a discussion of this concern and an analysis of Poland's experience with the 1990-1991 stabilization program, see Calvo and Coricelli (1993).
[12] See the proposal advocated in McKinnon (1991).

efficient than the former approach; at worst, it could quickly degenerate into case-by-case negotiation. Also, such a rule could deprive commercial banks from a potentially useful learning experience.

Nevertheless, a general approach that has considerable appeal for economies in transition, especially for the new states that broke away from the ruble area, is the establishment of a currency board—adopted in Estonia in 1992.[13] The variant—followed currently in Argentina—that seems particularly relevant would impose a foreign exchange cover only on new money issue, excluding the initial money stock. A major advantage of this option is that it obviates information on money demand and ensures price stability, dispensing with central bank expertise in discretionary monetary control. Furthermore, this could be a useful step for Central and East European economies that intend to move toward a fixed exchange rate-based money control, with a view to joining eventually a common currency area within the context of the Economic and Monetary Union (EMU).

Choice of Fiscal Instruments

Much like in the monetary sphere, the use of fiscal tools is handicapped at both the state-owned enterprise level and the policymaking level. The problem is, of course, exacerbated by the initial absence of an appropriate administrative machinery to collect taxes from state-owned enterprises (previously mostly effected passively through the banking system) and the embryonic private sector, and by the lack of an effective budgetary process and control.

Declining output and incomes have led to a sharp fall in tax revenue from state-owned enterprises. However, the high apparent (downward) elasticity of revenue to GDP, in real terms, in some countries suggests that this decline can in part be traced to similar pressures as those giving rise to the accumulation of interenterprise arrears. As a matter of fact, in a number of countries faced with relatively high tax rates, state-owned enterprises have accumulated sizable arrears in enterprise income tax and payroll tax payments, without the threat of bankruptcy. At the same time, fiscal authorities found it difficult to end industry-specific subsidies and case-by-case transfers to loss-making enterprises, especially when threatened by large-scale layoffs of redundant workers. Fiscal policymaking, again, carries the heavy legacy of central planning in a number of countries through conditioned reflexes in granting

[13] See the persuasive arguments in Osband and Villanueva (1992). However, a number of operational aspects of such an arrangement, including the ability to affect a necessary real exchange rate action, are yet to be tested. For a discussion of the case of Estonia, see Bennett (1993).

subsidies and tax preferences to enterprises, including foreign investors, identified as 'winners.'

More generally, once the budget is formulated, the fiscal authority finds it difficult to adjust expenditure or to adopt tax measures in response to an unanticipated revenue shortfall.[14] This can be explained in part by past rigidities of plan targets expressed in volume terms, regardless of financial constraints. Hence the need for a flexible mechanism to adjust actual budget outlays below appropriations any time during the fiscal year, in line with actual revenue flows. To this end, some economies in transition—Bulgaria, Czechoslovakia, Poland, and more recently the Baltic states—have resorted, in the context of stabilization programs, with considerable success, to cash rationing. Earlier, a system of cash limits was used in several industrial countries (United Kingdom and other Commonwealth countries) in the second half of the 1970s to meet the public sector borrowing requirement by containing the nominal growth of government expenditures in the face of inflation. A more drastic variant was adopted in certain Latin American countries to limit noninterest outlays to the actual monthly flow of revenue; in those cases, the immediate goal was to maintain a strict balanced budget target as part of a heterodox adjustment program to end hyperinflation.

However, the immediate adjustment burden imposed by cash rationing in economies in transition is much heavier than comparable techniques used elsewhere insofar as it is applied during a sudden fall in activity—which may look like a free fall from the perspective of policymakers. Such a process seems particularly burdensome in these economies where in the past prioritization of budget outlays subject to a financial constraint was an alien concept. Thus, in an attempt to implement cash rationing, the wrong programs may survive the ax, while productive expenditures are shelved. A related shortcoming is that the sharper the expenditure cuts, the more likely is the buildup of payment arrears that cannot be sustained indefinitely.

Beyond the initial transition stage, as output and prices tend to stabilize, cash rationing is to be abandoned, possibly in favor of formal rules to limit the budget deficit. More important is the case, particularly in the new independent states, for eliminating domestic bank-financed deficits. Such a fiscal rule can contribute to a significant reduction in the inflation tax and a

[14] Rapid response is also made difficult by the need to implement a large set of fiscal reform measures almost simultaneously. For an overview of these measures, see Kopits (1991) and the essays in Tanzi (1992, 1993). A recent discussion of the lessons derived from the experience with fiscal adjustment in Central and Eastern Europe can be found in Kopits (1993).

sustained growth performance.[15] Moreover, observance of this rule would be an integral part of a currency board arrangement. For the long run, economies in transition that desire membership of the European Union are implicitly committed to the eventual convergence of their budget and debt position relative to GDP, in line with the fiscal rules set under EMU.

An additional area where a fiscal instrument seems indispensable in the initial stages of transition relates to incomes policy. As observed earlier, the lack of cost-consciousness of state-owned enterprises coupled with the proliferation of various forms of employee participation in management (including the efforts of former party-appointed managers to retain their positions or effectively become owners of the enterprise in the event of privatization) generates considerable wage pressures, fueling inflation in the wake of the initial round of price adjustments. To contain these wage pressures, various forms of tax-based incomes policy were adopted, following the example of Hungary and Poland during the earlier market-oriented reforms. Although similar to the tax-based incomes policies introduced in some West European countries in the 1970s, in economies in transition the tax was imposed at highly progressive marginal rates (of up to several hundred percent) on wage increments above a certain threshold. The tax was found to be most effective and least damaging to labor productivity when applied on increments in the state-owned enterprises' wage bill, above a predetermined average increment consistent with the inflation target—as done, for instance, in Czechoslovakia and Poland in 1990-1991. The rationale for defining the tax base in terms of excess increases in the wage bill (rather than in the average wage) is to permit enterprises to grant significant wage awards to productive employees or to lay off nonproductive employees. While this approach could encourage much needed market-determined wage differentiation within state-owned enterprises, it would not be conducive to wage restructuring among state-owned enterprises to reflect interenterprise productivity differentials. Mainly because of this shortcoming on allocative efficiency grounds, tax-based incomes policies should be relied upon only on a temporary basis, until the advent of an effective collective bargaining mechanism—applied at present in Hungary.

[15] Indonesia stands out as a remarkable case where broad adherence to a rule prohibiting domestic deficit financing over the last two decades—following the external payments crisis and high inflation in the mid-1960s—contributed to the deceleration in inflation and a significant growth rate. The procyclical bias of the rule was apparently mitigated with extrabudgetary activities.

Is Stabilization Compatible with the Democratic Process?

An issue that requires discussion—especially in the context of the present volume—involves the relationship between macroeconomic management and democratic governance. Admittedly, this issue commands widespread attention in practically any economic environment, as exemplified by the perennial debate over central bank independence in the pursuit of price stability. However, it is of particular interest during postsocialist transformation where the need for restrictive fiscal and monetary stance may not be adequately addressed through the nascent democratic institutions. In countries undergoing transformation, the executive branch is often headed by weak and unstable coalitions, members of the legislature seek primarily to protect special interests, while the judiciary branch is neither technically nor constitutionally equipped to deal with market-based institutions. Furthermore, the democratic process itself is fragile and may be strained by politically extreme forces fed by economic hardship, social tensions and ethnic conflict. These conditions are not likely to be conducive to prolonged macroeconomic adjustment; indeed, in some countries, adjustment fatigue may set in even before the adoption of critical measures. Hence, an impasse may emerge when widely splintered political factions prevent the formation of a government for several months at a time.

The potential conflict between stabilization and the democratic process may be solved through legislative authorization for the government to take contingency measures in the fiscal area and for the central bank to take appropriate corrective action, to meet macroeconomic goals as well as the agreed-upon budgetary and monetary targets, when confronted, for example, with unanticipated shortfalls in tax revenue or claims on government spending. In this regard, the legislative enactment of a fiscal rule—disallowing domestic bank-financed deficits—possibly in the context of a currency board, implies delegation of taxing and spending authority to the government, without compromising the democratic process.[16]

This short-run tradeoff, however, does not invalidate the much broader complementarity over the medium to long run between economic liberali-

[16] In 1992, at the time of the currency reform, Estonia's legislature did in fact delegate considerable authority to the Monetary Reform Committee, and subsequently to the government to implement the currency board and a balanced budget—if necessary through cash rationing of expenditure. More commonly, in a number of economies in transition caretaker governments have assumed responsibility for adhering to a fiscal target, mainly by recourse to cash rationing, in the midst of a political crisis.

zation and the evolution of democratic institutions.[17] Indeed, durable market-oriented reform of the budgetary process, the tax system, social security schemes, and banking regulations, among others, must be predicated on an open and often prolonged legislative and public debate to create the necessary consensus.[18] However, legislation can be protracted and does not necessarily yield economically sound institutions. Clearly, action on a range of fundamental laws in these areas is likely to be slow and awkward given the congestion, magnitude, and technical complexity of the legislative agenda and the inexperience of lawmakers. At the same time, powerful interest groups seek to prevent enactment of reform measures aimed at closing loopholes in taxation and social entitlements, at eliminating rent-seeking budgetary practices, including procurement, and streamlining the inherited regulatory maze.

Concluding Observations

Given an extended history of central planning, institutional impediments associated with the state enterprise sector and a number of specific technical impediments, the authorities in economies in transition are at a disadvantage in formulating, let alone implementing effectively and efficiently, fiscal and monetary policies for macro stabilization purposes. The latter task is daunting for the best analysts anywhere, as reflected in the twin pressures on an unprecedented scale in modern times, of a collapse in activity and of the specter of hyperinflation. Moreover, insofar as possible, caution is needed to avoid a liquidity crunch that can contribute to a yet steeper output fall.

Under the circumstances, a number of relatively simple policy instruments stand out for their effectiveness. In the fiscal area, reliance on cash limits on noninterest expenditures, according to actual revenue performance, could, over time, be backed with an explicit rule that forbids domestic bank financing of the budget deficit. At the same time, to contain a looming wage-price spiral, it is necessary at the initial stage to rely on taxes on excess wage-bill increases. By necessity, the main instruments of monetary control will continue to be

[17] See the review of Fukuyama (1992) in Buchanan (1992). Despite the overall complementarity between economic and political evolution toward market and democratic institutions, respectively, there are many episodes of economic liberalization not matched by political liberalization, as illustrated, for example, by the pre-transition economic reform under one-party rule in Hungary and Poland.

[18] All along, of course, the democratic process needs to be subject to constitutional limits, which must be established in these economies as soon as possible. See Buchanan (1994).

ceilings on bank credits, supported by an active interest rate policy. Alternatively, in some countries, especially among the new independent states, consideration should be given to establishing currency boards, to ensure price stability, which in turn should lead to sustainable growth over the medium term.

A number of problems plaguing macroeconomic policymaking in the transformation from plan to market is not altogether unfamiliar to market-oriented economies, albeit on a far smaller scale. By the same token, the monetary and fiscal instruments applied during the transition have precedents of a much milder variety in industrial or developing market economies. In any event, these instruments are to be used only on a temporary basis in the initial stage of the transition partly because of their adverse implications for allocative efficiency and partly because of the loss in their effectiveness tends to erode over time. In the meantime, it is essential that authorities persevere in the implementation of well-designed structural reform measures in the financial sector and public finances, which will permit the application of market-based monetary and fiscal policies.

To conclude, monetary and fiscal management may be in conflict with democratic governance in the short run. This trade-off may require the legislative authorization for the government and the central bank to take whatever corrective action is necessary to contain inflationary pressures at the least output cost. This approach need not preclude the democratic process —within constitutional limits—that should buttress market-oriented structural reform during the transformation.

References

Bennett, A.G. (1993) The Operation of the Estonian Currency Board. *IMF Staff Papers* 40: 451-470.

Blommestein, H.J. (1994) *Experience and Lessons of Advanced Market Economies.* In this volume.

Bredenkamp, H. (1993) Conducting Monetary and Credit Policy in the Former Soviet Union: Some Issues and Options. Washington, D.C.: International Monetary Fund. IMF Working Paper WP/93/23.

Bruno, M. (1992) Stabilization and Reform in Eastern Europe: A Preliminary Evaluation. *IMF Staff Papers* 39: 741-777.

Buchanan, J.M. (1992) The Triumph of Economic Science: Chimera or Reality? Fairfax: Center for Study of Public Choice. mimeo.

Calvo, G.A. and F. Coricelli (1993) Output Collapse in Eastern Europe: The Role of Credit. *IMF Staff Papers* 40: 32-52.

Fukuyama, F. (1992) *The End of History and the Last Man.* New York: Free Press.

Harberger, A.C., M.R. Darby, S. Edwards, G. Kopits, and R.I. McKinnon (1992) Central and Eastern Europe in Transition. *Contemporary Policy Issues* 10: 1-20.

Kopits, G. (1991) *Fiscal Reform in European Economies in Transition.* In: P. Marer and S. Zecchini (eds.) *The Transformation to a Market Economy, Volume II.* Paris: OECD. 359-388.

Kopits, G. (1993) *Lessons in Fiscal Consolidation.* In: H. Siebert (ed.) *Overcoming the Transformation Crisis: Lessons from Eastern Europe for the Successor States of the Soviet Union.* Kiel: Institut für Weltwirtschaft.

Kornai, J. (1980) *Economics of Shortage.* Amsterdam: North Holland.

Kornai, J. (1992) The Postsocialist Transition and the State: Reflections in the Light of Hungarian Fiscal Problems. *American Economic Review, Papers and Proceedings* 82: 1-21.

Lane, T.D. (1994) *Financial Sector Reforms: Banking, Securities, and Payments.* In this volume.

McKinnon, R.I. (1991) *The Order of Economic Liberalization: Financial Control in the Transition to a Market Economy.* Baltimore: Johns Hopkins University Press.

Osband, K., and D. Villanueva (1992) Independent Currency Authorities: An Analytical Primer. *IMF Staff Papers* 40: 202-216.

Sundararajan, V. (1991) *Financial Sector Reform and Central Banking in Centrally Planned Economies.* In: P. Downes and R. Vaez-Zadeh (eds.) *The Evolving Role of Central Banks.* Washington, D.C.: International Monetary Fund.

Tanzi, V. (ed.) (1992) *Fiscal Policies in Economies in Transition.* Washington, D.C.: International Monetary Fund.

Tanzi, V. (ed.) (1993) *Transition to Market: Studies in Fiscal Reform.* Washington, D.C.: International Monetary Fund.

13

Financial Sector Reforms: Banking, Securities, and Payments

Timothy D. Lane*

Reform of the financial system is a vital part of the economic transformation that is currently taking place in the formerly centrally planned economies of Central and Eastern Europe. The financial sector cannot be regarded as just another sector in need of reform, but as one whose restructuring is critical to the success of reforms in many other areas.

The importance of the financial sector stems first of all from its ability to channel resources from surplus units, which are saving, to deficit units, which are spending more than their current revenues. Creating attractive vehicles for domestic savings is particularly crucial to satisfy the formerly-planned economies' vast need for investment, associated with the restructuring of other sectors of these economies; given these countries' limited access to international capital markets, most of the needed savings will have to be generated domestically. Moreover, the need for these scarce savings to be allocated efficiently to their most productive uses requires a complete change in the basis on which these countries' financial institutions have made lending decisions in the past. This calls first of all for substantial changes in banking systems. It also calls for development of non-bank financial activity—including securities markets—to supplement the banks as a means of channelling savings toward productive investment; the appropriate speed,

* The author thanks Gérard Bélanger, Ashok Lahiri, and Michael Spencer for helpful comments; any remaining errors are the author's responsibility. Views expressed are those of the author, and do not necessarily represent those of the International Monetary Fund.

H. J. Blommestein and B. Steunenberg (eds.), Government and Markets, 247–267.

nature, and scope of securities market development remains a subject of debate.

An additional reason for concern over reforming the financial system is its central place in the macroeconomy, associated with the creation of money.[1] Monetary policy has assumed a leading role in stabilization programs in transitional socialist economies, designed to check the inflation that all of these countries have, to varying degrees, experienced; this inflation has been associated particularly with price liberalization together with the fiscal and other strains of the transition itself.[2] Under these stabilization programs, monetary policy has often had to effect abrupt changes in the rate of nominal credit expansion, which have led in many cases to temporary real reductions in credit. Under the existing financial structure, this real credit contraction has been distributed across borrowers in an arbitrary, probably distortionary way—with much of the allowed flow of credit being pre-empted by the capitalization of interest on outstanding debts of state enterprises. It is possible that this misallocation of a limited stock of credit has exacerbated the declines in output that have taken place in these countries (Calvo and Coricelli 1992). Financial sector reform seeks to ensure that the impact of monetary policy is distributed more efficiently across the economy. Here, an important goal is to move toward market-based implementation of monetary policy, so that to the extent that credit is limited, it is allocated only to credit-worthy borrowers and rationed mainly by its price (Khan and Sundararajan 1991).

Another aspect of financial activity that is particularly vital to the development of a market economy is the payments mechanism, which permits transactions to be carried out efficiently and thereby permits economic activity to be specialized. A payment system is related to the role of a medium of exchange: it permits the separation of the act of purchase from the act of sale. In modern payments systems, payments are often initially made through credit, with final settlement in 'good funds' taking place later. This means, however, that some party has to bear the risk associated with the possibility that a payor may default before settlement has been effected; this also creates the possibility that the payment system can be abused, by making payments without having the funds available. The integrity of the payment system therefore depends on dealing carefully with the associated risks, and

[1] The appropriate role of monetary and fiscal policy in transitional economies is discussed by Kopits (1994).

[2] Some macroeconomic aspects of reform programs are reviewed, for example, for Poland by Lane (1992), for Hungary by Boote and Somogyi (1991), for Czechoslovakia by Aghevli et al. (1992), and for Romania by Demekas and Khan (1991).

requiring that settlement take place frequently enough to impose discipline on the payors.

This chapter explores some issues in financial sector reform, broadly conceived as including the reform of banks, the appropriate development of securities markets, and the modernization of the payment system. An issue that runs through this discussion is the critical importance of building *financial discipline*—put simply, the requirement that debt contracts be enforced.

Another common theme is the need for *institution building*. Many formerly centrally-planned economies lack the basic institutional structure of a market economy. The deficiencies include the legal framework, law enforcement, supervision and regulation, and policymaking. This means establishing a framework of rules within which a decentralized economic system can function, replacing a system in which the state is involved in every level of decision making. As pointed out by Buchanan (1994), this means limiting the scope of the democratic process—at a time when newly-constituted democratic governments are tempted to use their new power to pursue social betterment. In some cases, it also means recognizing the limitations of the market, for example establishing supervisory and regulatory structures to limit moral hazard in cases where market discipline is not enough.

Financial Discipline

Establishing financial discipline is a pervasive issue in financial development, particularly in transitional socialist economies. Under central planning, essentially all allocation decisions were made through the plan itself. Enterprises were only 'ostensible enterprises,' which did not make independent decisions but merely fulfilled the prescriptions of the planners (Beksiak 1989). In this context, the financial sector only served a record-keeping device, a check on whether the planned transactions had, in fact, been carried out. Enterprises were subject to 'soft budget constraints,' since any losses were underwritten through easy credit and subsidies, while the state appropriated any profits (Kornai 1980). Money was not fungible: cash and deposits were kept separate, and were subject to separate (cash and credit) plans; moreover, an enterprise could not spend its deposits at will. Circulation of money to households was also kept separate from that to enterprises.

The dismantling of central planning which took place in many Central and Eastern European countries in the 1980s or early 1990s led into a no man's land of 'neither plan nor market': enterprises were no longer subject to the discipline of the plan, but they still faced soft budget constraints. Credit was still given to underwrite losses, and even where bankruptcy laws were formally passed, the enforceability of credit contracts was obviously limited. Moreover, high inflation combined with controlled nominal interest rates implied that in many cases real interest rates were glaringly negative. In this environment—which still characterizes most socialist economies in transition—there is a need for a new form of discipline: financial discipline, which requires that borrowers obtain funds only at market interest rates, and only to the extent that they are expected ultimately to be able to service the debts they incur.

Financial discipline is essential for all other aspects of financial market reform to work. In the absence of financial discipline, the system cannot efficiently allocate savings among competing investment opportunities, since borrowers that may not have to repay their debts do not take the interest cost adequately into account (Dooley and Isard 1991). Likewise, market-based monetary policy depends on market discipline: in the absence of discipline, increasing interest rates do not check borrowing—on the contrary, they lead debtors to borrow ever more to pay the interest on their outstanding debt.[3] The payment system also cannot function without some kind of discipline: the payment system is ultimately a means of transferring claims on goods and services, and discipline is needed to ensure that the payee can ultimately make good on these claims.

Market-based financial discipline requires that three main conditions be met (see Lane 1993):

1. Markets must be free and open. This implies not only liberalization of market activity, but also requires that particular borrowers must not face 'captive markets' for their debt—as exemplified by the 'pocket banks' established by particular state enterprises after the liberalization of banking regulations in the then Soviet Union in the late 1980s.
2. Information pertaining to borrowers' creditworthiness must be readily available to lenders. This condition is needed first of all to ensure that borrowers are charged interest rates that appropriately reflect default risks, and that uncreditworthy borrowers are ultimately excluded from further borrowing. Adequate information is also needed to avoid contagion effects—that is, to ensure that creditworthy borrowers are not excluded from the market just because of defaults by other borrowers

[3] Other aspects of stabilization policies are also affected by financial discipline. In particular, many Central and Eastern European countries have introduced tax-based incomes policies to forestall the state enterprises' tendency, in the absence of financial discipline, to pay excessive wages at the public's expense. The absence of financial discipline may itself vitiate these incomes policies, however, as state enterprises may still pay excess wages and either fail to pay the tax, or borrow or run down their capital to pay the tax (see Coricelli and Lane 1993).

with some similar characteristics.[4] In this regard, the development of modern, standardized accounting systems is essential in ensuring that financial markets can do their work.

3. There must be no prospect of bailout of a delinquent borrower. If a bailout is anticipated, lenders believe that they will be unharmed by any default; they will therefore not refuse to lend to insolvent borrowers, nor require a higher interest rate to compensate for default risk. The prospect of bailout is the Achilles' heel of market discipline. What makes the no-bailout condition so difficult to satisfy is the problem of credibility: in many cases bailouts are considered beneficial ex post—to compensate groups whose protection from loss is socially or politically important, or to prevent one default from having systemic effects. Thus, even though there might be a gain in social welfare if the authorities could irrevocably bind themselves not to bail out borrowers, they often have strong motives to renege on any such commitment. Bailouts have frequently accounted for failures of financial discipline in market economies—such as during the recent Savings and Loan crisis in the U.S.: since depositors were protected by deposit insurance from default risk, funds kept flowing into insolvent institutions, and were often used for excessively risky ventures, exacerbating the crisis.

These three conditions are needed to ensure that market-based financial discipline works. For it to work *smoothly*, a further condition is needed: the borrower must respond in a timely manner to, or preferably anticipate, the higher interest rate spreads that lenders begin to charge as debt mounts toward levels that will be difficult to service. In the absence of such rational behavior on borrowers' part, market discipline is harsh: it can then only work by completely excluding prodigal borrowers from the market.

Bad and Good Debts

In reforming socialist economies, a serious handicap to market-based financial discipline is the existence of bad debts, including both bank loans and inter-enterprise claims. In some cases, their origin is in the arbitrary pattern of borrowing dictated under central planning, which saddled enterprises with debt without regard to their capacity to service the debts. In some cases, these historic debts have been largely eradicated by inflation, and most cases, they have been greatly augmented after the fall of Communism, as these economies have begun their liberalization and reform programs: price and trade

[4] This point is made in another context in Goldstein et al. (1991).

liberalization have exposed the fact that many enterprises are not viable at world prices (Hughes and Hare 1991); the breakdown of trading arrangements within the Council for Mutual Economic Assistance (CMEA) has also led to the contraction of enterprises in sectors that specialized in selling in the sheltered CMEA market (Rodrik 1992). In several countries, the state enterprises have been labor-dominated, and have chosen to protect workers from the risk of unemployment, maintaining their employment despite a sharp contraction in demand for their output (Lane 1994). In many countries the monetary authorities have also attempted to establish positive real interest rates, and in the absence of financial discipline this has led credit to burgeon through interest capitalization. All these developments increased the demand for credit, and in the absence of financial discipline, this demand has to a large extent been satisfied—if not through the banking system, then through the accumulation of inter-enterprise arrears (Clifton and Khan 1992). The result has been an overhang of bad debt that in many countries has been so large that the solvency of the banks has been in doubt, and in some cases the tangle of inter-enterprise claims has made it difficult to assess any enterprises' creditworthiness, and impeded the legitimate use of trade credit.[5]

The magnitude of the bad debt problem is impossible to assess accurately in the absence of financial discipline, since the payment or non-payment of loans then conveys limited information about creditworthiness: an insolvent borrower can continue to service debt by borrowing, while a solvent one can run up arrears with impunity, using this as a means of financing other activities.

The solvency of banks and other institutions is essential to their efficient operation, due to a moral hazard problem. If a bank, for example, is insolvent, its managers have an incentive to take excessive risks, as they face a one-way bet: if a risky venture is successful, they may be able to bring themselves back to solvency and keep a portion of any gains, while if it fails it is only their creditors who lose. This moral hazard problem applies not only to banks—whose opportunity to participate in risky ventures is almost unlimited—but also to any other kind of firm whose managers' liability for losses is limited. This problem makes it imperative that most banks and enterprises either be brought to solvency somehow, be shut down, or be controlled very

[5] The seriousness of the problem of inter-enterprise arrears has varied across countries: in Hungary at end-1991, gross arrears were relatively modest (6% of GDP), larger in Czechoslovakia, Poland and Yugoslavia (from 17 to 22% of GDP) and enormous in Romania (53% of GDP). In Russia, arrears reached 3.5 trillion rubles by mid-1992. It is possible that some of these arrears may be voluntary, as the classification of arrears—usually as trade credits that remain unpaid after a specified period of time—is arbitrary.

directly and strictly in all their activities; the third alternative cannot, of course, be adopted indefinitely for many firms if the move toward a market economy is to be a real one.

Proposed solutions to these problems have varied. Some have argued that the authorities should simply enforce debt contracts, and use the bankruptcy process used to deal with insolvent debtors. An exception may be made in the case of banks, whose central role in the payments system, together with the obvious political difficulty of wiping out a sizeable fraction of bank deposits, may warrant some measures to recapitalize them rather than shutting many of them down.

There have also been proposals for wiping the slate clean, either by erasing all outstanding debts or by socializing them—that is, taking them on as a liability of the government (Levine and Scott 1992). Clearly, bankruptcy is a costly mechanism, which should only be used to the extent that it is an efficient way of weeding out inviable enterprises, as well as to the extent that the *prospect*—of bankruptcy disciplines borrowers and lenders. To the extent that old debts are an artifact of the old regime—including the highly distorted prices that determined enterprises' profitability in the past—they do not convey much information about the borrowers' current viability. Moreover, there is a general rule about bailouts: if there needs to be a bailout, there should be only one, and it should be now. Clearly, market discipline would be impaired much less by implementing a general bailout immediately, while creating the conditions for avoiding any future bailouts, than by attempting to maintain an unsustainable situation in which there is a transparent need for a bailout in the future—although of course avoiding future bailouts is easier said than done. There is also another consideration: enterprises that are actually insolvent—whether because of the inviability of their economic activities or because of a crippling debt burden—have no incentive to maximize profits, and unless they are shut down immediately, will constitute a further drain on the economy. If it is not known which enterprises are fundamentally inviable, universal debt cancellation or debt socialization could, simply by increasing the proportion of enterprises that are solvent, increase the fraction of economic activity that is guided by the profit motive, and thus bring about some increase in economic efficiency.

A counter-argument is that debt may itself serve as a disciplining device, in an environment in which the managers' interests may not coincide with those of the ultimate owners of the company. Such a divergence of interests occurs even within private companies, where managers may seek their own rewards or aggrandizement at their shareholders' expense; in well-functioning market economies, a complex set of incentive mechanisms limits—but can never completely eliminate—this divergence of interests. It is usually even more of a problem in state enterprises in reforming socialist economies, where managers are often beholden to workers, and may seek to raise wages and protect employment at the expense of the enterprise's titular owner, the state (see Lane 1994, Coricelli and Lane 1993).

In this context, debt may play a role in disciplining managers and constraining them to behave in a way that is more in line with the enterprise's owners. Debt requires that periodic interest payments be made to creditors, and that further borrowing must be agreed to specifically. An important function of debt is therefore to impound a firm's free cash flow, which management might otherwise try to appropriate or to channel into projects or acquisitions whose return is low but which increase the resources under the management's control. This function of debt has been identified in market economies (Jensen 1986). It appears to be particularly important in sectors of the economy which may be generating high revenues but in which investment should be shrinking.[6] The state sectors of reforming socialist economies surely have these characteristics: many state enterprises enjoy market power, are potentially quite profitable, and may have substantial assets (particularly, in the early stage of transition, large inventories accumulated as a store of value); however, the long-run inefficiency of state ownership, and the obsolete capital with which many of these enterprises are equipped, suggests that they should shrink over time—particularly as the reforms progress, bringing wage levels up toward levels in developed Western countries, and thus making these enterprises' wasteful techniques increasingly unsuitable. The ability of management (and in many cases workers, to whom the management is frequently beholden) to appropriate the assets of the company is also almost completely unchecked, given the lack of supervision of these enterprises by their titular owner, the state. Under these circumstances, an overhang of debt may serve a valuable function: to force the enterprises, through debt, to pay out some of their revenues, rather than allowing them to use these resources to stay larger than is efficient, and rather than permitting various insiders to appropriate them. This idea that debt may play a disciplining role suggests that there may be risks in a universal debt writeoff, or in taking all enterprise debts onto the state budget. For one thing, the benefits of such a debt writeoff may be reaped immediately by the workers through higher wages—especially when enterprises are labor-dominated—and by the managers through other benefits. Moreover, in the case of unprofitable firms which have accumulated debts to finance their losses, a debt writeoff might

[6] Jensen (1986) identified the U.S. oil and tobacco industries as sectors with these characteristics. He cited the (largely unsuccessful) diversification of large firms in these sectors away from their primary areas of activity as illustrating the dangers of free cash flow, and the subsequent debt-creating buyouts of some of these firms as examples of the creation of debt to discipline management.

enable them to accumulate new debts, in order to postpone painful restructuring and in some cases to delay their inevitable demise. This appears, for example, to have been the consequence of the real debt writeoff—the sharp reduction in the real value of outstanding debt—that was associated with the initial price jump at the start of the 1990 reform program in Poland, and to a lesser extent in other countries; the resulting 'paper profits' appear to have enabled many enterprises to pay wages in excess of the legal norm, to postpone needed adjustments, and in most cases to avoid shutdown (see Lane 1992, 1994; Coricelli and Revenga 1992).

How will this differ with privatization? It is often assumed that, as the enterprises are privatized, they will immediately begin to behave as profit-maximizing entities.[7] However, it is only realistic to recognize that any of the proposed schemes for mass privatization will give rise to rather weak control of management by shareholders—either because shareholding is widely dispersed across individuals, because it is channelled though mutual funds and other institutions whose incentives to monitor management are less strong than those of private owners, or because the government, or governmental institutions such as pension funds, retains a large interest in the ostensibly-privatized companies.[8] Under these circumstances, freeing the newly-privatized enterprises of their old debt, while it sounds like a laudable objective, has the drawback of removing the new management's need to pay out some of its returns to debt-holders—and increases the danger that the management can turn most of these enterprises' assets to their own rather than their shareholders' benefit.

The foregoing line of argument suggests that bad debt impairs financial discipline, but good debt may strengthen it. This makes the bad debt problem much more difficult to solve, since it implies that one must be judicious in how much of enterprise debt to write off. This means trying to avoid leaving enterprises a debt burden that most of them cannot service, but also to avoid writing off debts that they will ultimately (even with difficulty) be able to service.

7 Some proposals for privatization are discussed, for instance, by Borensztein and Kumar (1990), Lipton and Sachs (1990), Blanchard and Layard (1990), and Frydman and Rapaczynski (1990). While all these authors discuss the incentive problems—which provide the rationale for complex privatization schemes rather than a simple uniform distribution of shares to the whole population—they do not claim to solve them.

8 Demsetz and Lehn (1985) find, for example, that a highly concentrated ownership structure is conducive to efficiency in industries in which there is a high degree of uncertainty—which surely also typifies most industries in formerly centrally planned economies.

The other main reason for being judicious in any debt cancellation is the fiscal constraint. Any writeoff or socialization of enterprise debts—unless it is combined with a corresponding writeoff of deposits or other liabilities—entails an increase in the debt that must be serviced by the state budget. If enterprises (including banks) could be privatized by selling shares in a large and efficient equity market, any debt writeoff would of course be fully offset by an increase in privatization proceeds, but if equity markets are not efficient, and/or if (as is likely to be the case) privatization takes place largely through give-aways, debt cancellation or socialization inevitably means an increase in the fiscal burden. This is of concern in any country, but especially so in the reforming socialist economies, whose tax bases are narrow, their tax administration cumbersome, and their ability to resort to either domestic or foreign capital markets for financing limited.[9] A large unnecessary socialization of debt would therefore mean an increase in distortionary taxation, probably including increased resort to the inflation tax.[10]

The conclusion of this discussion is that there is no good alternative to undertaking a speedy but careful assessment of the magnitude of the bad debt problem in each country. Such an assessment should if necessary be used as the basis for an immediate reduction of enterprise debts outstanding as of a particular cut-off date—a reduction which should be partial, but should be judged sufficient to remove the need for any further general bailout. After this has been done, attempts should be made to enforce credit contracts, and to make it clear that they will be enforced.

The Role of Banks and Securities Markets

Financial sector reforms can be divided into two parts: the reform of banks and the development of non-bank finance. Bank reform begins with the rather haphazard banking system that resulted from the devolution, during the period 1987-1990, of central banks' commercial banking activities onto newly established institutions, which created a two-tier banking system. In some countries, there has also been new entry of banks, either private or state-owned. The general area of bank restructuring has received a good deal of attention in Central and Eastern Europe, along with technical and other assistance from international financial institutions.[11]

[9] This is illustrated, for example, by the piecemeal approach that the U.S. authorities have recently been taking to failures of banks and Savings and Loan Associations.

[10] The weaknesses of the tax structure of formerly planned economies is reviewed by Tanzi (1991).

[11] Many of these issues are also discussed by Rybczynski (1994).

A fundamental issue of bank restructuring is whether viable banking firms can be created out of what are in many cases the district operations of the erstwhile monobank. The problems are not just how to deal with bad loans and recapitalize the banks, as discussed in the previous section. They also include dealing with the portfolio imbalances that arise when the existing banks have been made to specialize in particular categories of borrowers or lenders, and often to specialize either in borrowing or lending but not both—resulting in poor diversification, both geographically and across sectors, as well as often heavy dependence on the central bank for funds. There is an issue of whether these imbalances should be allowed to work themselves out through ongoing lending and, where possible, through interbank transactions, or whether they should be addressed through some kind of general portfolio reallocation. An alternative would be to regard these state banks as dinosaurs whose extinction is inevitable; from this perspective, measures should concentrate on limiting the damage associated with these banks' demise, setting up an appropriate environment in which the state banks can wither away and newly-formed banks can take over.

Even if one takes the view that the state banking sector should shrink over time, this does not provide practical guidance for immediate policy toward the banks. Replacing the old state banks with new banks will inevitably take time, since an abrupt failure of most or all of the large state banks would have extremely disruptive consequences. Meanwhile, the continuation of financial flows and the functioning of the payment system require that state banks continue to operate as efficiently as possible. For this reason, a great deal of energy has been put into the improving the existing banking systems. To start with, there has been attention to making these banks' operations more efficient: by training their management and staff, improving their computing facilities, introducing 'twinning' arrangements to facilitate technology transfer, and so forth. There has also been attention to prudential supervision: introducing standardized accounting systems to provide reliable data to be used by regulators, as well as establishing the relevant legal and administrative structures. Prudential regulation focuses on the enforcement of the capital adequacy standards recommended by the Bank for International Settlements. Competition is another concern: in most of the reforming socialist economies, there are few banks of any substantial size, and competition among these banks has been limited by their geographical and functional specialization, as well as by entrenched customer relationships with state enterprises.[12] The enormous interest rate dispersion in many countries—with borrowing rates at some banks sometimes exceeding lending rates at others—attest to the

[12] An extreme example is the 'pocket bank,' owned and controlled by particular enterprises, that are numerous in Russia and elsewhere.

segmentation of the markets, which limits competition. Another issue that has been given much thought—but no action as yet—is the privatization of the state banks (Thorne 1991). Privatization is viewed as an essential step in increasing banks' efficiency: private owners would care about banks' profitability, and could exert pressure for market-oriented lending decisions.

It is clear that, without a resolution of the bad loan problem—or a conclusion that it is not fatal, i.e. that most banks are still solvent—all the other measures mentioned will be either impossible to implement successfully or largely irrelevant to the efficiency of the banking system. A well-diversified portfolio is of little use to an insolvent bank. Technical improvements will be accepted only grudgingly by a bank that expects that either it or its losses will be liquidated, while competition is also a dull spur for such a bank. Likewise, prudential regulation of banks with negative capital has little meaning; for such banks, much more pervasive controls are needed to prevent imprudent behavior. Privatization generally also requires that banks be recapitalized first: there are precedents in other countries for the sale of insolvent banks, at negative prices, but that would require that there be enough other solvent institutions to be the purchasers—otherwise, the outcome would be larger, less competitive, but still perhaps insolvent institutions.[13]

What about securities markets? The problems with establishing efficient banks suggests that perhaps the banks' role should be attenuated—and accordingly that securities markets be established quickly and given the key position in the financial system.

Some progress has been made in establishing securities markets in reforming socialist countries. Central banks in some countries have begun to establish money markets—issuing Treasury Bills and central bank paper and entering into repurchase agreements for bills of exchange and other short-term instruments; these can play a role in the provision of liquidity to banks, and provide instruments that may later be used for market-based implementation of monetary policy.

In several reforming socialist countries, stock exchanges have also been established, trading initially in shares of privatized or mixed-ownership companies. To some extent, the latter development reflects the power of a stock exchange as a symbol of the rebirth of capitalism.[14] Can a stock exchange in a reforming socialist country be more than a symbol? Can it play a real role in the allocation of savings in the economy?

[13] There are examples of this procedure in the resolution of failed banks and Savings and Loan Associations in the U.S. Some approaches to dealing with problem banks are discussed in Fries (1990).

[14] This is illustrated by the fact that the Warsaw stock exchange is located in the former Communist Party Headquarters building.

To address this question it is important to consider how a stock market, despite a widely diffused structure of ownership, creates incentives for the efficient allocation of resources in a market economy. Shareholders can influence management through their possibility of 'exit' through the sale of their shares; this is the basic link that allows the stock market to act as a market for corporate control.[15] Dissatisfied shareholders sell their shares, driving the price down and making it advantageous for an outside group to buy up the shares and take over the management (Manne 1965). For this to work, there are several requirements. One is that relevant information be available to shareholders. This means both that the information must be made public—that is, that accounts providing relevant data on the firms' performance be published—and that the shareholders must have an incentive to monitor the firm's performance. If ownership is widely diffused—as is likely in reforming socialist economies, due to the relatively egalitarian distribution of wealth—any one shareholder's incentive to engage in such monitoring is relatively weak.[16] In developed market economies, other institutions such as market information services have emerged to reduce individual investors' cost of obtaining information, and institutional investors such as mutual funds play a role in concentrating interest in obtaining such information; all these arrangements, however, take time to emerge.

For securities markets to become a market for corporate control, it is also necessary that they be liquid, so that shares can be sold at short notice at the prevailing market price; without this condition—which securities markets in economics in transition do not seem likely to be able to satisfy soon—the shareholder's right of exit is hardly meaningful. Liquidity is also essential in encouraging investors to hold equities to begin with: if shares cannot be readily bought and sold at the prevailing price, they will be unattractive as a store of value, and this will make it difficult for firms to raise funds by issuing equity. Liquidity feeds on itself: if a market is deeper, assets traded there become more attractive, bringing more prospective buyers and sellers into the market, and further deepening the market. Markets typically must be in existence for some time before this synergy begins to work. Moreover, the liquidity of stock markets depends in turn on the liquidity of money markets. It also depends crucially on the development of banks, and their ability to supply funds flexibly at short notice to dealers and other specialist traders, who in turn make markets in equities and other securities. Moreover, given the present state of the banking system, the increased competition posed by rapid security market development might threaten their viability, in the

[15] 'Exit' in the sense used by Hirschman (1970).

[16] Demsetz (1986) discusses the importance of concentrated ownership holdings in providing incentives for shareholders to monitor management performance.

absence of an adequate restructuring of the banks. Thus, the development of securities markets cannot be viewed as an alternative to the development of an efficient banking sector; rather, the latter is a prerequisite for the former to go very far.

Some observers have suggested that, because of the limitations of securities markets, banks must play a dominant role in corporate control as well as in providing financing to enterprises. They have urged that formerly planned economies adopt an 'insider' model of corporate finance—something like the German model of universal banking, or the Japanese main bank system—in which banks have an intimate relationship with the firms to which they lend, having extensive shareholdings and placing their representatives on companies' governing boards (Corbett and Mayer 1991; Hoshi et al. 1992). Another aspect of these systems is the extensive cross-shareholdings among different companies. The alleged virtues of these systems are that they avoid the 'free rider' problem in monitoring enterprise performance, since the banks' stake as major creditors and in some cases as shareholders is sufficiently large to give them the incentive to monitor; these systems also, it is argued, give banks a longer-term perspective by locking them into loan contracts, rather than shares that they can sell tomorrow; they avoid the waste of resources in launching and fighting hostile takeovers; they create a greater incentive to restructure troubled enterprises, rather than simply letting them fail; and they avoid dealing with the problem of asset valuation, given the uncertainties associated with economic transition and the novelty of equity markets.

Clearly, banks play an important controlling role in all modern capitalist financial systems—in the 'Anglo-Saxon' systems as well as in the 'Teutonic' and Japanese ones. The role they play has been characterized as 'delegated monitoring,' which is particularly important in an environment with asymmetrical information, where firms' managers know more about their own operations than outsiders do (Diamond 1984). Banks watch their borrowers closely, which enables them to enter into more efficient risk-sharing arrangements without being cheated. Because banks are able to diversify the risks associated with their borrowers' activities, they can then issue fixed-interest claims which they will satisfy on pain of cumbersome and costly bankruptcy proceedings. Banks' specialization in monitoring is related to the fact that they typically issue short-term 'inside' debt. In this context, inside debt means that the bank has access to information about the firm that is not publicly available; it has been argued that it is important that this debt be short-term so that the borrower's ability to pay must be re-evaluated frequently (Fama 1985).

Clearly, given the uncertainties of transition and the time it takes to develop other non-bank financial institutions and markets, bank lending will perforce be particularly important in reforming socialist economies. However, there are some dangers in introducing a full-fledged insider system, of the German or Japanese variety, in the context of Central and Eastern Europe. For one thing, the banks typically do not even have the internal organizational efficiency and expertise needed to function effectively as outside lending institutions, let alone the extensive managerial and financial skills needed to participate directly in enterprise management in the capacity of universal banks. Another problem is the danger that bank ownership and control of companies, and cross-shareholdings, might be viewed as an easier substitute for privatization—which could essentially amount to preserving the status quo. This phenomenon has been discussed by Kornai, who calls it 'pseudo-reform': he characterizes such arrangements—including enterprise cross-ownership, ownership by state-owned banks, and 'institutional ownership' by state pension funds, insurance companies or city councils—as 'hand(ing) over the ownership rights held by this state organization to another state organization, which in turn continues to spend the money of the state irresponsibly' (Kornai 1990: 71). Thus, although an insider system might have certain benefits once private property and competition have been firmly established, there is the danger that it would sidetrack the reforms on the way to a market economy.[17] This is a particularly salient issue given that, in fact, most of these countries have had insider systems under socialism as well, and that breaking the control of the old insider networks (viz. the former *nomenklatura*) is widely viewed as an important political goal in many of the reforming socialist countries.

Another potential drawback of the insider system, even if it is combined with privatization and competition, is the threat to the soundness of the banking system that may result from extensive shareholdings by banks, and from inside dealings. This was illustrated by the bank reforms in Chile in the 1970s, which liberalized its banking sector according to the universal banking model while maintaining government guarantees on deposits. Industrial firms were allowed to own banks, and banks were allowed to lend to their parent firms—permitting arrangements such as the 'bicycle' whereby a firm would use a bank loan to buy a controlling interest in the same bank. The scope for self-dealing, and for imprudent behavior at public expense was enormous; much of this behavior was uncovered in the financial collapse that occurred with the onset of the debt crisis in 1982 (Eastwood and Durski 1992). There is no reason to think that entrepreneurs in Central and Eastern Europe would be any less adept at exploiting the opportunities associated with unrestricted

[17] Competition in banking and in product markets is a precondition for an insider system to work, according to Corbett and Mayer (1991).

cross-ownership of shares—particularly given that the regulatory structures are in their infancy.

In conclusion, it would be unrealistic to base all hopes for financial development on securities markets; securities markets themselves depend on the existence of an efficient banking system to permit them to become liquid enough to play an important role in financing and in enterprise control. Moreover, banks' function of delegated monitoring is important in all advanced market economies. This suggests that scarce resources should be devoted to developing the banking system first, and only later to the development of equity and other securities markets. However, it seems risky to promote an insider model of enterprise control in an environment in which privatization has not yet taken place, competition in banking and product markets have not yet been established, and the existing insider networks involving state banks and state enterprises have not yet been broken, and in which adequate regulatory safeguards against self-dealing have not yet been introduced.

The Payment System

The payment system is a linchpin of a market economy, as it permits economic agents to undertake transactions in goods, services, and assets. An essential aspect of banks' role stems from their ability to undertake payments on behalf of their customers. For the payment system to function efficiently, there must be both an effective means of transferring funds among banks and the means for other economic agents to obtain access to these facilities.[18]

In most of the formerly planned economies of Central and Eastern Europe, the payment systems have typically been inefficient. This is largely because speedy settlement of transactions was not important under central planning, since the plan did not attach a time value to money, did not require that firms have funds available to make transactions that were authorized under the plan, and did not enable them to make use of available funds for purposes that were not included in the plan. Moreover, the facilities for interbank payments were not developed because, under the monobank system, most banking simply involved branches of the national bank.[19] Even after the monobanks were dissolved, the weakness of competition and the profit motive among the banks onto which their commercial banking functions were devolved—as well as the soft budget constraint that their customers in the enterprise sector

[18] These issues are discussed in more detail in Folkerts-Landau et al. (1993).

[19] The exception is the specialized banks—state savings banks, agricultural development banks, foreign exchange banks and so on—that existed alongside the monobank in most socialist countries.

continued to face—meant that these banks also had little incentive to speed up payments. These circumstances, together with the primitive facilities for telecommunications—or even the postal services, which were often still used for clearing checks and other payment orders—meant that long and variable payment delays were widespread.

In improving the payment system, several considerations are important. Clearly, improvements in computer hardware and software, and other facilities for processing payments are necessary. Moreover, there is room for encouraging arrangements such as clearing houses—which permit payment orders in different directions to be canceled against each other, and only their net amount transferred among banks. However, as the foregoing discussion suggests, the provision of technical capabilities is not all that is needed: banks also need to have the incentive to make payments quickly—which depends on the hardening of budget constraints and the stiffening of competition. The authorities also need to insist on periodic settlement, otherwise the system permits an automatic extension of credit to the banks; this is an important step toward establishing discipline in the system.[20]

In reforming the payment system, there is also a need to address some policy issues related to the allocation of risk among the participants. Specifically, the question that arises is what would happen if a bank participating in the payments system were to fail. Here, there are essentially three alternatives. One is that each payment undertaken must be accompanied by the transfer of good funds—a rule that avoids credit risk in the system, but at the risk of creating bottlenecks (if for instance Bank B awaits a payment from Bank A before its payment to Bank C can be made, but A cannot pay until it receives funds due from C); a Western example is the Swiss interbank clearing system. A second alternative is one in which payments are made even when the payer does not have funds immediately available, but these payments are not final until the end of some period when settlement is due for any net imbalance; in this case, if a participating bank fails before the final settlement is made, all payments made by that bank are unwound, and the payees join the ranks of other unsatisfied creditors. This arrangement imposes credit risk on participants—and in particular entails the danger that credit risk could become systemic as the failure of one participant imposes losses that lead to a failure of another participant, and so on, potentially leading to a chain of bankrupt-

[20] An example of the failure of settlement is the Bulgarian case, where banks' end-1989 clearing balances were still unsettled by August 1990. Another example is the Polish foreign exchange settlement system in 1990, which in effect permitted the foreign exchange bank to obtain credit from the National Bank of Poland, which by August 1990 amounted to around 40 percent of net domestic credit.

cies (Humphrey 1986). It also has the danger that a bank whose creditworthiness is doubtful but that is not actually insolvent would effectively be excluded from the payment system, as other banks refused to deal with it; this loss of access could be fatal to the bank, making the market's doubts about its creditworthiness self-fulfilling. Such an unwinding rule was used in the Clearing House Interbank Payments System (CHIPS) in the U.S., but was replaced in the early 1990s by a rule for sharing credit risks among all the participants in the clearing house. Another alternative is an arrangement under which the system is underwritten by the central bank, which extends credit to participants but requires that they have good funds available by the end of some interval. For example, in the Fedwire system, the U.S. Federal Reserve allows participating banks to run 'daylight overdrafts,' requiring that they settle in good funds by the end of the day. This creates the risk that banks on the verge of failure might deliberately make a large volume of payments through the payment system, with the effect of shifting credit losses from their creditors to the central bank. If such a system is adopted, it must be accompanied by close monitoring of the creditworthiness of participants, as well as by limits on the size of daylight overdrafts allowed (Folkerts-Landau 1991).

It is essential that countries that wish to upgrade their payment mechanisms take these issues of risk allocation into account in designing their systems, weighing the risk of payment bottlenecks associated with a system that insists that the payor has good funds available against the risks of abuse of the system by failing institutions that result from systems that issue daylight overdrafts to participants. In the absence of strong prudential safeguards, and when securities markets have not developed enough to necessitate many large-volume transactions, there is much to recommend a system that permits its participants to incur no (or very limited) overdrafts; this would enforce discipline in the payments mechanism.

Conclusion

In moving to a market economy, the central control that existed in a planned economy must be replaced with financial discipline—which means allowing decentralized economic decision-making while imposing hard budget constraints. The need for financial discipline was illustrated in the discussion of solutions to the bad debt problem: it was argued that bad debts weaken financial discipline, but good debts can strengthen it. It was also illustrated in the role of banks and securities markets, both of which play a role in monitoring enterprise management and in gathering information that may be used to determine whether and on what terms enterprises should obtain funds. Securities markets can potentially discipline enterprises management by acting as markets for corporate control, but banks also play a role of delegated monitoring—supervising their debtors' behavior and prospects. Finally, in the context of the payment system, periodic settlement was viewed as a means of enforcing discipline. In all of these spheres, another key aspect of reform is to build institutions within which decentralized activity can take place. These would include both rules and supervisory structures. An appropriate legal and regulatory framework is essential in cases in which market-based financial discipline is limited. The effective working of a decentralized economy also requires setting appropriate constitutional limits for the state's activities.

A sound, smoothly functioning financial system—the goal of these reforms—is key to allocating savings, facilitating transactions, and governing the use of resources in a nascent market economy.

References

Aghevli, B.B., E. Borensztein and T. Van der Willigen (1992) Stabilization and Structural Reform in the Czech and Slovak Federal Republic: First Stage. Washington, D.C.: International Monetary Fund. IMF Occasional Paper No. 92.

Beksiak, J. (1989) *Role and Functioning of the Enterprise in Poland.* In: *Economic Reforms in the European Centrally Planned Economies.* New York: United Nations. 42-50.

Blanchard, O. and R. Layard (1990) *Economic Change in Poland.* In: *The Polish Transformation: Programme and Progress.* London: Centre for Research into Communist Economies. 63-83.

Boote, A. and J. Somogyi (1991) Economic Reform in Hungary Since 1968. Washington, D.C.: International Monetary Fund. IMF Occasional Paper No. 83.

Borensztein, E. and M.S. Kumar (1990) Proposals for Privatization in Eastern Europe. *IMF Staff Papers* 38: 300-326.

Buchanan, J.M. (1994) *Democracy Within Constitutional Limits.* In this volume.

Calvo, G.A. and F. Coricelli (1992) Stagflationary Effects of Stabilization Programs in Reforming Socialist Economies: Enterprise-Side versus Household-Side Effects. *World Bank Economic Review* 6: 71-90.

Clifton, E. and M.S. Khan (1992) Inter-Enterprise Arrears in Transforming Economies: The Case of Romania. Washington, D.C.: International Monetary Fund. mimeo.

Corbett, J. and C.P. Mayer (1991) Financial Reform in Eastern Europe: Progress with the Wrong Model. London: Centre for Economic Policy Research. Working Paper No. 603.

Coricelli, F. and A. Revenga (eds.) (1992) *Wage Policy During the Transition to a Market Economy: Poland 1990-91.* Washington, D.C.: World Bank. Discussion Paper No. 158.

Coricelli, F. and T.D. Lane (1993) Wage Controls During the Transition from Central Planning to a Market Economy. *World Bank Research Observer* 8: 195-210.

Demekas, D.G. and M.S. Khan (1991) The Rumanian Economic Reform Program. Washington, D.C.: International Monetary Fund. IMF Occasional Paper No. 89.

Demsetz, H. (1986) Corporate Control, Insider Trading, and Rates of Return. *American Economic Review, Papers and Proceedings* 76: 313-316.

Demsetz, H. and K. Lehn (1985) The Structure of Corporate Ownership: Causes and Consequences. *Journal of Political Economy* 93: 1155-1177.

Diamond, D.W. (1984) Financial Intermediation and Delegated Monitoring. *Review of Economic Studies* 51: 393-414.

Dooley, M. and P. Isard (1991) Establishing Incentive Structures and Planning Agencies that Support Market-Oriented Transformations. Washington, D.C.: International Monetary Fund. IMF Working Paper WP/91/113.

Eastwood, R. and A. Durski (1992) Financial Reform in Poland: Some Parallels with Chilean Experience 1973-83, paper presented at conference on Macroeconomic Stabilization and the Internationalization of the Polish Economy, Warsaw University.

Fama, E.F. (1985) What's Special About Banks? *Journal of Monetary Economics* 15: 29-39.

Folkerts-Landau, D. (1991) *Systemic Financial Risk in Payment Systems.* In: *Determinants and Systemic Consequences of International Capital Flows.* Washington, D.C.: International Monetary Fund. IMF Occasional Paper No. 77. 46-67.

Folkerts-Landau, D., P. Garber and T. Lane (1993) Payment System Reform in Formerly Centrally-Planned Economies. *Journal of Banking and Finance* 17: 849-868.

Fries, S.M. (1990) Issues in the Reform of Deposit Insurance and Regulation of Depository Institutions. Washington, D.C.: International Monetary Fund. IMF Working Paper WP/91/74.

Frydman, R. and A. Rapaczynski (1990) Markets and Institutions in Large-Scale Privatizations: An Approach to Economic Transformations in Eastern Europe. New York: New York University. mimeo.

Goldstein, M., D.J. Mathieson and T. Lane (1991) Determinants and Systemic Consequences of International Capital Flows. In: *Determinants and Systemic Consequences of International Capital Flows.* Washington, D.C.: International Monetary Fund. IMF Occasional Paper No. 77. 1-45.

Hirschman, A.O. (1970) *Exit, Voice, and Loyalty: Responses to Decline in Firms, Organizations, and States.* Cambridge: Harvard University Press.

Hoshi, T., A. Kashyap and G. Loveman (1992) Lessons from the Japanese Main Bank System for Financial System Reform in Poland, paper presented at conference on Bank Structure and Competition, Federal Reserve Bank of Chicago, May.

Hughes, G. and P. Hare (1991) The International Competitiveness of Industries in Bulgaria, Czechoslovakia, Hungary and Poland. London: Centre for Economic Policy Research. Division Paper No. 543.

Humphrey, D.B. (1986) *Payments Finality and the Risk of Settlement Failure.* In: A. Saunders and L.B. White (eds.) *Technology and the Regulation of Financial Markets: Securities, Futures, and Banking.* Lexington: Lexington Books. 97-120.

Jensen, M.C. (1986) Agency Costs of Free Cash Flow, Corporate Finance, and Takeovers. *American Economic Review, Papers and Proceedings* 76: 323-329.

Khan, M.S. and V. Sundararajan (1991) Financial Sector Reforms and Monetary Policy. Washington, D.C.: International Monetary Fund. IMF Working Paper WP/91/127.

Kopits, G. (1994) *Monetary and Fiscal Management During the Transformation Process*. In this volume.

Kornai, J. (1980) *Economics of Shortage*. Amsterdam: North-Holland.

Kornai, J. (1990) *The Road to a Free Economy. Shifting from a Socialist System: The Case of Hungary*. New York: Norton.

Lane, T.D. (1994) Wage Controls and Employment in a Reforming Socialist Economy. *Journal of Comparative Economics*. forthcoming.

Lane, T.D. (1992) Inflation Stabilization and Economic Transformation in Poland: The First Year. *Carnegie-Rochester Conference Series on Public Policy* 36: 105-156.

Lane, T.D. (1993) Market Discipline. *IMF Staff Papers* 40: 53-88.

Levine, R. and D. Scott (1992) Old Debts and New Beginnings: A Policy Choice in Transitional Socialist Economies. Washington, D.C.: World Bank. Financial Policy and Systems Policy Research Working Paper WPS 876.

Lipton, D. and J. Sachs (1990) Privatization in Eastern Europe: The Case of Poland. *Brookings Papers on Economic Activity* 1990: 293-341.

Manne, H.G. (1965) Mergers and the Market for Corporate Control. *Journal of Political Economy* 73: 110-120.

Rodrik, D. (1992) Making Sense of the Soviet Trade Shock in Eastern Europe: A Framework and Some Estimates. London: Centre for Economic Policy Research. Discussion Paper No. 705.

Rybczynski, T.M. (1994) *The Role of Banks and Financial Markets in the Process of Privatization*. In this volume.

Tanzi, V. (1991) Tax Reform in Economies in Transition: A Brief Introduction to the Main Issues. Washington, D.C.: International Monetary Fund. IMF Working Paper WP/91/23.

Thorne, A. (1991) Issues in Reforming Financial Systems in Eastern Europe: The Case of Bulgaria. Washington, D.C.: World Bank. mimeo.

14

Labor in Transition to a Market Economy

Cees van Beers and Jules Theeuwes

Rosa Luxemburg claimed that 'the realization of socialism will be the end of economics as a science.' Her prediction was wrong. Actually the reverse is closer to the truth: The end of communism gives an enormous jolt to economics as a science. The transition in Eastern Europe not only has far-reaching human and social implications, but also can be interpreted as a huge economic laboratory. Eastern Europe could be seen as the economists' superconductive super collider. It is not a neat laboratory situation, and testing economic theories and ideas about transition from a command economy to a market economy will be more trial-and-error than well set up research procedures.

Transition problems on the scale of Eastern Europe are not something that economists are familiar with. It has elements of development economics but is not exactly the same. Transition is not about development from a low to high growth economy but about changing one system into another. It is comparable with transition from a war economy to a peace economy such as Western Europe experienced in the forties and fifties. But, again, it is not the same because Western economies already had the whole set-up of a capitalist market economy ready to go and for most East European countries the capitalist experience was completely eliminated after the Second World War. The macroeconomic stabilization problems of East European economies have a Latin American flavor (high budget deficit, galloping inflation) but in Eastern Europe they are only part of a much larger array of problems. The economic infrastructure needs to be changed completely. Economists have notions and ideas but not one big 'plan de campagne' which could guide these economies flawlessly through transition.

H. J. Blommestein and B. Steunenberg (eds.), Government and Markets, 269–290.

This chapter will concentrate on one special but important part of the required change in economic infrastructure, the change to completely different labor market institutions. A labor market as such did not exist under socialism because it implied that one would treat a worker like a 'commodity.' Socialism did not allow talk about demand for and supply of labor. Yet labor is a very important factor of production in any economic system. *Having the right person in the right place while earning a fair wage* would be, in a nutshell, what one wants an economic system to achieve for its workers at the micro-economic market level.

At the more aggregate, macro level one would like the labor market to provide jobs for all those who want to work and to have a growth path for real wages that balances the requirements of real income growth and full employment.

The transition problems in Eastern Europe regarding the labor market will be analyzed along these micro and macro objectives. These are ideal objectives. Centrally planned economies in the beginning of the transition phase from 'planning' to 'market' will be far away from these aims. First, we will elaborate on the objectives to be achieved in an ideal and efficient labor market. We then discuss practical problems in achieving the micro and macro objectives during the transition phase of the former centrally planned economies. Finally, we ponder why labor market institutions play an important role in the transition of the labor market.

Objectives for Labor[1]

In the ideal world of neoclassical economics, flexible wages, perfect information and highly mobile labor ensure Pareto-optimal allocation. This is a static efficiency situation. All workers willing to work at the equilibrium wage rate are working the number of hours and the sort of job that let them attain the highest possible level of utility, given their earning capacity and preferences for work. All firms can hire the amount of workers they need at the equilibrium wage rate and employ people in jobs in which their productive capacities are best used. The allocation of workers over jobs is Pareto-perfect in the sense that one cannot increase any worker's utility or productivity by reallocating, without at the same time decreasing the level of utility or productivity of another worker. Pareto-optimal allocation of the labor market gives a specific meaning to the more general requirement: 'The right person in the right place.'

Wages achieve two goals. The wage rate compensates for the disutility of

[1] This section extends Theeuwes (1989).

work, and at the same time remunerates a person for his productive contribution. Under perfect conditions a person's wage represents the value society attaches to his productive time. It is, economically speaking, the 'right' wage, which does not mean that is an ethically fair wage.

Pareto-optimal allocation and equilibrium wages on the labor market are a package deal. They go hand in hand: A labor market in equilibrium is Pareto-optimal and a labor market can be Pareto-optimal only if it is in equilibrium. The optimal characteristics of such a perfect market equilibrium can be described in terms of equalities of marginal rates of transformation in production and consumption. In no way should one expect these perfect properties to hold for any particular labor market at any particular time. For instance, it is assumed that labor is perfectly mobile and reacts friction-free to the smallest wage differential in a system of completely flexible wages. It would be absurd to claim that this is a realistic description of the real world. Still the properties of this perfect neoclassical model of the labor market are useful as a background for judging the functioning of actual labor markets. One would like actual labor markets to exhibit at least some of the better properties that characterize perfect labor markets. This ideal framework will guide us in analyzing labor market transition problems.

In the perfect neoclassical world involuntary unemployment is a theoretical impossibility. In the real world it is all too painfully present. The imperfections and the dynamics of the real world will always create unemployment. Unemployment is an unavoidable consequence of a dynamic market economy operating in a stochastic environment, being constantly bombarded with demand and supply shocks. But underlying this fluctuating unemployment experience is a natural or equilibrium amount of unemployment. The natural rate of unemployment was originally defined by Friedman (1968) as

> the level that would be ground out by the Walrasian system of general equilibrium equations, provided there is embedded in them the actual structure characteristics of the labor and commodity markets, including market imperfections, stochastic variability in demands and supplies, the cost of gathering information about job vacancies and labor availabilities, the cost of mobility and so on.

An aggregate labor market objective would be to have the smallest possible natural rate of unemployment.

In a dynamic world wages will always change. Real wages will hopefully grow. One can only hope for a growth path of real wages along which the economy balances real income and employment growth at the same time. Equilibrium unemployment and balanced real wage growth are properties for the aggregate economy that we will use to reflect on practical transition problems.

We propose to translate static Pareto-optimality and the desirable conditions of a dynamic and stochastic economy into the following practical objectives, two at the micro level (1-2) and two at the aggregate level (3-4):[2]

1. correct allocation,
2. just wage structure,
3. equilibrium unemployment, and
4. sustainable wage inflation.

We will discuss each of these objectives in turn and show how they play a role in the transition from a planned economy to a market economy.

Transition, Allocation and Wage Structure

According to Le Blanc (1991) economies in transition still have a number of characteristics of a command type economy. Command economies can be characterized by:

1. *Central planning* meaning central allocation of production factors. This allocation, however is based upon unreliable statistical information and political preferences. Thus local adjustments are almost certainly necessary.
2. *Continuous wage drift* takes place within the framework of rigid income structures. Highly subsidized prices are administratively fixed.
3. *Public ownership* of land and other productive assets are mostly organized in large state enterprises even in the agricultural sector. Uncertainty in the production processes leads to excess equipment and excess stocks.
4. *Overemphasized heavy industries* which are managed in a technocratic way. Lack of market incentives causes absence of any inducement in product innovation in all sectors except military production.

On the other hand the more important elements of transition are:

1. *Macroeconomic stabilization*: growing budget deficits largely financed by monetary means resulting in a huge monetary overhang. Money has no exchange value neither internally nor externally. What is needed is a tough policy to tackle and gain control of the monetary and fiscal situation.
2. *Price and market reforms*: price liberalization, liberalization of labor and

[2] Similar problems are present in goods markets, where it is also necessary to translate the theoretical conditions for Pareto-optimality into practical guidelines for 'workable competition.' See, for instance, Clark (1940) for an early and influential contribution.

capital markets; financial sector reform. End of system of phantom prices for goods and factors. Steep increase in prices will reduce monetary overhang.
3. *Private sector development*: establishment of efficient property rights; demonopolization and promotion of competition; privatization and restructuring of state enterprises.
4. *Redefinition of role of the state*: involves legal reforms at the constitutional level (see also Buchanan in this volume), reform of legal institutions and information and control mechanisms (accounting, audit). Social security legislation is a complementary element in the total reform package.
5. *Opening up* to the competition of international markets.

Next we will first discuss the microeconomic transition problems and then the macroeconomic problems in an economy in transition from a command economy to a market economy. As explained above there are two practical objectives at the micro level: a correct allocation and a fair wage structure.

Correct Allocation

Making sure that the right person is at work in the right place is easy to define in a static environment, but hard to grasp in a dynamic economy. A static situation implies that productive characteristics and job preferences of the population are given. Also given is production technology and hence the distribution of jobs and job requirements.

Perfect allocation means that a person is working in the job where he is most productive, given his preferences. If there is perfect knowledge of both personal job characteristics and job requirements and if people are perfectly mobile, it should not be hard to allocate people and jobs in a perfect way. Problems arise when knowledge is not complete and mobility is not perfect. What to do when people get stuck in the wrong place?

In a dynamic surrounding, perfect allocation becomes even more problematic to define. In the long run people are more mobile, both geographically and functionally. One can always retrain or school people or encourage them to move. Old jobs disappear and new jobs appear. Through shifts in demand or technological innovation some jobs or industries have to be closed down, whereas at the same time new production opportunities require different skills. It is hard to define perfect allocation in such a context, but one expects that policies which encourage the working force to adapt to changes are desirable.

An important aspect of transition will be huge shifts in the structure of employment. Non-competitive production units will close down, laying off workers, profitable units will open up and emerge from the restructuring process at another place requiring different skills. To ease the reallocation of workers, mobility should be smooth and wage differentials should be allowed to arise in order to signal shortages. Socialist economies are coming from a situation in which the mechanism of the soft budget constraint (firms would always be compensated for losses) created implicitly an economy-wide 'employment subsidy program.' Surpluses in profitable firms were channeled to inefficient firms to subsidize employment. For quite a number of jobs this implicit subsidy drove a wedge between labor costs and value of marginal product. Hence labor inputs were not valued at their social opportunity cost which lead to huge misallocation. Part of the transition problems will be related to reallocating labor in a more efficient way.

Job mobility is extremely low in socialist economies. Whereas market economies have labor turnover rates between 15 and 20%, socialist economies experience only a fraction of that.[3] Vodopivec (1991: 145), for instance, mentions a 1% rate for Poland. Two problems can be seen regarding mobility. In most East European economies there is a housing shortage and housing was heavily subsidized. Workers are tied to their houses. Hence the housing market situation could substantially hinder regional mobility. A more general problem which also occurs in Western economies is that most of the adaption in the labor market is usually done by new entrants. Seniors in the labor market have in some sense established rights. The huge upheaval of East European economies, however, will require older workers to be both geographically and functionally mobile.

East European economies usually have a well-qualified labor force. Compared with OECD countries, they would be in the middle range according to educational qualification (see Boeri and Keese 1992). This will certainly be helpful for transition. Another advantage for East European economies is that they have paid and still pay a great deal of attention to vocational training (for example, comparable to Germany). Much (re-)schooling and training will have to take place but the educational conditions seem to be favorable.

Finally, one would expect a large rise in the number of self-employed (although this might in some cases be the underground economy coming above ground). There are two reasons for this phenomenon: (1) a pull factor, people who expect to be unemployed for a long time and live in countries with or without very limited social benefits are forced to start self-employment; (2) a push factor, people starting self-employment expect to earn more than in their previous labor force state (employed as wage earners, unemployed, out of labor force). This is a very desirable development as the

[3] Percentage of labor force changing jobs in a given year.

development of a competitive market economy will mainly rest on the pillars of private small- and medium-sized enterprises.

Fair wage structure

In the neoclassical model the wage rate is the maidservant of allocation. Wages should be perfectly flexible, and their level should function as a signal for shortages or excesses of the labor market, and as an incentive to change supply and demand. In that sense, wage rates are merciless and without any ethical foundation. Increases in the wage level should also be appropriate to allow for the right amount of investment in both physical and human capital. If one requires the wage rate to be helpful for allocation, or at least not to interfere with it, this will quite often contradict any ethical claim a society might have as to the level of the wage rate.

To the neoclassical economist a wage rate is just another price. This, however, is too narrow a view of the function of wages in society. There has always been room for wages to be influenced by non-economic forces —whether by custom, or by any other principle which affects what bargaining parties think to be just or right. Economic forces do affect wages, but only when they are strong enough to overcome these social forces. Wages have a triple role: (1) providing a fair reward, fair with respect to the effort put into the job and compared to what others in similar functions or with similar characteristics are getting; (2) taking care of allocation on the labor market, for instance, increase when there is a shortage, decrease when there are too many workers; and (3) motivating workers.

Economies in transition will have to set up institutions for collective bargaining and will have to regulate collective action much differently from the way they did before transition. They first have to make sure that managers (employers) have real power during the bargaining process to stop unrealistic wage demands. Managers have to run against 'hard budgets' if they accept unprofitable wage increases.

Recently, much attention has been paid in labor economics to the level of centralization in collective bargaining. Empirical work has started on the performance of different labor market institutions considering the optimal degree of centralization/decentralization of labor contract negotiations. According to Calmfors and Driffill (1988) both strongly centralized corporatist bargaining structures (for example, Sweden and Austria) and strongly decentralized negotiations (for example, U.S. and Japan) lead to more favorable inflation and unemployment levels than countries which are neither centralized nor decentralized (for example, the Netherlands). In strongly centralized bargaining, parties can internalize the macroeconomic effects of their negotiations. Decentralized bargaining has the advantage of a competitive structure. These results give some guidance to countries in transition when choosing their bargaining institutions. The wage bargaining institutions that have to emerge in East Europe may strongly differ between the countries depending on their own specific and historic characteristics.

The picture of wage dispersion in the East versus the West is mixed (see Boeri and Keese 1992). Vodopivec (1991: 149) argues that workers in socialist countries hold strong egalitarian sentiments with respect to earnings. In general there seems to be lower wage dispersion than in the West, but at the same time the low/high skill differential seems to be higher and there is less male/female wage equality. An increase in wage inequality during the transition period is to be expected. Flanagan (1992) argues in favor of an income policy in these countries during the transition phase.

The third role of wages, 'providing productive incentives' has been changing in Western economies. Blinder (1990), reviewing the evidence in his book on paying for productivity, argues that if society could start over again in designing a pay system that would encourage high productivity it would be most unlikely to choose the payment system that is valid in most OECD countries, for instance, payment by input. Yet, in the postwar period most countries witnessed a structural decline of wage payments by output. Those incentive systems are too simple to be effective in increasingly sophisticated production processes. In its place came group incentives and schemes that gave workers a financial interest in the overall performance of the firm (for example, profit-sharing and employee profit sharing plans). The link between productivity the latter schemes is somewhat doubtful. Most important and most difficult are managerial incentives in transition. Managers are pivotal in transition, their motivation helps motivate others. Good managers are always scarce and are certainly scarce in an environment that was until recently not very congenial toward them. Note that East European economies could be said to have suffered from a 'full employment syndrome,' guaranteeing all workers permanent jobs. This syndrome will certainly have reduced incentives to work hard.

Equilibrium Unemployment and Wage Inflation during and after Transition

We defined the practical objectives at the macro side of the economy as: (1) equilibrium unemployment; and (2) sustainable wage inflation. In OECD countries it was thought in the 1960s that economic decisionmakers could choose between a high wage inflation/low unemployment economy and a low wage inflation/high unemployment one, depending on their preferences. When in the beginning of the seventies Western economies experienced stagflation—high wage inflation *and* high unemployment—the idea of a trade-off dropped from sight. Attention concentrated more on long-run equilibrium unemployment and sustainable wage inflation. To capture these two objectives two concepts have been introduced in the literature: (1) the natural rate of unemployment; and (2) the non-accelerating inflation rate of unemployment. The first one was introduced by Friedman (1968) and the second one by the so-called New Keynesian way of thinking about unemployment and inflation. Both are equilibrium concepts. Governments trying to push unemployment below the natural rate of unemployment or the non-acceleration inflation rate of unemployment were confronted with unsustainable accelerating inflation. These two concepts originate from different schools of economic thought. However, their main implication—the existence of an equilibrium unemployment level and a non-accelerating inflation rate—is the same.

Actually, the non-acceleration inflation rate of unemployment is a long-term concept. It means that in the long run the economy in equilibrium will show an unemployment level as defined by the non-acceleration inflation rate of unemployment. In the short-term the economy will probably not be in equilibrium as all kind of internal and external shocks will continually work out on an economy. Although the non-acceleration inflation rate of unemployment is a theoretical variable, unobservable in practice, it represents an ideal situation that offers us a reference point for analysis.

Three questions need to be answered in this respect:

1. What determines the non-acceleration inflation rate of unemployment in general?
2. Did a non-acceleration inflation rate of unemployment exist before 1989 in the centrally planned economies and does a non-acceleration inflation rate of unemployment emerge during the transition phase from plan to market?
3. How remote are the economies in transition in Eastern Europe to the non-acceleration inflation rate of unemployment?

The existence of a non-acceleration inflation rate of unemployment indicates that labor markets do not function smoothly in the neoclassical way as described in the previous section. There are impediments to the complete clearing of the labor markets. These impediments are the result of the tension between the desired achievement of an optimal (for example, output maximizing) allocation of resources on the one hand and a distribution of output according to government preferences on the other. This tension has resulted in the OECD countries in all kinds of labor market institutions and government policies aimed at correcting the outcome of the functioning of a completely free labor market. The equilibrium unemployment as described by the non-acceleration inflation rate of unemployment can be thought to consist of two components, search unemployment and structural unemployment. The first one always exists at any moment as people quit their jobs and look for another. This takes some (short) time. Structural employment is mainly caused by labor market institutions and government policy aimed at protecting the labor force, for instance, minimum wages (see also Economic Commission for Europe 1991: 185-204).

By definition there was no structural unemployment in the East European countries in the pre-1989 period. Under socialism full employment—defined as no unemployment at all—was guaranteed for the state employees which comprised the majority of the labor force. That means that all workers willing to work at the going wage rate were able to find a job. There were implicit incentives in the centrally planned economies to maximize labor input in the production process. The systematic emergence of shortages in the production process, sanctions against managers when they appeared unable to fulfill the plan targets, gave rise to the creation of a reservoir of labor in the production units. Therefore, the demand for labor was larger than necessary to fulfill the plan targets in case of more certainty in deliveries and *much* larger than in the case of enterprises with a profit maximization objective. Inflation—accelerating or non-accelerating—did not exist as the central planner determined the prices conform the plan targets.[4] Consequently, a non-acceleration inflation rate of unemployment, as defined in a market economy, did not exist unless one is willing to define a non-acceleration inflation rate of unemployment with zero unemployment and no inflation.

After the collapse of 1989 the situation emerged of an economy with features inherited from the central plan period, but without a central plan, and an economy exposed to international market forces. For example, even though there was no longer a central planner for the new governments there was still pressure to maintain subsidized energy prices for the energy-intensive producing state enterprises. Even now (in Russia, for instance) it appears very difficult to abolish the state subsidies to these companies that are financed by money creation. This situation can be considered as 'neither market nor plan' (see also Borensztein et al. 1990: 2).

As the state enterprises were no longer centrally controlled but had to work in an environment that did not give appropriate incentives for efficient production, the ultimate result was: (1) a substantial decline in output and (2) an increase in unemployment. As can be seen from Table 14.1 and Table 14.2, it appears that output has declined substantially more than employment. An important reason for this phenomenon is that managers of the enterprises

[4] The price structure resulting from this behavior showed so many distortions that there were a lot of products produced revealing negative value added (see also Economics Focus: Russia's Value Gap. *The Economist* 24 October 1992: 69).

Table 14.1. Employment in Total Industry of Three East European Countries (1985=100)

	1988	1989	1990	1991
Czecho Slovakia				
Q1	101	102	98	87
Q2	101	102	99	83
Q3	101	101	98	80
Q4	101	100	93	NA
Hungary				
Q1	95	91	84	75
Q2	94	90	83	73
Q3	94	89	81	NA
Q4	94	88	79	NA
Poland				
Q1	95	92	87	80
Q2	95	91	84	78
Q3	94	90	81	76
Q4	94	88	78	NA

Note: Q stands for quarter; NA means not available.
Source: OECD 1991.

have often been appointed during the communist period and their loyalty to the Communist party has been a prerequisite to get an appointment. The future of this management personnel is very uncertain. They do not know whether they will still be in charge in one or two years when the privatization and restructuring of these big companies will start.

Therefore, management is not interested in the future of the firm. They have only one goal at this moment, which is to avoid as many risks as possible regarding their own positions. They have an incentive to strengthen their positions in the companies by choosing the side of the laborers and, thus, still maximize, or protect employment. That explains why, until now, the number of laborers that have been laid off is not large (see also Rutkowski 1990).

Another reason for this phenomenon is the decline of real wages, as price liberalization gave rise to price increases. At the same time, the weakness of the existing trade unions gave governments the opportunity to restrict wage

Table 14.2. Total Industrial Production of Three East European Countries (1985=100)

	1988	1989	1990	1991
Czecho Slovakia				
Q1	109.8	111.1	107.9	96.6
Q2	108.8	109.7	106.2	82.3
Q3	106.3	107.9	102.5	70.8
Q4	105.8	107.0	102.9	NA
Hungary				
Q1	102.6	100.6	92.9	81.6
Q2	103.6	102.1	90.5	71.7
Q3	99.9	94.5	84.4	NA
Q4	103.9	93.6	89.2	NA
Poland				
Q1	114.3	117.8	82.2	77.4
Q2	114.1	113.1	78.2	67.9
Q3	107.5	99.9	79.3	NA
Q4	115.1	107.6	87.0	NA

Note: Q stands for quarter; NA means not available.
Source: OECD 1991.

increases.[5]

As stated earlier the non-acceleration inflation rate of unemployment is a long-term concept determined by institutional and policy factors. Therefore, it is of importance to distinguish the analysis in two periods: (1) the short-term and (2) the long-term. The main concern in the short term is to achieve goals of price liberalization and stabilization. The liberalization of administered prices resulted in an accelerating inflation, especially in Poland in the recent past and today in Russia (the Big Bang). This reaction is nothing more than a signal to eliminate the shortages in these economies. The consequence of this will be—given nominal wage controls—that real wages will decline. Aggregated demand will decrease, resulting in substantial output and employment decline. The decrease of the aggregated demand is a (insufficient) brake on the price increases. Elimination of price controls also implies abolishing all kinds of subsidies on the prices of state enterprises' inputs. Production of

[5] In Poland, for instance, norms were set. If an enterprise exceeded these norms they had to pay penalty taxes that were sometimes 500% of the amount that exceeded the norm.

goods that are heavily subsidized will be eliminated (energy is a famous example). This gives a supply shock, that is, aggregated supply will decline and therefore output and employment will fall even further, and prices will increase further.

These developments cannot be considered an equilibrium situation. Unemployment is increasing along with an accelerating inflation in an economy in transition in the short term. The non-acceleration inflation rate of unemployment in economies in transition will be determined by the same factors as in a market economy. However, these factors, which are labor market institutions and structural government policies, are still undefined in these economies, which implies that the non-acceleration inflation rate of unemployment in East European labor markets is difficult to define.

In the longer term during the transition phase, every type of structural reform should be undertaken, especially privatization of the state corporations and restructuring. A re-allocation of labor from sectors with a comparative disadvantage to sectors with comparative advantage is necessary. This re-allocation will be substantial and therefore a substantial increase in unemployment can be expected. The immediate effect of eliminating the distortions in the price structure will be the collapse of sectors having a comparative disadvantage valued at world prices. The rise of new sectors with a comparative advantage will take some time after a number of institutional reforms have worked out. A kind of J-curve effect for unemployment can be expected. Tight monetary and fiscal policy, and elimination of state subsidies to the state enterprises will give the right incentives to dampen inflation. So, it may be expected that prices and, therefore, real wages will be under 'control' rather quickly but unemployment can be expected to increase substantially. The non-acceleration inflation rate of unemployment will not be influenced by unemployment and inflation resulting from demand restraining policies.[6] The structural imbalances caused by institutional impediments give rise to a higher non-acceleration inflation rate of unemployment. The ultimate and stable non-acceleration inflation rate of unemployment will emerge only after the privatization and restructuring process has been finished and worked out completely.

As stated above, it is difficult to define the level of unemployment and the wage inflation that can be considered dynamic equilibrium values in East European labor markets. However, we think that the non-acceleration inflation rate of unemployment in a labor market bearing the features of the East

[6] We think that the phenomenon of hysteresis, for example, increasing actual long-term unemployment will increase the non-accelerating inflation rate of unemployment, will not be a major problem for economies in transition as the structural reforms over the long term will probably eliminate long-term unemployment.

European markets is larger than that found in a 'typical' OECD labor market. This statement is motivated by a very important characteristic of the labor force in a former centrally planned economy: Its *very low* regional mobility (see, also, the previous section). This phenomenon is due to the rent control of housing in the central plan period. Artificially low rents result in a short supply of houses. Here we have an example how government policies in the short term—elimination of state subsidies and rent control in the housing market—can reduce the non-acceleration inflation rate of unemployment in the longer term. Increasing regional mobility will lessen the structural component of unemployment.

It is difficult to guess whether the non-acceleration inflation rate of unemployment in East European labor markets will eventually become smaller than in the OECD countries. On the one side factors like increasing regional mobility of the labor force and complete privatization of state enterprises in sectors having a competitive advantage can be expected to reduce the non-acceleration inflation rate of unemployment. However, at the institutional front several new labor market institutions will emerge, which will probably increase the non-acceleration inflation rate of unemployment. An example is the weak position of the trade unions at present (see also Svejnar 1993: 163). It is quite likely that in the future the trade unions will gain influence within the firms and, therefore, exert a stronger influence on the bargaining process wage with government and the employers. An increase in wage inflation and equilibrium unemployment can be expected from this rise of union power.

Labor Market Institutions[7]

In his recent review article on the role of institutions in economic history North (1991: 97) defines institutions as '...humanly devised constraints that structure political, economic and social interaction. They consist of both informal constraints (sanctions, taboos, customs, traditions and codes of conduct) and formal rules (constitutions, laws, property rights).' Institutions 'raise the benefits of cooperative solutions or the costs of defection' and they 'reduce transaction costs and production costs per exchange so that the potential gains from trade are realizable' (1991: 98). In the same article North warns against the view that institutions in society will always develop in an optimal direction, creating an environment that induces increasing productivity. History is full of examples of 'economies that failed to produce a set of

[7] This discussion on the importance of labor market institutions is partly based on Flanagan, Hartog and Theeuwes (1993).

economic rules of the game (with enforcement) that induce sustained economic growth' (North 1991: 98). To illustrate this he compares the existence, for thousand of years (until today) of the Suq in North Africa and the Middle East with its 'inefficient' forms of bargaining and the much more impersonal and efficient market economy of Western Europe. Sometimes society can get stuck with inefficient institutions.

Looking across market economies one is struck by the diversity in labor market institutions. One can only assume that they have been arrived at by historical accident such as strikes, wars, revolutions, crises. At such moments in history dominant aggregate preferences establish new institutions. When Solidarity stimulated worker-managed firms in Poland, it gave a new lease on life to the moribund worker councils (see Schaffer 1992). Once established, institutions are hard to change. Only the erosion of time and experience can weed out inefficient institutions. International competition can speed up the process. Changing institutions seems to be a very costly operation. Obviously, the East European countries have arrived at such a historic moment in which they can pick new labor market institutions.

It is very important for the (East European) economies in transition to build the 'right' labor market institutions like wage bargaining systems, minimum wage provisions and unemployment insurance systems, consistent with their own economic and social environment. Once these institutions have been established, they cannot be substantially changed for a long time.

Therefore, the choice for 'right' labor market institutions puts an enormous restriction on the ways—no matter how different they may be in several countries—to promote development of competitive markets (see also Blommestein 1994).

We will organize our discussion on the choice of labor market institutions in economies in transition along those special features of labor markets which 'explain' the existence of so many institutions in this market.

Many social restrictions and legal regulations govern the employment relation because this relation has a number of special features that other exchange relations do not. These special features of buying and selling labor services require a completely different set-up. There are at least five special characteristics of the employment relation.

Personal involvement. When selling labor services a person has to come along for the execution of the contract. When selling carrots, the seller usually does not care who the buyer is or what happens to the carrots afterward. Also, the carrots themselves do not care. When selling labor services the working conditions and the working environment become very important to the worker and can influence the wage that a worker is willing to accept. Socialist countries restricted the choices of workers in the labor market en they had to work in the social sector as there were hardly any opportunities in the private sector; they had to work full-time rather than part-time (Vodopivec 1991: 127).

Labor compensation has both a pecuniary and a non-pecuniary element. Comparing different countries, it is obvious that they choose different mixes of monetary and non-monetary compensation, of wages and fringe benefits, without necessarily having different unit labor costs (see Hartog and Theeuwes 1993). East European economies will have to place themselves on this pecuniary/non-pecuniary spectrum, while at the same time watching their level of labor cost as their economies become more vulnerable to international competition. Socialist countries used to have huge fringe benefits such as extensive programs for health and housing. In Western economies the recent rise in fringe benefits (as compared to pecuniary remuneration) is mainly due to the tax system.

Directly related to personal involvement is the level of effort that the employee exerts at his or her job. The employee can vary this level and has an interest to do so. The employer on the other hand is interested in a high level of effort but, at the same time, is unable to control this level to a sufficient degree (there is a problem of asymmetric information). Balancing the desired effort level of both parties requires intricate incentive schemes, performance monitoring arrangements, codes of conduct, mutual trust and so on. Williamson (1992), in his lectures on the global aspects of transition, stresses that motivation (or the lack thereof) was one of the major reasons why planning did not work. Labor market institutions in the centrally planned economies of Eastern Europe were so restrictive that they were an impediment to work motivation. They were strongly governed by political priorities of the governments such as guaranteeing firm specific employment (see also Svejnar 1991: 124). Laborers could not be fired, even in the case of neglect of duty, which is not a stimulus to increasing personal labor effort.

Obviously the personal involvement aspect of the work relation and the inherent danger of exploitation and alienation was an important reason for Marxists to treat the employment contract much differently from other relations and transactions in the economy. Yet, whereas trade unions or work councils in the West often represent the 'voice' or the social preferences of the employees in a work environment, a similar institution was unavailable in Eastern Europe. Trade unions were not independent enough.

Long-term relationship. An important characteristic of most employment relationships nowadays is their long-term character. When employer and employee start off with each other, chances are they will be together for a large number of years. To illustrate: the number of employees in the same job for five years and longer, as a percentage of total employment in 1984/1985 was in Germany, 63%; France, 57%; U.K., 62%; U.S., 40%; and Japan, 67%.

This long-term dimension implies that investing in each other might be very profitable for both parties; at the same time, the long-term relationship makes them hostages to each other. A worker learning the ropes of the production process of his employer specializes his human capital. This reduces the attractiveness of outside opportunities, increasingly so as time goes by. The employer spending resources on the training of an employee runs the risk that this investment will be lost if the employee suddenly decides to quit. As they mutually want to protect their investment in each other and their long-term relationship, labor market institutions develop to do just that. Seniority rules, promotion priorities, dismissal provisions are examples that come to mind. Western labor markets recognize quite early that labor was a quasi-fixed factor of production.

Command economies were notorious for their labor hoarding. Rutkowski (1990: 18) calculates that in Poland in the late eighties hoarding applied to about one-fourth of the labor force. The general picture for most East European countries would in effect be 20-30% of employment. Note that at the same time there was a shortage of labor in other sectors of the labor market. A long-term relationship in a labor hoarding setting is not very productive. The whole idea of a long-term relationship is not so much protection of employment but rather mutual investment and benefits. A long-term relationship is guaranteed but unproductive in command economies whereas it is convened and profitable in market economies.

Wage is price is income. As already stressed before, the wage is obviously more than just the market price of labor. For most individuals and households labor income is, if not the only, then certainly the most important source of income. Hence the price of labor is a crucial determinant of one's income position, and public policies often confound equity and allocational objectives. Anti-poverty policies or broader income distribution policies often try to achieve their goals through altering the price of labor. Minimum wage laws are the obvious case in point.

But there is more. Participants in the labor market often have a notion about what seems to be the 'fair' or 'just' wage for the kind of work they are doing. Hicks (1955) was among the first to develop this notion in modern labor economics. Recent contributions in the same vein are by Akerlof (1982) and Frank (1985). Also, 'just' wage differentials between occupations seem to be important considerations. It would seem to us that there exists no other market where relativities are so important. These considerations might set desirable wage differentials that one will try to protect against market forces. Note that Marxian economics recognizes the same double role for wages. In his Critique of the Gotha Program, Marx himself proposes not only 'from each according to his ability, to each according to his needs' but also 'to everyone according to his work.'

Command economies had an enormous system of state regulation consisting of rules for the total wage bill and tariff system (see Vodopivec 1991). The history of wage regulation is the history of the continual search for a 'perfect' system. This top-down regulatory system will have to be replaced by a system of collective bargaining.

In Eastern Europe the pre-1989 wage structure has collapsed. It was not difficult to prophecy that the exposure of the former centrally planned economies to market forces would not leave the wage structure untouched. As the strong regulation of wages by central governments disappears it may be expected that wage disparities will become larger. However, elements of fairness in wage distribution cannot be eliminated. When dispersion in wages increases continually, in the sense that a small (large) group of people earn very high (rather low) wages, the majority of the people may vote against further reform. This would be an enormous drawback against the transition process.

Economies in transition will need new institutions to accommodate the exit of firms and workers instead of the huge national bargaining system for employment subsidies.

Labor demand is derived demand. The demand for production factors is always labeled 'derived demand,' implying that the vagaries of product markets determine the fortunes of the factor markets. Prosperous firms have vacancies. Slumps on the product markets create reorganizations, layoffs and if worse comes to worst, even shutdowns. This creates a dependency for employees that is beyond their control. At the same time they seem to be risk averse and are not interested in sharing the uncertainties on the demand side (or there is an asymmetry in the ability of dealing with risks). Employees usually want stable labor income or, at most, one-sided variation, that is, they will gladly participate in profit-sharing but not in loss-sharing.

The approach of modern 'contract theory' in labor economics is based on the same 'stylized fact': Workers are risk-averse and employers are risk-neutral. Hence labor contracts are written in which insurance for workers is an essential element.

When firms in transition shift from soft budget constraints (with guaranteed bail out) to hard budget constraints they will no longer be able to hold onto unproductive labor. Hence workers in Eastern Europe will face much more employment uncertainty and, therefore, income uncertainty, than in the past. Although this move is unavoidable it calls for new labor market institutions (implicit contracts) that 'insure' against employment uncertainty.

Power relations. The view that employers bring superior power to the employment relationship provides a foundation for many private and public labor market institutions. Individual workers are seen as powerless compared to the employer. They are assumed to have less choice in labor markets than the employer. A coalition of workers may redress the power balance. Labor unions (or public policy) may establish a 'countervailing power,' to use Galbraith's durable term. In this way, labor markets become bilateral monopolies. In the pre-1989 period, trade unions existed but had no real power. Many of them survived after 1989 but their position remained weak.

This mental picture of the 'weak worker' versus the 'strong employer' also applies to other areas of the labor market. In many countries labor law is mostly biased in favor of the worker or some subgroups of workers (children, women). In some countries bluecollar workers are treated differently than whitecollar. Most of these provisions in labor law were established in times when capitalism was ugly and workers were untrained or uneducated and desperately poor. Some of these provisions would seem to be archaic for well-educated, high wage earners. In the former communist economies of Eastern Europe the contrast between employers and employees did not exist in the sense as described above. In the new post-1989 situation, especially when privatization programs start working, the contrasts between management (employers) and employees will emerge. And employers will need the protection of unions and/or the government.

These special characteristics of the employment relationship can help one to understand and can even explain the existence and importance of formal (legal) and informal labor market institutions. The 'special' character of the employment relationship is underscored even further if we look at the labor market from the viewpoint of market failures. There are several reasons why markets fail to achieve economic efficiency. Market failure is generally accepted as sufficient reason for government intervention. Important examples of market failure are monopoly (or in general, noncompetitive) situations, public goods and external effects. Governmental intervention and regulation is also accepted for equity reasons and in the case of merit goods.

Monopsony power at the demand side of labor has been historically offset to some extent by trade union power, creating a bilateral monopoly situation. Power relations, certainly when the division is very unequal, are often a sufficient reason for government to regulate or control the process of bargaining. Often the relationship between employer and employee is seen as one of unequal power and national labor law frequently has provisions that favors or protects the weaker party.

Many characteristics of the labor market have a public good property. Working conditions have a (local) public goods aspect. Work councils at the firm or plant level in which employees are consulted on working conditions are institutions that can channel the preferences of employees concerning working conditions. Public goods, such as a collective bargaining system that regulates the rhythm and ritual of collective agreements or the presence of official mediators in labor conflicts, are institutions which might benefit all parties.

Strikes are an obvious example of a labor market phenomenon which often has negative external effects for third parties. Merit good aspects are present in safety regulations, in restrictions on working time, provisions for holidays and so on. Macroeconomic externalities are an argument in corporatist institutions whereby the government consults with representatives of unions and employers' associations on social and economic policy questions.

Besides market failure there are also strong equity arguments for labor market intervention. Society usually has strong ideas about the fairness of wage differentials. The social insurance system does not just provide insurance but is also motivated by the desire to compensate the unemployed, sick and disabled for their bad luck at the labor market. Discrimination and comparable worth legislation is also motivated by equity considerations.

As it should be clear, organizing the labor market sector will be among the hardest sectors to set up in an economy in transition. A system of flexible wages and perfectly mobile labor, which is what neoclassical economics would prescribe, is not feasible. Labor markets are much too specialized for a simple application of the law of supply and demand. What economies need is a set of institutions that take care of the special characteristics and objectives in the labor market, in accordance with social preferences for fair income distribution, a satisfying and stable work environment, job security, human capital investment, worker protection and so on.

Conclusions

Institutions in society can be seen as a system consisting of three overlapping circles of legislation (such as labor law and strike law), self-regulation (such as collective bargaining, co-determination and work councils) and ethics (such as a fair wage notion). Institutions determine the ground rules of an economic system. East European countries in transition are on the verge of redesigning their economy and the choice of institutions is a very important one. In this contribution we discussed why institutions are important in the labor market and how they have to be organized so as to achieve a set of optimal microeconomic and macroeconomic goals. We analyzed four labor market objectives: (1) correct allocation; (2) just wage structure; (3) equilibrium unemployment; and (4) sustainable wage inflation. We discussed the problems and pitfalls of economies in transition in their choice of a set of labor market institutions which would allow them to achieve these goals as best as possible. The same goals are valid for West European economies. Economies in transition can learn from the failures in Western labor markets and combine the best Western policies and institutional choices with their own historic heritage and social preference in an idiosyncratic mix of labor market institutions.

References

Akerlof, G.A. (1982) Labor Contracts as a Partial Gift Exchange. *Quarterly Journal of Economics* 69: 543-569.

Blanchard, O., R. Dornbusch, P. Krugman, R. Layard, and L. Summers (1991) *Reforms in Eastern Europe*. Cambridge: MIT Press.

Blinder, A.S. (1990) *Paying for Productivity: A Look at the Evidence*. Washington, D.C.: Brookings Institution.

Blommestein, H.J. (1994) *Markets and Government in Advanced Market Economies: Experiences and Lessons*. In this volume.

Boeri, T. and M. Keese (1992) Labour Markets and Transition in Central and Eastern Europe. *OECD Economic Studies* 18: 133-163.

Borensztein, E., D.G. Demekas and J.D. Ostry (1993) An Empirical Analysis of the Output Decline in Three Eastern European Countries. *IMF Staff Papers* 40: 1-31.

Bruno, M. (1992) Stabilization and Reform in Eastern Europe. A Preliminary Evaluation. *IMF Staff Papers* 39: 741-777.

Calmfors, L. and J. Driffill (1988) Centralisation of Wage Bargaining and Macroeconomic Performance. *Economic Policy* 6: 12-61.

Clark, J.M. (1940) Towards a Concept of Workable Competition. *American Economic Review* 58: 241-256.

Economic Commission for Europe (1991) Economic Survey of Europe in 1990-1991. New York.

Flanagan, R. (1992) Wages and Wage Policies in Market Economies: Lessons for Central and Eastern Europe. *OECD Economic Studies* 18: 105-132.

Flanagan, R., J. Hartog and J.J.M. Theeuwes (1993) *Institutions and the Labour Market: Many Questions, Some Answers*. In: J. Hartog and J.J.M. Theeuwes (eds.) *Comparative Labour Market Institutions and Contracts*. Amsterdam: North Holland, Amsterdam.

Frank, R.H. (1985) *Choosing the Right Pond: Human Behavior and the Quest for Status*. New York: Oxford University Press.

Friedman, M. (1968) The Role of Monetary Policy. *American Economic Review* 58: 1-17.

Hartog, J. and J.J.M. Theeuwes (eds.) (1993) *Comparative Labour Market Institutions and Contracts*. Amsterdam: North Holland.

Hicks, J.R. (1955) Economic Foundations of Wage Policy. *Economic Journal* 65: 389-404.

Le Blanc, B. (1991) Economies in Transition. Tilburg: Center for Economic Research. mimeo.

North, D.C. (1991) Institutions. *Journal of Economic Perspectives* 5: 97-112.

OECD (1991) *Short-Term Economic Statistics Central and Eastern Europe.* Paris: Centre for Cooperation with the European Economies in Transition.

Rutkowski, M. (1990) Labour Hoarding and Future Open Unemployment in Eastern Europe: The Case of Polish Industry. London: Center for Economic Performance. mimeo.

Svejnar, J. (1991) Microeconomic Issues in the Transition to a Market Economy. *Journal of Economic Perspectives* 5: 123-138.

Svejnar, J. (1993) *Labor Market Adjustment in Transitional Economies.* In: *Proceedings of the World Bank Annual Conference on Development Economics 1992.* Washington, D.C.: The World Bank. 157-168.

Schaffer, M.E. (1992) The Polish State-Owned Enterprise Sector and the Recession in 1990. London: Centre for Economic Performance. Working Paper No. 191.

Theeuwes, J.J.M. (1989) *On Reducing Unemployment.* In: F. Muller and W.J. Zwezerijen (eds.) *The Role of Economic Policy in Society.* The Hague: Universitaire Pers Rotterdam.

Vodopivec, M. (1991) The Labor Market and the Transition of Socialist Economies. *Comparative Economic Studies* 33: 123-158.

Williamson, J. (1992) The Eastern Transition to a Market Economy: A Global Perspective. London: Center for Economic Performance. mimeo.

15

Financial Management in the Health Sector

Peter B. Boorsma and Ron J.H.A. Crijns*

All Central and East European countries have embarked upon large privatization programs. Although the elaboration of specific issues shows interesting differences (see OECD 1992) these programs show a common concern for the transfer of property rights in the (formerly public) business sector (comprising inter alia industry, banking and finance, and retail services).

This leaves open the question of whether the Central and East European countries will privatize other parts of the former public sector and if so, in what way. Leaving aside the specific sectors of agriculture (privatization meets problems in the former Soviet Union but not in Central European countries) and finance, the question is raised whether it might be useful to privatize sectors like public utilities or—coming more to the point—education, health, law enforcement or other sectors that will remain more or less within the public domain in the future.

Although it is not argued that these last sectors are suitable cases for privatization, there is certainly room for the introduction of more market-like mechanisms and incentives, i.e. for the introduction of a watered-down version of privatization, in the sense of introducing more private initiative and responsibility.[1] It is commonly accepted that the newly privatized companies

* The authors express their gratitude to M. Peter van der Hoek and both editors for their critical remarks.

[1] The ongoing privatization processes in the Central and East European countries all relate to the selling of ownership. This is termed privatization in the strict sense. In the Netherlands and other countries privatization in a broader sense might imply all modes of introducing private initiative (Boorsma and Mol 1983; Boorsma 1985) into

H. J. Blommestein and B. Steunenberg (eds.), Government and Markets, 291–310.

have to apply modern business techniques such as cost accounting, marketing, price setting, capital budgeting and financing. In many publications (see, for instance, OECD 1993) on privatization in the former communist countries these aspects have been stressed thoroughly enough. But the Central and East European countries have to change the functioning and performance of governmental organizations, too. Changes are taking place in the form of decentralization and devolution of power. Other changes to the external organization of the public sector might include the building of other types of institutions, like social insurance funds and semi-public or parastatal organizations, which are so common in countries like the U.K. (quangos), Belgium or the Netherlands.

In regard to those organizations which remain more or less within the public domain, not only are such organizational changes taking place or will take place, internal changes are also necessary in respect of their internal organization, organizational procedures, budgeting, cost accounting, tariff setting and so on.

Since it is absolutely impossible to deal with several sectors and different functions in one contribution, this chapter will deal with the reorganization of the health sectors in the Central and East European countries, and with the necessity to introduce public financial management to achieve a better resource allocation and improved cost containment.

This chapter is organized as follows. First, we give some information on the health sector in the Central and East European countries. Presenting a complete review in this chapter is impossible for several reasons. Not only are there finite limits to a contribution, one also is confronted with the large number of countries and the institutional variety, the difficulties in obtaining reliable information on institutional reforms in health care and in obtaining reliable data.

In the next section we argue that the Central and East European countries, will face rising health costs, which demonstrates the necessity of institutional change in this part of the governmental sector, not only to improve quality of the health services, but for cost containment reasons as well. We discuss the topic of public financial management of the health sector. Again the qualification is added that it is impossible to treat the topic thoroughly. No information is available on financial management in the strict sense, in health institutions in the different Central and East European countries (nor, for the same reason is it available for OECD countries). Three levels of public financial management will be distinguished. It is one of the postulates that many OECD countries, and probably the Central and East European countries

the public sector. Thus privatization might refer to contracting out, the use of user fees, hiving off, the use of volunteers, etc. (see also LeGrand and Robinson 1984).

as well, give enough attention to the macro level but certainly not to the meso level, which might cause problems because of the interrelatedness of the sectors.

In this chapter, we will not try to summarize the changes going on in the Central and East European countries. Rather, a framework will be sketched and some questions raised to help the administrators of Central and East European countries in their reforms. In setting up a framework, there is of course the question of the starting point or reference. In this contribution system elements in Western European countries in general and the Netherlands in particular are quite often mentioned. This starting point might be acceptable since these societies are characterized as social democracies, where market economies function with rather strong state interference in sectors like education and health. Such a society might be a better point of reference for health than a more liberal society such as the U.S., which is currently changing its health system toward European models (Aaron 1991; Reagan 1992).

Some Characteristics of the Health Sector

This section gives some information on health in Central and East European countries sketching the contours for comparison with OECD systems.[2]

The first characteristic of the health sector in the Central and East European countries has been organized in a very centralized way, leaving little room for decisionmaking on the lower levels (apart from medical decisions, of

[2] The view given here is based on the following sources: Grote Winkler Prins Encyclopedie, September 1990; The New Encyclopedia Britannia, 13th Ed. 1989 (in this respect more outdated); Country Profiles 1991-1992, Annual Survey of Political and Economic Background, The Economist Intelligence Unit; description of the health sector in Central and East European countries by the Netherlands Foreign Trade Agency, The Hague, 1991-1992; Sovjetunion 1980-1991, Bilanz der letzten Jahren, Statistisches Bundesambt, März, 1992; CSFR Health Statistics Yearbook 1991, Institute of Health Information and Statistics, Prague, 1991; Czech National Council, Dept. on General Health Care Insurance, 6th of Dec. 1991, Prague. Statistical Yearbook 1989, Hungarian Central Statistical Offices; Länderbericht Ungarn 1992, Statistisches Bundesambt, Mai 1991; Poland Statistical Data, Central Statistical Office, 1989, Warszawa 1989; The World Bank Atlas 1991, The World Bank, Washington D.C.; The World Bank (1992), Poland, Health System Reforms: meeting the challenge. Länderbericht, Staaten Mittel- un Osteuropas 1991, Statistisches Bundesambt, Wiesbaden, April 1991; Länderbericht Albaniën 1990, Statistisches Bundesambt, Wiesbaden, Juli 1990.

With special thanks to Mrs. J.M.A. Bakkenes, Economische Voorlichtingsdienst (Netherlands Foreign Trade Agency), The Hague, who kindly helped us to gather information.

course). That is not to say that deconcentration did not take place. On the contrary (see, for instance, Bulgaria (Länderbericht Bulgaria 1991) or Rumania), in many countries regional health centers, like those in Italy, were active and functioned as focal points, playing the central role, which in most Western countries is played by the general practitioners. In Poland, for instance, most of the health care programs are financed by 49 regional (or *voivodship*) health authorities, which receive their budget directly from the Department of Finance, not the Ministry of Health. These *voivodships* fund the 400 local integrated health units or ZOZs (World Bank 1992). Apart from these regional/local programs the largest share (80%) of health expenditure is paid by the Ministry of Health, covering the outlays of drugs, hospitals, sanatoria and so on.

In the Anglo-Saxon literature the distinction between decentralization and deconcentration is not always made. In our view, most Central and East European health systems were centralized, which implies that most decisions on investments, new buildings, allocation of specializations and so on were taken at the central level, where the central actor was using deconcentrated, i.e. regional, units.

As a consequence of the latter, Central and East European health systems are very bureaucratic, a second characteristic, implying a lot of paperwork for doctors, patients and administrators. The other side of the coin is, that for many Central and East European health systems poor management exists, not only on the macro level but also on the institutional level. Mismanagement is caused by many factors, one of which is that different systems may co-exist, as in Poland, where besides the major health programs financed by the Ministry for Health, other ministries have parallel health systems; these systems are not coordinated, there are wasteful duplications and so on. Another factor is that in most countries there is no monitoring or linkage of the outcome of clinical management with the performance of services.

Not only are the Central and East European health systems very centralized in their decisionmaking, they are all—one hardly needs to say—'national health systems,' in the U.K. This third characteristic means that all hospitals and other institutes and health centers are publicly owned and publicly funded, and that all people working in health care are public employees. Some countries show some differences at the margin, for instance, if doctors are allowed to work some hours on a private basis. In Poland, for example, a small private sector existed with doctors' cooperatives (World Bank 1992). In the former Soviet Union, an unquantified private sector existed in the form of a black market, where patients were paying a price to physicians in better hospitals to get treatment, to which they were not entitled (Kleemans 1992). The public character of the health sector in these countries also encompasses

Table 15.2. Infant mortality per 1,000 live births.

	1987	1988
Countries:		
Albania	28.2	25.2
Bulgaria	14.7	-
Czechoslovakia	13.1	-
Hungary	-	16
Poland	-	16
USSR	25.4	
Rumania	-	24
Netherlands	-	8

Source: see Table 15.1.

This gives rise to the casual remark that the former communist regimes have probably deliberately decided to increase quantitative standards such as the number of doctors and hospital beds per 1,000 inhabitants, while neglecting qualitative aspects of health, since in international comparisons with 'capitalist regimes' political success was measured with such indicators, besides, of course indicators such as infant mortality and life expectancy. At least this approach, well-known from the international literature on Soviet economics as moral hazard, might explain the quantitative increase in supply levels, while at the same time buildings and equipment were deteriorating. The Hungarian National Institute for Medical Information (1990) mentions the 'institutional interestedness in quantitative indicators.'

Table 15.3. Indicators of health-care availability per 10,000 inhabitants (1989).

	physicians	hospital-beds	dentists
Countries:			
Albania (1988)	14.1	60.6	3.4
Bulgaria	38.1	99.9	6.7
Czechoslovakia	37.0	102.9	5.5
Hungary	33.8	93.6	3.9
Poland	20.9	69.7	6.4
USSR	44.4	132.4	4.9
Rumania	21.1	88.9	3.1
Netherlands	24.2	115.0	5.3

Source: Ministerie van W.V.C. en CBS (1991: 186), Statistisches Bundesambt (1991: 54). National Institute for Medical Information (1990: 11).

In many Central and East European countries state funding has become an insufficient and unstable source for the financing of health services, characteristic seven, compelling governments to find other sources like social insurance premiums and private co-payments.

Formerly communist regimes were stressing quantitative measures, such as the number of beds, doctors, and dentists, characteristic number eight. This led to the neglect of technological developments[5] and may explain 'overcrowding at hospitals' (National Institute, Budapest 1990). Another consequence of this moral hazard (stressing criteria such as the number of doctors and beds) is the lack of modern medicine and medical appliances and equipment (see, for instance, Poland).

Central Expectation: Rising Costs

It is well known that differences in health costs between countries may be traced to different causes, not necessarily to differences in health quality. Nevertheless, it is quite common practice to compare health expenditures as a percentage of GDP. It is well known that this figure says something about the relative standard of living, with Western European countries falling in the 8 to 10% range.

Table 15.4 gives data for six Central and East European countries for 1987. From this table one may infer that health expenditures, as a percentage of GDP, are much higher in The Netherlands than in the Central and East European countries. The Dutch figure is normal for countries like France, Germany and Denmark, while the Central and East European countries' figures are more in line with figures for countries like Spain and Portugal (OECD 1992). Another interesting difference is between the Central European countries, showing higher expenditures, and the Eastern European countries, Rumania ranking lowest.

It is to be expected that the costs for health in all Central and East European countries will show rising trends, not only in absolute cost terms, but also in relative terms as a percentage of GDP. This expectation is based on the following arguments.

In the first place, Central and East European countries have adopted market-oriented economies with policies of deregulation and privatization in order to achieve higher standards of living as well as democracy. From Western experience it might be learned that a rise in GDP will reveal a rise in health costs as a percentage of GDP. To put it another way, macroeconomically, medical consumption turns out to be income elastic (see Boorsma 1991;

[5] In so far as this statement is correct, the result will be relatively long in-hospital stays, compared with Western Europe.

Table 15.4. Health-care expenditures as a percentage of GDP

	1987
Countries	
Bulgaria	4.7
Czechoslovakia	5.8
Hungary	5.3
Poland	5.7
USSR (1989 % NNP)	3.8
Rumania (1989)	2.4
Netherlands	8.5

Source: World Health Organization (1991: 8350, World Bank (1991: ii; 1992: 38), Ryan (1992: 229), Ministerie van W.V.C. en CBS (1990: 195).

OECD 1987). A rise in welfare will induce a greater rise in medical demand.

Second, the expected rise in welfare will give rise to a phenomenon known as Baumol's 'disease.'[6] The rise in wages will be evidenced in the industrial sector by rising productivity; the more or less corresponding wage increases in the public and semi-public sector (health included) will give rise to price increases. As a consequence, the nominal cost increases (price rises) in the health sector will exceed those in the industrial sector. This argument is a part of the explanation for the rise in relative health costs, mentioned above, apart from the rise in demand.

In the third place, another cost-increasing factor stressed in Western countries is the aging of the population, as health expenditures for the elderly are much higher than for younger people. This factor is certainly relevant for countries like Hungary[7], the Baltics and the other relatively developed parts of Eastern Europe (Schepin et al. 1992), Bulgaria and other countries.

In Western countries, the fourth argument, which is relevant for Central and East European countries too, is associated with advancing medical technology, giving rise to new demands and new expectations.

In the fifth place, an extra dimension is given to the last argument, since in the Central and East European countries as previously stated shortages of existing technology and medicine persist. Take Bulgaria as an example, which, in its 1989-1990 Reform, formulated goals for the achievement of in-

[6] For an extensive treatment of the phenomenon, although not using this name, see OECD (1987).

[7] Negative natural increase rates of -1.7 since 1985 (The National Institute for Medical Information 1990).

ternational standards in diagnosis and therapy and the termination of medicine shortages.[8]

In the sixth place, several sources state that many health institutes, such as hospitals, face severe arrears in maintenance/major renovation which requires substantial investment.

Seventh, in many Western countries, such as the Netherlands, Belgium and Spain, decisions on major investments in high-tech, capital-intensive equipment and in specialized (e.g. academic) hospitals are taken at a central level to avoid overcapacity and improve cost containment. Belgium is an interesting case for the Central and East European countries, as the federalization of the country into three more-or-less independent parts leads to the doubling (or tripling) of such expensive investment decisions. Such indications also exist for Canada (with one of the best health systems in the world): since health care is a responsibility of the provinces, total administrative costs seem to be high.

Indeed, since the democratization of the Central and East European countries nationalism has given rise to many newly independent or semi-independent states and regions. This will also lead to the doubling or multiplication of investments, to rising administrative costs, and to some overcapacity of services for the area as a whole.

In the eighth place, the opening up of Central and East European economies to tourism, travel, news and so on, will lead to a faster spread of new ideas and cultural standards. It is expected that the levels of personal ambition for health, life expectancy, elderly care and so on will rise to Western standards. Improvements which raise life expectancy will definitely induce the rise in health costs as a percentage of GNP.

The overall conclusion (or central hypothesis) is that the Central and East European countries will face rising health costs as a percentage of GDP, not only because of the rise in welfare but also because of the decline in health, the existing shortages and the costs of overdue maintenance.

Public Financial Management: Three Levels

If this central hypothesis of an inevitable and substantial rise of health costs is plausible, the necessity of public financial management for the health system has been demonstrated. Such management has to be substantiated at several levels to be fully effective: on the macro level, on the institutional (meso)

[8] It remains to be seen whether the right policy approach has been chosen to achieve the latter goal.

level and on the individual (micro) level.[9] As one studies the reports on health reform in the Central and East European countries one cannot escape the impression that much attention is given to some macro questions but not to all aspects on the three levels, the meso level being especially disregarded. In the existing literature on health economics a good deal of attention has been spent on the macro and micro aspects.[10] For this reason only a few aspects will be treated in this chapter. But just a few topics for the meso level will be mentioned as well, not only because of the limits of this chapter, but more because this public financial management approach on the meso level is rather terra incognita, even more so for the Central and East European countries.

On the *macro* level public financial management—known as allocation—implies the *choice of a funding mechanism.* Up until now or recently, the Central and East European countries have been funding their health sector from central financial means, mostly from central taxes. The same is true in Western countries with a national health system such as the U.K. and Portugal, and Spain has been increasing part of the funding (or 'financing' as most authors say) from taxes since 1986. Instead of taxes, the funding might come from social insurance funds, 'financed' by premiums, and/or private insurance funds. A third income source is direct payments from users. There is an argument for financing health by central taxes. In that case, central government has to weigh extra health expenditures against other governmental priorities or against an extra tax burden. This may preclude practices like those in the Netherlands where central government is making decisions on health expenditures, although funding is by social and private insurance companies, paid for by premiums. But if health is paid for by central gov-

[9] This distinction is not made in the literature on Public Finance. As a matter of fact, almost all the major textbooks following Musgrave (1961) give attention to stabilization or the macro budgetary policy, to distributional questions, and to allocation, using welfare economics as the paradigm to analyze public expenditures and taxes. Efficiency, in Musgrave's approach, is confined to allocational efficiency, neglecting other kinds of efficiency.

The literature on business economics is restricted to companies operating in the market, giving no attention to financial management of organizations working in the public sector.

So there is a need for a theory of public financial management, applying the concepts and theories of business economics to public organizations but taking into account the special characteristics of the public sector. The number of textbooks in this field is small (see, for instance, Coe 1989, Miller 1991).

[10] See, for instance, Feldstein (1983) or OECD (1987). The last publication gives a rather detailed treatment of many relevant questions for these two levels, comparing OECD countries.

ernment or by one central social insurance fund, there is no cost-economizing incentive in the funding mechanism. The same is true if there are several social insurance funds, each with its own regional monopoly. For this reason Dutch government has decided to end the regional monopoly of social insurance funds and to induce competition with private insurance companies.[11]

It seems that some Central and East European countries decided to introduce insurance plans besides the central funding from taxes, not so much to achieve competitive incentives and cost containment, but to acquire more income sources to improve health systems. If a Central and East European country decides upon the introduction of social insurance funds, then the question of the number of social funds arises. If a country is opting for one social fund for all citizens (like Hungary) or for all citizens with an income below a certain level, which agency will control the costs of such a new public monopoly? A General Accounting Office might conclude on the righteousness of the outlays, but that leaves open the room for inefficiencies. If a country opens the health sector to private insurance companies, the government also has to prevent cartels and excessively high premiums. That implies a Western-type legislation on competition and cartels.

If Central and East European countries decide to substitute insurance plans for tax funding of health, the next macro decision is whether *insurance* is provided *by social funds or by private firms*: roughly the choice between the Bismarck and the American approach. Central and East European countries will find in Western economies many models to use as an example. Assuming Central and East European countries will not adopt the American model, with maximum room for private insurance plans and minimum public provisions, these countries might learn from the models existing in Germany, the Netherlands, France and so on (see OECD 1987).

The Dutch model is mentioned as a mix of ideas. First of all, there is an obligatory social insurance against exceptionally costly medical risks, compulsory for all. There are then three systems: one for wage earners up to a certain income level, one for civil servants working with provinces and municipalities, and one for wage earners above the income level and for independents and the self-employed. The first two are obligatory and are paid by income-related premiums, while the last is on a voluntary base with 'nominal,' non-income-related premiums.

The Netherlands has decided to enlarge the compulsory social insurance to a basic insurance package, equal for all citizens, while they are free to take supplementary insurance on a voluntary basis. This basic insurance package,

[11] Suggested by Commissie Structuur en Financiering Gezondheidszorg (1987).

which will be provided by competing insurance funds and not-for-profit firms, will be paid mainly by income-related social premiums and partly by flat-rate premiums (the price as the competitive instrument). This new approach was decided on in 1987-1989 and has been implemented stepwise since 1989 in a policy which will end in 1995.[12]

For Central and East European countries, choices to be made are again whether private insurers will have room to provide services, and if so, if they can strive for profit or not. According to ILO and European Union rules, a large part of health care has to be provided for by public or social organizations, at least by not-for-profit companies. If the Central and East European countries should follow these rules, there is the Scylla of inefficiency: many empirical findings in the health sector show the relative inefficiency of public organizations compared with private for-profit organizations. Another choice is whether the social insurance is offered by governmental funds or by non-governmental parastatal funds. According to Kleemans (1991) the former Soviet Union has opted for social health funds for employees (and their families), funded by employer-paid premiums related to the employee's income: roughly the Western European model. As in the new Dutch approach, the insurance funds contract physicians' services, specifying the price-performance. Public insurance funds are needed for the unemployed, to be funded by central funds and by the regional social funds (a solidarity payment) (Kleemans 1991). But according to Schepin et al. (1992), the former Soviet Union is still funding health from taxes, with experimental schemes in Leningrad and two other cities. The new insurance scheme is a voluntary one, but has been compulsory since 1993. Hungary, likewise, chose at the end of the eighties for funding by the Social Insurance Fund, which has recently (1991) been split into a Pension Fund and a Health Insurance Fund. As in the the former Societ Union this Fund does not cover all groups, especially the small self-employed and those unemployed who are not entitled to unemployment allowances.

The Czech and the Slovakian republics have introduced National Health Insurance Services, which are 90% funded by the state from central taxes. These funds are governed by boards, with representatives from the state, cities, companies and citizens. (See, for instance, Czech National Council 1991). These new institutions might turn out to be more efficient because of the participation of employers and citizens in the Board, but the monopoly character will hinder efficiency.

Since 1991 Lithuania has the SoDra, a national Social Insurance System, covering only employees (workers) and other active persons, such as the

[12] Anno Februari 1994 it is politically not clear what the future will be for the restructuring; resistance to it is growing.

military, representatives, retirees, and farmers. The Fund is partly paid by the state from taxes and partly by premiums. Nowadays, plans for the unemployed are absent.

Hungary seems to have a universal and comprehensive National Social Insurance.

The Central and East European countries face the decision about the *ownership* of hospitals, nursing homes, practices of general practitioners, physician practices and so on. The 1989 OECD study gives ample information on this subject, too. In most Western European countries hospitals are not-for-profit and are owned by the state, provinces or municipalities, or by church organizations such as Roman Catholic congregations or by other private initiative institutions. Privately-owned, for-profit hospitals do exist, but marginally, however on an increasing scale in countries such as the U.K. and the Netherlands. The type of organization is interesting from a public financial management point of view. Studies indicate that for-profit institutions tend to be more efficient than not-for-profit ones, while private, not-for-profit institutions tend to be more efficient than public ones.

Each society has to make many choices on the *micro* level, too. For example, do citizens have an *own risk* in an insurance scheme, and if so, is such an own risk obligatory or optional? An obligatory own risk will confront each medical consumer with (part of) the costs of his or her demands. This will partly relieve the public sector of the burden of rising medical costs, treating health not only as a public but also as a private good. An obligatory own risk will also lead to some decline in medical demands from citizens. If insurance schemes treat own risk as optional, there is the possibility of risk selection.

Another issue at the micro level (and, from the funding perspective, at the macro level as well) is the choice for *direct payments* or user fees, not only to decrease the financial burden for the public sector, but also to influence the medical demands of the patients. It has been stated that medical supply in all Central and East European countries is free of charge, with some exceptions at the margin, notably for part of the cost of pharmaceuticals. Just as in Western regimes, Central and East European countries face the question of raising the importance of user fees. In Western countries resistance is fed by equity considerations, but these are at odds with efficiency, since a free supply induces overconsumption. See, for instance, Hungary, (Länderbericht): the CSFR is considering the introduction of a user fee for specific treatments and for 'not directly necessary treatment.'[13]

[13] The use of such formulations lures a system into new bureaucracies, as has been proven in the Netherlands, with its very detailed regulatory system for tariffs, prices and so on.

Other choices at the micro level pertain, for instance, to the mode of *disbursement* to physicians. In the Central and East European countries physicians used to be salary-earners, while in Western Europe other systems exist, sometimes within one country, such as a capitation basis or a service-for-fee basis. The Dutch system clearly shows the allocational differences. The general practitioners in the Netherlands earn a fixed annual amount per head for their socially insured patients, regardless of the number of visits and treatments. For their privately insured patients they earn a fee per service. It has been proven that socially insured patients will be referred to a specialist at a faster rate than privately insured patients. This referral behavior is to be expected from economic theory, although other explanations (like differences in health) probably also play a role. This has the consequence of higher than necessary health costs. The large majority of specialists in Dutch hospitals are working as independent, self-employed persons, hiring facilities in the hospital. They are paid by the insurers per treatment. This disbursement mode, from the economic point of view, gives an incentive to the extra supply of services and rising costs. Overall the Central and East European countries might be advised to pay the general practitioners on a service-for-fee basis and to imburse the specialists on a capitation basis. Another option is to have the specialists as wage earners in the hospital.

Financial Management at Institution Level

As stated, there is quite a lot of literature and research on the macro and micro allocational aspects of health systems. But that is not the case with aspects such as administration, control and cost accounting within institutes. More generally speaking, the theory of cost accounting and financial accounting has been developed for market firms, while the adaption to public organizations has been underdeveloped (Boorsma 1986, 1992). These topics form the rather new discipline of public financial management in the strict sense. This section will give attention to a few items, which might be important for Central and East European countries. In their health reform plans, most Central and East European countries are concentrating on financing reform, a macro level element of public financial management. But to reach an overall efficient and effective system the *meso* level needs attention, too.

Is a health institute *funded* with a budget, based on general distribution criteria like number of persons in the area, or is it funded via market criteria like number of services and tariffs? The budgeting of health organizations is an interesting problem, implying the risk of moral hazard and adverse selection. If the expenses are reimbursable on presentation of a detailed account, inefficiency will be inevitable. If more objective criteria are used for an a priori budgeting, there is the danger of over-imbursing certain hospitals and under-imbursing others. If these institutes have to compete, there exists the problem of *cost pricing*, just as in a market firm. Now, the Netherlands provides an interesting case. In the ongoing reform, started in 1989, hospitals in the future will have to compete for contracts with insurers. The latter will compare price (tariff) and quality, as in any market place. The same will be relevant for other categories of health care providers. To set its tariffs, an institute has to calculate cost prices, per diem per bed for general care and nursing, and per treatment. If cost prices are calculated on a historical cost basis—which in the public sector in many countries is general practice—the cost price for older institutes will be lower, sometimes much lower, than for younger institutes. There will be an incentive for the insurers to contract within a certain region with the older institutes which, implies that the latter will receive imbursement that does not cover the integral costs on a current market price base.

Apart from this specific problem it is clear that *cost accounting* becomes an important task for hospitals in such an institutional setting. Again the question is raised under which setting health institutions in the Central and East European countries will have to function in the near future.

Another but related topic on the meso level is that of *internal budgeting*, meaning, to make up plans and to control operations and costs of implementation. Again the literature on public financial management is rather scant in regard to the health sector. To point out the importance of the topic we turn again to the Netherlands. Since 1983 the government has decided, in order to contain increasing costs, to set a ceiling on hospital income, which has since been termed an (external) budget.[14]

Because of the introduction of such a cost ceiling, hospital management has faced the need to set up internal budgeting systems. After the introduction of rather management-poor budgets, such as individual ceilings per specialist, which, after all, were not binding, more advanced internal budgeting systems seem to be evolving recently. These tend to be based on absorption cost-accounting techniques, although other techniques are used at the same time because of the difficulties involved in absorption costing. Since the number of treatments is extremely high, a large number of different cost prices have to be calculated, which is almost impossible with absorption costing. A great

[14] Often there is the confusion that institutions are receiving the budget. The institutions are receiving, as stated, their income from insurers as the vector of services multiplied by the vector of tariffs, but the total amount of income is capped by the government by the ceiling or budget. It is, by the way, interesting to note that the Slovakian Department of Health has installed budget ceilings for certain costs. But again, it is not sure whether this relates to a ceiling to income from tariffs or to a maximum budget received from the government.

deal could probably be learned from pricing techniques used in big warehouses or department stores, where the price is set by adding to the (variable) direct costs, a margin to cover the remaining costs and profit, while this margin will be different for different product groups.

The need for developing a public financial management theory for the health sector, not only for Central and East European countries but also for Western countries, might also be inferred from the next topic, in the field of capital market transactions.

If a health institution needs *investment capital* there are several sources. In the Central and East European countries investment capital will be provided by government, as in countries with a national health system such as the U.K. A second option is that an institute can receive a loan from national, provincial or municipal government, or some other public organization. The third possibility is that a health institution can borrow on the capital market. The last option is a regular practice in the Netherlands, where market loans were received under full governmental and provincial guarantees, making loans riskless for capital providers. Recently, however, guarantees are no longer provided (suggested by Boorsma 1985), making loans to hospitals risky. This becomes even more relevant since hospitals will have to compete in the future as mentioned above.

This combination of changes in institutions has downgraded bond loans to health institutions to very risky financing transactions. The implication is that economic managers of such institutions have to draft a business plan which must be sound enough to persuade a banker. So the Central and East European countries are facing the question of how to provide health institutions with capital: the financing problem in the strict sense. Will central government provide capital a fonds perdu out of the central budget, or do they have to borrow on the capital markets? With or without government guarantee? Do they have the possibility of setting tariffs at a level which makes reservation of own capital possible? What about private hospitals with equity capital and a for-profit character in competition with non-profit social hospitals?

The type of management and *organization procedures* have to be changed, from central to decentral, with delegation of responsibility for quality, cost control, and performance. Recent Russian experiments in the regions of Leningrad, Kemerovo and Kuibyshev stress the need for organizational changes, besides changes in financing health (Schepin et al. 1992).[15]

Attention also has to be given to the *accountability* aspects, for instance, via the information given in the income statement and balance sheet, the

[15] Even leasing arrangements are mentioned as a modern off-balance financing technique.

financial accounting. What will be the standards for the balance sheet evaluation of assets like hospital buildings, or outmoded medical equipment? What kind of information may be expected in the annual report of social insurance companies? It is interesting to note that as a corollary of the health system reform in the Netherlands, where many social insurance funds have merged or are merging, the existing and remaining funds are hesitant to give extensive information about their operations, as they used to do.

It is also easier in this field to point out topics and raise questions than to answer them: the state of the art is one reason for this.

Conclusions

Summing up, besides the privatization programs for (formerly public) business units in industry, finance, agriculture and retail, Central and East European countries face the problem of reorganizing other sectors like public utilities, health and education, introducing modern administration techniques, market-like incentives, and to some extent, transferring property rights. This chapter has focused on the health sector.

We mentioned some problems and aspects of health systems in the Central and East European countries and formulated the central expectation that Central and East European countries will show a large rise in costs of the health sector, not only in absolute terms but also as a percentage of GDP. Besides the causes known from Western countries—rising welfare and rising demands, rising relative prices, progressing medical technology and the aging of the population—some specific causes are mentioned, like existing shortages of specific medicine and high-tech equipment, the need to renew written-off and outmoded hospitals, the decline in life expectancy and the breaking-up of nations into more independent countries. In our opinion these specific arguments for a rapid future rise in health costs in Central and East European countries have not been signaled elsewhere.

The fully public and strongly centralized health systems might be reorganized, not only decentralizing decision-making to lower levels but also introducing more market elements and market-like incentives.[16] We treated some topics and aspects of public financial management at the macro and the micro level. Public financial management in the strict sense, at the meso level, is rather underdeveloped not only for Central and East European countries but for developed Western economies, too, and not only in the health sector but

[16] That is not to say that the Central and East European countries are not already working on it. To mention some examples, Bulgaria in 1989-1990 and Poland in 1990 have embarked on reform programs for their health system, while Hungary has for a long time been reconsidering the shortcomings of its system.

also in other typical public sectors such as education, law enforcement, and public works. This chapter dealt with some topics, such as the need for cost accounting, internal budgeting, capital financing, the ownership of hospitals and others.

The number of problems to be solved by Central and East European governments in restructuring the sectors which remain in the public realm is large. The implication is that the new Central and East European market economies still need qualitatively highly equipped governments for the building of many institutions which seem so common to Western economies, such as social insurance funds, tariff setting in hospitals, imbursement modes for independent doctors, and so on.

References

Aaron, H.J. (1991) *Serious and Unstable Condition.* Washington, D.C.: Brookings Institution.

Baur, E. and R. Enz (eds.) (1993) *Sigma: Health Care in Eight Countries: Growth of expenditure a problem for social insurance systems and private insurers.* Zürich: Swiss Re. 1-36.

Boorsma, P.B. (1985) *Versterking van het economische denken in de gezondheidszorg* In: J. ter Beek (ed.) *Ziekenhuismanagement in strategisch perspectief.* Lochem: De Tijdstroom. 9-23.

Boorsma, P.B. (1986) *Privatisering.* In: F.K.M. van Nispen and D.P. Noordhoek (eds.) *De grote operaties.* Deventer: Kluwer. 83-111.

Boorsma, P.B. (1991) Economische groei en (de kosten van) de gezondheidszorg. *Openbare uitgaven* 23: 235-243.

Boorsma, P.B. (1992) Economic and monetary union and public financial management: The Dutch 'public financial revolution,' paper for the Conference 'Effective Efficient Management in the New Europe,' Ireland.

Boorsma, P.B. and N.P. Mol (1983) *Privatisering.* Den Haag: Stichting Maatschappij en Onderneming.

Coe, Ch.K. (1989) *Public Financial Management.* Englewood Cliffs: Prentice Hall.

Commissie Structuur en Financiering Gezondheidszorg (1987) *Bereidheid tot verandering* (Willingness to Change). Den Haag: Staatsuitgeverij.

Feldstein, P.J. (1983) *Health care economics.* New York: Wiley.

Kleemans, C.H.M. (1991) Stelselherziening, zo noemen ze dat ook in Rusland. *Het Ziekenhuis* 8: 298-300.

LeGrand, J. and R. Robinson (eds.) (1984) *Privatization and the Welfare State.* London: Allen and Unwin.

Miller, G.J. (1991) *Government Financial Management Theory.* New York: Marcel Dekker.

Ministerie van W.V.C. en CBS (1990) *Vademecum Gezondheidsstatistiek Nederland 1991*. Voorburg.

Ministerie van W.V.C. en CBS (1991) *Vademecum Gezondheidsstatistiek Nederland 1992*. Voorburg.

Musgrave, R.A. (1961) *The Theory of Public Finance*. New York: McGraw-Hill.

Statistisches Bundesambt (1991) *Länderbericht, Staaten Mittel- und Osteuropas 1991*. Wiesbaden.

National Institute for Medical Information (1990) *Reports on Albania, Bulgaria, Hungary, Czeck and Slovak Federal Republic, Poland*. Budapest.

OECD (1987) *Financing and Delivering Health Care*. Paris.

OECD (1992) *The Reform of Health Care: A Comparative Analysis of Seven OECD Countries*. Paris.

OECD (1993) *Trends and Policies in Privatisation*. Paris.

Reagan, M. (1992) *Curing the Crisis: Options for America's Health Care*. Boulder: Westview Press.

Ryan, M. (1991) Policy and Administration in the Soviet Health Service. *Social Policy and Administration* 25: 227-237.

Schepin, O.P., V.Y. Semenow and I. Sheiman (1992) *Health Care Reform in Russia*. York: University of York.

World Bank (1991) *Staff Appraisal Report Rumania*. Washington D.C.

World Bank (1992) *Poland, Health System Reform: Meeting the Challenge*. Washington D.C.

World Health Organization (1991) *Social Equity And Health In Non-Market Economies*. Copenhagen: Regional Office For Europe.

Author Index

Subject Index